A TRAILS BO

GREAT
MIDWEST
COUNTRY ESCAPES
FARMS, FOODS, AND FESTIVALS

NINA GADOMSKI

TRAILS BOOKS
Black Earth, Wisconsin

Library of Congress Control Number: 2004116031
ISBN: 1-931599-52-1

Photos: Nina Gadomski, unless otherwise noted
Editor: Stan Stoga
Maps: Mapping Specialists
Cover Photo: Michael Shedlock

Printed in the United States of America by Versa Press.

10 09 08 07 06 05   6 5 4 3 2 1

TRAILS BOOKS
A division of Trails Media Group, Inc.
P.O. Box 317 • Black Earth, WI 53515
(800) 236-8088 • e-mail: books@wistrails.com
www.trailsbooks.com

To my mother, Stella, who once kept a cow.

Contents

Introduction

This book is intended for people who like to poke around in the Midwest's pioneer past, traveling to places that reflect this tradition in the way they grow, sell, and celebrate food of all sorts. Farms, of course, play a major role in the book's tours but are not the only attractions. You might also find yourself in a museum that is devoted to local agricultural history, or picking cherries in the morning and eating locally harvested smoked fish in the afternoon. You might be climbing a silo, touring the mansion of a nationally known agriculturist, buying sacks of cornmeal at the mill where it was ground, or eating the famous cream puffs at the Wisconsin State Fair.

Local food in all its bounty is an important focus of the book. You can sample it on the run, eat it at local restaurants, and have your fill during special events. And you will certainly be taking some home. So before heading out on one of these country escapes, be sure to clean out the trunk of your car to make room for all the colors, textures, and tastes of a Midwest bounty: Amish noodles, apples, asparagus, baking mixes, bison meat, blue raspberry licorices, bushels of vegetables, brandy-laced ice cream toppings, breads, cheeses, ciders, cornmeals, dried fruits, dried herbs, dried morels, elderberry wine, fruit butters, fudge, gourds, honeys, horseradishes, Indian corns, jams, jellies, kale, maple creams, mustards, navy beans, nuts, old-fashioned ribbon and horehound candies, pancake mixes, pickled vegetables, pie fillings, pies, pumpkins, quick bread recipes, relishes, salsas, sauces, sausages, smoked herrings, sorghum, soup mixes, turkey jerky, Vidalia onion dressings, vine-ripened tomatoes, whitefish dips, yarns, yellow squashes, and zucchinis. Other products are also bound to catch your eye, from goat's milk soaps to toy tractors.

What Is in the Book?

Each of the book's 45 tours in various regions of six states is based upon a theme, such as "Asparagus." But the tours are hardly limited to one food or food-related subject; their coverage of an area is as inclusive as possible. The Hart-Mears area of Michigan, for example, is known for its asparagus, but the local folks recently hosted their first apple festival, and that is included as well. Furthermore, local attractions that are unrelated to the theme, but that draw visitors because they are such great fun, are also mentioned. One tour within each state is designated as a Country-in-the-City tour. Its purpose is to show that Midwestern cities of all sizes are trying to recall their agricultural roots in the form of farmers' markets, specialty food shops, and farm re-creations.

Some of the tours are extensive, and some involve long-distance driving. Some of the point-to-point directions given in the tours are as specific as possible; others are offered for general reference only. Depending on several factors, you may want to plan your own itinerary. For one thing, not every suggested site or event will appeal to everyone. My hope, however, is that you find yourself lingering at a farm longer than you expected to. Sometimes, just the smell of freshly baled hay, or your child's unexpected kinship with a calf, will make it harder to leave than you would have thought possible. It could also happen that you get to talking to an organic farmer or a baker of artisan breads. Or you may get to talking to your son about the huge combine he saw, and, well, suddenly the sun is setting in the sky. Then, too, you will undoubtedly discover additional places on your own, places that become yours as you explore the highways and byways of these Midwestern states.

A word about hours of operation: they vary. Many of the places are family owned and therefore more likely to have irregular hours. Many are also dependent on the seasons, so if you want to pick apples off a tree, you have to go in late summer or autumn. But when exactly? It depends on the latitude, the variety of the apple, and especially the weather during the growing season. Most places are open on weekends, especially throughout the growing season, but of course there are exceptions. Amish-owned businesses are never open on Sunday, and some places that depend on Amish workers or simply wish to show respect for the local Amish community may follow suit. Of course, variances in hours of operation are a small price to pay for uniqueness and direct contact. The best advice is to call ahead and visit Web sites.

The book also includes listings of special events that celebrate the farms and the foods, the harvest and the ethnic heritage. These events are the great state fairs and the regionally commemorative county fairs, the cheese days and the tractor pulls and the antique engine demonstrations, the breakfasts on the farm, the pumpkin fests that you can only have in the autumn, the horse shows, the farmers' markets. There are also listings for places to eat and places to stay. In many cases, these are in keeping with some aspect of the overall theme of agricultural tourism.

Who Is the Book For?

City people. For those who are more used to feeling the heat of concrete than the coolness of earth beneath their feet, this book can take them back to the places where growing things, and raising things, fill the hours of each day. It is said that with each passing generation, people are less and less likely to have a chance to visit their own grandparents' farms. By visiting places in this book, they can re-establish connections that may have been lost.

Country people. For those who spend their lives surrounded by farms, this book may be able to show them something new of a world that is already familiar. It may suggest visits to places where they can learn more about how work gets done, or used to get done, on the American farm. It may give them a reason to celebrate what is all around them.

Parents. For those who want their children to know something of the American farm and are looking for a way to introduce them to better nutrition, there are many useful resources within these pages. Perhaps they are planning a trip to an area that is known for its great swimming lakes. Well, while there, they can broaden the scope of the family vacation to include a visit to a cherry orchard or a café that is known for baking great pies made from the local cherry crop. Their children will learn where milk and cheese and butter come from, and they will pick up fun facts, such as knowing that goats prefer to nibble rather than bite. Their children are the ones who will grow up knowing that there is not only work, but also reward, on an American farm.

Seniors. Those who smile at the sight of a cream separator—or any vestige of a bygone era that few people seem to recognize today—will find inspiration here. Those who want to get away and explore Midwest back roads at their own pace will find plenty of opportunities to do just that. And who cares if a few days turn into a week? Older adults who are in search of their ethnic roots, as they were put down by pioneer ancestors long ago, will find ways to reconnect. And these same people will undoubtedly enjoy discovering that the traditional ways and places can be reinvented without loss to original character, and so a barn becomes a bed and breakfast, and a cornfield becomes a maze.

Couples, friends. Adventuresome folks out on a lark to discover the latest gourmet flavors will also enjoy taking the tours. These are the style-conscious twenty- or thirty-somethings who know that a pair of antique tin ladles might be just the thing for their kitchen redesign. People who care that the eggs they buy are from chickens that spend their lives ranging freely, and that the beef they barbecue has come from cattle that were pasture-fed. And people who value regional cuisine, whether it is wild rice from a northern Minnesota lake, or sausage gravy and biscuits from a cozy southern Indiana restaurant. Foodies, bon vivants, connoisseurs—call them what you will—these people know there is no substitute for the real thing.

Most important, the book is full of the stories of Midwesterners who had dreams of following an agrarian way of life and chose to make them happen. Some of them grew up in the family business. As adults, they looked around at the alternatives and knew that this was something good, something they could make even better, and something they could use to open the way for others to experience farm life. Other people learned that a place was up for sale, perhaps in disrepair, and found a way to buy and preserve it and make it work for a new market. Still others started completely on their own, fresh out of college or much later in life, with this wild idea to start a buffalo ranch, a soup-mix operation, or an inn that once was a gristmill. Some of the people found that their ideas were regarded as crazy. Yet against the current, they jumped in heart-first, swam furiously, and succeeded. For their pluck, defiance, and strength, the Midwestern landscapes and Great Lakes seascapes have become fascinating, story-rich places to visit. A book like this is only possible because of them.

No matter who you are or where you live, and whether the American Heartland is a place you can find in your own backyard or at the end of a long flight, you are invited to take the time to discover its homegrown goodness. It's still here, within these pages, and just up the road.

$\mathcal{A}cknowledgments$

I would like to extend special thanks to my family for always being there: my mother Stella, sister Elizabeth and brother Steve. Also, my sister Linda, brother-in-law Larry, and Kristin, Courtney, Eric and Alexander. I am grateful to Dennis for his votes of confidence, shared need for country places and unwavering love. And Desiree, who could not read, but who did not need any explanations. Special thanks also go out to Edward Moskal of the Polish National Alliance, Therese Ramirez, Karen Miller, and Janie and Andy Crawford.

Thank you, too, to Stan Stoga and Erika Reise.

I would also like to thank the fine people at many convention and visitors bureaus and chamber of commerce offices who helped me. In Wisconsin, thanks go out to Kathleen Galas, Manitowoc VCB; Joy Gieseke, Mineral Point Chamber; Wendy Haase, Greater Milwaukee CVB; Denny Moyer, Sheboygan County CVB; Eric Prise, Tomah Chamber/CVB; Noreen Rueckert, Green County Tourism; Jane ann Savaske, Merrill Area Chamber; Kim Straka, Greater Madison CVB; Kim Swisher, Tomahawk Regional Chamber. In Minnesota, Suzette Bush, Brainerd Baxter Lodging Association; Andrea Downing, Braham Pie Day; Sue Hegarty, Eagan CVB; Chuck Lennon, Explore Minnesota Tourism. In Iowa, Joel Akason, Oskaloosa Area Chamber; Kari Burns, Winneshiek County CVB; Stacey Glandon, Villages of Van Buren; Robin Hennes, Amana Colonies CVB; Rob Johnson, Des Moines CVB; Jan Paulsen, Danish Windmill Corporation; Angie Watson, Ice Cream Capital of the World Visitor Center. In Illinois, Theresa Binion, Arthur Amish Country Visitors Center; Charlotte Doehler-Morrison, the Quad Cities CVB; Susan Foster, Arcola Chamber; Marge Heissinger, Central Illinois Tourism Development Office; Carol Hoffman, Southernmost Illinois Tourism Bureau; Barbara Kleiss, Tuscola Tourism Office; Amy Trimble, Blackhawk Waterways CVB; Beverly VanDerZyl, Galena/Jo Daviess County CVB; Amy Watson, Bloomington-Normal Area CVB; Pat White, Southwestern Illinois Tourism Bureau. In Indiana, David Dabagia, LaPorte County CVB; Jennifer Dinga, Porter County Convention, Recreation & Visitor Commission; Jackie Hughes, Elkhart County CVB; Kathleen Linderman, Historic New Harmony; Kate Mejaski, Brown County CVB; Pam Sanders, Parke County CVB; Michael Schug, Indianapolis Convention & Visitors Association; Nicole Twigg, Harrison County CVB. In Michigan, Sandra Kay Coats, Hart-Silver Lake-Mears Chamber; David Creighton, Michigan Grape and Wine Industry Council; Linda Dougherty of Lake Michigan Carferry (*S.S. Badger*); Phyllis Dowsett, Southwestern Michigan Tourist Council; Jamie Furbush, Frankenmuth Chamber and CVB; Barbara Kravitz, Grand Rapids/Kent County CVB; Amy Lalewicz and Jacqueline Merta, Charlevoix Area Chamber; Tim Meloche, Marx Layne & Company; Teri Pearce, Battle Creek/Calhoun County VCB.

For granting permission to reprint recipes, thanks go to: Kim Billiard, Warrens

Cranberry Festival Inc., Warrens, Wisconsin; David M. Braswell, Corner George Inn Bed & Breakfast, Maeystown, Illinois; Russell Carter & family, Red Wagon Farm, Park Rapids, Minnesota;William M. Deming, City of Portage, Celery Flats Interpretive Center, Portage, Michigan; Lary Eckert, Eckert's Inc., Belleville, Illinois; Carl Ehrmann, Colony Inn Restaurant, Amana Iowa; Phyllis Hoegh, Our House Bed & Breakfast, Elk Horn, Iowa; Craig Kirkwood & Dan L. Seltenright, Elkhart County Parks, Bonneyville Mill, Bristol, Indiana; Charles M. "Mike" Mainland, Blueberries of Indiana, LaPorte, Indiana; Lori Murphy, Murphy's Gardens, Galena, Illinois; Michael Roeder, Vectren Corporation, Evansville, Indiana; Andy Rogers, Nashville House, Nashville, Indiana; Holly Sorge, Iowa Egg Council, Urbandale, Iowa; Angela Pletcher Stillson, Amish Acres, Nappanee, Indiana; Dee Windell, Kintner House Inn, Corydon, Indiana.

Finally, I will always treasure the memories of the unforgettable people whom I was privileged to meet and learn from and laugh with along the way.

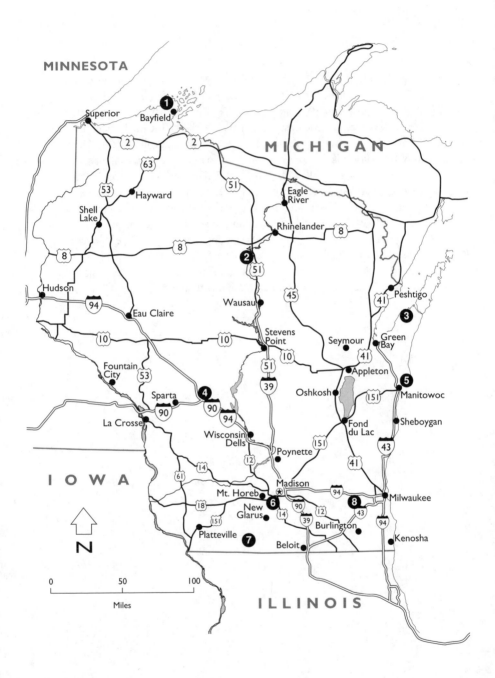

MINNESOTA

MICHIGAN

Superior

Bayfield

(2)   (2)

(63)

(53)   Hayward

Shell
Lake   Eagle
(51)   River

Rhinelander   (8)

(8)   (8)

Hudson   (2)

(94)   (51)

Eau Claire   Wausau   (45)

(10)   Peshtigo

(10)   (10)   (41)

Stevens   Seymour   Green
Point   Bay

(51)   (10)   (41)

Fountain   (39)   Appleton
City   (53)   (5)

Sparta   (4)   Oshkosh   (151)   Manitowoc

(90)   (90)   (94)

La Crosse   Fond   Sheboygan
du Lac

Wisconsin
Dells   (151)   (43)

Poynette   (41)

I O W A   (14)   (12)

(61)   Madison

Mt. Horeb   (94)   (8)

N   (18)   New   (90) (12)   (43)   Milwaukee

Glarus   (14) (39)

(151)   Burlington   (94)

Platteville   (7)   Kenosha

Beloit

0   50   100

Miles   I L L I N O I S

Wisconsin

The Dairy State is known the world over for master cheese making, but did you know it also produces crops like cranberries and sphagnum moss? Wisconsin always manages to make its farmscapes things of beauty, so just passing by them on a country drive is downright uplifting and rewarding. But your sense of taste deserves a reward too, so go ahead and pick the tart cherries right off the trees, and enjoy restaurants where the bounty of the surrounding land forms the heart of ingredients-based cooking.

1. BAYFIELD'S GREAT NORTHERN HARVESTS

The top of Wisconsin pushes out into Lake Superior as if it cannot get close enough to the cold, clear water. This is Bayfield County, and all of Wisconsin is south of here. The nearest major city is Duluth, Minnesota. Most of the tour centers around Bayfield, where grand Victorian residences march down to Lake Superior, and sailboats chafe against their moorings. Up above the harbor, Bayfield's farming community thrives in the lofty, fertile hills. This is where the lake effect tempers the climate enough to make all the apple, berry, and flower farms so productive this far north. It is what inspires 50,000 people to gather each October to celebrate the harvest at the end of another fine growing season. And it is what makes that first bite into an apple, which spent its summer warmed by the breath of Lake Superior, such a crisp, juicy reward.

The Fields

Follow the Orchard Circle auto tour as mapped out by the Bayfield Chamber of Commerce, (800) 447-4094, www.bayfield.org, to a dozen or so orchards, each one as individual as its owners. Since the orchards are nestled close together and the entire tour has an estimated circumference of less than 10 miles, you do not have to drive endlessly to experience them all. Many orchards welcome visitors to pick their own fruit and make memories to last a lifetime. If you have kids along, they will remember too. And then, as you feel the stretch of dormant muscles and talk and laugh the hours away, you begin dreaming of the pies, cobblers, and pancakes to come.

From downtown Bayfield, you could begin orchard hopping at Washington Avenue and Highway 13. Go west on Washington, make a right onto Betzold Road, and after a half mile, pull into the **James Erickson Orchard and Country Store**, 86600 Betzold Road, Bayfield, (715) 779-5438, which sits on about 200 acres. Choose from pre-picked or u-pick apples, also strawberries earlier in the season. Cortlands are especially popular for their tart, crisp flavor and keeping

The well-stocked shelves of Erickson Orchard's country store, Bayfield.

quality, and the newer Honeycrisp sells well. Inside the shop is an intriguing selection of fruit jams, jellies, and marmalades in flavors limited only by the founder's imagination, and made from local fruits in flavors like raspberry-rhubarb, rosy red rhubarb, pear, blueberry, cherry-blueberry, crabapple jelly, and country apple marmalade. Also look for the farm's own fresh-pressed apple cider, pancake mixes, wild rice soups, and Vidalia onion dressings. Try the sweet, homemade apple donuts if there are any left.

Just up the road, you come to **Betzold Orchard**, 87380 Betzold Road, Bayfield, (715) 779-3207. Here some of the first apple trees that were planted, back in the 1920s, still bear their delicious fruit, a variety called Wealthy. The owner says a ripe Wealthy apple is one of the best eating varieties, but it also excels in pies and sauces. Pre-picked and u-pick Cortland, McIntosh, Spartan, Honeycrisp, and some other varieties are available.

Next up, **Bayfield Apple Company**, 87540 County Road J, Bayfield, (800) 363-4JAM, (715) 779-5700, is unmistakable for fresh, intensely apple aromas and tastes, especially when they are cooking up another batch of apple butter. Apple mustard is another signature treat, along with jams and jellies starring the orchard's own apples and raspberries. It is rare and refreshing to find places that make *and* grow their own foodstuffs, but Bayfield Apple Company is one of these. And here the clever orchard dog has cultivated a particularly fruitful relationship with the UPS driver, who always delivers a biscuit along with the regular packages.

Go south on County Road J and follow it to **Johnson's Good Earth Gardens**, 87185 County Road J, Bayfield, (715) 779-5564. This colorful reinvention of an abandoned apple orchard tops its fence posts with birdhouses and grows ever-lasting flowers that are fertilized, in part, with fish trimmings supplied by Bayfield fishermen. See where the flowers hang in the drying shed; they call it the upside-down garden. Pick small-production blueberries or blackberries from about July through mid-August. Neighboring Bayfield Apple Company puts up Johnson's gooseberry and currant jams that you can buy here in finished form. Fresh herbs are seasonally available.

Continue south to **Hauser's Superior View Farm**, 86565 County Road J, Bayfield, (715) 779-5404, www.superiorviewfarm.com, which has been around since 1908. Here and there, big old dogs are flopped down on the ground like thick throw rugs. Beginning in August, pick your own apples and picnic in the orchard. Poke around Hauser's trademark red Sears barn with two flights of stairs to the top for a view toward the lake and a peek into the family attic where hundreds of feed caps hang from nails in the rafters. The barn's lower level is the shop festooned with crayon messages from schoolchildren, as well as newspaper clippings and family photos that chronicle the history of the farm. Shop for the farm's own dry to sweet apple and pear wines, honey meads, and farmhouse cider wines made with blueberries, blackberries, cranberries, and raspberries. There are also handmade soaps and fruit preserves in uncommon flavors like Bluebarb, Dewberry, and Mission Cherry.

Apple Hill Orchard, 34980 County Road J, Bayfield, (715) 779-5425, offers pre-picked and u-pick fruit, and next comes **Sunset Valley Orchard**, Rt. 1 Box 207, Bayfield, (715) 779-5510. When no one is around, visitors are invited to pop into the tiny wooden shop for self-service on the honor system.

Just to the north is **Highland Valley Farm**, 87080 Valley Road, Bayfield, (715) 779-5446, where a decorative row of apple trees parallels the curved drive. Look for u-pick blueberries, pre-picked raspberries, honey, and maple syrup that has been produced from their own sugar bush since 2003.

Blue Vista Farm, HCR 64 Box 71A, Bayfield, (715) 779-5400, attracts visitors who love fresh blueberries and raspberries and long-distance views of blue hills sloping down to the lake. The barn is a classic. Built about 1910 when this site was a dairy farm, the barn housed livestock up until the 1950s. Today, visitors are welcome to enjoy its historic charm, cool stone foundation, and views of grazing horses while picking their own apples from late August through November, including Cortlands and Galas, from the 1,000-tree orchard. Come in July or August to pick berries among the clean rows. Look for fresh-cut flowers from June through October, everlastings from August to December, and enjoy the herb, butterfly, and lemon gardens throughout the growing season. Shop for organic preserves and pre-picked fruits from June through December.

Back in town at Washington Avenue and Broad Street, an intriguing bit of Bayfield's apple-growing history can be found at the **Apple Shed**. Looking like the mouth of an above-ground cave, this previously abandoned storage cellar

3

is a relic of the 1920s. Learn why William Knight abandoned his shed, and don't miss the nature trail that snakes past primeval ferns and beneath the 1912 Iron Bridge.

The Bay

Now let's travel down to the bay side of Bayfield. Commercial fishing began in this area when the American Fur Company set up shop in 1856, shipping salted fish in barrels to eastern markets. Soak up the history inside the **Bayfield Maritime Museum**, Bayfield Boat Barn, on First Street across from the Bayfield marina, (715) 779-9919 (May through October), (715) 779-3925 (October through May).

Heard about the area's whitefish livers? They are something of a local tradition. Some consider them to be addictive, while others find the texture to be somewhat of a challenge. At any rate, this nautical delicacy has a mild taste that is easy to like, and some of the restaurants are happy to lure you in with the novelty of it. **Greunke's First Street Inn**, 17 Rittenhouse Avenue, Bayfield, (715) 779-5480, has been serving them since the 1940s, and they are available deep-fried or sautéed with peppers and onions. At the flamingo-pink eatery called **Maggie's**, 257 Manypenny Avenue, Bayfield, (715) 779-5641, www.maggies-bayfield.com, they serve up a plate of whitefish livers sautéed with green peppers, onions, and mushrooms.

Two waterfront fish markets, neighbors to one another, supply the restaurants and also sell direct. **Bay Fisheries**, 207 Wilson Avenue (next to the Coast Guard Station), Bayfield, (715) 779-3910, has fresh lake trout, whitefish, smoked fish, and smoked fish dip. The occasional fresh walleye comes in. **Bodin Fisheries**, 208 Wilson Avenue, Bayfield, (715) 779-3301 (closed on Sundays unless it is a holiday) offers fresh, frozen, and smoked fish, along with herring caviar and whitefish livers at a very affordable price. Ted Chaney, plant manager, says whitefish livers are considered to be something of a delicacy. They can be frozen or refrigerated, then grilled or deep-fried. One of Chaney's favorite cooking methods is to parboil the whitefish livers, then roll them in flour, salt, and pepper before sautéing. Right before they are done (10 to 12 minutes over medium-high heat), he throws in sliced green, red, and yellow peppers and onions, then sets the dish aside, covered, for three to four minutes before eating hot, or later as the filling for a cold sandwich.

Hills and all, Bayfield is a great walking town, where you can pop in and out of ice cream shops and a little place called **Sweet Sailing**, 120 Rittenhouse Avenue, Bayfield, (715) 779-3682. Shop for homemade fudge in distinctive flavors like Big Bay Turtle and Lake Superior Agate with chocolate pebbles. With something like 34 kinds of saltwater taffy, you can afford to be picky. Don't miss the gourmet mustards and regional cookbooks and travel guides. Before leaving Bayfield, enjoy sitting down to a meal that features the local flavor.

Offshore, the 22 Apostle Islands bob in the water like big, green apples. Take your pick of a number of interesting ways to get to the islands: ferry, excursion boat, sailboat, multi-masted schooner, or kayak. Sailboat adventures are available, too, and range from half days to overnights. Passengers are welcome to help crew by trimming sails, steering, and handling dock lines, or they can just lay back and feel the wind in their hair and the spray on their faces.

Small museums that shed light on agriculture and commercial fishing, among other local histories, have cropped up across Ashland and Bayfield County; here is a sampling of what they call the hidden treasures. **Bayfield Heritage Center Historical Museum and Research Facility**, 30 North Broad Street, Bayfield, (715) 779-5958, www.bayfieldheritage.org, maintains a collection of artifacts and archival materials related to the history of the area with themes of settlement, agriculture, logging and lumbering, transportation and tourism. **Hokenson Brothers Fishery Museum**, at Little Sand Bay off Highway 13, about 13 miles north of Bayfield, (715) 779-3397, is a restored commercial fishing facility offering guided or self-guided tours. Learn about the tools and techniques of a family fishery that proved to be more successful for the brothers than farming had been. **Port Wing Heritage Hall**, Memorial Park, Highway 13, Port Wing, (715) 774-3949, is another newer center, and it is located on the western coast of the peninsula, 33 miles from Little Sand Bay. **Northern Great Lakes Visitor Center**, 29270 County Road G, Ashland, (715) 685-9983, runs a 28-minute video on the eras of farming, logging, shipping, and mining. You could also get an insightful audiotape tour for your car ride here. Ashland is 23 miles south of Bayfield, down the east coast of the peninsula.

From shiny red apples to saltwater taffy to the cold northern beauty of a

Old Rittenhouse Inn, Bayfield.

freshwater lake, Bayfield should top your list for a Wisconsin getaway of great northern harvests from the land and the sea.

SPECIAL EVENTS

Big Top Chautauqua Tent Theatre, (888) 244-8368, www.bigtop.org. June through September. The blue-and-white striped tent sets the stage for everything from big-name entertainment to original musical histories that capture the spirit of the region. "Riding the Wind" lures you back to the days of sailors and lumberjacks, with song and drama and stirring photographs.

Top of the North Farm and Garden Show and 4-H Dairy Breakfast, Bay Area Civic Center, Ashland, (800) 284-9484. Early April.

Scandinavian Heritage Day, Bay Area Civic Center, Ashland, (800) 284-9484. Mid-May. Cultural displays, food, music, dancing.

Chequamegon Chefs Exhibition, Madeline Island, (888) 475-3386. Mid-June.

Manomin Fest and Pow-Wow, Bad River Chippewa Reservation, Odanah, www.badriver.com. August. Help celebrate the wild rice harvest, sample ethnic foods at the Bad River Lodge and Casino, (800) 795-7121, learn about the fish hatchery, and consider that over 95 percent of this 124,234-acre reservation remains undeveloped and wild. Ten miles east of Ashland on Highway 2.

Bayfield Apple Festival, (800) 447-4094. Three days on the first weekend in October. Biggest apple festival in the American Heartland. Apple slices drenched with melted caramel, fritters, pies, tortes, tarts, sundaes, cider, bratwurst. Pie-making contest and sampling as you help choose the winner. Orchard Lane for the kids. Apple peeling contest. 400-member high school band parade. Park at the orchards, shuttle to the festival grounds. Fisherman's boil and dance on Saturday. Free pony rides at Hauser's Superior View Farm.

Red Cliff Cultural Days and Powwow, three miles north of Bayfield on Highway 13. July 4th weekend. Traditional Ojibwe storytelling, singing, dancing, canoe making, leather tanning, beading, teepees, wigwams, fish boil. Everyone is welcome to this great Woodland Indian cultural event.

PLACES TO EAT

Greunke's First Street Inn, 17 Rittenhouse Avenue, Bayfield, (715) 779-5480, www.greunkesinn.com. Berry pancakes, trout, steaks, chicken, burgers, etc. Call ahead to reserve a place at the traditional Wisconsin fish boil: whitefish steaks, baby red potatoes, onions, served with a buffet of coleslaw, dark breads and homemade rolls, melted butter, lemon, and a Bayfield fruit dessert that follows the growing season from strawberry shortcake to raspberry shortcake to apple crisp. Quaint bed-and-breakfast inn too.

Lotta's Lakeside Café, 792 Main Street, La Pointe (Madeline Island), (715) 747-2033. Fresh ingredients, simple atmosphere, lotta fun.

Old Rittenhouse Inn, 301 Rittenhouse Avenue, (715) 779-5111. Regional cuisine, elegant style. Lunch choices include a Lake Superior trout sandwich

---

FIELD NOTES

Homestead Garden

With acreage totaling nearly a baker's dozen, Homestead Garden is a deliciously natural stop about 13 miles south of Bayfield along Highway 13 near Washburn. Owner Peg Lukasiewicz offers fresh, northern-grown lettuces, radishes, green onions, specialty potatoes, eating and pickling cucumbers, carrots, beets, and green and yellow beans. "I like to cut them in half, brush them with olive oil, add Parmesan, and grill them," she says of the zucchinis. She grows some apples as well, and says that for it to live up to its name, a Red Delicious should be "dribble-down-your-chin juicy, but not mealy, because that means it's already past its prime."

Visitors on their way to cottage stays or camping adventures on the Apostle Islands like to pick up trail mixes like the snacky date-nut rolls that fly off the shelves. "It's nothing but ground dates rolled in coconut with almond on top. It's high-energy but low-fat," Lukasiewicz explains.

Homestead Garden also sells fresh chicken eggs that are laid by fowl that forage by means of a traveling pen. It is not free-range, but it offers the birds fresh pecking grounds in the outdoor environment while employing them for seed-bed preparation and keeping them safe. Lukasiewicz likes the traveling pen method because it is sustainable. Also look for Wisconsin cheeses, pancake mixes, Amish products, and bulk mixes and cereals.

Tending one of the many naturally grown crops at Homestead Garden, near Washburn.

"My motto has been, expand only as we can afford to. And everything has to pay for itself, which in my mind, that's sustainable agriculture. There will always be three fields out of production and rejuvenating," says Lukasiewicz. 🐎

———————————•———•———

that is lightly seasoned and baked and a cheeseburger that is seasoned with cracked pepper, fresh herbs, and sea salt. Seasonal soups, mesclun salad with blackberry vinaigrette. For dessert, enjoy fresh fruit and berry creations, then a self-guided house tour (you can't do Bayfield without doing this).

The Egg Toss Bakery Café, 41 Manypenny Avenue, Bayfield, (715) 779-5181, www.eggtoss-bayfield.com.

Wild Rice Restaurant, 84860 Old San Road, Bayfield, (715) 779-9881, www.wildricerestaurant.com. Creamy wild rice soup with house-smoked chicken and Granny Smith apples, crispy pan-fried Lake Superior whitefish and trout with wheat pilaf and citrus soy butter, and more such finery coming out of this kitchen.

PLACES TO STAY

Old Rittenhouse Inn, 301 Rittenhouse Avenue, Bayfield, (715) 779-5111, www.rittenhouseinn.com. Classic 1890 mansion looks down from a lofty perch but welcomes all to enjoy its bygone-era splendor. Flower baskets pose on the wraparound porch like colorful carousel horses. The luscious guestrooms and two third-floor suites come complete with bay views. Continental breakfast served in the dining room includes their own line of fruit preserves.

White Seagull Bed and Breakfast and Homes on Madeline Island, (800) 977-2624, www.islandrental.com.

Winfield Inn and Gardens, 225 East Lynde Avenue, Bayfield, (715) 779-3252, www.winfieldinn.com. Views! In-room refrigerator, cable TV, A/C, second floor rooms have private balconies. Twenty additional rental homes and condos available.

2. INTO THE NORTH WOODS

Start off a great North Woods getaway with a Friday fish fry. It's a tradition that caught on a long time ago and still runs as deep as the cold, blue lakes. At almost any supper club, tavern, or VFW Hall, the pros will gladly reel you in with their version. They are tossing the breaded cod and perch into the hot oil and sending an aroma clear up into the pines, an aroma that would crunch if you could bite into it. And you can bet they are scooping up the coleslaw, French fries, and rolls with butter, and pushing the plates out of the kitchen as fast as anyone can close the menu, prop elbows onto the red-checkered tablecloth, and say, "I'll have the fish fry."

Tomahawk is about 40 miles due north of busy, vibrant Wausau, and pretty near nowhere else. For those who don't know where Wausau is, think straight up Highway 39/51 to north-central Wisconsin. The tour also includes a drive into Price County to the northwest, and here you will find a surprising range of farming venues.

Fish

Once upon a time, Debbie and Bill Eastwood fled Chicagoland to start frying up the fish at **Tomahawk Lodge, Resort, and Supper Club**, N10985 County Road CC (three miles northwest of downtown), Tomahawk, (715) 453-3452, (888) 412-1022, www.tomlodge.com, just as previous owners had been doing since the early 1930s. Apparently the regulars approved, or didn't know that a couple of Illinois people were behind the counter, because they keep coming back. The place is just what you would expect from a genuinely old North Woods eatery, and a bonus is that Frank Sinatra croons in the background. The fish fry gets going at 5:00 p.m. and ends whenever it ends, which is usually around 10:00 p.m. Expect a crowd as you settle down to tuck into the all-you-can-eat deep-fried sno cod. If you fall in love with the lake view, you can always rent a lakeside cabin.

Perched on a dusty hill some three miles from Tomahawk Lodge, Resort, and Supper Club at the junction of Highways 8 and CC, **Sportsland Pub and Chili Pepper Café**, W8995 U.S. Highway 8, Tomahawk, (715) 453-6867, is a vintage-1960s roadside pub where locals park their North Woods toys out front. When the current owners bought the café a few years back, it had been closed and needed work. Sure, they fixed it up, but they stopped way short of cutesy. Come in, sit down, and order. The fish fry is all-you-can-eat haddock or walleye. They also offer fried bluegill and lake perch (a plateful, not all-you-can-eat), as well as the Fisherman's Platter with a little of everything including shrimp, which is a nice change but still from the sea. It is a lot of food, choice of potato, soup, and salad bar included.

Drive north several miles from downtown Tomahawk on Highway 51 to **Bootleggers Supper Club**, 2001 Indian Pine Point Road, Tomahawk, (715) 453-7971. It's all log construction on a peninsula, with lots of glass overlooking Lake Nokomis. Eat indoors or out on the deck that sits above a grassy slope and a sandy beach. Al Capone once hid away here, and you can bet there was a tunnel to the lookout that is now a benign ice cream shop.

Nearby, **Schaefer's Wharf**, 1969 County Road L, Tomahawk, (715) 453-2768, is another beautiful spot that takes full advantage of its lakeside locale. Piers and a garden lead up to the deck, and brightly clad boaters docking for a meal or gasoline seem to bring the essence of summer in their wake. The fish fry is a beer-battered three-piece cod (now with a thinner batter that does not hold a lot of grease) with French fries, coleslaw, and rye bread. Fish and chips and deep-fried or boiled shrimp are alternate choices. Dine outside or in. A few miles south of downtown Tomahawk is **Big Moose Supper Club**, N8796 Business Highway 51 South, Tomahawk, (715) 453-6667. You can't miss the moose out front, and don't trip over the boots that some cowboy checked at the door long ago, for there they remain, stuffed with dirt or cement or something, offering no explanation, asking none in return. Never mind the boots. The fish is all-you-can-eat cod, and there is a salad bar. The view out back is of a sparkly, blue, and very northern lake.

But if you want to catch your own fish, consider that Lincoln County has 726 lakes and 246 streams, with 318 miles of trout streams and 120 miles of sport fishing waters. Many of the waterways offer public access and fish on the order of bass, muskie, northern pike, and panfish. Walleye can be found in some of the county lakes and flowages, most of which offer public access. The 110-acre **Bradley Park**, West Spirit Avenue, Tomahawk, has a children's fishing pond with fishing piers, playground equipment, and picnic spots complete with grills.

Forests

If you head west on Highway 8 from Tomahawk and cross the Lincoln County border into Price County, you can get a taste of North Woods heritage. It is **Knox Creek Heritage Center**, N4517 West Knox Road, Brantwood, (715) 564-2520, which opened in 1995 and honors the farming and logging cultures of the region. The furnished circa-1900 farmhouse was built using round tree trunks as studs and roughhewn timber for the walls. A nice touch is an etched glass window featuring a plowing scene. Displays inside the Keto House depict a logging camp and other history. The summer kitchen has an old wood cookstove, the shed houses tractors, plows, and a sleigh for hauling logs, and the sauna represents a lifestyle of Finnish immigrants. Hike or bike the Heritage Trail past Timberland Christmas Trees, Brantwood Bison, and an intriguing mix of historic sites that give a clue to a wilder past.

Price County is loaded with possibilities for farm tours and source-direct purchases with a distinctive North Woods flavor. Always call ahead if you wish to arrange a tour. Following is a fast rundown of what is available in this area. **Jump River Shepards Dairy**, N3584 County Road I, Catawba, (715) 474-3485, sells breeding stock, pets, vegetables, cheese, lamb, beef, rabbit, and chicken meats. **West View Dairy and Sugarbush**, W1681 Highway 86, Ogema, (715) 564-2527 or 2616, sells maple syrup, wreaths, and roping. **Heikkinen Bros. Tree Farm**, N5100 Venison Drive, Brantwood, (715) 564-2278, offers Christmas trees. **Northern Wisconsin Maid Sugarbush**, W8052 Maple Ridge Road, Park Falls, (715) 762-4796, has maple syrup and other maple products, hand-picked berry jams, pancake mixes, honey, and jelly for sale. About 12,000 taps get the juice out of the maple trees that spread across two hundred acres. Go in spring for the syrup-making open house, and again on Thanksgiving weekend for

Mmmaple

The folks at Maple Hollow know their syrup. Here are some tidbits of information that they have gathered about their favorite product.

The three grades of maple syrup that you can buy are: Light Amber (make cream or candy with it), Medium Amber (drench pancakes with it), Dark Amber (make-no-mistake it's maple). By the way, pure maple syrup has only 40 calories per tablespoon compared to 60 in corn syrup and 54 in sugar.

They tap the sap when the days are warm and sunny and above 40 degrees, the nights are frosty, and sap is flowing. Tapping does not hurt the trees, as the Native Americans who thought of the idea well knew.

Do the math: you need 30 to 50 gallons of sap for one gallon of maple syrup. Each tap generates about 10 gallons of sap per season, or one quart of maple syrup, depending on the sugar content of the sap.

So give your palate and your pancakes a taste of the real thing—pure, American maple syrup. And then you will know why it is so widely imitated. 🐎

Maple syrup, along with many tasty items that go with it, at Maple Hollow, near Merrill.

"Christmas at the Sugar Cabin." Finally, **Shady Knoll Farms**, W2502 Shady Knoll Road, Park Falls, (715) 762-1875, offers produce, garden plants, beef, and the company of friendly critters.

To the east in Forest County, hop aboard the Lumberjack Special steam train to **Camp Five Museum**, 5480 Connor Farm Road, Laona, (715) 674-3414, (800) 774-3414, www.camp5museum.org, which is the actual site of a former logging camp. The logging history includes a frying pan that measures three feet in diameter—big enough to satisfy the legendary appetites of North Woods lumbermen whose harvest was timber. A blacksmith forges souvenir horseshoes, and the 1900 Cracker Barrel Country Store has all the provisions a fair-weather lumberjack needs. Open end of June through very early September and closed on Sundays. Reopens for Fall Festival late September through early October.

The Lincoln County Forest has 101,000 acres of great forestland. And when it comes to great eats, the woods deliver the goods. About 29 miles south of Tomahawk and 12 miles northeast of Merrill, **Maple Hollow**, W1887 Robinson Drive, Merrill, (715) 536-7251, www.explorewisconsin.com/maplehollow, has been processing pure maple syrup from their own sugar bush since 1889. From Highway C, which runs east-west a little north of Merrill proper, go south for a very short distance on Town Hall Road and turn right onto Robinson Drive. It is northeast of Merrill and a little west of Doering. Imagine fresh pancakes dripping with pure maple syrup, banana-nut bread slathered with maple cream, or maple candy glistening with sugar. Get it all at Maple Hollow, a third-generation family operation where apple-red buildings complement the cool green of maple leaves. They are not open on weekends except by appointment, so plan to visit on a Friday, since you will be in town anyway for the fish fry.

Maple Hollow's sugar bush consists of about three thousand trees across acres of beautiful forestland. A sugar bush, in case you don't know, is a stand of sugar maples that a grower taps. Don't look for buckets hanging from taps, though, because the trees give up their sap to tubes that pipe it directly into the syrup house. Wood fires boil it down to syrup density, which is about 40 gallons of sap to one gallon of syrup. There are more technical details, but in the end, know that you can buy the thick, finished product in a variety of sizes and nuances. Specialty table syrups are blended with cane sugar syrup for less intensity of maple flavor and a lower price. The stone-ground multigrain flours of the Heritage Pancake Mixes are jazzed up with cranberries, blueberries, blackberries, buttermilk, and other tasty tidbits. Honey is available but not from any resident honeybees. Seems the local black bear population proved incapable of keeping its paws out of the cookie-jar hives, and so Maple Hollow has to stick to producing maple products. Maple Hollow also sells cookbooks and equipment to those who wish to make their own maple syrup, and they will help you get started. Trees are tapped only during March and April, so that would be a great time to see the activity on an informal tour, but for sales and general camaraderie, they are open all year.

Dairyfest and Rodeo Days

Be sure to visit Merrill in late June for **Dairyfest**, held at the Lincoln County Fairgrounds, Sales Street north of Highway 64, Merrill, (715) 536-9474. It happens only one Sunday each year, and the highlight is the June Dairy Breakfast, which generates lines out the door. No wonder. For a few bucks, they serve up the breakfast of eggs, sausage, potato pancakes, pancakes with pure maple syrup, cheese, applesauce, juice, milk (chocolate and white), and coffee. It is all prepared by alumni of the FFA (Future Farmers of America) and the Agri-Business Committee. These are people whose business is farm-fresh food, so you know you are in good hands. See who wins the recipe contest, purchase ice cream from the Little Red Barn, watch square dancing, get a free horse-drawn wagon ride or tractor-pulled hayrack ride, and the very little people in your party can saddle up on miniature horses. Young calves, bunnies, chicks, and similar critters make up the small petting zoo, and the Humane Society sells fresh-baked goods.

Lincoln County Rodeo Days is the really big draw on the same weekend, and starts at the fairgrounds on the day before. Grandstand performances by the Professional Rodeo Cowboys Association include Bareback and Saddle Bronc, Calf Roping, Ladies' Barrel Racing, Steer Wrestling, Team Roping, and Bull Riding. Youngsters (human and animal) work off energy at the Children's Mutton Bustin' (sheep rides for prizes) and the Calf Scramble (grab a ribbon off the tail for prizes). Find out what Mounted Shooting is all about, and kick up your own heels at the Saturday night dance. Call (715) 675-6043, (715) 536-9336 or (877) 90-PARKS or visit www.lincolncountyrodeo.com.

Around these parts, visitors learn what the residents have known for a long time, that the Friday fish fry is a fine thing, and it is just the beginning of a great Weekend in the North Woods of Wisconsin.

SPECIAL EVENTS

Ethnic events at Knox Creek Heritage Center, N4517 West Knox Road, Brantwood, www.pricecountywi.net. Midsummer Celebration, Late June, maypole, Scandinavian foods, bonfire. A Country Afternoon, second Saturday in September, old-time crafts and demonstrations, baking and costume contests, homemade bread sale. Finnish Independence Day, December 6, *mojakka* (stew) dinner cooked outdoors in an iron kettle over an open fire.

Dairy Breakfast, www.pricecountywi.net. June. Free eggs, pancakes, pure maple syrup, sausages, and dairy products. Open barn, petting zoo, music. Held on different farms every year.

Ancient Skills for the Trail and Classroom, Treehaven, 2540 Pickerel Creek Road, Tomahawk, (715) 453-4106, www.uwsp.edu/cnr/treehaven. End of June.

Sign up in advance to acquire new skills that are as old as the ages.

Charity events, including brat, pork chop, and steak fries, happen all over the North Woods, as well as fish boils, chicken barbeques, and pancake breakfasts. Call the chambers of commerce and tourism offices for details.

PLACES TO STAY

AmericInn Lodge and Suites, 3300 East Main Street, Merrill, (715) 536-7979. Exceptionally clean, complimentary continental breakfast, indoor pool complex.

Palmquist's "The Farm," N5136 River Road, Brantwood, (715) 564-2558, (800) 519-2558, www.palmquistfarm.com. Eight hundred acres of North Woods farmland, this dream getaway is a working beef and tree farm that welcomes guests with a variety of rustic lodging styles with contemporary comforts, saunas, and Finnish specialties at every meal. Stay in the turn-of-the-century farmhouse, the newer White Pine Inn, or a variety of inviting cabins. Guests enjoy hayrides, hiking, biking, and fishing opportunities. Bring your horse if you have one, and they'll accommodate him too. Home-cooked meals are served family/buffet style in the farmhouse kitchen and dining rooms, and include meats, soups, vegetables, salads, and Finnish specialties.

Pine Cone Ranch Resort, N11668 Lamer Road, Tomahawk, (715) 453-3991, www.pineconeranchresort.com. An aptly named rustic resort on spring-fed lake with sandy beach. Clean, modern cottages. Fishing boat included.

Super 8 Motel, 108 West Mohawk Drive and Business 51, Tomahawk, (715) 453-5210. Indoor pool, whirlpool, continental breakfast. Clean, comfortable, convenient.

Timm's Hill Bed and Breakfast, North 2036 County Road C, Ogema, (715) 767-5288. Year-round accommodations, but also guided tours of syrup making available during late March/early April, and choose and cut your own Christmas trees late in the year.

3. BEFORE THE DOOR

From the sweet-tart pucker of Montmorency cherries to the fiery triumph of a whitefish boil-over, Door County has long had a way with food. Door County's next-door neighbor, Kewaunee County, is less well known but no stranger to farm experiences or regional foods. Anyone who has ever zoomed through Kewaunee County on their way up to The Door might want to consider stopping next time for a taste of what's cooking, smoking, boiling down, or fermenting in and around its small towns. And the Kewaunee County countryside, as you will discover on a back-roads drive, is home to dairy cows, big old barns, and fields that grow good, healthy crops right down to the shoreline of Lake Michigan. About eight miles west of the town of Kewaunee, one of Wisconsin's Rustic Roads leads you past the remains of a lime kiln, an old flour mill, weathered barns, and an old German home.

Heritage Farm, south of Kewaunee.

Kewaunee County is located along Wisconsin's east coast, on land that sticks out of the mainland like a pie knife. The town of Kewaunee is the county seat and a busy waterfront city located 29 miles east of Green Bay.

Around Kewaunee

Start a tour of Kewaunee County from the southern end by first visiting **Heritage Farm**, N2251 Highway 42 (five miles south of downtown), Kewaunee, (920) 388-0604. From the roots of an 1876 Czech farmstead, there is emerging a celebration of traditional Midwestern agriculture. It is not a living history farm or museum, but more like an event-oriented center. The big event is Farm Fest, and it is all about the traditions, stories, food, music, and landscape of the Midwestern farm, and it spans eight weeks in summer. In a recent season, Farm Fest sprang to life with a country fair, old-fashioned school picnic, visit-the-farm weekend with tours, dairy, and cheese vat demonstrations, butter making, milk bottling, brunch, a trout boil, and more.

Following a schedule of themes, there are also old-time cook stove threshing meals, square dancing to the Sugar on the Floor Barn Dance Orchestra, and a variety of ethnic heritage celebrations. Some events occur on weekdays throughout the season, but on every weekend during Farm Fest, visitors can enjoy wagon rides, a farm animal petting zoo, and foods from the Summer Kitchen. Come autumn, the local 4-H kids swoop down on the barn with creepy props and rigging that transform it into a haunting Halloween experience. When this happens, one can almost see the ghosts of the early Czech farmers scratching their heads in confusion.

Drive southwest 5 miles on Highway 42 and County Road G to **Norman General Store**, E3296 County Road G, Kewaunee, (920) 388-4580, www.norman generalstorebb.com. Closed on Sundays except by appointment. Located on a quiet country crossroads, this outpost will please anyone in the market for gourmet foods, quilt fabrics, sewing notions, and home décor items. You may be interested in purchasing a cheese box that is silk screened with the Norman General Store logo and made by the last U.S. maker of these wares, in a nearby Wisconsin town called Denmark. Feast your senses on handmade soaps in yummy colors, hand-woven rag rugs, hand-dipped beeswax candles, put-up vegetables and maple syrup, and set a few floorboards to creaking. The store is old, having been built by immigrant Czech farmers about 1870. The current owners are former dairy farmers who carefully researched their store and proudly reopened it in 1998.

The proprietors of Norman General Store are likely to recommend a stop at the nearby **Silver-B Maple Syrup Farm**, N1460 County Road B, Kewaunee, (920) 388-2910. This grassroots enterprise taps into a local resource and comes up with a product that enhances the flavor of other foods, from pancakes to home-baked bread. Each spring, they start with three thousand taps, catching the sap in buckets before sending it through the stainless steel evaporator. Drop by during the annual spring open house to enjoy the woodland setting, a tour of the sugar shack, and an ice cream sundae topped with the house specialty.

Now, it's on to Kewaunee. The **Kewaunee County Historical Museum**, 613 Dodge Street, Court House Square, Kewaunee, (920) 388-7176, counts a few farm-related artifacts among its collection. Located very close to the museum, **Fiala's Fish Market**, 216 Milwaukee Street, Kewaunee, (920) 388-3701, sits right on Lake Michigan and offers fresh and smoked fish and spreads at incredibly reasonable prices. In the summer of 2003, **Barnsite Art Studio and Gallery**, 109 Duvall Street, Kewaunee, (920) 388-4391, www.barnsiteartstudio .com, sponsored a juried exhibition having the theme of "Barns and Farms." This exhibition attracted artists from across the country and brought together—under one barn roof—a collection of fine arts that became a feast for the eyes and the heart. One thing was clear—how much farms mean to people all over America. It was held in conjunction with the traveling Smithsonian Exhibit, "Barn Again: Celebrating an American Icon," and it was so successful that they began repeating it. Barnsite is an art school and gallery housed in a 5,200-square-foot red barn that was built of hand-hewn posts and beams. From Fiala's, the studio is about a mile north on Highway 42; turn right onto Duvall.

Leave Kewaunee now and go northwest about 11 miles to the Casco and Luxemburg area, where apple and cherry orchards paint the towns red. **Hillside Apples**, E2237 Highway 54, Casco, (920) 837-7440, offers pre-picked or u-pick McIntosh, Cortland, and other varieties. Load up on fresh cider, caramel apples, jams, jellies, honey, and maple syrup. The autumn Harvest Festival includes free horse-drawn wagon rides to the orchard and to the pumpkin patch.

Algoma

Take Highway 54 northeast from Casco for 10 miles into the fishing village of Algoma on the Lake Michigan shore. Algoma has transformed a fish shanty into a history lesson, a brewery into a winery, and dreams into realities. It is a big bite for a small town. Let's start with the dreams.

The same folks who run the Heritage Farm south of Kewaunee opened a fully certified, commercial-grade kitchen that local growers and entrepreneurs rent in order to produce their specialty foods of choice. It is a great savings for them and a chance for visitors to stop in and see what's cooking. It might be coffee one day and powdered mushrooms for use in soups and stews the next. Plus, they have retail shelves with some of these finished products for sale, along with the works of local artisans. Choices change with the seasons and according to who is realizing what culinary dream, but may include elk summer sausage and snack sticks, fresh produce, jams, jellies, pickled and canned foods, and baked goods. There are scheduled and TBA demonstrations of cooking, a sprinkling of by-reservation Meet the Chef dinners, and sometimes samples that come fresh from this, the **Farm Market Kitchen**, 520 Parkway Street, Algoma, (920) 487-9750. Call ahead.

Housed in a Civil War-era stone building with four stories, red velvet drapes, underground arched cellars, and a sealed-off tunnel, the **von Stiehl Winery**, 115 Navarino Street, Algoma, (920) 487-5208, (800) 955-5208, www.vonstiehl.com, offers free tasting and nominal-fee tours. The wines are made from traditional *vinifera* grapes grown on the west coast, French hybrids from the American Heartland, and regional fruits including apples (Door County), blackberries (Pacific

The historic structure housing the Art Dettman Fish Shanty is just to the left of the old Chicago fireboat in Algoma.

17

Northwest), blueberries (Michigan), and cranberries (central Wisconsin). The semi-sweet Private Reserve Cherry wine has an especially intense cherry taste with a finish that lingers. It's made from Door County cherries, as are the four other cherry wines that represent a legacy of winemaking going back to the late founder.

Located across the riverfront from the winery, the **Art Dettman Fish Shanty** is the green tarpaper structure that is listed on the National Register and once served the commercial fishing industry as a handy storage spot for nets and gear. Back in 1897, the fishing fleet of Algoma was the largest on Lake Michigan. Today, people who love to hear the old fish stories gather at the shanty when former commercial fishermen, historians, musicians, actors and others bring it back to life on scheduled Saturdays. To check for current availability of Saturdays at the Shanty, or to schedule a visit to the shanty where information boards also tell the stories, call (920) 487-3443.

All this talk of fish makes a visit to **Bearcat's Fish House**, 295 Fourth Street, Highway 42 Bridge, Algoma, (920) 487-2372, (920) 487-3549, the next best stop. It is two-tenths of a mile from the winery. Cases are stocked with smoked chubs, whitefish, trout, salmon, bluefins, carp, blind robins, and spreads. They buy from some 30 commercial fishermen across the Great Lakes. Smoked cuts include steaks, fillets, and whole fish, and some are seasoned with brown sugar, Cajun spices, or lemon pepper. All smoking is done on the premises using real wood, and Bearcat and Linda say it is the only way to smoke. Bring in your own fresh catch for custom smoking done right.

From Algoma, drive north on County Road S to **Wienke's Cherry Acres Farm Market**, 292 County Road S, Algoma, (920) 487-5722, the fun side of this work-

Beach at Algoma Beach Motel, Algoma.

ing family farm. A big barn is filled to the rafters with homegrown produce such as fingerling potatoes, preserved products, Upper Peninsula pasties, condiments galore, and chickens, ducks, geese, or turkeys by special order. You will not believe the array of preserved products, from blueberry applesauce to Super Hot Dill Spears with Super Hot Peppers. The cherry jam/jelly choices include cherry, hot cherry, whole cherry, cherry apricot, cherry blueberry, cherry raspberry, cherry rhubarb, cranberry cherry, and strawberry cherry. They also have cherry summer sausage, brats, and links. Less than one-quarter mile to the south, **Renard's Cheese Factory and Outlet Store**, 248 County Road S, Algoma, (920) 743-6626, (920) 487-2825, offers tours (call ahead) of the cheese-making and curd-cutting processes.

Door County
Kewaunee County is indeed coming into its own, but of course you cannot ignore The Door. Following is a whirlwind tour of popular food and farm attractions, beginning in Forestville at the southern end of Door County, and on up to Washington Island, which covers roughly 70 miles. Hang on, here goes. Inland off Highway 42, stop in to **Country Ovens**, 229 East Main Street, Forestville, (920) 856-6767, www.countryovens.com. Their Cherry De-Lite brand of dried cherries is made on-site. They also offer cherry juices, syrups, sprinkles, and baking mixes. Once dried, the cherries pack the equivalent oomph of eight pounds of fresh cherries. The folks at Country Ovens recommend adding dried cherries to: barbeque sauce before grilling chicken or ribs, rice pilaf, oatmeal, regular cherry pie, and cream cheese. Munch on free samples as you learn the answers to questions such as, how long do dried cherries last? For a history lesson on the local cherry crop and the fish boil, visit the **Door County Historical Museum**, 18 North Fourth Avenue, Sturgeon Bay, (920) 743-5809. From Country Ovens, it is a 13-mile drive.

Anyone who thinks kids have little interest in farms hasn't seen the excitement levels go through the roof at **The Farm**. It is located four miles north of Sturgeon Bay on 4285 Highway 57, Sturgeon Bay, (920) 743-6666. From the din in the gift shop when it is time to choose that one best souvenir, to the picture-perfect grin that lights up a little one's face when a piglet suckles milk from a baby bottle, The Farm connects even city kids with country critters. Continue the farm theme at **Dairy View Country Store**, 5169 County Road I, Sturgeon Bay, (920) 743-9779, www.dairyview.com, where you can not only eat ice cream, but also watch cows being milked for it.

Continuing north, you can buy whole pies that are fresh baked or frozen at **Sweetie Pies**, located at the Settlement Shops just south of Fish Creek on Highway 42, (920) 868-2743. **Lautenbach's Orchard Country**, 9197 Highway 42, Fish Creek, (920) 868-3479, grew from a fruit-piled wagon to a very-cherry farm market that today offers orchard tours and the experience of an on-site winery. See the trademark roof-eating goats at **Al Johnson's Swedish Restaurant**, 700 North Bay Shore Drive, Sister Bay, (920) 854-2626, where you can dine on Swedish pancakes with lingonberries. Getting close to the top of the Door now, stop at **Berry Best Foods and Fish**, 12266 Highway 42, Ellison Bay, (920) 854-4443, where they catch and smoke fish, grow their own berries, and bake them into delicious treats. **Bea's Ho-Made Products**, 763 Highway 42, Gills Rock, (920) 854-2268, makes jams, jellies, pickles, and pies and invites you to "watch us make your product." Cross "Death's Door" on the ferry to the 14,000-acre Washington Island, where farming and commercial fishing are still practiced. The **Washington Island Farm Museum**, RR 1, Jackson Harbor Road, Washington Island, (920) 847-2179, is comprised of five original island buildings on three acres with field machinery, a forge and sawmill, and homemaking artifacts. Have a picnic, then set out for a tour of the **Double K-W Ostrich Farm**, W1928 West Harbor Road, Washington Island, (920) 847-3202, which also features a petting zoo and ostrich products for sale. Finally, go to **Field Wood Farm**, RR 1 Box 225, Washington Island, (920) 847-2490, for a trail ride atop a rare Icelandic horse. It's closed some days in June and September for supply trips; hey, it's an island.

Putting it all together, now you know that on this trip, you can pick cherries right off the tree, eat cherries dried, baked into a pie, or mixed into ice cream, and stock up on more cherry condiments than you ever thought existed. Among other delights, you can visit a couple of farms, poke around an old fish shanty, and thrill to a whitefish boil. And you can discover the undiscovered charms of Kewaunee County.

SPECIAL EVENTS

Shepherd's Market, Whitefish Bay Farm, 2831 Clark Lake Road (County Road WD), near Jacksonport, (920) 743-1560. Mid-May. Fiber event with demonstrations of spinning and weaving.

Cherry Fest, Lakeside Park, Highway 57, Jacksonport, www.doorbell.net/jhs/events.htm. Early August. Fresh cherry bakery, historical display, arts, crafts, foods, music.

Shanty Days Celebration of the Lake, Algoma. www.algoma.org/shantydays. Early August. Fishing contest with Youth and Shore classes, nominal entry fees with prizes just for entering. Call Kevin Naze, (920) 487-2433. Parade, Friday evening fish boil, food tents/booths (shanty chili, hot pork sandwiches, fish plates/sandwiches with perch, smelt, and whitefish, authentic chicken booyah, Belgian *trippe*, hot roasted corn on the cob, roasted nuts, Farm Market Kitchen offerings, etc.), entertainment, street market fair.

KeLe Alpacas the Fun Side, E1870 Pine Grove Road (approximately 10 miles west of Kewaunee), Kewaunee, www.alpacanation.com/KeLeAlpacas.asp. This private alpaca farm hosts this special day to learn about alpacas and their role in agriculture. Join the llamas on a picnic in the pasture.

Agricultural Heritage Days, Kewaunee County Fairgrounds, Luxemburg. Near end of September. Old-fashioned demonstrations of steam engines, antique tractor and horse pulls, rides behind steam engine Big Jim, petting zoo, farm antiques, and the Cookstove Ladies serving foods from wood stoves.

Scarecrow Fest, Garden Angels, N6695 Highway 42 (three miles south of town), Algoma, (920) 487-2530. Early October. Scarecrow voting, pumpkins, produce, fall decorations, alpacas, steam engine, children's games like Prize in the Haystack. Garden Angels is a barn-based gardening shop. Meals served up in the Farm Market Kitchen include breakfast (sausage, pumpkin pancakes) and lunch (sausage sandwich, chili, pumpkin ice cream, spiced cherry topping, hot cider and chocolate, etc.).

PLACES TO EAT

Tradition runs deep at the classic Door County fish boil, a dinner event that harkens back to the days when fishermen and farmers fed the lumberjacks and settlers. Specifics vary among the restaurants, but generally include locally caught whitefish, little potatoes and onions, coleslaw, lemon, melted butter, and Door County cherry pie. Cooking occurs over an open fire, and just before the fish, potatoes, and onions are removed from the kettle, the Master Boiler adds fuel to make the fish oils boil over the rim and light up the night. Restaurants that are serious about their fish boil include the **Old Post Office Restaurant,** 10040 Water Highway 42, Ephraim, (920) 854-4034; **Pelletier's Restaurant,** 4199 Main Street, Fish Creek, (920) 868-3313; **Sandpiper Restaurant,** 8166 State Highway 57, Baileys Harbor, (920) 839-2528; **The Viking Grill and Lounge,** 12029 Highway 42, Ellison Bay, (920) 854-2998; and **The White Gull Inn,** 4225 Main Street, Fish Creek, (920) 868-3517. Most prefer that you make reservations in advance.

Birchwood Inn, E3902 County Road F, Kewaunee, (920) 388-0240. Sunday brunch features baked and broasted chicken, barbeque meatballs, ham, porkies, eggs, Belgian waffles, potatoes and vegetables.

Karsten Inn Restaurant "Zum Engel", The Historic Karsten Inn, 122 Ellis Street, Kewaunee, (920) 388-3800. German buffet each Saturday night, 1800s bar. A former housekeeper, Agatha, has been reported to knock over sugar bowls and salt shakers to the vexation of the kitchen staff. But no one gives Agatha the pink slip; she died decades ago.

Not Licked Yet, 4054 Main Street, Fish Creek, (920) 868-2617. Frozen custard in endless flavors, playground, creek side. Summer hot spot.

The Cookery, Main Street (Highway 42), Fish Creek, (920) 868-3634, www.cookeryfishcreek.com. Breakfast, lunch, dinner. Cute country décor with emphasis on Door County flavors. French toast with cherry sauce, whitefish chowder. Take home a whole cherry pie from The Pantry.

PLACES TO STAY

Algoma Beach Motel, 1500 Lake Street, Algoma, (888) 254-6621, www.harbor walk.com. No road between your balcony and the stretch of sandy beach. On Sunday mornings, awaken to the sounds of seagulls and church bells.

Century Farm Motel, 10068 Highway 57, Sister Bay, (920) 854-4069. Motel

Wish you were here

Door County has over three thousand acres of Montmorency cherry orchards. It is easy to plan a summer vacation around cherry-picking, because the tart fruits ripen from mid-July to mid-August. Just ask the Miller family of Kenilworth, Illinois.

"We went cherry picking, kids and grandparents too, great fun and delicious results! Two full buckets and three cherry pies came home with us. We love cherries! Whether you are a child sitting on your daddy's shoulders to pick cherries, or a grandparent who serves as the 'taste tester,' it's great family fun!" says Karen Miller, whose husband Tim and children Sara and T.J. all get in on the fun.

So what does the Miller family do with their bounty? "We eat them 'alone' or on French vanilla ice cream. The ones we bring home we use for baking cherry muffins or bread, sometimes a cherry crisp, and often for cherry smoothies or shakes," Karen Miller explains.

But for her family, the true reward is sweeter still. "The best feeling is being able to pull out a bag of Door County cherries from the freezer in the middle of a Chicago winter and share the memories of our summer day," Miller says.

The Wisconsin Red Cherry Growers, Inc. recommends calling the Door County Chamber of Commerce at (920) 743-4456 for current picking dates.

---

on country farm 10 miles south of town. Four individual units for up to five people. Picnic area.

Froghollow Farm Bed and Breakfast, N17W1029 Jackson Harbor Road (near Sievers School), Washington Island, (920) 847-2835, www.froghollowfarm.com. Drift off to sleep in this historic, renovated farmhouse on five country/island acres. Private baths, breakfast on the deck.

Norman General Store and Bed and Breakfast, E3296 County Road G, Kewaunee, (920) 388-4580, www.normangeneralstorebb.com. Cozy accommodations with furnishings gathered from the area. Former dairy farmers, the innkeepers are happy to offer suggestions for agricultural attractions and share stories of local history. Two-bedroom Summer Kitchen includes, true to its name, a full kitchen.

The Inn at Windmill Farm, 3829 Fairview Road, Baileys Harbor, (920) 868-9282, www.1900windmillfarm.com. Baileys Harbor is quiet to begin with; a stay at this 10-acre farm with original barns and windmill is a real escape. Full cooked breakfast, adults only.

The Washington Hotel, Restaurant, and Culinary School, W14N0354 Range Line Road, Detroit Harbor (by Gislason Beach), Washington Island, (920) 847-2169, www.thewashingtonhotel.com. This century-old hotel was built to accommodate ships' captains. Hand-carved beds with organic cotton sheets, steam showers, herb garden, brick-oven breakfasts. Also available are restaurant meals that feature brick-oven cooking, island produce, lake fish, and more local/artisanal foods. The school offers single and multi-day classes and drop-in demos.

The Wickman Farm, Homestead Road, Washington Island, (847) 256-1664, (920) 847-2478. 1872 log cabin on Detroit Harbor. NOTE: The cabin has no street address. There are only four cottages on Homestead Road; the cabin is the only one built of log. Currently it is the only accommodation available. The farm is one and one-half blocks away. It dates to 1875.

Whitefish Bay Farm Bed and Breakfast, 3831 Clark Lake Road (County Road WD), Sturgeon Bay, (920) 743-1560, www.whitefishbayfarm.com. Restored 1908 farmhouse on 80 acres with Corriedale sheep. Next to Whitefish Dunes State Park.

4. CRANBERRY COUNTRY

The Tomah Convention and Visitor's Bureau reports that settlers who first set eyes on the cranberry called it the craneberry because to them, the flowering vine nodded like the head of the elegant marshland bird. And long before this romantic notion took flight, Native Americans were eating cranberries fresh, ground, or mashed with cornmeal and baked. They also sweetened the refreshingly tart fruits with maple syrup or honey, and mixed them with wild game to make the survival food known as pemmican.

Today even as the latest tropical fruit comes into favor, the cranberry remains special for its zingy taste, nutritional value, and traditional place on the Thanksgiving table. It is also one of the few major fruits native to North America, and Wisconsin is one of its leading national producers. As you'll discover, the cranberry even finds its way into refreshing ice cream and savory condiments. In Monroe County, which accounts for a healthy percentage of the Badger State's annual production, the cranberry even has its own museums and festivals.

This tour focuses on Monroe County. However, the area around Wisconsin Rapids (52 miles northeast of Tomah) would also be worth a visit, as it offers the Cranberry Highway, a museum, and harvest tours. But that's another trip. You will find Monroe County, and the town of Tomah, about equidistant from both Madison to the southeast (98 miles) and Eau Claire to the northwest (81 miles). Monroe County is located in the west-central part of Wisconsin, just one county east of the Minnesota border.

Tomah

Tomah rolls out the cranberry-red carpet with a remarkable range of ways to try cranberries—eating, drinking, air freshening, decorating, and learning. Tomah's sprawling **Cranberry Country Lodge** opened in 2003 with an indoor water park, tasteful cranberry décor, and the Cranberry Canteen that offers jumbo cranberry muffins with Wisconsin butter in the morning, cranberry cocktails in the evening, and sandwich fare (cranberry honey mustard, anyone?) in between.

Fern Kennedy of **Humbird Cheese Mart** remembers what the northern edge of Tomah was like some 30 years ago. Back then, she and her husband first opened their cheese shop at the point where I-90 and I-94 finally go their separate ways. As Kennedy recalls, it was nothing but peaceful hayfields all around. However, it was also a popular mid-point stop between Milwaukee and the Twin Cities, and so there the enterprising couple began offering quality Wisconsin cheese from area farms. Today the intersection is all grown up, and Humbird Cheese Mart, I-94 and Highway 21, Exit 143, Tomah, (608) 372-6069, (888) 684-5353, www.humbirdcheese.com, is housed in a stylized barn and silo. Cheese remains the staple product, but browse around to discover an amazing range of specialty foods, from savory to sweet, that are prepared with cranberries: mustard, syrup, muffin mix, fruit preserves, horseradish, coffee, cranberry-vanilla-pecan fudge, and cheesecake. Don't miss the serving pieces made of hand-blown cranberry glass. It's not cheap, but it is gorgeous.

Next door, the **Cranberry Country Mall**, I-94 & Highway 21, Tomah, (608) 372-7853, (888) 757-0044, www.tomah.com/antiquemall, offers gifts such as cranberry-scented traveler's candles and cranberry glass pieces. If you ask about *antique* cranberry glass, they might send you north to the Wisconsin Cranberry Discovery Center in Warrens. But first, dig a little deeper into Tomah and pick up insight into the history of cranberry farming at the **Tomah Area Historical Society Museum**, 1112 Superior Avenue (the main north-south street, a.k.a. Highway 12), Tomah, (608) 372-1880. Closed on Sundays. Enjoy learning of the area's farming, lumbering, manufacturing and railroad/transportation history.

Continue south on Superior Avenue and left on Highway 12/16 East to **Burnstad's European Village and Café**, 701 East Clifton Street, Tomah, (608) 372-3277. This is not only an encapsulated old-world shopping experience with eighteenth-century street lamps, but it also houses the All Wisconsin Shop with its extensive collection of cranberry-themed items and specialty foods. Shop at the village's supermarket and break there for lunch.

Tucked into the loft of **This Old Barn** is **Cranberries and Such**, 16005 Holiday Road, Tomah, (608) 374-3330. This charming gift shop is located four miles east of Burnstad's in rural Tomah, and there is also a petting zoo with llamas, horses, goats, and pot-bellied pigs. To get there from Burnstad's, continue east on Highway 12 for about 4 miles.

Cranberry Marshes

Now it's on to the low-growing cranberry marshes, reached by way of the 45-mile route mapped out by the Tomah CVB. These are strictly commercial operations and viewable from the road. Feast your eyes upon a remarkable form of agriculture that's only practiced in Massachusetts, New Jersey, Oregon, Washington, and, uniquely in the American Heartland, Wisconsin.

Heading east on Highway 21, drive four miles to the **Tomah Ocean Spray Receiving Station**, which is the largest such facility in the world. During harvest season, you can arrange for an insightful tour (alas, Monday–Friday only) by calling (608) 372-7824. Learn what it takes to clean and grade millions of pounds of berries each day during peak production. Learn why a good berry bounces, and how computers help to sort individual berries according to color. In general terms, they consider a bumper crop to be four berries per vine, and a bed should last 20 to 25 years before it requires replanting.

The drive goes north for seven miles on County Road N, passing four cranberry marshes along the way. Taking a few turns and continuing north, you pass the Jim Potter marshes that belong to the oldest family of growers in this area, and that they share with nesting herons. You also pass by the building that until recently housed the Cranberry Expo Ltd. Museum and Gift Shop, which has moved to the village of Warrens and become the Wisconsin Cranberry Discovery Center.

The **Wetherby Cranberry Company**, 3365 Auger Road, Warrens, (608) 378-4813, is a special place for visitors. Family-owned since 1903, Wetherby sells fresh cranberries directly from its on-site warehouse from late September through mid-November. What a rare treat! And, you don't have to pull up with a truck—they offer sizes from one to 30 pounds. But there is more. They host the Public Cranberry Harvest Day on the first Saturday morning in October, rain or shine. It is an opportunity to watch the harvest and listen as family members interpret and answer questions. No admission, no reservations, lots of fun.

Eventually, you come to Warrens, a tiny village that has been dubbed the Cranberry Capital of Wisconsin because it has the largest concentration of cranberry marshes in the state, producing about 40,000,000 pounds of cranberries each year on more than 6,500 acres within a 15-mile radius. Warrens is right up near the top of Monroe County.

Here is the **Wisconsin Cranberry Discovery Center**, 204 Main Street, Warrens, (608) 378-4878, and it is appropriately housed in a former cranberry warehouse. A video explains the farming practices that are unique to cranberry growing. For instance, the vines are self-pollinating, but some growers also rent honeybees and bumblebees. Also, since the beds are close to the ground, frost damage is always a concern until the vines go dormant, then sprinkler irrigation applies water that freezes to protect the hardy but still vulnerable plants. View antique machinery that many of the local growers had designed, built, and used throughout the decades. Included are hand rakes, horse clogs, water reels, and harvest boats that show the evolution of the industry. Antique cranberry glass is also on display, much of it having originated in Switzerland and the Czech Republic. Check out the Wisconsin Cranberry Taste Test Kitchen. Shop for contemporary cranberry glass vases and other pieces, cranberry wines, mustards, sauces, dried cranberries, candies, pie, ice cream, cookbooks, and coloring books.

Drop into the **Warrens Cranberry Festival Office** a few blocks away on Pine to get information and buy festival souvenirs like older cook booklets and embroidered key chains. Pick up the Cranberry Country tour map; suggested routes cover some of the same ground as the Tomah map, but this one also pinpoints the locations of cranberry marshes in and around Warrens. Additional points of interest in the Warrens area include the Cliffstar Receiving Plant, the Double K Korral, the Moseley Fruit and Vegetable Farm, and a sphagnum moss drying bed. They call sphagnum moss Wisconsin's invisible crop because it is important but no one seems to know it is grown here.

Back Roads

Depending on which direction you are traveling, you may be able to explore even more regional sites. Take a guided trail ride at **Red Ridge Ranch**, two miles east of Mauston (Mauston is 29 miles southeast of Tomah) 4881 State Road 82, (608) 847-2273, www.redridgeranch.com, through 250 acres of rolling farmland and hills next to the Lemonweir River. Pony rides are available for youngsters. Thirty-four miles southwest of Tomah around Cashton, there lies an Amish community where a guide service called **Down a Country Road**, (608) 654-5318, offers step-on tours, but never on Sunday. Observe cheese making at **Old Country Wisconsin Cheese**, S 510 County Road D, Cashton, (608) 654-5411, (888) 320-9469, www.oldcountrycheese.com, where they produce fresh curds daily and remain as one of the few cheese factories that handle only fresh can milk. That's the stuff that comes direct from Bessie, Clover, and Buttercup, and Amish farmers deliver it as if were still the nineteenth century. Farther southwest is **Norskedalen Nature and Heritage Center**, N455 O Opus Road, County Road T, Coon Valley, preserving natural beauty and pioneer Norwegian-American farming with relocated log structures that depict a turn-of-the-century farmstead. Coon Valley is 46 miles southwest of Tomah. Somewhat east, **Kickapoo Valley Ranch**, E11761 County Road P, La Farge, (608) 625-6222, www.kvranch .com, sits in the lap of 8,500 acres of preserved, unglaciated land and offers 45 miles of trails. Reservations are recommended. The town of La Farge is 35 miles southwest of Tomah.

So come to Monroe County and cultivate your own appreciation for the tart little cranberry. Learn about the specialized farming techniques that produce seas of red toward the autumn of each year. And come on Thanksgiving, when the bright red cranberries bounce into the produce section of your local grocery

FRESH FROM THE FIELD
Tips from Cranberry Country

Since cranberries are highly seasonal, buy extra bags and simply pop them as is into the freezer, where they keep well up to a year. When ready to use, rinse the berries with water but don't thaw. Cranberries are great in recipes, requiring no seed, skin, or stem removal, and add an extra burst of flavor that makes ordinary recipes special and distinctive. Plus, although cranberries are a native Midwestern fruit, they are not used as commonly as, say, apples, so culinary kudos are sure to roll your way. The Wisconsin State Cranberry Growers Association says 12 ounces of cranberries equal three cups, and you can chop the little red devils in a food processor to save time. For lots more information, visit www.wiscran.org, www.cranberryinstitute.org, and www.oceanspray.com.

store, you can recall your weekend visit to the beautiful cranberry marshes where farmers raise their crops and herons make their nests.

SPECIAL EVENTS

Butterfest, Sparta, (608) 269-BUTR, www.spartabutterfest.com. Second weekend in June. Butter making demonstration, milking contest, lumberjack breakfast, quilt show, horseshoe tournament, horse-drawn wagon rides, softball tournament, parade.

Wisconsin Dairyland National Tractor/Truck Pull, Recreation Park, Tomah, (608) 372-2081, (800) 948-6624, www.tomahtractorpull.com. Late June. Said to be the biggest in the country.

Warrens Cranberry Festival (Cranfest), (608) 378-4200, www.cranfest.com. Late September. A granddaddy event. Rooms in Tomah sell out for this one. Enjoy very-berry activities like cranberry marsh and museum tours, the Wisconsin cranberry recipe contest, the Cranberry fry pan, the biggest cranberry contest, and viewing of the cranberry video. Partake of cranberry cream puffs and lots of other foods like lamb and pork sandwiches, chicken dinners, and ethnic specialties. The food booths number close to a hundred. Shop among an additional hundred farmers' market booths. There are fresh cranberries and cranberry products for sale all over the place. The pancake breakfast features cranberry syrup. Not to distract you, but there are also 650 art/craft booths, 350 antique/flea market booths, a carnival, a two-hour parade that resonates with

---

FIELD TO TABLE

Crunchy cranberry clumpers

This recipe is from Betty Brockman, from "Year-Round Cranberry Recipes," courtesy of Warrens Cranberry Festival, Inc., Warrens, Wisconsin.

1 pound Ambrosia Alabaster White Confectionery Coating (white chocolate)
3 cups Post Cranberry Almond Crunch cereal
1/2 cup sweetened dried cranberries
1/2 cup sliced almonds

Melt white coating and stir until smooth. Stir in cereal, sweetened dried cranberries, and almonds. Use teaspoon to drop on waxed paper, creating your own size of cluster. May garnish with additional chopped sweetened dried cranberries. 🦃

---

marching bands, live music, and where else could you hope to see people dressed up as cranberries?

PLACES TO EAT

Countyline Bar and Supper Club, W3686 Monroe Road (2 miles north of Warrens), Warrens, (608) 378-4767.

Cranberry Cabin Café, 212 Market Street, Warrens, (608) 378-4144.

Mr. Ed's Tee Pee, 812 Superior Avenue, Tomah, (608) 372-0888.

PLACES TO STAY

Cranberry Country Lodge, 319 Wittig Road, Tomah, (608) 374-2801, (800) 243-9874, www.cranberrycountrylodge.com. Make like a cranberry and get water-logged in the two-story water park with its swimming pools, giant hot tub, and 16-foot spiral slide. Kids have a ball in the prize redemption arcade as parents relax at umbrella tables. Not for kids only, though. Rustic theme, convenient location, all suites. You can run in flip-flops to the Cranberry Cupboard, (608) 374-2800, for convenience foods and a small selection of cranberry stuff.

Lark Inn, 229 North Superior Avenue, Tomah, (608) 372-5981, (800) 447-5275, www.larkinn.com. Rustic décor with country quilts on the beds and a convenient general store/deli. Continental breakfast.

Sunnyfield Farm Bed and Breakfast, N6692 Batko Road (5 miles from I-90/94 on Batko Road), Camp Douglas, (608) 427-3686, (888) 839-0232, www.sunnyfield.net. Slumber in the lumber, the native oak and maple that once grew on this farm, that is. The house was built back in the day by Otto Nettlebeck, who fired up a sawmill with a steam engine that was fueled by wood, and built the house that you enjoy today. Hardwood floors, 10-foot ceilings, hand-carved woodwork, spacious rooms, and windows in their original state. Four guestrooms, full country breakfast.

5. A LAKE MICHIGAN SHORE LUNCH OF SORTS

Sandwiched between Milwaukee and Door County on Wisconsin's sunrise coast, there are three cities that have the makings for a nice lunch complete with dessert. There is the Sheboygan brat, brought to you by Sheboygan. About 29 miles to the north, some of the healthiest breads ever to come out of an oven are coming out of Natural Ovens of Manitowoc, all golden brown and steamy and fragrant. And it is said that the classic American ice cream sundae was invented seven miles north of Manitowoc, right there in Two Rivers.

Brats

First up is Sheboygan. Set foot in this old German town and you will find that there are two kinds of bratwursts in the world. There is the brat, and then there is the Sheboygan brat. You can get the Sheboygan brat any number of ways—from a Sheboygan specialty shop or grocery store, in a Sheboygan restaurant, or at a Sheboygan brat fry. Among the many things to learn while in town is that the terms "brat fry" and "fry out" have special meaning in Sheboygan.

Let's say you are out touring the Sheboygan County Historical Museum, 3110 Erie Avenue, Sheboygan, (920) 458-1103. Somewhere in between the 1890s Schuchardt Barn that is full of rural agricultural displays, and the Bodenstab Cheese Factory that dates from 1867, you have gotten a craving for a Sheboygan brat. Soon enough you are driving down to the unassuming retail outlet of Old Wisconsin Sausage Company, 2107 South 17th Street (at Union Avenue), Sheboygan, (920) 458-4304. Here you can buy direct, and the selection is good.

For more brats direct from the source, pick up Highway 43 north to Miesfeld's Market, 4811 Venture Drive, Sheboygan, (920) 565-6328, www.miesfelds.com. Miesfeld's is eight miles north of Old Wisconsin Sausage Company. From Highway 43, take Exit 128 West onto Highway 42, about one-half mile to Venture Drive. Now into the third generation, the proprietors of this old-fashioned meat market still use Grandpa's old-world recipes as they have since 1941, except now they do it in a sparkling new building complete with a drive-thru. Pepper bacon and apple pie bacon are favorites, along with hams, summer sausages, and brats, plus they are branching out to make sausages of ethnic origins other than the German. All curing and smoking is done on-site, and this is

Loaves, hot and fresh, from the Natural Ovens Bakery in Manitowoc.

the old-line sausage maker's only location, although they distribute to regional supermarkets. Miesfeld's has won over 60 state and national awards for the sausages, with the Grand Champion Bratwurst voted Best in Wisconsin and second in the country for two consecutive years.

Which brings you to the search for the hard roll. Follow your nose four miles southeast of Miesfeld's to **Johnston Bakery**, 1227 Superior Avenue, Sheboygan, (920) 458-3342, or to the nearby **City Bakery**, 1102 Michigan Avenue, Sheboygan, (920) 457-4493. Visit a Sheboygan grocery store for the recommended butter, mustard, ketchup, sliced dill pickles, and onions, but not sauerkraut, to plop on top.

Oh, is the sun setting already? Better find that brat fryer . . . they've got them at the beautiful **Kohler-Andrae State Park**, 1020 Beach Park Lane, Sheboygan, (920) 451-4080. The park is located 11 miles south of the bakeries at the southern end of Sheboygan, and right on the lakefront.

Of course, you can make it very easy on yourself and order an honest-to-goodness Sheboygan brat at a local restaurant.

The third way to get your brat is to attend a special event, and one special event you don't want to miss while running around Sheboygan is the brat fry. Fortunately, you don't have to. The Sheboygan brat fry does not happen at 7:00 a.m. on the third Sunday of August in odd-numbered years, weather permitting. It happens on January 1 when hundreds of the town's bravest (choose your own adjective if this one does not seem right) jump into the lake for their inaugural Polar Bear Swim. And it keeps happening, all over town, almost any time there is an event going on. Sometimes the brat fry *is* the event; but even when Sheboyganites have something else to celebrate, like fine art, you can pretty much figure they will be frying brats too.

Breads

Now let's go get some of that great Natural Ovens bread direct from the bakery, and maybe even some of their fresh-baked cookies and bagels too. It is about 29 miles north, but first, you may wish to stop halfway up at **Whispering Orchards and McIntosh Café**, W1650 County Road MM, Cleveland, (920) 693-8584. Whispering Orchards is a farm market in a country setting with farm animals, orchard, corn maze, and lunch with apple pie. It is open daily most of the year, so it is hardly just an autumn thing. If you can make a long weekend of it, the best time to visit **Natural Ovens Bakery**, 4300 County Road CR, Manitowoc, (920) 758-2500, (800) 558-3535, www.naturalovens.com, is on a weekday, because that is when they give free, guided tours of the bakery operation. The schedule is Monday, Wednesday through Friday, 9:00, 10:00, and 11:00 a.m. Highway 43 gets you there.

Natural Ovens is a corporate enterprise based on one couple's refusal to bake with chemical additives, preservatives, and processes. Watch as white-clad bakers heft bags of recently milled whole-wheat flour, stone-ground hard white wheat, oat bran, millet, and other feel-good ingredients into mixers. Ground flaxseed and ground sorghum seed are key ingredients in many of the breads. By the time the dough is shaped into loaves, it has risen three times, representing a slow method that enhances flavor and increases B vitamins as the yeast happily grows and grows. Three thousand loaves bake each hour in the 106-foot-long hearth oven. The tour includes samples, and afterward, you can purchase breads, bagels, rolls, muffins, cookies, cereals, and mixes, as well as books, including some eye-openers written by the owners. Breads include 7-Grain Herb, Sunny Millet, Happiness with raisins, pecans, and cinnamon, Hunger Filler, and other golden-brown goldmines, and each comes with a newsletter—a new issue every week. The chocolate raspberry cookies are addictive.

Don't miss the bakery's own **Farm and Food Museum.** Buy some sheep feed before strolling over to the farm, where you can commune with the resident sheep, Belgian parade horses, chickens, donkeys, and rabbits in their pastures and barnyards. Donations are accepted. Housed in farm buildings, the museum takes a long look at agricultural history, all the way back to earliest recorded time. Enjoy the collection of two-cylinder John Deere tractors, and give the early 1900s hand mill a spin. The granary and log barn were built in 1857, and the 1920 smokehouse has yet to give up its pungent aroma. In the 1920–1960 Farm Machinery Building, life-size farmer sculptures—the work of one artist—slouch and otherwise hang about their equipment as if about to tend another field or call it a day and head in to supper.

Beyond the Shore

Meander on the farm-filled back roads to **Pine River Dairy**, 10115 English Lake Road, Manitowoc, (920) 758-2233, www.pineriverdairy.com, which is one of only a dozen butter factories left in Wisconsin. To get there from Natural Ovens, drive southwest on Highway 42, make a right at the eight silos and continue 2.5 miles on English Lake Road. It is about seven miles total. Almost unbelievably, Pine River Dairy has been around since 1877, and owned by the Olm family since 1932. It is open on Saturdays from 8:00 a.m. to 1:00 p.m., and closed on Sundays. Plunk down a quarter for a hand-dipped ice cream cone (cotton candy, strawberry, praline pecan, Mississippi mud pie, etc.) and begin deciding among over 250 varieties of cheese. Peek in the observation window as a worker wields a huge bowl of fluffy butter fresh from the churn. A by-product of cheese making, cream is put into pasteurization vessels where it pasteurizes overnight. From there it is pumped into the churns, removed, and shaped into blocks of butter. You can buy it here, along with flavored versions, at stock-up prices.

Go north now for 5 miles to **Pinecrest Historical Village**, 924 Pine Crest Lane (just south off County Road JJ), Manitowoc, (920) 684-5110, www.mchistsoc.org /pinecrest.htm. It is easy to imagine children dressed in calico dresses and little suits, escaped from school, free to race across the Village Green that stretches out as grassy and long as summer itself. With its tidy sense of community shaded by white pines, its tools polished and ready for craftsmen and shopkeepers and farmers to take up, Pinecrest Historical Village has the ability to fuel any nostalgic notion of our pioneer past. Who smokes their own meats, dries their own green beans, or hangs around the blacksmith shop anymore? Here is the Old Midwest. You can live it, for a time.

Pinecrest Historical Village sprang to life on a donated farm. Most of the buildings that you see were collected from farms around the county. The buildings' histories are tied to the lives of settlers and descendants, and the interpretive audiotape reenacts their own voices. The Witt Blacksmith Shop has been made fully operational for demonstrations, but even if nothing is going on, the audiotape brings all the materials to life, from the forge to the farrier box. The circa-1927 Benzinger-Rehrauer Sawmill is still used to cut lumber for repairs needed at Pinecrest. As timber ran out and agriculture replaced logging operations in the Manitowoc area, many earlier sawmills were converted to gristmills, but this one has retained its original nature. The 1920s Sladky Bee House is an uncommon farm building that sat atop a vaulted cellar, a resourceful arrangement that kept the bees warm in winter. Don't miss the exhibit of millstones along the nature trail.

Just Desserts

You've been promised dessert, so let's go get it. For those who would have started the tour with dessert, start reading here.

Topping many a list of classic dessert favorites is the ice cream sundae, a most civilized way to eat ice cream that is said to have been invented right here in Two Rivers, which is just seven miles north of Manitowoc. How did they do it? Here's the inside scoop. Key events came together at the right time and in the right place to bring the ice cream sundae to the world. Seems that in 1881, soda fountain owner Ed Berner was asked to top a dish of ice cream with chocolate sauce instead of serving the usual ice cream soda. This new-fangled version became a popular treat, but it was deemed good enough to be served only on Sundays. Until one day a little girl who had developed a taste for the concoction came along and proposed that on other days, couldn't they simply pretend it was Sunday? So the adults decided that would proba-bly be okay. Then a glassware salesman came along and placed a product order for an item that he spelled "sundae dishes." Well, *voila!* The ice cream sundae was officially born.

Today, you can order an ice cream sundae in its hometown, and on any day that you feel like spooning up some of that cold, creamy goodness with hot fudge/marshmallow/butterscotch sauce and a cherry on top. Don't miss an opportunity to relive ice cream history at **Ed Berner's Ice Cream Parlor**, which has been specially created as a replica and is located a little over one block one-tenth of a mile from the original. You can find it inside the Historic Wash-ington House, 17th and Jefferson streets (one block east of Highway 42), Two Rivers, (920) 793-2490, (888) 857-3529.

All in all, this trip is a wonderful way of experiencing three original con-tributions that Wisconsin has made to the food world, all within a 40-mile stretch along the sunrise-coast lakeshore.

SPECIAL EVENTS

Flapjack Day at Maywood, Ellwood H. May Environmental Park, Sheboy-gan, (920) 459-3906. March. Guided tour of the maple forest, samples of maple syrup, horse-drawn carriage rides, crafts.

Johnsonville Sausage Fest, Village of Johnsonville, (920) 893-3054. First Sunday after July 4th. Sausages, of course. Polka, big band, and German music in ballroom, tent, and firehouse.

Jaycees Brat Days, Kiwanis Park, Sheboygan, (920) 803-8980, www.sheboygan jaycees.com. First Saturday in August. This ultimate tribute sizzles with the heat of fryers, the brat-eating contest, the brat-cooking challenge, tons of live music, carnival rides, and more summer fun.

Food and Wine Experience, Kohler, (800) 344-2838, www.destinationkohler .com. Late October/early November. Food presentations, wine tastings, nation-al food and wine celebrities, book signings.

PLACES TO EAT

Sheboygan (and Kohler) restaurants that happily fry (grill) authentic She-boygan brats:

FULL STEAM AHEAD
The S.S. Badger

From May through early October, people and their vehicles cross the 60-mile-wide belly of Lake Michigan between Ludington, Michigan, and Manitowoc aboard the S.S. *Badger.*

For the four-hour crossing, this venerable car ferry features a lot of room to roam indoors and out, a gift shop, a mini-museum, a movie lounge, and a playroom. Early and late in the season, some passengers can overnight in a private stateroom while the ship is docked in Ludington.

Breakfast in the Upper Deck Café entices passengers with fresh fruit, scrambled eggs, French toast, sausage links, baked ham, buttermilk biscuits and sausage gravy, hash browns, English muffins, fresh-baked Danish, and baked apples. Passengers, up early to make sure they do not miss the boat back to the Wisconsin side, find the fragrant and colorful spread particularly welcoming.

As of 2004, passengers "Cruise and Learn" their way across the lake. An expert is aboard to share the secrets of, say, Great Lakes ships and shipwrecks, lighthouses, or fisheries and ecosystems. Plus, an officer of the ship may be talking about the shipboard lifestyle. But as ever, there are rounds of Badger Bingo. 🦡

Brisco County Wood Grill, 539 Riverfront Drive, Sheboygan, (920) 803-6915. Also charcoal/apple wood grilled Black Angus beef.

Happy Days, 2538 North 15th Street, Sheboygan, (920) 208-0615.

Horse and Plow, The American Club, Kohler, (920) 457-8888. A dozen Wisconsin beers on tap, 80 bottled beers.

Jumes Restaurant, 504 North Eighth Street, Sheboygan, (920) 452-4914. Fifties-style.

Rupp's at Riverdale, 5008 South 12th Street, Sheboygan, (920) 457-6444. Sunday buffet.

Rupp's Lodge, 925 North Eighth Street, Sheboygan, (920) 459-8155. Sheboygan's oldest restaurant.

Sy's Family Restaurant, 1735 Calumet Drive, Sheboygan, (920) 452-7850.

Beernsten's, 108 North Eighth Street, Manitowoc, (920) 684-9616, www .beernstens.com. The black walnut candy cases and booths, olive nut sandwich, and Kewpie Doll Special Sundae say it is the 1930s. Make time for this old-fashioned ice cream parlor serving Special Sundaes in 30+ sweet renditions of its own vanilla, chocolate, and strawberry ice cream. Other requisite ingredients include marshmallow, chocolate, butterscotch, and fruit toppings; nuts, maple, fruits, whipped cream, cherries, sprinkles, and Beernsten's own Chocolate Pigs.

Cedar Ridge Restaurant, 9215 County Road Z (I-43 Exit 164), Maribel, (800) 881-8691, www.foodspot.com/cedarridge. Friday night land and sea buffet, Sunday buffet. Scheduled trout boil April through October. Mini-farm over the wooden bridge past antique machinery and pond.

Warrens Restaurant, 905 Washington Street, Manitowoc, (920) 682-2533. Breakfast, lunch, dinner, everything cooked fresh and available anytime you are.

PLACES TO STAY

Harbor Winds Hotel, 905 South Eighth Street, Sheboygan, (920) 452-9000. The only hotel on the Riverfront Boardwalk offers proximity to the lake and complimentary breakfast bar.

Harmony Hills in the Hollow Bed and Breakfast, W7625 County Road N, Plymouth, (920) 528-8233. Victorian farmhouse leans toward luxury on 40 acres. Full breakfast.

Hillwind Farm, N4922 Hillwind Road, Plymouth, (920) 892-2199. Four guest rooms.

Holiday Inn, 4601 Calumet Avenue, Manitowoc, (920) 682-6000. Contemporary skylight lobby, 203 rooms including balcony rooms and suites. Indoor pool/whirlpool, sauna, exercise and game rooms.

6. COUNTRY IN THE CITY: THIS IS MADISON?

Cows on campus. Restaurant chefs who believe the quality of the ingredients is as important as the cooking. A farmers' market that many consider to be the best in the Midwest. This is Madison? Oh yes, and if you are willing to drive a short distance into the surrounding countryside, you could also enjoy visits to a trout fishing farm and a mustard museum, of all things. So make a mad dash for Madison, which is located 75 miles west of Milwaukee in far south-central Wisconsin, and 145 miles from Chicago. Odds are you will fall madly in love with the quirky mix of college-town madness and Dairy State sensibility.

Ice Cream 101

First, a little schooling. The University of Wisconsin–Madison is a 933-acre campus and the epicenter of Madison's sometimes freewheeling style. Founded in 1848, the university is renowned for excellence in education and a long history of breakthroughs in research. In the College of Agricultural and Life Sciences alone they developed the butterfat test that became the standard for

Fresh eggs at the UW-Madison's Poultry Research Lab.

milk-quality measurement, discovered vitamin A and the B complex vitamins, pioneered land planning, and revolutionized animal reproduction (www.cals .wisc.edu /media/history/index.html).

Okay, that's great. But on a hot summer day, the one thing you would really like to know before you melt into the sidewalk is, where's the Babcock Hall Dairy Store?

In case you haven't heard, this is where the university makes its own ice cream. It is a campus hot spot and a Madison must-stop, so for a taste of college life, get on over to **Babcock Hall Dairy Store,** University of Wisconsin–Madison, 1605 Linden Drive, Madison, (608) 262-3045, www.wisc.edu/food sci/store. Babcock Hall Dairy Store is open weekdays plus Saturdays 10:00 a.m. to 1:30 p.m. (later on football Saturdays), and closed on Sundays. Educate your palate with dairy-fresh, premium-rich ice creams, sherbets, and frozen yogurts in cones or in a range of sizes to go, all at reasonable prices for the high quality. No additives, no preservatives, just premium-quality ice creams from resident cows.

A master cheese maker hangs out here, too, reserving some of the fresh, frothy milk for the production of specialty cheeses. Try dill Havarti, Gouda, or a signature cheddar. The oldest cheddar is aged two years; they just don't have the space to store more. Try *juustoleipa,* but just don't try to pronounce it. This Finnish-style cheese is baked and the resulting brown, crusty surface earned it the name that, roughly translated, means "bread cheese." Shop for trinkets like stuffed cows and cow pencils. On weekday mornings, head upstairs to the observation window and watch the dairy production plant in action. But do all of this lickety-split, because you can only park for a limited time out front if a spot is available. Otherwise, find a nearby metered lot (watch out for "permit required" lots) or a not-so-nearby parking ramp.

A few doors west at the **Dairy Cattle Instruction and Research Center,** 1815 Linden Drive, Madison, (608) 262-2271, view afternoon cow milking and learn facts such as how many pounds of ice cream the average person eats in a year, and how many gallons of milk a cow gives per milking. On weekdays at the nearby **Poultry Research Lab,** you may be able to buy a dozen fresh eggs for a bargain price if they are available at the time.

Veggies 101

Drive six miles west of the campus to the 572-acre **West Madison Agricultural Research Station,** 6972 West Mineral Point Road, Madison, (608) 262-2257. It is one of the university's dozen outposts statewide, where field research happens under natural climatic conditions. No cows here, but, bed after bed of flowers, fruits, vegetables, and ornamental grasses, all labeled, offer a sneak peek into the possible future of horticulture and home gardens of this zone. The bulk of the acreage is planted in grain crops for academic researchers and also for the campus cows, but you are welcome to take a free, self-guided tour of the horticultural beds. You may see varieties of kale and Swiss chard that are planted together to demonstrate ornamentation and practicality. Farther on, look for berry bushes, grape vines, and apple trees. You need not be an avid gardener to enjoy wandering among the neat rows and taking in the long views of rolling hills.

Street Smarts

Back in the heart of Madison, just east of the campus and adjacent to the can't-miss-it State Capitol on the isthmus between Lake Mendota and Lake Monona, visit the **State Historical Society Museum of Wisconsin**, 30 North Carroll Street, Madison, (608) 264-6555, www.wisconsinhistory.org/museum, located seven miles from the research station. Closed on Sundays.

Half a block over, take the little ones to **Madison Children's Museum**, 100 State Street, Madison, (608) 256-6445, www.madisonchildrensmuseum.org. In keeping with the cow theme, the Milking Parlor has cows that are always happy to get a good milking (no matter whether this happens 50 times a day or the standard two; it is all the same to fiberglass cows). In the Toddler Barnyard, little ones enjoy books, puzzles, costumes, and foam building blocks. Agricultural education continues in the Let's Grow! area with opportunities for children to plant produce then sell their harvest at the farmers' market.

There are interesting shops scattered about Madison too. Since 1949, the **House of Wisconsin Cheese**, 107 State Street, Madison, (608) 255-5204, www.houseofwisconsincheese.com, has been purveying cheese from selected Wisconsin cheese makers. These range from the traditional to the specialty, from cranberry cheddar to aged stinky brick. They also sell fun stuff like cheese cutouts shaped like cows, tractors, and barns, and foam cheesehead gear (hats, neckties). The Web site describes the line as "amazingly popular," as if even they can't believe it. Another great in-town shop is **Seed Savers Garden Store**, 1919 Monroe Street, Madison, (608) 280-8149, one of the most unique garden supply stores you could hope to find. That's because it is a venture of the remarkable Seed Savers Exchange of Decorah, Iowa. It is the kind of place that uses Amish-built seed racks to display its collections of heirloom vegetable, flower, and herb seeds. **Lakeside Fibers**, 402 West Lakeside Street, Madison, (608) 257-2999, www.lakesidefibers.com, specializes in natural and organic yarns and fibers, many from Wisconsin, for the knitter and weaver.

Madison is growing a reputation for its emphasis on fresh ingredients that come in right from the fields. You see it at the **Dane County Farmers' Market**, and you see it in the restaurants that are the most celebrated. The restaurateurs who pay attention to where their—and your—food comes from simply cannot help but express their passion for what is fresh, and for what is grown locally. So stay for lunch and get a taste of why this makes such a difference in your dining experience.

School's Out

For some outlying fun on a real working dairy farm, visit **Hinchley's Dairy Farm**, 2844 Highway 73, Cambridge, (608) 764-5090, www.hinchleydairyfarmtours .com. It is about 20 miles east of Madison. There is an admission fee for the tour that can last from one to three hours, including an antique tractor ride and lots of hands-on opportunities to hold, pet, and feed the farm's critters. Spring brings baby animals, or go in autumn for pumpkins, hayrides, and haunted barn tours (additional fees apply). Ten miles to the south of Madison, **Eplegaarden**, 2227 Fitchburg Road, Fitchburg, (608) 845-5966, www.eplegaarden.com, offers raspberry, apple, and pumpkin picking with a Norwegian accent, *ja*.

Twelve miles south of Madison, immerse yourself in a farm experience and catch your own dinner at **Century Trout Farm**, 882 Highway 14, Oregon, (608) 835-9712, www.wistrout.com. This squeaky-clean, family-friendly farm welcomes visitors to fish for trout in a spring-fed pond that never freezes. The rolling farmland setting is picturesque. Trout is priced by the inch, and you can choose to have them dress and clean it for you. Not far away, visit **A–Z Sheep Farm**, 1820 Schuster Road, Oregon, (608) 835-5553, www.a-zfarm.com. These farm folks very much want to educate visitors about sheep shearing (February), baby lambs (March), and sheep in pasture (later in the year). The approach they take to farming is at once humane, environmentally sound, and economical, with lambs being pasture-raised without hormones or growth stimulants. Wool is available for spinning, weaving, crafts, and blankets, and the best time to buy it is at shearing.

And then there is the **Mount Horeb Mustard Museum**, 100 West Main Street, Mount Horeb, (608) 437-3986, (800) 438-6878, www.mustardmuseum .com. Mount Horeb is 24 miles west of Madison, and there you can feast your eyes on the world's largest collection of mustards, some 3,600 from all over the planet. Walk your taste buds to the adjoining shop, where they invite visitors to taste-drive the mustards that are offered for sale. The mustards from Wisconsin Wilderness in Milwaukee are big on Wisconsin ingredients such as cranberries. Don't overlook their garlic balsamic version, either.

Madison's country-in-the-city side is alive and well and easy to like. It is about university-made ice cream and cheese, and a host of fresh, local ingredients piled high at the farmers' market and on your restaurant plate. It is about all of the things that help make a city as down-to-earth as it is sophisticated.

SPECIAL EVENTS

Dane County Farmers' Market, Capitol Square, Madison, (608) 455-1999, www.madfarmmkt.org. Saturday mornings 6:00 a.m. to 2:00 p.m. during the growing season. Bring each of your senses to the largest producer-only farmers' market in the American Heartland. Enough said? How about juicy, red strawberries, real Wisconsin cheeses, pasture-fed meats, and specialty and baked goods.

Midwest Horse Fair, Alliant Energy Center, 1919 Alliant Energy Center Way, Madison, (920) 623-4322, www.midwesthorsefair.com. Mid-April. It is a fair, not a show, so you can buy horsey stuff including a horse. Return later in April for the Great Midwest Alpaca Festival.

Dane County Fair, Alliant Energy Center, 1919 Alliant Energy Center Way, Madison, (608) 224-0500, www.danecountyfair.com. Mid-July. Commercial marketplace, youth exhibits, carnival, critters.

Wisconsin Sheep and Wool Festival, Jefferson, www.wisbc.com. Mid-September. Wisconsin SpinIn, fiber arts classes, country store (books, roving, blankets, spinning wheels, more), crook and whistle stock dog trials, sheep shearing demonstrations, State Make-It-Yourself With Wool Competition, lamb barbeque and auction, quilt show, livestock sales, sheep raising information, children's activities.

World Dairy Expo, Alliant Energy Center, 1919 Alliant Energy Center Way, Madison, (608) 224-6455. End of September/early October. It is a trade show and exhibition of some of the finest cattle from across North America, but anyone can go. Shows and sales of world-class livestock, the very latest in dairy technology and equipment, educational seminars on dairy management, virtual farm tours.

One Saturday each year (in 2003 it was in August), have a **Field Day** at the West Madison Agricultural Research Station, 6972 West Mineral Point Road, Madison, (608) 262-2257. Growers attend, but home gardeners and the generally curious are welcome as well for informal chats and discussions and a tour.

PLACES TO EAT

Harvest, 21 North Pinckney Street, Madison, (608) 255-6075, www.harvestrestaurant.com. Dinner only. Located across the street from the State Capitol, this stylish storefront offers American and French cuisine created with organic beef, pasture-fed pork from a Wisconsin specialty farm, and hand-selected Farmers' Market veggies.

Heartland Grill, Sheraton Hotel, 706 John Nolen Drive, Madison, (608) 258-9505. National hotel restaurant balances classic offerings with prairie décor and some Midwest regional specials like sautéed pork loin, Wisconsin brook trout, slow-roasted prime rib, and Rotisserie Duck with Door County Cherry Sauce.

L'Etoile, 25 North Pinckney Street, Madison, (608) 251-0500, www.letoilerestaurant.com. When you dine at L'Etoile, you are never far from the farm. This is French cuisine with a passion for ingredients that are individually sourced from the fields and pastures of the American Heartland, as well as other regions from around the world. If you order something with eggs, they are probably organic or laid by pastured poultry. Savor dinner, or opt for the more casual, street-level Bakery and Market Café, (608) 251-2700, which is no stranger to locally grown ingredients, either.

Guest house and resident Katahdin sheep at the Speckled Hen Inn B&B, Madison.

Morels, 4635 Chalet Street, Middleton, (608) 836-7151. From Highway 12, go west 4 miles on Airport Road. Dinner. Wisconsin cuisine featuring wild and tame ingredients from the state and from other parts of the American Heartland, such as morel mushrooms and game. How's this for an appetizer: Forest Mushroom Pâté mixes roasted mushrooms with garlic, then serves them alongside red-waxed Wisconsin cheddar and toasted beer bread. Now you are ready for Breast of Pheasant au Morels in puff pastry with wild rice pilaf and brandy cream and morel sauce. Panned walleye pike, char grilled filet mignon, and stuffed quail may also be on the menu.

Old Feed Mill, 114 Cramer Street, Mazomanie, (608) 795-4909, (888) 345-4909, www.oldfeedmill.com. Off Highway 14 between Madison and Spring Green. They call it good, basic Midwestern food, and they serve it up in a stone flour mill that was originally built in 1857. Get comfortable with pot roast, meat loaf, pot pie, and cider-roasted chicken.

Quivey's Grove, 6261 Nesbitt Road, Madison, (608) 273-4900, www.quiveys grove.com. Traditional Wisconsin dishes are prepared and served fresh in the Stone House (dinner) and the legitimately rustic Stable Grill (lunch, dinner) on this 1856 estate that was once a 130-acre farm. Whet your appetite with the Wisconsin sausage sampler. Springdale Chicken Salad is mixed field greens tossed with honey mustard dressing, fried chicken, and a signature muffin.

Named for a small town, Black Earth Trout is filets baked with dill, green onion, and mustard butter. The fish actually comes from a southeastern Wisconsin farm where artesian springwater supplies the ponds. The roast pork loin sandwich is flavored with cranberry mustard. Rock-walled tunnel, wine cellar, outdoor fish fries.

PLACES TO STAY

Annie's Garden Bed and Breakfast, 2117 Sheridan Drive, Madison, (608) 244-2224, www.bbinternet.com/annies. Madison's first B&B is a cedar shake and stucco craftsman-style home that accepts only one reservation at a time for the ultimate in privacy. Neither the natural world nor Madison is very far away. DVD surround-sound theater furnished with microwave oven and plenty of popcorn. Full breakfast.

Othala Valley Inn, 3192 County Road JG/N, Mount Horeb, (608) 437-2141, www.othalavalley.com. In Norwegian, the name means "home and wisdom of the ancestors." In southern Wisconsin, it means being surrounded by an organic farm with Scottish Highland cattle, Jacob sheep, and heirloom chickens. Lodging in the contemporary home includes full organic breakfast, guest living room with fireplace, and other amenities. Or choose the cabin with similar amenities except for the full kitchen where guests can cook their own meals.

The Speckled Hen Inn Bed and Breakfast, 5525 Portage Road, Madison, (608) 244-9368, www.speckledheninn.com. From the porch that stretches out and invites you to do the same, the view of grazing sheep unfolds like a living postcard. The sheep are a breed called Katahdin, a circa-1950s American creation that sheds its own hair and requires no shearing. Farmers, who raise Katahdin for meat and not fiber, find they have less work on their hands. They also have ewes that typically bear twins and take good care of them (some breeds are sheepish when it comes to the mothering instinct). Two llamas mingle among the flock and actually function as volunteer sentries and shepherds—not to mention pasture ornamentation. Speckled hens also make their home here.

Beautifully appointed rooms; three of the four feature whirlpool tubs. Fifty acres, places to walk, exceptional common areas: home theater, galley kitchen with snacks, sodas, and wine, and a gazebo. Full breakfasts feature Wisconsin cheeses, fresh fruits, maybe a quiche or a Dutch baby pancake (very light, not too sweet, lightly sprinkled with powdered sugar, baked with cinnamon-sprinkled apples in the center) and crispy bacon. Fresh-ground, locally roasted coffee.

7. A EUROPEAN HOLIDAY IN SOUTHERN WISCONSIN

From the wiener schnitzel, Swiss *roesti*, and fondue of New Glarus to the old-world cheese making all over Green County, a weekend in southwestern Wisconsin puts one in mind of a European holiday. Along the back roads, you will see plenty of Holstein, Brown Swiss, and Jersey cows grazing in the farm-scapes. All that milk and cheese must be ready in time for the hugely popular Breakfast on the Farm event in spring, as well as Cheese Days in autumn, when selected farms around Monroe throw open the barn doors and show everyone why this part of the New World has not lost the best of the Old.

Did you know that Green County has a lot more cows than people? And that the average Green County cow produces over 25,000 10-ounce glasses of milk a year? Find out stuff like this when you sign up for a weekend **Farm to Feast Culinary Getaway**; contact the Monroe Chamber of Commerce & Industry, (800) 838-1603, www.farmtofeast.com. Fill your weekend with cooking demonstrations, tours of the local foodmakers, a visit to a dairy farm and overnight accommodations. Selected weekends are available. Then, watch some of the finest cheese making in the world take place before your eyes during a cheese factory tour or via a peek through an observation window.

Enjoy it all in peaceful, quiet, southwestern Wisconsin. Green County shares a border with Illinois to the south, and with Madison's Dane County to the north. But your European holiday would not be complete without a venture out to Mineral Point, which is located in neighboring Iowa County. Mineral Point has not lost sight of its unique Cornish miner heritage, especially when it comes to heritage foods like pasties and figgyhobbin.

Browntown

Starting in the southwestern part of Green County, visit **Chula Vista Cheese Company**, 2923 Mayer Road, Browntown, (608) 439-5211. Muenster, Swiss, Cheddar, Colby, and flavored cheeses, some with Mexican heat.

Monroe

From Browntown, head east for 7 miles to Monroe, which is anchored by a stunning courthouse and quaint town square. Monroe has always been home to the Swiss Colony, that famous purveyor of cheeses and other specialty foods that got its start way back in 1926. If you have ever hefted the Swiss Colony's mouthwateringly photographed catalog, you know this company is serious about food. Divine combinations of cheeses, sausages, mustards, breads, and breakfast specialties make you want to eat the pages. The red velvet cake, deep-dish caramel apple pie, caramel pecan brownie cheesecake, home-style bars, fruit jewels, old-fashioned butter toffee, and baklava are just about the limit of what anyone should be expected to resist. You cannot take a factory tour of the **Swiss Colony** while in Monroe, but you can browse inside their **Seventh Avenue Outlet**, 652 Eighth Street, Monroe, (608) 328-8836.

Franklin Cheese Cooperative, W7256 Franklin Road, Monroe, (608) 325-3725, was established in 1890. Specialties include farmer and flavored Muenster cheeses. **Roth Kase USA** (Alp and Dell is the store name), 657 Second

Street, Monroe, (608) 328-3355, (800) ALP-DELL, offers both tours and a vast observation window. Specialties include blue, Fontina, Gruyère, Havarti, Raclette, Rofumo, smoked cheese. Roth Kase USA represents the first American maker of European mountain cheeses Fontina (Italian) and Gruyère (Swiss). Gruyère is full-flavored and good for quiches and fondues.

At **Torkelson's Prairie Hill Cheese Plant**, N398 Twin Grove Road, Monroe, (608) 325-2918, specialties include Muenster, brick, Colby, Monterey Jack. **Chalet Cheese Cooperative**, N4858 County Road N, Monroe, (608) 325-4343, is the only factory in America that still makes the famously aromatic yet surprisingly mild Limburger. Chalet Cheese Cooperative was established before the majority of the people alive in the world today were. **Deppeler Cheese Factory**, W6805 Deppeler Road, Monroe, (608) 325-6311, specializes in Swiss and Baby Swiss varieties. **Klondike Cheese Company**, Junction House Tavern (outlet), N3696 Highway 81, Monroe, (608) 325-3226, was established in the late 1800s. Fetas are sold under the Odyssey label in plain, pepper, Mediterranean herb, and tomato/basil varieties.

Yes, it is a big block of cheese makers in the space of a single county, but did you know that in 1910, Green County alone had over two hundred cheese factories? Find out about those glory days inside the local museums, one of which devotes its entire exhibit space to cheese making. It is the **Historic Cheese-making Center**, 2108 Seventh Avenue (Highway 69), Monroe, (608) 325-4636, (888) 222-9111, and it is located inside a restored train depot and sports telltale copper vats out front. The friendly folks inside are happy to share their knowledge of Monroe's favorite subject. Hard to get them to play the Swiss harp, though. Exhibits include cheese-making and dairying artifacts and photographs, and there is a great selection of regional books for sale.

The **Green County Historical Society Museum**, 1617 Ninth Street, Monroe, (608) 325-2924, has a display case stuffed with Cheese Days memorabilia going back to the 19th century. During the Civil War, this former church was used to store wheat and wool for the Union soldiers. It is a little over a mile north and then east from the Historic Cheese-making Center.

Juda and Brodhead

From Monroe, let's head to Juda and Brodhead. Juda is home to the **Maple Leaf Cheese Factory Outlet**, W2616 Highway 11/81, Juda, (608) 934-1237, which was established in 1910. Edam, Gouda, queso blanco, and flavored cheeses like cranberry Cheddar are the order of the day. If you are looking for great prices along with great flavors, look here. Continue on Highway 11 toward Brodhead, which sits at Green County's eastern border. Four miles west of town, be sure to visit **Decatur Dairy**, W1668 County F, Brodhead, (608) 897-8661. Specialties include the newer Stettler Swiss, Havarti, Muenster, brick, Asadero, farmer, Amish Swiss, fresh curds. **Decatur Dairy** has been a cooperative since 1946, and is currently supplied by 75 farmers. The **Brodhead Depot Museum**, 1108 First Center

Bernese mountain architecture and flower boxes adorn Chalet Landhaus, New Glarus.

Avenue, Brodhead, (608) 897-4150, devotes a corner to cheese-making history because the community's Goldenrod Creamery was once a neighbor.

Monticello

County Road F and WI-39 will get you from Brodhead to Monticello. There, you can visit the **Swiss Heritage Cheese Factory**, 114 East Coates Avenue, Monticello, (608) 938-4455. Specialties of the house include brick, Muenster, farmer, and breaded curds that are ready to deep-fry. This cheese factory was established in the 1930s. At **Silver-Lewis Cheese Cooperative**, W3705 County EE, Monticello, (608) 938-4813, specialties include Gmur brick and Muenster. Stand on the rubber mat and peek in to see what is happening on any given day.

New Glarus

Located almost six miles north of Monticello, New Glarus has a charm all its own, based on its Swiss heritage that you can see in the architecture, the music, the food, and especially the people. Focusing on the heritage, the **Swiss Historical Village**, 612 Seventh Avenue, New Glarus, (608) 527-2317, www.swisshistorical village.com, recreates the early life of immigrants who ventured here from their alpine homeland in 1845. Village buildings include an 1890s cheese factory, smokehouse and sausage shop, blacksmith shop, general store, and 10 others.

At the cheese factory, the guide explains that the cheese-making process started with farmers who carried or hauled their cans of milk to the cheese factory. First, the cheese maker poured the milk into a weighing tank to properly credit the farmer. Next, he collected it in a copper cheese kettle and lit a fire to heat it to about 112 degrees. To make a wheel of Swiss cheese, he added rennet to begin the curdling process. Rennet is a product made from the stomach of a calf; the enzymes promote the curdling process. At this point, he stirred and cut up the curds with a cheese harp, and eventually they reached the consistency of pudding. Then he dipped cheesecloth underneath to gather and tie up the curds and hoist this up like a bag. The by-product of whey was often returned to the farmer for pig feed; today's whey often goes into animal feed as well. The process continued at the press table, where the cheesecloth was changed and pressure was applied to squeeze out the last of the liquid. Once solidified, the dried curds went into a salt brine for a few days, where the rind began to form. From there, it went to the curing cellar, aged for a couple of months, and got its characteristic holes.

A bit of poking around in the quaint shops of New Glarus yields perfect foodstuffs to pair with your cheddars and Gruyères. How about smoked sausages? **Reuf's Meat Market**, 538 First Street, New Glarus, (608) 527-2554, www.ruefsmeatmarket.com, makes sausages according to old family recipes, stuffing them by hand into natural casings and smoking them for the finest flavor. Swiss specialties include *kalberwurst* and *landjaegger*.

Also try **Hoesly's Meats**, 219 Industrial Drive, New Glarus, (608) 527-2513, for award-winning natural casing wieners, jerky, and *braunschweiger*. **Maple Leaf Cheese and Chocolate Haus**, 554 First Street, New Glarus, (608) 527-2000, www.wischeese.com, sells local cheeses and sausages, and has set up a Swiss Cooking Corner with ingredients and cookbooks. Pick up hearth breads at **The New Glarus Bakery**, 534 First Street, New Glarus, (608) 527-2916, www.newglarusbakery.com, which is another revered institution around here. At **Robert's European Imports**, 102 Fifth Avenue, New Glarus, (800) 968-2517, www.shopswiss.com, buy Swiss cowbells that are small enough for your rearview mirror or big enough for your own neck. Also shop for fondue and raclette sets. **The Bramble Patch**, 19 Fifth Avenue (in the Fifth Avenue Shoppes), New Glarus, (608) 558-8366, www.thebramblepatch.biz, stocks maple syrup, Amish jams, gourmet mustards, and honey.

If shopping makes you thirsty, hop into **New Glarus Brewery Co.**, 119 County W, New Glarus, (608) 527-5850, www.newglarusbrewing.com, for a free tour and nominal-fee tasting of their handcrafted beers. The brew house that found its way here from Germany has a story all its own. Seems a brewery owner who was retiring had sold his property to developers but had not found a buyer for his beautiful copper brew house, except for a scrap-metal dealer who had but one use for it. Just a week before the dealer was scheduled to pick it up, along came the Careys, and the old brewer was so relieved that he sold it to them for way below market value. The brewery has been open since 1993 and the awards keep piling up. The brewery's Spotted Cow brand is a Wisconsin farmhouse ale brewed with flaked barley and Wisconsin malts and a bit of corn tossed in. There is no mistaking the intense Montmorency cherry flavor in the Belgian Red brand. A whopping 1.4 pounds of Door County cherries go into every bottle, then it is aged in oak tanks. Raspberries and apples find their way into other beers. Enjoy the rich coffee flavor and color of Coffee Stout, a seasonal beer. Norski Honey Bock features clover honey harvested over the hill in Verona.

Mineral Point

It is time to leave Green County and discover the Cornish heritage of Mineral Point, located about 30 miles west of New Glarus in Iowa County. From the far southwest of England, Cornish settlers first arrived in Mineral Point in 1830, coming to work the lead mines in search of a better life. Some of the stone cottages they built survive today.

Experience these at **Pendarvis State Historic Site**, 114 Shake Rag Street, Mineral Point, (608) 987-2122, (866) 944-7483, www.pendarvis.wisconsinhistory .org. This great site sheds light on a little-known yet fascinating pocket of Midwestern history. The museum store offers English teas, teacups, teapots, tinware, and toffees. Across the street, the former Merry Christmas Mine site is accessible to walkers, although the old mine shafts have been filled in and only a few artifacts remain. It is possible to imagine a Cornish miner heading off to work with his metal lunch bucket, a Cornish pasty and its fragrant steam tucked inside. The Cornish pasty, a flaky-crusted meat pie that was picked up and eaten by hand, would have been welcome convenience food for a miner working under dark and cramped conditions. Beginning in 1940, one of the Pendarvis cottages served restaurant-style meals, and Cornish pasties were a menu favorite. The eatery closed in 1971, but today's visitors to Mineral Point can taste something of the miner's experience by ordering a pasty at some of the restaurants in town.

Among the artist studios and stone architecture that make Mineral Point so delightful, there is **Ivey's Pharmacy**, 128 High Street, Mineral Point, (608) 987-2336. Unexpectedly, this very old-line business carries saffron, a favorite spice of the Cornish people. Other great, unique points of interest are the zinc dog, **Shake Rag Alley**, **Mineral Point's Root Cellar**, and **The Barn Shops** that are comfortably housed in a picturesque 3,500-square-foot limestone barn.

In summary, this tour highlights cheese factories that adhere to the utmost standards of excellence, where you can sample some of the finest cheeses that are available anywhere, perhaps with a wee dram of ale or a clear glass of wine. You can partake of foods that are prepared just as they were centuries ago and

---

Crawford Farm

It is the third week of July, and warm on Crawford Farm in Green County. Sheep bleat on the hillside pastures, their voices scaling from deep baritones to insistent, childish wails. Great Pyrenees puppies tumble over one another like cotton balls at play. Whiskey, the older dog that jealously guards his own energy in anticipation of the coming night's work, looks on in soldierly detachment.

After buying their farm in 1988, Chicagoans Janie and Andy Crawford quickly began to grow a reputation for excellence among a certain coterie of Midwest regional chefs who are driving the farmer-chef connection and achieving celebrity status in the process. Such chefs are Crawford Farm's best customers. "It's restaurants that are interested in really supporting farmers, because my product is fairly expensive. It's several high-end restaurants in Chicago, and a couple of forward-thinking restaurants in Madison," Janie Crawford says. So even though Crawford Farm is not open to the public, you can sample its products at some of the best restaurants around.

Here the business of raising the best lamb for discerning markets means things are done a little differently. Crawford explains, "We don't use conventional meat breeds, and we're much happier with the texture and flavor of the breeds we select. A lot of this stems from this soil and this grass, but also the way we select the breeds. These are animals that do really well in this climate and are very suited to our operation, which is a non-confinement operation."

Crawford tells more about how things are done, and not done, on this farm. "Our sheep are outside all year except for lambing, which we do primarily in the deep winter. So that happens in the barn. Or if you're an old sheep and past being able to stay outside, you go to the barn. It's the principle in shepherding to actively cull so you keep your flock at its prime. We don't do that, though. We figure that after they've given their years of producing lambs for us, they might as well get to retire," she says.

For Janie Crawford, life didn't even hint at this turn. "My grandfather was a cotton farmer in Texas, but no one in my family taught me anything about farming. I always knew I wanted to do something in the country, though, but I didn't know what it was going to be. I certainly didn't know it was going to be sheep, because there were not sheep in the area where I grew up. So I've just come to the sheep later in life, and

I adore them. And now the pigs. I would eventually like to have three things going on the farm. The third thing will probably be poultry."

The farm dogs are Great Pyrenees, and their job is to protect the sheep. Only thing is, they do it at night—and loudly. "They're nocturnal, which makes it a little tough on houseguests because the dogs clock in at sundown, and they'll be up all night barking. I don't really care anymore; it's just white noise to me," she explains.

A clarion call blares from the direction of a nearby pen, but it is not a dog. Crawford does not look surprised. "That's Pocket," she explains, her attention already focused on the curly bundle that stares and bleats with all its might.

The chat ends. It is time to see about the flock.

Note: Not open to the public. 🐾

---

half a world away. You can motor through the velvety countryside and maybe tour a farm. Through it all, you can no doubt feel the hospitality of the *Wilkommen* mat that is always out in this part of the world.

SPECIAL EVENTS

Breakfast on the Farm, Green County, (608) 325-4636. Last Saturday in May. Join thousands of other hungry folks for a legendary farm breakfast including Wisconsin cheese, eggs, pork sausage, homemade coffee cake, strawberry sundae, milk, juice, coffee. Cow-milking contest, petting zoo, live music, crafts. The host dairy farm changes each year; it probably takes a year just to wash the dishes.

Dairy Day, second to last Saturday in June. This event mooves around each year among 11 Green County communities. Cattle show, dairy queen and princess, dairy foods.

Green County Fair, www.greencountyfair.net. Mid-July. Championship livestock shown by 4-H'ers, rodeo, harness racing, demolition derby, carnival, grandstand entertainment.

Cheese Days, Monroe, (608) 325-7771, (800) 307-7208. Third weekend in September, even-numbered years only. Fun, educational, thoughtfully organized, and dirt-cheap bus tours out to the cheese factories and family farms in the countryside. Sample cheese and kick up your heels to the lively sounds of a polka band. Enjoy yodeling and Swiss folk costumes. Eat cheese.

Cornish Festival and Celtic Celebration, Mineral Point, (608) 987-3201, www.mineralpoint.com. Last weekend in September. Bus tours; pasty banquet with Cornish entertainment (pre-registration strongly suggested); traditional pub night at Pendarvis Friday night (singing, imbibing, live music); Crowdy Crawn storytelling and demonstrations of spinning, sock knitting, and apple pressing; Taste of Mineral Point; Bagpipe-led procession.

Old Time Demonstrations, Swiss Historical Village, New Glarus, (608) 527-

2317, www.swisshistoricalvillage.com. Mid-October. Watch skilled artisans make cheese, sausage, brooms, and candles in the tidy buildings of the village. Also observe activities of blacksmithing and beekeeping. Taste and purchase the Swiss holiday cookies called *bratzeli*.

PLACES TO EAT

Baumgartner Cheese Store and Tavern, somewhere on the square, Monroe, (608) 325-6157. Limburger cheese sandwiches and lots more lunch fare in rustic surroundings that feel like a hug. Since 1931.

Brewery Creek, 23 Commerce Street, Mineral Point, (608) 987-3298, www.brewerycreek.com. From scratch/local ingredients in the salads, burgers, pastas, salmons, and steaks, lots of vegetarian dishes, pub brews, pub atmosphere. Hunker down in this 1854 limestone warehouse.

Dining Room at 209 Main, Monticello, (608) 938-2200, www.209main.com. Dinner only. Fresh, local, seasonal, Midwestern regional cooking. Unusual to find this emphasis in a tiny, off-the-beaten-path small town.

Glarner Stube, 518 First Street, New Glarus, (608) 527-2216. Swiss and American cuisine. Popular with the locals.

New Glarus Hotel Restaurant, 100 Sixth Avenue, New Glarus, (608) 527-5244, (800) 727-9477, www.newglarushotel.com. Lunch, dinner. Swiss specialties, Green County cheeses, local wines, weekend polka bands. Built in 1853.

Pointer Café, 809 Ridge Street, Mineral Point, (608) 987-3733. Melt-y Wisconsin cheese tops the burgers. The Cornish pasty comes with soup or salad and a dinner roll. Lots of other choices, and you could wake up to breakfast at, say, two in the afternoon.

Red Rooster Café, 158 High Street, Mineral Point, (608) 987-9936. American fare in this vintage twentieth-century storefront café straight out of Mayberry. Ah, but the Cornish specialties are rare treats in the American Heartland. Their pasty is a thick hunk of flaky pastry stuffed with potatoes, rutabagas, onions, cubed steak, and seasoning slowly baked to a golden brown. Add breaded cheese curds as a side, and finish up with Figgyhobbin for dessert: raisins, nuts, brown sugar and cinnamon, rolled up in a pastry crust. Roosters everywhere, and customers buy the menus as souvenirs.

Shake Rag Alley Coffee House, 18 Shake Rag Street, Mineral Point, (608) 987-3292. Enjoy sandwiches, soups, and quiches indoors amid the history or outdoors among the gardens.

PLACES TO STAY

Chalet Landhaus, 801 Highway 69, New Glarus, (608) 527-5234, (800) 944-1716, www.chaletlandhaus.com. From Bernese mountain architecture to red-and-white flower boxes and European-style breakfasts with sliced cheeses and meats, guests are transported to another world, except that motel-style conveniences make you feel right at home.

Country House, a Bed and Breakfast Inn, 180 Highway 69, New Glarus, (608) 527-5399. Renovated 1892 farmhouse on 50 acres. Four guestrooms, private baths, full breakfast under candlelight chandeliers, walking trails in the woods.

Gasthaus Motel, 685 30th Street, Monroe, (608) 328-8395, www.gasthaus motel.com. Cute, clean, and convenient but not costly.

Hoch Haus, 218 Second Street, New Glarus, (608) 527-4019, www.hoch haus.homestead.com. Swiss/German breakfast buffet with local breads, cheeses, and meats, fruit or juice, yogurt, eggs, muesli, and cereal.

Honeywind Farm Bed and Breakfast, W8247 County Road P, Browntown, (608) 325-5215, www.wbba.org/inns/BB257.htm. Breathe the fresh country air on three hundred acres of farmland with pasture, woodland, and the Honey Creek.

Inn Serendipity, W7843 County Road P, Browntown, (608) 329-7056, www .innserendipity.com. Five-acre organic farm with chickens, llamas, labyrinth. Full vegetarian breakfast starring the inn's own fresh produce.

Maple Wood Lodge, 2950 State Highway 39, Mineral Point, (608) 987-2324, www.maplewoodlodge.com. When you make a reservation, they'll give you directions to Maple Wood's country-hideaway location. The sign whispers "Maple Wood" and leads you past a Holstein herd and a prairie that is guarded by redwing blackbirds in the spring. The three-bedroom, timber-frame lodge nests in a flower garden where Tootsie the Cat might yawn from his flower box and, later, accompany you on a moonlit walk through the private forest. Twenty-six acres in all. Fireplace, hot tub, fully-equipped kitchen, TV/DVD/VCR, old books, local artwork including a handcrafted woodpecker drilling a high beam. This is a *whole-house rental,* so no other guests, no neighbors in sight.

Swiss Aire Motel, 1200 Highway 69, New Glarus, (800) 798-4391, www.swiss aire.com. Swiss-clean motel with outdoor pool and complimentary continental breakfast.

8. OLD WAYS IN THE NEW WORLD NEAR MILWAUKEE

The Kettle Moraine lands of southeastern Wisconsin are home to a 576-acre snapshot of the state's formative years, especially the land depressions called kettles. The region is also where Wisconsin's last electric trolley runs on a regular schedule, mostly for people out on a lark, but also, in a nod to community service, as a hauler of freight that includes agricultural products. There is a lot more to like here, from a barn painted with a smile as if the old building itself relishes the farm-fresh foods that are stashed inside, to places where visitors can pick fruits, ride horses, and get all mushy over baby animals. Put it all together, and you have a region proudly retaining its rural character, and all so surprisingly close to Milwaukee and Chicago. How close? From Milwaukee to Eagle it is about 38 miles, and from Chicago to Eagle it is about 100 miles. These distances are not all that far, but they are truly a world away.

Apples being stewed at Koepsell Farm, one of three German farmsteads at Old World Wisconsin, Eagle.

The Old World

The main attraction of this tour is **Old World Wisconsin**, S103 W37890 Highway 67, Eagle, (262) 594-6300, www.shsw.wisc.edu. Drive 1.5 miles south of Eagle, and park among the pines. Enter a world where wool is dyed with Queen Anne's lace, where children chase wooden hoops across meadows, and where the aroma of squirrel stew calls hungry farmers in to supper. These are just a few of the scenes you can become part of at Old World Wisconsin, which is nothing short of the state's grandest tribute to its own ethnic heritage and pioneer spirit.

All told, Old World Wisconsin has 10 farmsteads and a village. Each of the structures was trucked in from somewhere in the state and restored, and their histories are thoroughly documented so the costumed interpreters who populate them can tell you lots of things. The village is full of the businesses that would have helped to sustain the farmers' needs, from horseshoes and hardtack to a sense of community and the occasional gossip. It all adds up to over 65 buildings, and in between is a heavily forested landscape with a few miles of trails that visitors share with wild turkeys, deer, and sandhill cranes. It is not unusual to see evidence of their passing, from feathers to footprints.

The hiking is great, with views of woodlands, marshes, grasslands, and the Hidden Kettle Pond. Combine hikes with rides aboard the open-air tram, which runs every 20 to 30 minutes along the gravel roads. Stops are clearly marked on the colorful map obtained at the Visitors' Center complex of historic buildings. At the Visitors' Center, they also set you up with a taped audio tour that adds depth to your experience. Plus, there is a gift shop where you can buy the house brand of honey, jam, and syrup, a recently published book about Old World Wisconsin, nineteenth-century reproductions of household items, cards, toys, and games. Many of the handcrafted items for sale are made on the premises. Also watch the orientation video, have lunch in the rare octagonal barn, and enjoy a dinner theater performance.

First in the Old World tour is the African-American area, which depicts the lives of freed and runaway slaves in the early integrated rural community of Beetown (Grant County). An interpreter takes on the character of Mary Anna Hoffman and guides you through the experience as it is told through a church and two cemeteries.

Next up is the German area that features three farmsteads showing a range of structural characteristics from 1860 to 1880. There the aroma of baking bread is frequently wafting about the air of the Kessel Bakehouse, and you can sometimes catch a demonstration of rye straw basket making, which is part of a unique cooking technique. Learn, too, about the extremely rare black kitchen that was used to cook vegetables, such as potatoes and rutabagas, for livestock. Meats were also smoked there, and breads were baked. You might also see Durham or Shorthorn oxen, which were among the earliest breeds of cattle brought from England to America. The earliest Midwestern farmers relied on the strength of oxen more than horses in order to help break up the tough prairie soil.

Stroll over to the Polish area, where one of the complex's most striking building constructions can be seen. Called stovewood, it involves setting logs in a way that shows the diameter, rather than the length, of each piece. The resulting circles are unusually decorative. The building's house-barn design provided shelter for the farmers together with their chickens, albeit in separate quarters. The house-barn was built around 1884 in Hofa Park, a Shawano County, Wisconsin community that was developed to attract Polish settlers.

On the 1845 Fossebrekke Farm within the Norwegian area, you can see feral pigs called Ossabaw Island Hogs that originated in Spain and were first brought to America in the 1500s. You may see a demonstration of wool processing at the 1865 Kvaale Farm where Cotswold sheep graze. While picking wool, the interpreter explains that the four kettles in which the wool is washed must be of similar temperature or the wool will felt. Once washed, the wool is gathered into cheesecloth and hung out to dry. After carding, the wool could be dyed, and the interpreter demonstrates the use of handy sources of dye color such as Queen Anne's lace to achieve a sea-green color, and black walnut hulls for taupe.

The Finnish area contains two farms highlighting the unique culture of these Scandinavian immigrants. There is, for example, the Ronkainen Sauna that was brought down from Douglas County in the far northwest corner of Wisconsin. A white stripe courses down the back of each of the farm's resident lineback cattle as if a particularly low-flying airplane stamped its contrail there.

For farmers, a hub like Crossroads Village would have been valued indeed. They could come in from the fields to have a wagon repaired, horses shod, or clothes washed and ironed. They could also lift their voices in song to the strains of a pump organ during a worship service, play checkers, bang a fist during a town hall meeting, visit in a Victorian parlor, and brighten their family's day with purchases of new shoes, fabric, and penny candy. For today's visitor, Crossroads Village provides a peek into that kind of experience. For an additional fee and by reservation, visitors can partake of a private dinner at Four Mile Inn, which in 1853 was a stagecoach stop in Dodge County. The festive evening event involves learning about nineteenth-century food preservation, cooking, and etiquette. After helping with preparations, diners enjoy a bountiful meal served by a costumed interpreter and host. This is followed by a personal tour of the inn, a round of parlor games, dessert, and coffee. Arrange for this special experience by calling (262) 594-6305.

If you've ever lamented the loss of skills that were once common, skills from rug making to log home building, take heart and learn them for yourself by signing up for an Old World Wisconsin Workshop. You could plan a weekend visit around one of these workshops, taking in all that the region has to offer and returning home with a hard-earned sense of satisfaction. Reserve your place by calling (262) 594-6305.

Processing wool at the Norwegian Kvaale Farm, Old World Wisconsin, Eagle.

The New World

Located very close to Old World Wisconsin, the Northern Unit of the Kettle Moraine State Forest preserves 30,000 acres of land that still bear evidence of Ice Age activity. Sometimes when a glacier melted, it left behind a land depression called a kettle; hence the name. Drive several miles westward to **Rushing Waters Fisheries**, N301 County Road H, Palmyra, (800) 378-7088, www.rushing waters.net, for on-farm rainbow trout fishing and smoked trout and salmon from their retail store. Artesian springs supply the 49-degree water to the ponds and antibiotics and chemicals are nowhere to be found. Also in the vicinity is **Swinging W Ranch**, S75 W36004 Wilton Road, Eagle, (262) 594-2416, where you can saddle up for trail rides, hayrides, and 20-mile overnight rides.

Another experience unique to this region is the ride aboard the **East Troy Electric Railroad**, 3238 West Main Street, East Troy, (262) 642-3263, www.east troyrr.org. East Troy is located 11 miles southeast of Eagle, to which you will backtrack the short distance from Palmyra, and it is off I-43. The train ride experience is about an hour roundtrip excursion (including a layover at either end) made possible by exquisite restoration efforts of interurban trolley cars that roll under clean electric power. Trains operate on set schedules to and from Mukwonago, and fees apply, although reservations are not needed. Book ahead, though, for the elegant, two-hour dinner train by calling (262) 642-3077.

Freight cars once used the line to transport goods, including farm produce and over 8,000 gallons of milk a day. Today the trolley whisks passengers through rolling countryside and, at the end of the line, rewards them with a stop at a local-food emporium. This is the smiling, pale yellow barn that houses **The**

After seeing the goodies inside, visitors know why the barn housing The Elegant Farmer, near Mukwonago, is smiling.

Elegant Farmer, on County Road ES just southwest of Mukwonago, (262) 363-6770, www.elegantfarmer.com. It is a second-generation family operation that concentrates on foods that might have come out of old-fashioned farm kitchens. Indeed, the owner, Farmer Dan, grew up on a farm and didn't want to lose that feeling. Nor did he want to lose those wonderful tastes, if the fragrant, bubbly Apple Pie Baked in a Paper Bag is any indication. The top crust is crunchy while the bottom crust is flaky, and the whole thing is drizzled with caramel. Cider-baked boneless ham is another delicious choice. It is cured with apple cider, then hickory smoked.

Want fresh fruit breads for tomorrow's breakfast? Then you should know that The Elegant Farmer's versions get fully a third of their weight from fruit and juice—the most they can pack into the recipe. Farmer Dan never forgot how his mother would cut thick slices of home-baked bread then slather on as much jelly as he wanted. But he does not just wax nostalgic over his memories, he also serves them to customers. So order up a thick, hot slice of bread, and pile on all the jelly you want in memory of a Wisconsin farmwife and her hungry little boy.

Browse, too, among the vast assortment of specialty foods, including fresh and smoked meats, Wisconsin cheeses, and preserved vegetables. And when the air turns crisp on autumn weekends, you can add "Cheap Fun" to the experience. This includes nominal-fee hayrides to the apple orchard and pumpkin/squash patch for u-pick opportunities, caramel-apple making, and cider sipping in the barn market. The best deal going is the Rotten Guarantee, which means that if the turning-orange or orange pumpkin you pick rots before Halloween, The Elegant Farmer will replace it.

After disembarking from the train back in East Troy, refresh yourself at **J. Lauber's Old Fashioned Ice Cream Parlor**, 2010 Church Street (Highway 120), East Troy, (262) 642-3679. Enjoy real ice creams (not soft serve), 20 flavors of malteds, and a candy counter straight out of the 1920s. Four miles east of East Troy, **Bower's Produce**, W490 State Road 20, East Troy, (262) 642-5244, satisfies every appetite with apples and ciders, vegetables, herbs, honeys, and maple syrups. Five and one-half miles northeast of East Troy, **Stacey Farms**, N8750 Thiede Road, East Troy, (877) 784-2578, www.staceyfarms.com, celebrates harvest time with u-pick pumpkins, pony rides and hayrides, a petting zoo, and a five-acre corn maze that is haunted according to an evening schedule (good news for your littlest goblins, who will be safely ghoul-free during the daylight hours). **Green Meadows Petting Farm**, 33603 High Drive, East Troy, (262) 534-2891, www.greanmeadowsfarmwi.com, can be found eight miles east of East Troy and three miles west of Waterford. It features a two-hour guided tour that includes cow milking, a pony ride, a tractor-drawn hayride, and a free pumpkin in October. Children especially enjoy the petting farm.

The eternally popular Lake Geneva area offers boatloads of fun on, in, and around the lake that owes much of its cleanliness, despite heavy use, to the fact that it is spring-fed. The town of Lake Geneva, which pulsates with life that surges up each weekend from Chicago, is located 20 miles south of East Troy. Take the yummy Ice Cream Social cruise aboard the Grand Belle of Geneva, or opt for full meal tours while feasting your eyes on the shoreline mansions. Call the **Lake Geneva Cruise Line** at (262) 248-6206 or (800) 558-5911; visit www.cruiselakegeneva.com. The resident critters of **Lake Geneva Horse Park and Petting Zoo**, Highways 50 and 67, Williams Bay, (262) 245-0770, www.lakegenevapettingzoo.com, will keep everyone entertained. Williams Bay is another lakeside town, and it is located on the northwestern shore. Enjoy the park's exotic animal show, the circus show, the baby barn, live tiger demos, and keeper talks. The horse farm part is a 110-acre home for the facility's magnificent Arabians. Recharge big and little batteries at the picnic/cookout area.

Watching the sun sparkle and then set over the waters of Lake Geneva makes a fine ending to this southeastern Wisconsin weekend that takes you out of the way and a little nostalgically into the region's agricultural past.

SPECIAL EVENTS

Sheep Shearing, Old World Wisconsin. Mid-May. The show unfolds at a fast clip as expert shearers relieve sheep of their winter coats.

Power Exposition, Old World Wisconsin. Early August. All the power of horses, oxen, and sheep is unleashed to make threshing machines, buggies, wagons, and a butter churn go.

Autumn on the Farms, Old World Wisconsin. Mid-October. Help Wisconsin's earliest farmers gather in the goods and get set for winter. Enjoy demonstrations of food preparation appropriate to the ethnicity and period of the various sites, such as: fresh fruit bottling and cottage cheese making at Crossroads Village; the processing of hearty sausages, sauerkraut, and horseradish in the German/Polish area; and cheese and soap making in the Norwegian/Danish area. Take in demonstrations of corn husk doll making, quilting, sawmilling, and fall plowing done by teams of draft horses. It all adds up to an exciting weekend down on the farm.

Chuck Wagon Cookouts, Clambakes and Lobster Boils, other culinary feasts, The Abbey Resort, Fontana, (262) 275-6811. Gather, eat.

Winemaker's Dinners and Tastings, Pig Roast, Octoberfest Sunday Brunch, other culinary feasts, Lake Lawn Resort, Delavan, (262) 728-5095.

Walworth County Farm Bureau Dairy Breakfast, Walworth County Fairgrounds, Elkhorn, (262) 723-3228. Mid-June.

Pork Chop Cookout, Walworth County Fairgrounds, (262) 723-5788. Mid-June. Sponsored by the Southeastern Wisconsin Pork Producers (a.k.a., folks who know pork).

Walworth County Fair, (262) 723-3228, www.walworthcountyfair.com. Late August/early September. Truck and tractor pulls, harness racing, demolition derby. The Barnyard Adventure Tent puts kids to work as they "Help the

Farmer." They can pick apples, plant seeds, milk "Helene the Holstein" cow and spread bedding for the farmer's livestock. This thing has been going on for over 150 years.

PLACES TO EAT

Clausing Barn Restaurant, Old World Wisconsin, (262) 594-6320. Reservations are recommended for the Friday night fish fry which includes unlimited deep-fried Alaskan pollack, hot German potato salad, potato pancakes, coleslaw, apple sauce, and pumpernickel bread.

Cotton Exchange, Highway 20/83, Waterford, (262) 534-9291. Classic steaks, ribs, and seafood, Friday night fish fry, Sunday prime rib buffet brunch.

PLACES TO STAY

Eagle Centre House Bed and Breakfast, W370 S9590 Highway 67, Eagle, (262) 363-4700, www.eagle-house.com. The big white house with the double verandah replicates an 1846 Greek Revival stagecoach inn and sits on 20 acres. Luxuriate amid both ends of the comfort spectrum—from wood-burning fireplaces and an 1862 Melodeon to whirlpool tubs and air conditioning.

Sleep Inn, 945 Greenwald Court, Mukwonago, (262) 363-9970. A convenient choice located 15 miles from Old World Wisconsin and eight miles from East Troy Electric Railroad Museum. Deluxe continental breakfast.

The Elliott House LLC, W1796 County Road J, East Troy, (262) 363-9666. Stay in this 1843 farmhouse surrounded by five acres. Three guestrooms, one with attached private bath, two with unattached private baths. Full breakfast served at the guests' convenience.

Milwaukee is a great place to stay. The Greater Milwaukee CVB makes it easy to choose; visit www.milwaukee.org. Milwaukee is also a great place to play. Each August, the Wisconsin State Fair, www.wistatefair.com, showcases the finest in agriculture, not to mention those famous cream puffs. Milwaukee keeps visitors hopping, with everything from brewery tours and brew pubs, to museums and multi-cultural celebrations. Enjoy!

Minnesota

Minnesota's famous Scandinavian heritage has its roots in agriculture that produces harvests from the land and the sea. On land, livestock leads the way in the state's agricultural output, but crops such as corn, soybeans, and hay are also very important. From the apples in the south to the wild rice of the north, Minnesota food products satisfy with a homegrown heartiness—and a gourmet touch—that keeps everyone well fed. Each year the Minnesota Department of Agriculture publishes the Minnesota Grown directory; download the latest edition at www.minnesotagrown.com.

9. NORTH WOODS FARMLANDS

Where sunlight sparkles on water that beads off the backs of loons, people do the things that end all too quickly, but that stay with them forever as the best memories. They swim, boat, and fish. They lick drippy ice cream on the beach. They build castles of sand.

And they get their picture taken with an emu.

An emu? Isn't that an Australian bird? Turns out that Minnesota's northern lake country harbors plenty of good, dry land in between all that water. Here and there, specialty and traditional farmers have found unique ways to make agriculture work this far north. Meet some of them on this tour, most of which is through Hubbard County. For visitors who are in search of a farm experience, a little insight into our common agricultural heritage and a fat strawberry or two, it is a great place to be. Find it all in far northwestern Minnesota just west of big, beautiful Leech Lake.

Back at the Ranches

We'll start in the Nevis area of Hubbard County, which is about 40 miles south of Bemidji, and where a couple of specialty ranches welcome visitors. Make advance reservations for a trail ride at **BK Ranch**, 30880 County Road 91, Nevis, (218) 652-3540, then from Dorset (the tongue-in-cheek Restaurant Capital of the World, where you can stop for a bite) drive 12 miles north on County Road 7. The BK Ranch trail experience is what you might wish more Midwestern trail rides could be like, because it takes you right into the heart of the North Woods. Picture winding paths with some ups and downs, and the creak of saddle leather as you ride through a bit of the 75,000 acres of the Paul Bunyan State Forest, or through a separate 160-acre parcel. Picture dense trees and ferns, open vistas, beaver lodges, and wildlife sightings. Picture, too, a can of bug spray.

The intimidating stare of a bison at the Northland Bison Ranch, Nevis.

It gets more exotic. A visit to **Northland Bison Ranch**, 22376 Glacial Ridge Trail, Nevis, (218) 652-3582, (877) 453-9499, www.northlandbison.com, offers a fee-based ride out to see, hear, and observe a bison herd. The ranch occupies an old farmstead site. From BK Ranch, it is about a 10-mile drive. Call ahead to reserve your seat in the air-conditioned bison bus and get set to learn all about North America's largest native mammal. Back at the Log Gallery, look for products that are handcrafted by Native Americans from the ranch's own tanned bison leather. View the short video and shop for the ranch's own USDA-inspected bison meat. You can also find chili and stew mixes, as well as North Woods jams and jellies, wild rice, honey, and syrups.

Now for that photo op with an emu, which will surely get attention when you haul out the family photo album. The **Heart of Minnesota Emu Ranch**, 24200 Fairwood Lane, Nevis, (218) 652-2303, www.emumagic.com, is located three-quarters of a mile west of Nevis on County Road 18. From there, go left for a block on Fairwood Drive and right on Fairwood Lane. It is a little over three miles from the bison ranch. This ranch focuses on emu production, education, and research. It has outdoor runs, five barns, four breeder huts, an incubation and chick rearing facility, and, on average, 450 birds. It has 40 acres with only five used for the birds and a thick planting of tall grasses that helps to minimize environmental impact. It may be possible to arrange a tour, so be sure to call ahead to check current availability. If you do go on a tour, you will find that the big birds are amusing because of their inquisitive nature and big, brown eyes that follow your every move.

The ranch utilizes most of the bird for a variety of products that are made

FIELD TO TABLE

Grandma's scalloped asparagus ...

A CARTER FAMILY FAVORITE

2 pounds asparagus, trimmed and cut into 1-inch pieces
2 cups milk
1/3 cup butter or margarine
1/4 cup flour
1/4 teaspoon salt
1/4 teaspoon pepper
4 hard-cooked eggs, sliced
1/2 cup shredded Cheddar cheese
1 cup cooked ham, chicken, or cubed beef
1/2 cup bread crumbs
2 tablespoons butter, melted

Cook asparagus in 1/2 cup boiling water for 3 minutes (asparagus will still be crisp). Drain, reserving liquid. Add milk to cooking liquid. In a medium saucepan, melt 1/3 cup butter, stir in flour, salt, and pepper. Stir in milk mixture all at once. Cook and stir until thickened and bubbly. Remove from heat. Cover bottom of a greased two-quart casserole with half of asparagus. Arrange half of eggs over asparagus. Put in half of meat. Spoon in half of sauce, sprinkle with half of cheese. Repeat layers. Sprinkle with bread crumbs and drizzle with butter. Bake in 425-degree oven for 20 minutes or until bubbly. Serve over rice, pasta, toast, or biscuits. Serves 4.

Recipe courtesy of Russell Carter and family, Red Wagon Farm, Porte Rapids.

to exacting standards. Their EmuMagic line includes pure, soothing emu oil that functions as an anti-inflammatory and a moisturizer with fatty acids. Other products include skin care lotions, lip balms, soaps, and topical veterinary products for livestock and pets.

Down on the Farms

Head west on Highway 34 for about 13 miles to Park Rapids, where additional specialty farms and a rustic downtown await discovery. During the growing

Carter's Red Wagon Farm Market, Park Rapids.

season, **Carter's Red Wagon Farm Market**, 16338 County 107, Park Rapids, brings the Carter family's farm to town as it has since 1956. Call (218) 732-4979 for information. It is a country market that captures the feel of being on a farm and yet is conveniently in town. Shop in the post-and-beam barn where the family stocks popcorn, caramel corn, a crunchy field corn snack, Minnesota-made chokecherry syrups, honey, condiments, egg noodles, red pasta sauces, hormone-free beef, Northland Bison Ranch meats, wild rice, and, of course, Carter's own fresh produce. Asparagus kicks off the season in May, then come the strawberries, followed by all kinds of peppers, tomatoes, onions, sweet corn, melons, squashes, and pumpkins. Carter's own strawberry freezer jam tastes like you are eating fresh strawberries, and it works great in layer cakes. Autumn brings Saturday pumpkin parties with scarecrow making, wooden-cow milking, a pumpkin propeller, a corn-strawbale-fence maze, wagon rides, and of course plenty of farm-fresh foods.

Continue the short drive to downtown Park Rapids. **The Trading Post**, 19866 US 71, Park Rapids, (218) 732-4509, is a great shop with wild rice, great-smelling cedar boxes, wildlife figurines, pottery, toys, miniatures, and classic northland souvenirs. At **Snyder's Park Pharmacy**, 101 North Main Street, Park Rapids, (218) 732-3343, order up a couple of scoops of ice cream at the soda fountain. **Aunt Belle's Confectionary**, 110 South Main Street, Park Rapids, (218) 732-7019, invites you to watch while they make the fudge and chocolates fresh daily. Sample their exclusive line of gourmet condiments, and mosey on back to Grandpa's Cabin for gourmet coffees, teas, and kitchen stuff. While in town, you might also note that the Fish Hook Mill Pond and Dam at Rice Park still shows evidence of the town's first sawmill and flour mill. Incidentally, Rice Park gets its name not from wild rice, but from town founder Franklin C. Rice. Now you know.

Here is an idea for an on-farm experience. The Carter family's **Red Wagon Farm**, which is separate from the market, is located southwest of Park Rapids, three miles west of the junction of Highway 71 and Highway 34, then 3.3 miles south on County Road 115. Once at the farm, you can hop aboard the fringed strawberry surrey for a ride out to the acres of strawberry fields, and pick your own from late June through July.

Not far past the Red Wagon Farm is **The Secret Garden**, 11059 County Road 14, Park Rapids, (800) 950-4409, www.secretgardengourmet.com. This sustainable farm is an imaginative venture in the middle of nowhere. Their staple products are original-recipe lines of soup and baking mixes in pretty packages. Their bestseller among the wild rice mixes is cream of wild rice soup, and other choices include creamy wild rice asparagus soup, wild rice cranberry pilaf, and Almond/Apricot Wild Rice Hot Dish/Stuffing Mix. They only buy Minnesota-harvested wild rice in an effort to support fellow producers.

Also check out their newer line of Mexican salsa mixes, classic vegetable and bean soup mixes, seasonings, dips, bread maker mixes (Hearty Lumberjack Beer Bread, anyone?), salad dressings, and gift baskets. The breakfast goodies are pure North Woods: maple syrup, wild rice pancake mix, wild chokecherry and wild blueberry fruit syrups, and homemade jams like wild plum. Pick your favorites from corrugated boxes (most of it goes by mail order), and you may be able to visit the test kitchen where new soups are developed, where bulk ingredients like two-thousand-pound bags of beans are stored, and where assembly takes place. You can visit the organic (not certified) garden to see how it is grown at this latitude, although none of it ends up in the mixes. You can also take a guided tour of their beef cattle farm. Call ahead for tour information.

In the Woods

Twenty-one miles north of downtown Park Rapids on Highway 71, **Itasca State Park**, Minnesota's oldest, draws crowds because only here can they actually walk across the Mississippi River. It is said that is why everyone comes to Itasca State Park, but that they come again for the towering trees, the 32,690 acres of pristine beauty, and the excursion boat ride. Just east of the park entrance at the top of the hill (use the frontage road) is **Rising Star Ranch**, Highway 71 North, Park Rapids, (218) 732-1749, offering trail rides, pony rides, and a free petting zoo with bison, fallow deer, llamas, rheas, miniature goats, calves, pigs, and rabbits.

In the mood for a little fruit of the vine? Drive east on Highway 71/200, then a bit south on Highway 64 for a total of about 23 miles to **Forestedge Winery**, 35295 State 64, Laporte, (218) 224-3535, www.forestedgewinery.com. Their unexpectedly complex fruit wines tend toward the dry side, which is exciting for fruit wines. The plum wine blends Minnesota-grown plums into a full-bodied dry wine. Headwaters Classic Red combines chokecherry and rhubarb into another dry wine that has a tart finish.

As you make the regional stops, don't neglect the scenery in between, for it is of interest too. Blaze your own trail, or drive on one that is designated, such as the 14-mile **Woodtick Trail**. It winds through the Chippewa National Forest and takes you past evidence of forgotten farmsteads. Actually, if you start at the west end, which is a few miles north of Hackensack where Highway 371 meets the Upper 10 Mile Lake Road, you only need to drive a half mile to see the farmstead area. To help get your bearings, know that Hackensack is located about 38 miles east of Park Rapids. The Woodtick Trail got its name because what early twentieth-century road builders remembered best about working in the area was the ticks. As you traverse the route, keep an eye out for open fields, windrows, and old homestead sites. Ticks too.

There are some more farms in the area that are available for visiting, but going for a swim in one of the finest lakes in the world is another great option. While there enjoying the cool of the water and the heat of the sun, you can build some of those sandcastle memories.

SPECIAL EVENTS

Lake Itasca Region Pioneer Farmer's Show, Itasca State Park, Park Rapids, http://pioneerfarmers.tripod.com. Last two Saturdays in June. Great old-fashioned stuff: 1937 Wallingford's store with shelf-stocked grocery containers, old logging photographs and equipment, functional sawmill, threshing, steam/gas /diesel engines, tractor pull, blacksmith shop, museums, gospel music, more.

Hubbard County Fair, Park Rapids. Mid-July. Open Class and 4-H livestock judging, canine agility show, tractor and ATV pulls, motocross racing, demolition derby.

Blueberry Festival, Lake George, www.lakegeorgemn.com/b_festival.htm. End of July. Blueberry pies, garden club pie sale, blueberry educational booth, pig roast, fireman bean feed, mini pedal tractor pull, blueberry ball.

Real Horse Power and a Little Ox Power, Forest History Center, County Road 76, accessible from Highways 169 South and 2 West, Grand Rapids, (218) 327-4482, www.mnhs.org/foresthistory. Authentically re-created 1900 logging camp. Board the moored river "wanigan," a floating cook shack for "river pigs" as they floated logs downstream to the mills. Demonstrations of animal handling, harnessing, log skidding, etc.

Lake Itasca Region Pioneer Farmers Reunion, Itasca State Park (north entrance) Park Rapids, http://pioneerfarmers.tripod.com . Mid-August. Old-time engines, logging/lumbering pageantry, corn shredding, silage chopping, blacksmithing, domestic arts and crafts, threshing, daily parades, live music, kids' tractor pull. Feast on full meals, Norwegian *lefse*, fry bread, corn on the cob. This event grows every year.

Leaning on the hoe

Golden sun settles on the blue-striped engineer's cap and faded coveralls of Paul Sturm, who is alone tending vegetables on the 40 acres of the **Antique Tractor and Engine Club** late one afternoon. He pulls up a bunch of radishes, leans on his hoe, and talks of the old days of farming in northern Minnesota. He says the earliest farmers planted wheat as their main crop, and that in this area, the Hubbard Prairie was a big producer. He talks of the changes the railroads brought, and without bothering to stop and think about it, rattles off all the old station-stops. He remembers how there used to be a lot of creameries around, and that most made butter.

He remembers the wild rice boom of the late 1960s, early 1970s. "The price of green-harvested wild rice went to about two dollars a pound. Everybody that could find a canoe went out ricing. There were those that were good at it, but a lot of the others swamped their canoes and got wet," he says wryly.

Antique threshing machines anchor the four corners of the club grounds, not far from a subdivision where children play ball. Sturm

Paul Sturm takes a break from hoeing vegetables at the Antique Tractor and Engine Club, Park Rapids.

remembers that when he was growing up, the farmers would get together and thresh 45 to 50 acres of wheat a day. "And the women cooked. Two or three would get together and help each other out." Sturm worked in farming for only a decade starting in the mid-1950s, but anyone could tell he's spent a lot more time than that observing it. "It isn't that hard to know," he says. "You hear people talking, you listen." 🐜

Field Days, Antique Tractor and Engine Club, County Road 6, Park Rapids. Mid-late August. Call the Park Rapids Area Chamber of Commerce at (800) 247-0054. Yesteryear farming of the 1920–30 era meant that the harvest was done by steam power. Demonstrations include threshing, corn picking, rope making, potato digging. All aboard for rides on the scale model locomotive and wagons. Enjoy the model 1930s farm and village with pavilion/kitchen, farmhouse, church, sawmill and planer, railroad, shingle mill, heritage garden, tractor-pull track, and productive fields.

PLACES TO EAT

Douglas Lodge, Itasca State Park, Park Rapids, (218) 266-2100. In addition to other menu items, the dining room offers northern delicacies like regional blueberries, wild rice, and walleye. Open Memorial Day through early October. Choose indoor or outdoor seating overlooking beautiful Lake Itasca.

Rapid River Logging Camp, Highway 71 North (turn on County Road 18, follow signs), 15073 County 18, Park Rapids (218) 732-3444. All-you-can-eat family-style meals suggest a logging-camp experience. Breakfast (flapjacks, ham, and eggs), lunch, and dinner (roast beef, ham, hamburgers, chicken and barbeque sandwiches, sides). Catch steam-powered sawmill demonstrations (call for hours).

Sun Porch, Summerhill Farm, 24013 U.S. Highway 71, seven miles north of Park Rapids, (218) 732-3865. Also seven gift shops.

The Hog & Hen Roadside Bar-B-Que, 24025 State Highway 34, two miles west of Nevis, (218) 652-0220. Barbeque ribs, turkey drumsticks, steak sticks, wings, sandwiches, homemade sides.

If some of the lakes around here don't make you think about food—Blueberry, Cranberry, Duck, Ham, Hungry Man, Kettle, Potato, Rice—the Restaurant Capital of the World surely will. Having only four restaurants with a resident population of 22, Dorset gets away with its claim of supremacy on a technicality— it has more restaurants *per capita* than anywhere in the country. Heck, it is not even a town. **Compañeros**, (218) 732-7624. Mexican fare. **Dorset Café**, (218) 732-4072. Broasted chicken, steak, salad bar. **Dorset General Store and La Pasta Italian Eatery**, (218) 732-0275. **Dorset House Restaurant**, (218) 732-5556. Pizza, evening buffet, homemade pies, soda fountain.

PLACES TO STAY

C'mon Inn, Highway 34 East, Park Rapids, (800) 258-6891. Conveniently located motel built of natural wood accented with local fieldstone. Some rooms have indoor balconies overlooking the indoor courtyard pool and whirlpool area. Continental breakfast.

Douglas Lodge, Itasca State Park, entrance is 21 miles north of Park Rapids on U.S. Highway 71, (218) 266-2122. Circa-1905 classic rustic lodge with fireplace lobby. Redecorated historic suites and guest rooms on the second floor. Or choose from among a variety of cabins by the lake and other accommodations.

LoonSong Bed and Breakfast, Lake Itasca #27, Park Rapids, (218) 266-3333, (888) 825-8135, www.bbhost.com/loonsongbnb. Perching on Heart Lake, which is known for bass, this newer B&B has four rooms with handmade quilts and a clean country look. Mornings are worth getting up for, with breakfasts ranging from eggs and Canadian bacon to Minnesota specialties like wild rice pancakes with fresh blueberries.

10. FAR SUPERIOR

Hiking from waterfall to waterfall. Snatching up a prized agate. Slipping into a sea kayak or canoe, gliding down an alpine slide or gondola, and riding horseback to a North Woods lunch before luxuriating in a hot tub beside a crackling fire.

It is easy to do the North Shore of Lake Superior without ever soaking up the story of its commercial fishing industry.

But amid the crash of waves, you can still hear the echoes of men who lived from one day to the next, men of independence and courage and providing. Theirs was a hard life, but an adventuresome one too. It was the scrape of a skiff safely returned to dry land with its hull full of fish. It was the raw, cold work of filleting and salting and icing. It was the inevitable return to the water to sell the day's catch to the packet boats bound for Duluth, because they were too heavy to pull up to the fish houses that clung to the rocky shores. Working for themselves and with their families in this way, the mostly Norwegian immigrants made their lives the stuff of untold legends, and at least one of their descendants recently decided to return to the sea.

Duluth

Let's start in Duluth. Tucked into the well of the bay that touches both Minnesota and Wisconsin, Duluth is the logical starting point for a North Shore adventure. There are many things to do in this busy port city. The **Great Lakes Aquarium**, 353 Harbor Drive, (218) 740-3474, www.glaquarium.org, which opened in recent years, should help you get your feet wet for the North Shore experience. Uniquely, this 62,382-square-foot fish tank is entirely devoted to interpretation of the freshwater environment.

You may be getting good and ready for a taste of the North Shore's legendary smoked fish. But before diving right in, how about taking a detour inland and straight north on County Road 4 from Duluth? About 50 miles of driving will get you to the **Eli Wirtanen Finnish Homestead,** a few miles south of the intersection of 4 and County Road 16, 5312 Markham Road, Makinen, 218-638-2859. Take the free, self-guided tour of the farm's 16 historic buildings that tell a story of early Finnish-American farmsteading in the North Woods of Minnesota. Eli Wirtanen (1870-1958) was an immigrant who built everything by hand, including the farmhouse, horse barn, shingle mill, well house, pigpen, smoke-hole bathhouse, and hay shed. The layout, construction and forest lifestyle still stand as testimony of his Finnish heritage.

Northbound
It is almost two hours and just over 50 miles to the next stop, Tom's Logging Camp, which is located 16 miles northeast of downtown Duluth. Ready? Return to County Road 4, this time turning left onto County Road 44, right onto County Road 37, left onto County Road 43, and staying straight to pick up US Highway 61 for just under one mile. Next, turn right onto County Road 258, left onto Minnesota Highway 61 going north and right onto Alseth Road which becomes County Road 290. Take a right onto North Shore Drive and you have arrived at **Tom's Logging Camp and Old Northwest Company Trading Post,** 5797 North Shore Drive, Duluth Township, (218) 525-4120, www.tomsloggingcamp.com. To get here as you are driving up from Duluth, choose the scenic route, not the expressway. Tom's is a classic family-vacation attraction that celebrates the region's logging heritage with camp buildings and a petting zoo amid a forest of spruce, balsam, birch, and pine.

The logging camp's Knife River Fishing Museum features old commercial fishing boats (one that was on the water as late as 1973), nets, and other historic equipment that still emits odors of herring and lake trout. The harness shop has an antique shoeing stall in working order and a bobsled that was used to haul food out to the loggers. In the cook shanty, mannequin lumbermen are just finishing up a big meal.

For smoked fish that you can enjoy at a beach picnic or take back home to share with friends, visit the handful of fish markets that are scattered like agates along the North Shore from Knife River to Grand Marais. Smoked herring, whitefish, trout, salmon, and other fish are sold by the pound as fillets, chunks, or dressed whole. The whitefish and herring are typically caught in Lake Superior. The distinctively intense flavor of smoked fish is almost meaty, which is good news for resolute meat-eaters who otherwise don't care much for fish.

Drive into the remote little community of Knife River, which sits three miles northeast of the logging camp. There, very close to where the waves break against the shore, is **Russ Kendall's Smoke House,** 149 North Shore Drive (Scenic Highway 61), Knife River, (218) 834-5995. The fragrant aroma of fish that has been carefully smoked to bronze perfection is a heady lure.

The owner says the place has been operated, at one time or another, as a casino, a tavern, and an ice cream parlor, but the anchor has always been the fish. House specialties are brown sugar trout and salmon. They say the smoking process takes about 12 hours in the old-fashioned ovens and over open fires, but it depends on the weather and the size of the fish. Eat your catch in the un-fussy dining area or pack it into your cooler. They also throw beef into the smoker for satisfying beef jerky that could be the ultimate car food. Also pick up a jar of juicy, red wild lingonberries from Sweden, if the local Scandinavians haven't already snapped them all up.

Next up on your left as you continue northeast is **Mel's Fish**, 223 Scenic Drive, Knife River, (218) 834-5858, www.superiorschoicefish.com. It is a neat, modern cottage on the outside, and an appropriately smoky fish house on the inside. The glass deli case tempts with a selection that includes freshly smoked whitefish, brown sugar salmon, and brown sugar trout. Also consider Minnesota specialty products like wild rice.

The market has been known for its smoked salmon for the last 30 years or so. Other offerings include homemade smoked beef jerky and turkey jerky and smoked (Wild) Alaska salmon lox spreads. Check out **Buddy's Wild Rice**, 724 Seventh Avenue, Two Harbors, (218) 834-5823 for an assortment of wild rice, pure maple syrup, honey, and over 50 kinds of jams and jellies.

Not far up the road, **Superior's Choice Fish Company**, 605 Seventh Avenue (Highway 61), Two Harbors, (218) 834-3719, www.superiorschoicefish.com, is in the log cabin. The shop is newer, but the operation is multi-generational, so they know their brines and smoking techniques. They use natural wood fires and brown sugar glazing. Poke a toothpick into flaky, fragrant samples of smoked whitefish, trout, and salmon to compare the flavors and decide which is to be your favorite. For example, salmon is the most expensive and tends to be drier than trout, which is oilier. Add a batch of batter-fried cheese curds to your fish selections, and you're set for lunch.

Four miles northeast, you come to busy Two Harbors. **Lou's Fish House**, 1319 Seventh Avenue, Two Harbors, (218) 834-5254, www.lousfish.com, pops up. By all means pull in, and if Jo Ann is at the counter, you are likely to get friendly patter and frank suggestions as you peer into the deli case. Lou and Jo Ann freshly smoke a variety of fish over a wood fire, including lake trout, Alaskan salmon, whitefish, herring, and ciscoe. The wood is from the North Woods, and includes sugar maple, birch, and alder.

Next is Beaver Bay, about 25 miles up the shore. Your destination? The **Lake Superior Sausage Company**, 309 Old Town Road, Beaver Bay, (218) 226-3540. This great shop offers a world of sausages from Polish to Polynesian. Where else could you find Boerwors (South African), English Bangers, Hungarian, Irish, Linquica (Hot Portuguese), New York Italian, Norwegian, Russian, Sicilian, chicken, duck, lamb, turkey, and vegetarian sausages? Something is fishy here too, for they also offer lake trout sausage and lake trout wild rice sausage.

Log cabin structure of Superior's Choice Fish Company, Two Harbors.

Commercial Fishing Museum

The next stop along the North Shore is a great little museum in Tofte, which is just over 30 miles from Beaver Bay and named for a small farming community in Norway. Get hooked on the fish stories inside the **North Shore Commercial Fishing Museum,** 7136 West Highway 61, Tofte, (218) 663-7804, www.commercialfishing museum.org, which replicates a twin-gabled fish house that once stood nearby. The museum and its *North Shore Commercial Fishing Museum Journal* tell the stories of independent fishermen more than those of large commercial operations. Stories of men in a steamer who got icebound for an entire winter, and of a teacher who braved isolation on Isle Royale. Learn that the heyday of North Shore commercial fishing began about 1880, and that it was a largely individual enterprise, the almost exclusive domain of Norwegian immigrants. It continued with their offspring, who grew up mending gill nets and hammering nails into fish boxes, and who eventually took up the oars alongside their fathers. Processing of the catch took place in the family's fish house that sat near the water's edge, and in the case of herring, it was a hard job of splitting the fish down the back before cleaning, washing, and layering it between handfuls of salt.

Just past the museum, what appears to be an ordinary gas station and convenience store is the **North Shore Market,** 7125 Highway 61, Tofte, (218) 663-7288. Walk back to the deli counter, where, instead of the usual pre-packaged stuff, you will find seasoned fish cakes made by the owner of a local restaurant, a selection of fish smoked by a third-generation family, a family-recipe fishcake batter, chicken and wild rice sausage, beef jerky dried in the market's own smoker, and ridiculously low prices for frozen duck and goose that would be perfect for the grill.

Far North

Nine miles beyond Tofte on Highway 61, you come to Lutsen, a crossroads community with an array of attractions that could keep you busy for days. The four peaks of the Lutsen Mountains have become an alpine playground with rides on all sides. Board the Mountain Tram for a swing through the treetops to the highest peak, where you can grab a bite at the deli and savor the one hundred-mile views. Ride a horse to a lunch of walleye, fried potatoes, and baked beans, or to a steak dinner cooked over an open fire. Both the lunch and dinner rides require parties of four people, or you can opt for a regular trail ride. Also zip around on the twisting alpine slide, the hiking trails, and the mountain bike trails.

Lutsen has not one but two maple syrup producers. **Caribou Cream**, 558 Caribou Trail, Lutsen, (218) 663-7841, sheds light on the ancient art of syruping, and offers pure maple syrup, maple candy, and pancake mix for sale. **Wild Country Maple Syrup**, 191 Barker Lake Road, Lutsen, (218) 663-8010, www.wildcountry maple.com, makes its award-winning product on a 320-acre sugar bush with almost 12,000 taps—the greatest such operation in the entire state.

Way up in sometimes-arty Grand Marais, which is about 110 breezy, breathtaking miles northeast of Duluth (and 18 miles beyond Lutsen), the folks at **Dockside Fish Market**, 418 West Highway 61, Grand Marais, (218) 387-2906, www.docksidefishmarket.com, are commercial fishermen *and* the people behind the counter. That is increasingly rare. They smoke lake trout, herring, salmon, and whitefish using brown sugar brine and local sugar maple wood. They also sell fresh fish, including walleye, halibut from Alaska, seasonal salmon from Alaska, shellfish, smoked fish spreads, smoked fish mousse, specialty seasonings and breadings, sauces like lingonberry horseradish and cucumber-chive horseradish, cheeses including an organic Gouda, wild rice, local maple syrup, and plenty more.

Grand Marais is also home to the **North House Folk School**, which teaches people how to build boats, cook fish chowder, bake bread, and acquire other practical, lost art skills. Call (218) 387-9762, (888) 387-9762 or visit www.north house.org for course information. Here's just a taste of what they've got cooking: the Chez Jude Culinary Workshops include North Shore Fish Cookery, Barbeque and Grilled Foods Cookery, Wood Roasted Foods Cookery, Artisan Breads for Hearth Ovens, and more. Don't be put off by the hearth oven thing; they teach you how to use baking stones in your good old convection model. You could also learn the art of "Making a Birch Bark Berry Basket," "Making a Broom-Corn Broom," or discover how to tap a tree in "Birch Sap is Arisin'— Let's Tap!" At the unusual school, you don't just sit around in a classroom acquiring skills. For example, the berry basket class begins with a trek to the forest to harvest birch bark, and involves boiling, peeling, and splitting pine root before you even begin to shape or stitch the basket.

The **Joynes Department Store and Ben Franklin**, 205 Wisconsin Street, Grand Marais, (218) 387-2233, is a bargain hunter's delight that is jam-packed with practical outdoor clothing, mad cows that moo insanely (unless they've all been

Sea Change

On the eve of retirement after a lifetime spent teaching industrial arts and later being a school superintendent, Dale Tormondsen was ready to be gone fishing. But not in the way other guys dream of. This grandson of Norwegian immigrants was taking up the oars of a commercial fishing boat, a skiff that he had built himself. Tormondsen never forgot the years he had spent working alongside his grandfather, pulling in a ton of herring a day using gill nets, and spending many hours choking and cleaning the catch that would be shipped to Duluth and destined for Chicago.

Today, Tormondsen spends about 20 hours a week fishing for herring up to two miles out from shore, going out at dawn and returning about 8:00 a.m. to process the fish that get caught in nets he sets each July and leaves in the water through the middle of autumn—before the lake's legendary November storms kick up. There is a trick to it.

"My nets are secured by rope to big iron anchors in four hundred feet of water. Lake Superior has a terrific current that typically goes from here to Duluth in a counterclockwise pattern. Sometimes it is so strong it drags the anchors or even will break the polyurethane rope," he explains.

A good day's catch is 10 to 15 pounds of cleaned fillets. To maintain his commercial fishing license, Tormondsen must net $1,500 each year. He says that has proven to be no problem, as both the catch and the market are good. "I usually charge about $3.75 per pound. I sell my catch to the local grocery store and to private individuals. Fish cakes are popular here amongst some of the locals, and typically people will order 10 pounds. If I catch too many, I sometimes go to the big grocery stores in Duluth."

Even so, Tormondsen says he does not do it for the money. "I give a lot of fish to seniors who are shut in," he adds.

Three summers after launching his second career, Tormondsen is still captivated despite the hard work and risk. "Being out on the lake all alone early in the morning with seagulls surrounding the boat, Carlton Peak looming above the shoreline, and watching for the silvery flash in the clear water, beats any other thing I have done for work or pleasure," he says.

But Tormondsen hasn't had time to get lonely out on the water. Hardly a week goes by when someone doesn't ask to join him. "Many tourists, locals, and summer residents are fascinated by commercial fishing. Today, for example, I had a gynecologist and another doctor who specializes in cancer at the University of Minnesota."

Seems he's still teaching, after all. 🐟

You can't beat the view of the North Woods and Lake Superior from the Lutsen Resort, Lutsen.

recalled), and foods that are special to Minnesota and Canada. The Malkins jam from Canada comes in a can with a plastic lid that keeps everything neat in the car. Joynes is not your typical Ben Franklin, but then, was any Ben Franklin you ever poked around in typical?

Keep going to the **Judge C. R. Magney State Park**, 4051 E. Highway 61, Grand Marais, (218) 387-3039, where the **Devil's Kettle Waterfall** runs amok on the Brule River. They say the falls swallows half the river's water and takes it to parts unknown. A mysteriously bottomless kettle? That's devilish, all right.

This tour takes you a long way, not only geographically but also in a way that has been known to change people's outlook on life. That is because, with its history of human bravery and independence set against a backdrop that is still wild, the North Shore of Lake Superior makes people want to return. Besides, that smoked fish is a draw that they cannot resist.

SPECIAL EVENTS

Lions Club Fisherman's Picnic. Grand Marais. First week of August. Four-day event featuring log sawing contest, tractor pull.

Rendezvous Days, Grand Portage National Monument, Grand Portage, (218) 387-2788. Second week of August. Wrap yourself up in the old fur-trading days at this re-created bayside trading post. Enjoy displays of birch bark, cedar, and spruce canoes that were built to harvest wild rice. Also enjoy Voyageur cooking and camping re-enactments, explorations of an authentic garden, and outdoor oven.

Lake County Fair, Two Harbors, (218) 834-8300. Late August. Horse show, animal barn, pie contest.

PLACES TO EAT

Angry Trout Café, 416 W. Highway 61, Grand Marais, (218) 387-1265. Offering fresh, local foods in a lakeside setting rendered special by the works of local artists and artisans, and doing business in a way that minimizes environmental impact. Your lunchtime fish sandwich is fresh-caught by local fishermen, grilled, and tucked into a multi-grain bun. The maple grilled chicken sandwich is brushed with their own maple syrup barbeque sauce. How many kids' menus offer to feed the little ones chicken nuggets made from free-range chickens, and where else does doing shots mean knocking back an ounce of pure maple syrup?

Coho Café, Bakery and Deli, 7126 W. Highway 61, Highway 61, Tofte, (218) 663-8032. Fresh, seasonal ingredients grown and harvested locally. Wake up to blueberry bread pudding topped with maple syrup. Sandwiches, salads for lunch, pastas for dinner. Creative pizzas, including one with wild rice sausage.

Emily's Restaurant and Inn, 218 Scenic Drive Highway 61, Knife River, (218) 834-5922. Summertime brings whitefish boils (served as a buffet; no theatrics a la Door County, Wisconsin) and whitefish chowder, and winter brings cozy fireside dining. Enjoy smoked salmon wrap for lunch, or smoked salmon fettuccini for dinner. Emily's also features salmon from nearby Mel's Fish, and panfried walleye. Enjoy views of the Knife River and the passing excursion train that chugs up from Duluth on its way to Two Harbors. Stay tuned; an inn is in the works.

Judy's Café, 623 Seventh Avenue, Two Harbors, (218) 834-4802. No-nonsense luncheonette really cooks at lunchtime when lots of customers are having breakfast, which is served all day. Some fish choices, including an ocean whitefish sandwich (breaded and deep-fried), a walleye pike entrée, and a Friday fish fry.

The Pie Place, 2017 West Highway 61, (on the way to downtown) Grand Marais, (218) 387-1513. The ever-fresh menu changes weekly and the concept is one of home-cooked gourmet with fresh produce, locally caught fish, and the meats from a local butcher. The menu has featured, for example, smoked salmon pâté, BLT with thick-cut maple-cured bacon, homemade sun-dried tomato cream cheese and wild rice oatmeal bread, Scandinavian Sweet Onion Pie with Jarlsberg cheese, and a fried egg dish whimsically called Caribou Eyes. Pies by the slice or whole to go are made daily; blackberry-peach is a specialty. The Pie Place brings to mind an old-fashioned family summer cottage with its row of windows overlooking Lake Superior.

PLACES TO STAY

Lutsen Resort, 7106 W. Highway 61, Lutsen, (218) 663-7212, (800) 258-8736, www.lutsenresort.com. Stay and play on a mile-long stretch of Lake Superior at the Poplar River, as guests have done since 1885. This is rustic resort living in a pristine natural setting. Exceptional programs are free to guests: sea kayak instruction, agate hunts, Voyageur history talks, beach campfire with marshmallow roast, naturalist hikes, more. On-site restaurant features Swedish meatballs, steaks, walleye, and other quality fish. Indoor pool complex, Poplar River fishing for steelhead, lake trout, and salmon (license and trout stamp required), 9-hole par-3 golf course, game room, etc. Newer, Scandinavian-chic condos are loaded with comfort and style. Lots of accommodation options: historic lodge, sea villas, log homes, condos.

Superior Shores Resort and Conference Center, 1521 Superior Shores Drive, Two Harbors, (218) 834-5671, (800) 242-1988, www.superiorshores.com. Located right on the water, this attractive property has the rustic look and all the amenities. Opt for a lodge room with full bath and TV/VCR; a lodge suite with full kitchen, gas fireplace, double whirlpool, and private deck with grill; or one of the lake homes that range in size from studio to three bedroom plus loft.

Temperance Traders North Shore Cabins and Gift Shop, 7759 W. Highway 61, Schroeder, (218) 663-0111, www.northshorecabins.com. Newer one- and two-bedroom cabins with knotty pine interior, full kitchen, satellite TV, and outdoor deck.

11. WILD RICE, WILD NORTH

This weekend, why not go off in search of something wild—wild rice, that is. The Minnesota DNR lists 74 Rice Lakes, Wild Rice Lakes, Big Rice Lakes, and Little Rice Lakes in Minnesota. More wild rice grows naturally in these cold northern waters than in any other state. Native Americans continue to hand-harvest the tasty and nutritious seed-heads. The wild rice that you buy is either called "lake," which means it grew naturally in a lake, or "cultivated," which means it was grown in a paddy as a field crop. Wild rice is a prized restaurant menu item. It is often served with chicken, and pheasant when you can get it, but it is also a fine accompaniment to another Minnesota swear-by—walleye. A pilaf of wild rice might include cranberries or blueberries, which are also native to the north.

When it comes to finding wild rice at or near its source, Crow Wing and Aitkin counties are good choices because you can see the wild rice in all its guises: growing naturally in the lake, under cultivation, in a museum, and on the store shelves. Besides, these counties are reasonable drives north of Minneapolis-Saint Paul, and you will always be within splashing distance of a swimming hole. One of the communities you will be "ricing" in is Baxter, which is about 130 miles from Minneapolis.

Wild Ways

Let's start in Aitkin County. An hour or so west and a little south of Duluth, and five miles south of McGregor on Highway 65, the Rice River flows over the top and past the eastern shore of Rice Lake, which is at the heart of the 18,064-acre **Rice Lake National Wildlife Refuge,** 36289 State Highway 65, McGregor, (218) 768-2402. It is bordered by the East Lake Indian Reservation. According to the U.S. Fish and Wildlife Service Web site for the refuge, every September, members of the Ojibwe band come to hand-harvest the *manomin* (wild rice) from canoes just as their ancestors did for an estimated 1,300 to 1,400 years, although in the past they would also camp in the area. Following harvest, the grain is dried by the curing or parching method, threshed underfoot to loosen it from the hull, and then winnowed, which means it is tossed into the air from a basket so that the chaff flies away and the good grain is retained for storage and eventual consumption.

For a peek into Ojibwe culture and history, and the significance of wild rice to their way of life, drive to the southwestern shore of Mille Lacs Lake. Highway 169 curves with the shoreline, and gawking at the water is a natural thing to do because of its beauty and proximity. Your destination is the **Mille Lacs Indian Museum**, 43411 Oodena Drive, Onamia, (320) 532-3632, www.mnhs.org. It is actually 12 miles north of the heart of Onamia, on the southwest shore of Lake Mille Lacs (Highway 169). The Grand Casino Mille Lacs is across the road; the crowds are over there.

At the museum's wild rice exhibit, a video shows how the seed heads are beaten from the tall grass stalks and into the boat. See the tools of the trade: sticks, a basket, and a round ball of reeds that would have been used to tie the plants together for protection against birds, rains, and winds. The exhibit is small and comes up near the end of your self-guided museum tour.

But references to wild rice are scattered throughout other exhibits as if to underscore how essential this food was to the Ojibwe. Look into the glass shadowboxes near the entrance, where handfuls of dried foods that the Indians would have harvested and eaten include grains of wild rice. A model of Rice Lake (one of them) shows where such harvests once occurred. As a guide takes you on a tour inside the Four Seasons Room, one life-size diorama shows individuals forever frozen in the timeless tasks required to harvest and process wild rice. Over in the trading post, displays show how the Indians used to set up roadside stands for nineteenth-century tourists. And along with birch bark baskets and canoes, they also sold wild rice. Today you can buy Ojibwe-harvested wild lake rice in the museum's gift shop.

You might be able to see wild rice growing in Lake Onamia, which is 10 miles south of the museum. Look near the shoreline.

Let's head to a farm-based museum in Brainerd, which is in Crow Wing County, and 32 miles northwest of the Ojibwe museum. Drive north on 169, then west on Highway 18 to **This Old Farm Antique Museum and Birch Ridge Village**, 17469 Highway 18, Brainerd, (218) 764-2915. You are on the Rademacher family farm, where dairy cows and sheep have yielded to Richard Rademacher's passion for collecting rural artifacts. Collected over 40-odd years, the items represent what it took to make a living in this area. Take a self-guided tour among buildings that have been brought in to comprise a village along with the original barn and threshing machine shed. There is a blacksmith shop, doctor and dentist offices, post office, filling station, fire station, and the Sweet Shoppe displaying an old soda fountain, popcorn popper, and children's toys. There is even a genuine, flat-bottom wooden rice boat on display. Although Rademacher never cared to go ricing, he always had his eye on one of the boats, and one day added it to his vast collection. Take a trip through the past, as well as through the seasonal 11-acre corn maze.

Richard Rademacher shows off a gleaming steam-powered tractor at This Old Farm Antique Museum, Brainerd.

Under Cultivation

You have seen it growing wild, you have seen it under glass, now let's go find wild rice growing as a farm crop, and buy it direct from a farmer, namely, **Ray Puetz Wild Rice**, 6545 County Road 45, Brainerd, (218) 829-8058. To get here from town, head south on 13th Street, which becomes County Road 45, for a total of almost seven miles. Do this navigating after you've called ahead, though, to make sure someone will be there. Three brands, all grown on-site, are available complete with recipes, along with crockery and gift tins with wild rice. Puetz is an amiable grower who has been cultivating wild rice at this farm since 1967. He harvests sometime in August, depending on the weather. Don't look for a lake—Puetz nurtures his crop chemical-free in paddies on the farm.

The cycle begins each autumn with preparation of the paddies, which are akin to fields at that stage, for seeding before winter freeze-up. He floods the paddies in the spring when water is plentiful, although he reports that some other growers prefer to do this step in the autumn. He keeps them flooded until sometime in July, when he begins to let the water level drop. This must be done gradually and with an eye toward wind, so the grasses don't get blown over. After the draining process, the crop finishes its ripening cycle. Don't look for a canoe or rice boat, however, as harvesting is all done by combine. After harvest, the crop is transported to local processing plants for drying, hull removal, and grading. Then it comes back for packaging and shipping to area retail outlets, as well as direct sales to you.

The wild life

Wild rice likes to stick close to shore, generally in water that is up to three feet deep. It is an annual, dropping seeds into the water each autumn in preparation for new growth the next spring. The Minnesota DNR reports that the state has 60,785 acres of the native grass, and that over half of it is in the north-central counties of Aitkin, Itasca, Cass, and Saint Louis. The agency also reports that the seeds—the part you eat—contain an antioxidant that some believe might help to reduce the risk of cancer. That is reason enough to keep lots of it around. The DNR, the Bureau of Indian Affairs, Ducks Unlimited, and other organizations have launched the Minnesota Wild Rice Management Planning Project to help stem the tide of decline. 🏃

At Retail

From Brainerd, drive about 10 miles north to **Christmas Point Wild Rice Company**, 14803 Edgewood Drive North, Baxter, (218) 828-0603, (800) 726-0613, www.christmaspoint.com. The shop, with its babbling pond and kayaks lashed to the wraparound deck, is pure North Woods. But it is hardly rough and hardly all wild rice. Christmas Point is a playground for gourmets, gourmands, and lakeside cottage redecorators. The owners stock handpicked and cultivated wild rices that are bagged and priced by the pound and all from Minnesota. Interesting wild rice soup mixes, which take all the guesswork out of cooking, include cheese and broccoli, mild white Cheddar, and red bean. Other mixes include cranberry wild rice stuffing and Italian garlic and herb quick bread. The fish batter mix has wild rice flour in it. Beyond wild rice, a variety of gourmet goodies are presented in such a way as to visually spark great menu ideas.

The region's grocery stores carry wild rice, including **Schaefer's Foods**, Highway 371 at County Roads 77 and 13, just south of Nisswa, (218) 963-2265. It is a handy stop on the way to the serious lake territory. From Christmas Point Wild Rice Company, it is a little over 12 easy miles north.

Wild rice is a classic accompaniment to fish—another traditional treat from the lakes of Minnesota. Walleye, also called walleye pike, is a favorite of the state, so much so that it is the state fish. It gets its rather unappetizing name not from any physical impediment, but from the silvery or milky cast to its eyes, which is simply characteristic of the species. Luckily the region north of Brainerd/Baxter is just flooded with lakes, and the **Nisswa Guides League**, (218) 963-2547, (877) 963-FISH, www.nisswaguides.com, has a string of experts ready to take you out

Wild rice and other Minnesota-made products inside the Christmas Point Wild Rice Company store, Baxter.

on the water. A handful of these guys are schoolteachers, so you are bound to learn something. Sign up for a half- or full-day adventure. If you like, they will clean your catch and even prepare a shore lunch. While in Nisswa, visit the cute gift shops for birch bark switch plate covers, cinnamon-scented pine cone candles, and gourmet bean dips from Minneapolis-based Old Fart Baked Bean Company.

In the next town north of Nisswa, about six miles up Highway 371, stop into **The Enchanted Cottage**, 4572 East Main Street, Pequot Lakes, (218) 568-5001, to check out their furniture that is fashioned from authentic barn wood. You may wish to have lunch in town, and then take County Road 11 east almost two miles to see **Rice Lake**, which is often abundant with wild rice, as well as the wildlife that loves to eat it. You might also be able to see wild rice growing in **Norway Lake** just north of the community of Pine River, which is slightly less than 10 miles north of Pequot Lakes and actually in Cass County. The wild rice stays close to the shoreline and can be viewed from the boat launch. Duckweed and bull-frogs can also be seen and heard. While in Pine River, stop in the IGA for more wild rice, and in the visitor center for more information.

In essence, this tour involves a hunt for something wild. Whether natural or cultivated, wild rice is a fascinating resource that has kept people, fish, and birds well fed for untold ages. Find out what the native people and animals of Minnesota have known for a long, long time. And bring some of it to your own table, for wild rice has a way of elevating meals to fine dining experiences.

SPECIAL EVENTS

Workshops and Demonstrations at Mille Lacs Indian Museum and Trading Post, (320) 532-3632. Pre-registration and payment required. Topics include Birch

Bark Basket, Loom Designs, Birch Bark Canoe Building Demonstration, Natural Dye Demonstration.

Nisswa-Stamman—A Scandinavian Folk Music Festival, Brainerd, www.niss wastamman.org. Early June. Great Scandinavian buffet. International gathering of musicians and dancers who fill your senses with traditional folk entertainment.

Free Corn on the Cob Feed, 12:00 noon, Don Adamson Field, Brainerd. Fourth of July.

Bean Hole Days, Bobberland Park, Pequot Lakes. Early July, on a weekday. This free bean feed amounts to more than a hill of beans—because all the cooking action happens underground. On the evening of the first day, they lower 150 gallons of Pequot Lakes Baked Beans into the ground to cook. The Bean Lowering is spiced up with children's games and hot dog stands. At high noon of the second day, witness the Bean Raising and the serving of the beans with lemonade and a roll. The tradition goes back to 1935, when local businessmen decided to sponsor a festival to thank the area farmers for their harvests.

Museum in Motion, This Old Farm Antique Museum and Birch Ridge Village, 17469 Highway 18, Brainerd, (218) 764-2915. Early August. Get all fired up about our rural American heritage as they power up the old farm equipment and turn back the hands of time.

Polka Fest, on Rat Lake in Larson's Barn, 47987 240th Avenue, McGregor, (218) 426-3648, www.larsonbarn.com. Early August. Kick up your heels and stamp your feet even if you don't know how to polka. Country, old-time, and other music from multiple bands. Food, camping.

Wild Rice Days, McGregor, (877) 768-3692, www.mcgregormn.com. End of August. VFW wild rice pancake breakfast, special wild rice foods, wild rice cooking contest, bake sale, pony rides, horse show/competition, parade, music, cloggers.

PLACES TO EAT

Here's a sample of area eateries featuring walleye and/or wild rice on their menus.

Kavanaugh's Resort and Restaurant, 1685 Kavanaugh Drive, East Gull Lake, (218) 829-5226, (800) 562-7061, www.kavanaughs.com. Fresh Salmon Nordique is broiled and served with lobster-based spinach cream sauce and wild rice. Walleye Vanessa is a broiled filet with shrimp sauce and wild rice. Overlooks Sylvan Lake.

Manhattan Beach Lodge, 39051 County Road 66, Manhattan Beach (on Big Trout Lake), (218) 692-3381, (800) 399-4360, www.mblodge.com. Minnesota world cuisine: walleye tacos (pan-fried and served in taco shells with red cabbage, onion, cilantro, coconut lime sauce), walleye shore lunch, walleye sandwich, walleye and wild rice cakes (served with lemon and remoulade sauce), thai walleye, honey pecan crusted, broiled almandine, Walleye World, and many more non-walleye choices.

Sibley Station, 31020 Government Drive, Pequot Lakes, (218) 568-4177. Pizza, pasta, sandwiches. Minnesota walleye is a house specialty. "World Famous" Hungarian Mushroom Soup. Chili in a homemade bread bowl that took five years to perfect. One month's chef's special was Minnesota Wild Meat Loaf stuffed with wild mushrooms and asiago cheese and topped with a wild mushroom shallot sauce.

The Dining Room at Grand View Lodge, 23521 Nokomis Avenue, Nisswa, (218) 963-2234, www.grandviewlodge.com. Walleye, wild rice soup.

Timberjack Smokehouse and Saloon, Highway 371 and County Road 168, Pequot Lakes, (218) 568-6070. Smokehouse on premises. Walleye sandwich, deep-fried or broiled walleye fillet, sides include wild rice blend.

PLACES TO STAY

AmericInn, 600 Dellwood Drive North, Brainerd/Baxter, (218) 829-3080. Indoor pool/sauna, continental breakfast. Convenient location.

Bay View Lodge, 12038 Harbor Lane, Crosslake, (218) 543-4182, (888) 543-4182. Originally a family farm where a grassy recreation area was used to grow crops. It became a resort back in the 1940s, starting with two cabins. May or September only for single-night stays.

Lost Lake Lodge, 7965 Lost Lake Road, Lake Shore, (218) 963-2681, (800) 450-2681, www.lostlake.com. Cabins on private Lost Lake and the Upper Gull Lake Narrows, in 80-acre woodland. Included in the family vacation packages are activities, watercraft, and two meals daily. Along with gourmet entrées that change daily, signature breads are on the menu. They are not just any breads—the lodge has its own working vintage gristmill that was rescued in Saint Paul and has the capability of producing several hundred pounds of flour/cornmeal each day. Wild rice pancakes for breakfast, anyone?

Pinecrest Cottage, 10818 53rd Avenue SW, Pillager, (218) 746-3936. Sleep tight beneath North Woods pines in this 1890s Scandinavian log cottage on a turn-of-the-century farm. Make your own breakfast in the fully-stocked kitchen that has eggs from the farm, homemade jams and jellies, and fresh-baked foods.

Whiteley Creek Homestead, 12349 Whiteley Creek Trail, Brainerd, (218) 829-0654, (877) 985-3275, www.whiteleycreek.com. Only three miles from Brainerd, yet secluded on 40 acres where you can canoe on-site and enjoy breakfast served in a railroad car. The Homestead has five guestrooms with private baths, including three cottages with fireplaces. Outdoor stone fireplace, rustic décor, 1930s–1940s cars and trucks for the vintage enthusiast.

12. PIE DAY! A SLICE OF AMERICANA

A math contest for fun? In summer? Before school starts? Yah, you betcha. It's called Pi R Squared, and along with lots of other pie-themed high jinks, it adds up to great fun at the annual **Pie Day** in Braham, Minnesota.

For a slice of Americana just 50 miles north of where Minneapolis got famous for bagging voluminous quantities of flour, visit the **Homemade Pie Capital of Minnesota**—also known as Braham. You might say this town is a little preoccupied with pie, but it has also been known to manufacture products such as eggbeaters and potato-harvesting equipment at one time or another.

Pie Day happens in Braham on the first Friday of every August, www .braham.com. Some five thousand people come to edify, classify, deify, and dignify pie. They happily consume over five hundred fruit and berry pies that some 150 local volunteers have spent weeks baking up from scratch. No ready-made crusts here, just lots of rolling pins and rolled-up sleeves. It is said that the rhubarb pies disappear first, not strawberry-rhubarb, just straight-up rhubarb. Rhubarb has also been called pie plant, and this particular rhubarb hails from the fields surrounding Braham. And over at the Park Café, they are baking more fruit pies, as well as heavenly cream pies, to help meet the demand.

Early on the morning of Pie Day, visitors and locals begin to gather in the VFW Hall for a pancake breakfast. By 8:00 a.m., excitement stirs the summer air as pie-contest hopefuls begin to deliver their fragrant entries to the Braham Evangelical Lutheran Church. Be sure to get to Freedom Park, where they start to serve pie and ice cream early.

Lots of other Pie Day merriment is also getting underway. About a hundred craft vendors and local organizations throw open the flaps of their tents, and food vendors open for business with their good, fresh smells—and pie puns are everywhere. Catch the Pie A(r)t Squared Art Show, where each of the works has to depict something about pie, from growing and harvesting of ingredients to celebrating Braham's status as the Homemade Pie Capital of Minnesota. Live musical entertainment is scheduled throughout the day and includes the sing-along Pie-Alluia Chorus. Also enjoy storytellers, children's poetry readings, door prize drawings, a fashion show, and a pie medallion hunt. There must be a pied piper around here somewhere. Naturally the cows of Braham—you knew this was coming—also make pies. For the Pie in the Pasture raffle, cows are let loose in a makeshift pasture in the park, and people take a chance on where given cows will go to work in given squares.

Back at the Lutheran church, a batch of home economists from General Mills and the Betty Crocker Kitchens are busy judging entries on appearance, taste, and texture, in the categories of baked single crust, baked double crust, fresh fruit, cream, and children's. When the winning pies are announced in the afternoon, they are auctioned off to hungry bidders. At that time, the judges also provide informative commentary. It wouldn't be a pie event without a pie-eating contest. Pie Day sponsors one such competition for the kids and another for the big kids. In order to win, you have to eat a whole graham-cracker crust pie filled with blueberries and blanketed with whipped cream. It is worth it to get your name engraved on a trophy that will sit in the hallowed halls of piedom—the Park Café.

All day long you've been listening to people singing about pie, watching people eat pie fast, wondering how someone gets up the nerve to dress up as a slice of pie, deciding which pie craft to buy, and figuring you'd seen it all. But as evening shadows begin to lengthen across Freedom Park, along comes what

---

Easy as pie

Andrea Downing, director and certified festival manager for Pie Day, offers a behind-the-scenes look at Pie Day preparations.

"The veteran pie bakers do the top crust and the crimping on the edge. Your first year as a volunteer, you're not working with crust. At first you're just mixing filling. And then you're getting the crust into the pans. As you get more experienced, you're working with the top crust. I wouldn't call it a pecking order, but there is definitely a hierarchy. You're working with people who are very good at it. So if you want to learn how to make a great pie, it's a great way to do it," Downing explains.

Of course, all the scratch pies are what make Pie Day go 'round.

"Pie Day connects us with a memory that people very often hold really dear, because a lot of people don't bake pies anymore. I'm finding that outside of small-town communities, pie is kind of a mystery to people. They love pie, but never figured out how to get a good crust or how to make a really great pie," she says.

---

could be the flakiest Pie Day event of all—the Pie Race. This is not your standard 5K. This is a relay race run by teams of four who strive to reach the finish line with a freshly rolled out piecrust. As they go, they have to run with pie and coffee, eat pie, mix pie dough, and roll out the crust.

As the earth turns and stars come out in the sky, Pie Day becomes Pie Night, and over at the Sweety Pie Dance, they are kicking up their heels to the strains of a live band. Others are gathering at the Fire Hall for scary Pie Night Movies.

Why Pie? Pie Day in Braham is comparatively fresh on the nation's food festival scene. The first Pie Day occurred in July of 1990. Some enterprising locals cooked it up when a series of events came together. Someone noticed that in 1921, the *Braham Journal* newspaper reported that the Ladies Civic Club held a Pie Social and donated the proceeds to beautify the town. Second, it is common knowledge around town that Braham has been a pie-lover's destination since the 1930s. Back then, folks tooling along between the Cities and Duluth and northern lakes would regularly satisfy their collective sweet tooth in the Park Café. Fortunately, the storefront eatery called the Park Café is still here, so today's foodies can still perform the time-honored ritual.

Fast forward to 1990, when the State of Minnesota encouraged communities to host special events during the calendar year after the date of July 1, sweetening the offer with a promise of special funding. Braham's town-wide Appreciation Day occurred in June, so it did not qualify. But then someone observed the Governor of Minnesota eating pie at the Park Café. The wheels began to turn. It wasn't long before the governor found himself pronouncing Braham as the Homemade Pie Capital of Minnesota.

PLACES TO EAT

Park Café, 124 South Main Street, Braham, (320) 396-3630. Breakfast, lunch, dinner, pie, coffee. Folks talk across tables, and the subject is pie as often as not. Look around; you will see thick slices of the stuff at almost every table.

Pizza Pub, 128 South Main Street, Braham, (320) 396-4112. Pizza pie.

PLACES TO STAY

Dakota Lodge Bed and Breakfast, RR 3, Box 178, Hinckley, (320) 384-6052, www.dakotalodge.com. Located on six acres, the guest accommodations include five rooms and one private luxury cabin suite, all with private baths. Four of the rooms have double whirlpools and fireplaces. Full breakfast.

Down Home Bed and Breakfast, RR 2, Box 177A, Hinckley, (320) 384-0396. This contemporary home sits on 40 acres and features three guest- rooms with private or shared baths. The coolest thing is that dog sled rides are available in season (the cold one) courtesy of resident Cadence Racing Huskies.

Oakhurst Inn, 212 Eighth Avenue S., Princeton, (763) 631-8727. The elegance of the turn-of-the-century era is yours in this 1906 Victorian manor with three guestrooms and two carriage house suites. All private baths. Full breakfast.

Rum River Country Bed and Breakfast, 5002 85th Avenue, Princeton, (763) 389-2679. Fresh country air and plenty of porches, fireplaces, antiques, and hand-crafted iron beds. Located next door to a crop farm where you can arrange for an agricultural experience. There are also 80 acres of riverlands to hike, canoe, and encounter wildlife. Breakfast includes the inn's own jams and jellies.

13. COUNTRY IN THE CITY: THIS IS MINNEAPOLIS-SAINT PAUL?

Minneapolis has one of the American Heartland's best stories to tell about food, and about itself. It is the story of wheat or, more familiarly, of old friends like Gold Medal, Betty Crocker, and the Pillsbury Doughboy. In recent years, the Minnesota Historical Society decided to shout out that story from the burned-out ruins of what was once among the world's largest flour mills and is now the great Mill City Museum. A little to the south, General Mills tells its story to children within the tantalizing confines of the country's largest mall, in a storybook version of a factory tour that has kids sliding down a spoon into a bowl of outsized Cheerios, and learning about cereal production in a way that is exciting and loud. And all around the region, there are more farm attractions than you can possibly pack into a single weekend.

Milling Around

In 2003, **Mill City Museum**, 704 South Second Street, Minneapolis, (612) 341-7555, www.millcitymuseum.org, opened as a 12,000-square-foot cultural icon. The museum is important because Minneapolis grew up around the mills that once lined this stretch of the Mississippi River, and for the half century from 1880 to 1930, the city led the world in flour milling. Railroad boxcars fed the mills with vast quantities of wheat. The mills in turn fed and created nationwide demand for their fine flours, cereals, and baking mixes.

You are in the Historic Mill District, which is one of those suddenly hot lifestyle addresses full of edgy condos and beautiful people. It is located downtown on the west bank of the Mississippi River, just north of the Hubert H. Humphrey Metrodome. One mill over, the Gold Medal Flour letters that proclaimed the premier brand of the Washburn Crosby Company will help you find the museum.

Mill City Museum rises like a phoenix from the ruins of the 1880 limestone Washburn A Mill (there were B and C mills) as it appeared after a 1991 fire. It was the world's largest when built in 1880, but supplanted in size when the Pillsbury A Mill went up across the river, just the next year. View the remnant of the Washburn A Mill from the museum's rooftop observation deck. In rebuilding, the architects did not ruin the ruins, but celebrated them as evidence of a dramatic event (the fire) in the ongoing life of the mill. What they refused to refine away is what you see, including surreal details like a door that leads nowhere, broken glass in some windows, twisted metal beams, all the raw scars. The result is a strangely beautiful tribute to Minneapolis' growth as a great mill town, and indeed to one of America's most beloved behemoths, General Mills. For it was here that the Washburn Crosby Company eventually came to be General Mills.

Mill City Museum teaches about three stages in the milling process: the movement of grain, the mechanical innards of the mill, and the finished products. In the Harvesting Wheat exhibit, visitors are invited to sit down at a threshers' dinner table that was sculpted by Saint Paul artist Kathleen Richert. Here they connect with farmers and learn about the challenges of wheat farming. Enter the Water Lab and don a raincoat to discover how the rush of water over Saint Anthony Falls ran the turbines to power the Washburn A Mill and its many neighbors. The Flour Tower gently whisks passengers eight stories skyward. Along the way, you see and hear the people and machines that once drove the mill to produce sacks and sacks of flour. Pull up a butter-pat stool and reminisce with vintage commercials, advertisements, packaging, and marketing.

Outside, the recently reclaimed riverfront tells its part of the milling story. Cross the Stone Arch Bridge that spans the river at a leisurely diagonal, and is closed to vehicular traffic. Down below by the canal is **Mill Ruins Park**, which is at once civilized and raw, manicured and crumbly, an archeological site with tunnels, trestles, and tailraces. Join a walking tour for a fee; for current information, visit www.minneapolisparks.org. Farther on, feel the spray and hear the thunder of Saint Anthony Falls.

Let's leave the mills behind and see what else the area has to offer. A most unusual piece of sculpture awaits your reaction on the same riverbank as Mill City Museum and about three miles west. The *Spoonbridge and Cherry* outdoor sculpture at Walker Art Center and Minneapolis Sculpture Garden, 725 Vineland Place, Minneapolis, (612) 375-7577, has probably gotten more publicity than any other piece at the 11-acre site. For who can resist the charm of a stainless steel spoon that is 52 feet long, long enough to span a stream of water, and big enough to hold a giant cherry?

Farms in the City

For some living farm history, drive about 14 miles north, taking I-94 to Highway 252, west on Highway 610 to Noble Parkway, north to 101st Avenue, and east about a block. You have found the Eidem Homestead at the **Brooklyn Park Historical Farm**, 4345 101st Avenue North, Brooklyn Park (North Metro region), (763) 493-8368, www.brooklynpark.org. This old farmstead was in the same family for 82 years, and now is down to 10 acres, but that is room enough for visitors who wish to get a taste of life as it was lived from 1890 to 1910. The structures include a farmhouse, barn, outhouse, chicken coop, windmill, and miscellaneous outbuildings. Period farm equipment and cropland add to the scene, as do resident pigs, chickens, cows, sheep, goats, ducks, geese, and cats. Costumed interpreters are busy cooking rhubarb sauce in spring and a Thanksgiving goose in autumn, and in between, there are folk dancing, music, hayrides, and children's games.

Over in Saint Paul—the other half of "the Cities"—visit the **Minnesota History Center**, 345 Kellogg Boulevard West, Saint Paul, (651) 296-6126, (800) 657-3773, www.mnhs.org. You have come about 24 miles southeast of Brooklyn Park. Learn what it cost to start a farm in the mid-1850s, and what that translates to in today's dollars. In Grainland, see what a grain elevator looks like on the inside, as a cutaway model illustrates that the elevator is a conveyor belt with scoops that lift the grain to storage bins above. Nearby, a towering climb-up/slide-down grain elevator is an utter kid magnet where youngsters pretend to be oats, corn, or wheat. Kids of all ages can enter the 24-ton boxcar that would have transported the grain to and fro. There is even a farm wagon to hop into. Downstairs, the History Center offers an array of Minnesota gifts (loon eggs, anyone?) and books. Café Minnesota offers a changing menu that includes Minnesota specialties like wild rice soup that is made with hand-harvested Minnesota lake rice.

Leaving the Minnesota History Center, visit **Gibbs Museum of Pioneer and Dakotah Life**, 2097 West Larpenteur Avenue, Falcon Heights, (651) 646-8629, www.rchs.com. It is almost eight miles northwest; take I-94 to Highway 280, and then take the Larpenteur Avenue exit. Learn why not one but two cultures are depicted across these acres. Tour a farmhouse, barns, replica sod house, and original soddy excavation site, garden of native corn (a variety that was grown in 1100 A.D.), beans, squash, and sunflowers, and pioneer garden of heritage seeds. Visit with the farm animals, from horses to chickens.

On Saturdays, buzz into the retail outlet of the family-owned **Cannon Bee Honey and Supply Company,** 6105 11th Avenue South, Minneapolis, (612) 861-8999, www.cannonbee.com, which keeps its own hives humming at 15 farm locations. Find the retail store one block north of the Crosstown Highway (County Road 62) at Portland Avenue, west of the Mississippi River and east of Edina, and about 13 miles from the Gibbs Museum. Liquid honey is just the beginning, and where else can you get it in basswood, buckwheat, clover, wildflower, orange blossom, and purple loosestrife flavors? Sip on a honey straw for a mess-free energy boost on the road.

It's All at the Mall

Let's take a break and go milling around at the **Mall of America,** 60 East Broadway, Bloomington, (952) 883-8800, (800) 879-3555, www.mallofamerica.com. Yes, it is easy to get to on a short drive southwest of the Cities' downtown core, or almost five miles south of Cannon Bee. How big is it? It is so big that you could park 32 Boeing 747s inside. It has so many shoppers breathing their way from store to entertainment venue that mall management doesn't bother to heat the place. Think-outside-the-mall venues include a seasonal petting zoo, nightclubs, and something called Cereal Adventure.

Inside the General Mills Cereal Adventure, at the Mall of America, Bloomington.

General Mills Cereal Adventure is a colorful, super-sized flight of fancy, the creative corporate answer to the demise of factory tours, where the idea is that cereal goes on an adventure from field to table, but as you follow its course, the adventure becomes your own. It begins in the farm field, where the seeds of grain are planted, grown, and harvested. The next step is milling into flour, followed by a trip to the ersatz cereal factory. But amid the flakiness, you learn about the cereal production. For an additional fee, you can create your own cereal, from selecting the grains to naming the product to coloring the box. Barring a PGA win, you can buy your way onto a Wheaties box and be on a par with the likes of Tiger Woods. The café supplies recipes for cereal treats, or you can buy these pre-made by the piece along with nutritious bowls of favorite General Mills cereals.

Back to the Farms

Just a few growing seasons ago, a brand new farm was built right in the Cities. It is the **Wells Fargo Family Farm**, and it adds a rural dimension to the Minnesota Zoo, 13000 Zoo Boulevard, Apple Valley, (952) 431-9500, www.mnzoo.org. The zoo's Apple Valley location is in the South Metro region just three communities east of Shakopee (and south of Minneapolis-Saint Paul and just southeast of Bloomington). From livestock breeds in danger of disappearing to clones that just keep reappearing, the Family Farm looks forward and back at the same time. Corporate logos of big names in American agriculture sprout up all over the farmyard, but since they are all related to the theme, they actually help to set the stage. What's more, grain elevators and barns have always borne signs (who can forget Mail Pouch tobacco?).

The Wells Fargo Family Farm, at the Minnesota Zoo, Apple Valley.

Outside of the silver grain elevator, hop aboard a wagon pulled either by a John Deere tractor or a pair of American Cream draft horses that are the color of fresh-whipped butter. The team represents the only breed of draft horse that has been developed in Iowa, and one that is rare and beautiful indeed. At a good clip, you can walk almost as quickly, but the ride is more fun, and if you have kids along, you already know which method of transportation you will be using. This farm is a barnyard full of education and fun. Inside the hog barn, farrowing pens are seasonally littered with piglets, and a cutout model of a pig showcases the myriad of products that utilize pig parts. Over in the silver machine shed, a timeline of American agriculture begins at the point when Christopher Columbus brought livestock to this land. It points out other key events that occurred in succeeding years: the invention of the McCormick reaper in 1831, the 1862 Homestead Act that made farmland available free to pioneers, and the 1985 Farm Aid concert that raised an estimated nine million dollars for beleaguered American farmers. Cap off your Family Farm visit within the classic white-frame farmhouse. Order lunch or a snack at the Farm Café, then eat it outside at a table on the wraparound porch.

On to the **Historic Holz Farm**, 4669 Manor Drive, Eagan. Turning left out of the Zoo drive, make a series of lefts: onto Mc Andrews Road, South Robert Trail, Todd Avenue, and Manor Drive, for a total of about five miles through a pleasantly suburban scene that swallowed up all farms but this one. Near as anyone can tell, the butter-yellow farmhouse of dairy farmers Otto and Ella Holz has hugged this hilltop since the early 1900s. The land slopes gently toward water, and red outbuildings dot the grassy slopes. When the childless Holzes passed away in the early 1990s, the house almost died too. Even an old refrigerator was sold at auction. But in 1996, farsighted locals bought the farm to rescue it from a looming bulldozer. Lots of people came forward to help, including the buyer of the old refrigerator, who donated it back to the farm, and once again it sits where it belongs in the farmhouse kitchen. Today the Holz Farm rests easy in its new role as a small-scale, late-1940s living history farm. Even residents of the surrounding subdivisions—where crops once grew—wander up the gravel road to explore the farm's beautiful five acres. Join them on a quiet journey into the past when the resident chickens may be outside, and when you can dream of summers gone by. For event information, call ahead to Friends of the Farm, (651) 681-4660.

If you have worked up an appetite from touring, drive about 5 miles west to **VonHanson's Meats**, 2141 Cliff Road, Eagan, (651) 687-9311, www.vonhansons .com. This new, old-fashioned meat market is a strip-mall surprise. It is actually part of a local chain and something of a Twin Cities legend, and they will have you believing you wandered into a bygone era. Butcher boys sport paper hats. Each store has its own smokehouse. Choose from the vast array of smoked and fresh meats including ring bologna, maple country sausage, smoked ham shanks, and marinated kabobs.

The Minneapolis-Saint Paul metro region has much to tell about itself, and much to offer visitors looking for the rural spirit amid skyscrapers and shopping malls. And many of them will be pleasantly surprised to find that so much of the country still resides in the Cities.

SPECIAL EVENTS

Macalester's Scottish Country Fair and Highland Games, Macalester College, Saint Paul, www.macalaster.edu. Early May. Aye, it's a bonny fair day when the lads and lasses come out to play. Traditional Scottish culture comes alive with sanctioned competitions in piping/drumming, Highland dance, Highland games, sheep-herding demonstrations. Live entertainment includes local/re-gional Celtic artists. The Scottish Marketplace offers heritage fare and a tasting tour.

Shepherd's Harvest Sheep and Wool Festival, Lake Elmo, http://burroak. hypermart.net/festival.htm. Early May. Sheep and llama exhibits, demonstrations of shearing and herding. Fiber arts classes, demonstration, competitions, and vendors.

Farmers' Fourth of July, Oliver H. Kelley Farm, 15788 Kelley Farm Road, Elk River, (763) 441-6896. Theatrical reading of the Farmers' Declaration of Independence, a Grange document dating back to 1873 (See **The Oliver H. Kelly Farm** section below for more information on the Grange). Enjoy sack races, hoops and sticks, and other nineteenth-century games, and bring a picnic lunch to enjoy on the farm's grounds. Return for Children's Day in mid-July and mid-August, when your little ones can try their hand at farm chores, also Pioneer Threshing Weekend at the end of August, when kids of all ages can pitch in by hauling oat bundles and filling grain sacks.

Minnesota State Fair, Minnesota State Fairgrounds, 1265 North Snelling Avenue, Falcon Heights, (651) 288-4400, www.mnstatefair.org. Late August–Labor Day Weekend. Here's what you could learn in the Agriculture and Horticulture Building on a single fair day: "Cooking with Honey," "Looking in the Hive," "Honey Harvesting," "Making Beeswax Candles." Pop into the Creative Activities Building to see what's cooking in Betty Crocker's Kitchen at the Fair. Take in special events, judgings, and demonstrations inside the livestock buildings, the Children's Barnyard (witness the birth of baby farm animals), Little Farm Hands, and the 4-H Building.

New in 2003, Little Farm Hands leads kids by the hand through the agricultural process. There are five miniature barns, a grain bin, tractor yard, four garden plots, an apple orchard, and a farmers' market, all connected by a self-guided pathway. It is all free, including the make-and-take. The general idea is for kids to grow/produce their own agricultural products that they can pretend to buy as finished items in the grocery store.

Speaking of food, consider these fair fare facts from the 2003 edition of the Minnesota State Fair: fairgoers put away 183,764 foot-long corn dogs and 515,900 regular-length corn dogs, 90,000 pork chops, 3,244,200 ounces of French fries,

2,600,000 individual curds of cheese, and 20,000 gallons of milk. Now it is your turn. How about Walleye on a Stick from this, the Land of Ten Thousand Lakes? They pack all of this farm and food fun into one event, in a major American city. What are you waiting for?

PLACES TO EAT

Dakota Bar and Grill, 1021 Bandana Boulevard, Saint Paul, (651) 642-1442. Most of the dishes are prepared with ingredients from Minnesota and Wisconsin.

Lake Elmo Inn, 3442 Lake Elmo Avenue, Lake Elmo, (651) 777-8495. Try Minnesota wild rice and duck soup, Amish-farm-raised chicken, walleye pike sautéed with artichokes and mushrooms in a wine sauce, rack of lamb, or Kobe beef stuffed with gorgonzola and served on a bed of carmelized onions.

Lexington Restaurant, 1096 Grand Avenue, Saint Paul, (651) 222-5878. Midwestern ringneck pheasant, wild rice.

The Whitney Grille, 150 Portland Avenue, Minneapolis, (612) 372-6405. Savor regional cuisine made from fresh, seasonal ingredients—along with riverfront views—in a former mill hailing from the Flour Milling Capital of the World era.

PLACES TO STAY

Chatsworth Bed and Breakfast, 984 Ashland Avenue, Saint Paul, (651) 227-4288, (877) 978-4837, www.bbonline.com/mn/chatsworth. In the Summit-University neighborhood 10 miles from the Mall of America. In-room A/C, parlor fireplace, front porch, full breakfast, access to 24-hour beverage pantry and bottomless plate of homemade cookies.

Hilton Garden Inn, 1975 Rahncliff Court, Eagan, (651) 686-4605. Microwave and refrigerator in each room. Breakfast available in the Great American Grill, convenient free shuttle to Mall of America and hop-skip to Minnesota Zoo.

The Covington Inn Bed and Breakfast, Pier 1, Harriet Island, Saint Paul, (651) 292-1411, www.covingtoninn.com. Yes, she's a boat. Yes, she rocks you to sleep on the ultimate waterbed. Yes, she's elegantly trimmed from stem to stern in mahogany, brass, and bronze. For 30 years since 1946, this towboat worked hard pushing river barges, but today she pampers guests. Four staterooms with private baths, fireplaces, A/C. Galley-cooked breakfasts.

The Prairie Farm Bed and Breakfast, 2334 175th Street, Lester Prairie, (320) 395-2055, (888) 470-1846. This restored 1918 farmhouse is loaded with antiques, including a classic car collection. Baths are private or shared. A river runs through the farm, and there are hiking trails for guests to enjoy. Full breakfast.

14. LOOKING FOR LAURA

Especially since the beloved NBC-TV series *Little House on the Prairie* premiered in 1974, most people at least know the Laura Ingalls Wilder name. The program was, of course, based on the books written by Laura Ingalls Wilder (1867-1957).

Farther afield

If the Cities haven't supplied enough of a farm fix, drive 30 miles, give or take 10, to:

Aamodt's Apple Farm, 6428 Manning Avenue North, Stillwater, (651) 439-3127, www.aamodtsapplefarm.com. 180-acre orchard with processing plant, renovated 1800s barn, gift shops, bakery, lunchroom where you can order apple cheese soup.

At the Farm, 8880 Highway 5, Waconia, (952) 442-4816, www.atthe farmwaconia.com. Shop for farm produce and farm antiques on this working farm. Even when the cold half-light of winter descends upon the American Heartland, you can always come here for fresh brown eggs and think of summer.

Gale Woods Farm, 7210 County Road 110 West, Minnetrista, (952) 472-9203. Learn about sustainable agriculture at this contemporary farm on a lake. The tour experience is self-guided, with educational displays provided. Chickens, sheep, and cattle call the place home. June through August, the barn is open on Sundays from 2:00 to 4:00 p.m., when chores are being done.

Grimm Farm, Grimm Road, Carver Park Reserve, 7025 Victoria Drive (west of Minneapolis via Highway 5 or Highway 7), Victoria, (763) 694-7650, www.threeriversparkdistrict.org/parks/grimmfarm.cfm#upcoming. The German immigrant who farmed here created the world's first winter-hardy strain of alfalfa, which, it is said, opened the way for the American Heartland to become a great dairy region. You can see the farm and surroundings when you visit the Carver Park Reserve, but the farm is only open during scheduled programs.

Hugo Animal Farm, 9441 180th Street North, Hugo, (651) 433-4455, www.hugoanimalfarm.com. Call ahead to visit this working family farm in October. The crisp-air fun includes hay rides to the pumpkin patch, goat milking, farm-animal petting, and a hay maze. Sign up for a tour.

The Oliver H. Kelley Farm, 15788 Kelley Farm Road, Elk River, (763) 441-6896, www.mnhs.org, is about 45 minutes from the Cities, on Highway 10 West and 169 North. In 1867, Farmer Kelley founded The Grange, a nationwide organization of farm families and rural Americans. Visit his former home, restored as it is to the 1850–1876 timeframe. There are heirloom vegetables to tend in the garden, butter to churn in the farmhouse, animals to visit, farmhands to shoot the breeze with, fields to plow in spring, hay to make in summer, and grain to thresh in autumn. 🐾

Many people grew up reading the books, which continue to be popular today. Given this almost universal awareness, you do not have to be an avid Laura fan to enjoy a weekend experience in Walnut Grove, Minnesota, where the family lived in the late nineteenth century. So make this stop along the Laura Ingalls Wilder Historic Highway, and read a chapter in a remarkable life.

On the Banks of Plum Creek tells of Laura's childhood in Walnut Grove. It is a southwestern Minnesota railroad town where the tallest structure is still the grain elevator, and where farm fields still wave in the wind. It is located about 160 miles southwest of Minneapolis-Saint Paul, and nowhere near the Twin Cities' urbanity. It was here that Charles (Pa), Caroline (Ma), Mary, Laura, and Carrie Ingalls first arrived in 1874, homesteading in the sod dugout that overlooked Plum Creek. But by 1876, drought and sun-darkening grasshopper plagues devastated Pa's hard-won wheat crops, so the family backtracked eastward, only to return the next year, living with another family and enriching Laura's storehouse of memories.

At the Farmstead

Drive 1.5 miles north of town on County Road 5 to the **Ingalls Homestead** site. It is actually located on a working farm that the Gordon family bought in 1947, not knowing at the time what they had on the back 40. The working parts of the Gordon family farm are private and not accessible to the public, but they do make a nice visual backdrop for your visit. So pay the nominal admission fee and drive on back to the site that is maintained in an unrestored and undisturbed state. Discover for yourself how effective and meaningful this approach can be. Take your time, because the attractions here gently invite you on a journey to imagine what life was like for a little girl and her pioneer family. Follow the interpretive signage to the sod dugout site, the spring, and Big Rock, each of which you can see, hear, and feel, just as Laura did. Consider how it would be to live in a sod dugout nestled alongside a winding creek. The earthen home is gone, but a deep depression remains to mark the site. Dip your toes into the cold, clear water of Plum Creek, but unlike Laura, you cannot drink or swim in it. Feel the prairie wind that has never stopped blowing.

One-tenth of a mile north of the Ingalls Homestead, stop to read the roadside marker that was erected to honor the Ingalls family and indeed all American pioneers.

Going to Town

The **Laura Ingalls Wilder Museum and Information Center**, 330 Eighth Street, Walnut Grove, (888) 528-7280, www.walnutgrove.org, is also easy to find, in town at the corner of Highway 14 and County Road 5. The museum appeals to both TV and book fans, but in different ways, and endeavors to clear up some facts of Laura's life that she changed in her books, which are categorized as works of historical fiction.

Begin at the red depot. Here the stories of Walnut Grove and the Ingalls family

Welcome to the world of Laura Ingalls Wilder, Walnut Grove.

unfold. Laura's Room has a red-and-white quilt that was stitched by Laura togeth-er with her daughter, Rose; information about Laura's life; and TV memorabilia. Newly opened in 2003, the walk-in dugout display is authentically furnished. You cannot miss the white Grandma's House for its onion dome cupola. Inside, the creaky doors and floorboards alone would be enough to take you backward in time. Butter churning is described, along with the myriad chores Laura and Mary had to do just to keep Ma's woodstove humming. The Early Settler's Home was moved from the property owned by a neighbor of the Ingalls family. Heritage Lane, a veritable agricultural museum, contains a covered wagon and a small army of the types of necessities that would have sustained the family on their migra-tions, farming tools such as a corn-husking sleeve (and directions for how to use it), early cloth feed bags, and a toy tractor collection. Although small and sym-bolic, the prairie plots just outside the door teem with life that buzzes about on delicate wings. Enjoy the colors, listen to the sounds, feel the textures, and imag-ine what the prairie would have been like on the grand scale that Laura knew.

The gift shop carries all of the books by Laura, along with books about her, and cookbooks of all kinds, including pioneer cookbooks and the community-project *Walnut Grove Cookbook*. Look for the Prairie Smoke barbeque sauce that is locally manufactured by Westbrook Walnut Grove High School students.

While living in Walnut Grove, the Ingalls family participated in town life, attending school and church and going shopping. A self-guided tour map points out key sites. Many of these, like the hotel where Laura once worked, are private homes now and not open to the public, but you are welcome to view them from the street. While in town, you may wish to do some shopping as well. Be sure to pop into **Weekend Innovations**, 311 Seventh Street, Walnut Grove, (507) 859-2170, www.walnutstation.org. No musty antiques or redundant gifts here; rather, there is locally handcrafted furniture that incorporates elements from rural buildings, and there are kitchen supplies, spices, and cookbooks. At **Nellie's Café**, you can stop for lunch and meet some locals. Nellie, of course, was Laura's blond-haired, sausage-curled nemesis.

Just outside of Walnut Grove, you can not only enjoy a picnic, but also a swim in pretty **Lake Laura**, which is located in **Plum Creek Park** and surrounded by farmland. The stocked lake has a sandy beach and changing facilities. The 205-acre park offers a 60-site campground with electrical hookups and playground equipment. Plum Creek lazes through it.

Going to Sanborn

Leaving Walnut Grove, drive east on Highway 14 (Laura Ingalls Wilder Historic Highway), then south on 71 to Sanborn, a distance of about 19 miles. On a gravel road called Magnolia Avenue, there is a farm where you can lose yourself in the pioneer lifestyle of Laura's day. This is **Sod House at Sanborn**, 12598 Magnolia Avenue, Sanborn, (507) 723-5138, www.sodhouse.org. For a fee, take the self-guided tour through sod houses, through the prairie, and through time, or make it a lifelong memory by staying overnight in the sod guesthouse. These sod houses, affectionately called soddys, are not frontier relics, but the fulfillment of one man's modern-day dream.

The tour is like a walk through a history book. A sign reports that an estimated one million sod houses dotted the pioneer-era prairies. But why did the pioneers build them? The prairie is, by definition, largely free of trees, and so the pioneer farmers had to come up with other building materials. Being pioneers, they came up with the most resourceful and inventive solution. As it turned out, the thickly root-tangled prairie sod that was giving them so much trouble when it came to agriculture worked beautifully as the walls and roofing of a home. So sod blocks were cut and pulled by a horse or ox, dried, and stacked grass-side-down like brick, to take shape as walls around the door and window frames. By contrast, the sod roof would have been laid grass-side-up. The modern-day soddys that you are looking at here were built just that way.

With a wooden floor, a wooden roof that sprouts grass, and 1880s-style furnishings, the guesthouse maintains a rustic feel that you can get a taste of on the daytime tour, but really feel during an overnight stay. The guesthouse is made of 350,000 pounds of sod with walls two feet thick. Wooden beams are part of its construction, and were taken from an 1890 Minneapolis flour mill. The guesthouse has separate sleeping and eating areas, although they are not divided by an interior wall. The bathroom is housed in a rustic, stand-alone structure commonly known as an outhouse, so you get two rooms and a path. It is a small price

Inside the Sod House B&B, Sanborn.

to pay for sleeping with a prairie at your doorstep, and actually part of the pioneer experience.

While in Sanborn, it is worth the short drive to the town center and **Deutschland Meats**, 141 South Main Street, Sanborn, (507) 648-3388. Owner Martin Ziegler, a native of the Black Forest region of Germany, was trained for three years to the highest standards of German sausage making before emigrating to America. In true pioneer spirit, he arrived with the skills and the recipes to succeed here. So stop and savor the old world atmosphere and the smokehouse smell. Think you've tasted bologna? Think again. Lyoner Bologna is the real thing. How about lunchmeat, such as *jagdwurst* (coarse) or *gelbwurst* (mild), for a sandwich on the road? *TeeWurst* is a cold smoked sausage spread, and wouldn't a couple of those bratwursts sizzle nicely on a grill? Marinated pork chops are seasoned from the inside, smoked, and fully cooked for an easy dinner. Chicken is free-range, beef is certified Black Angus. Ziegler says you can taste the difference, but in order to achieve it, he needs the combination of the best product and the German craftsmanship.

Covering More Ground

Now drive almost 50 miles west on the Laura Ingalls Wilder Historic Highway and north on Highway 59 to the town of Marshall and the **Walnut Grove Mercantile**, 1501 East Lyon Street (off Highway 23), Marshall, (507) 929-3127, www.walnutgrovemerc.com. Closed Sundays. The Klein family, which began bee-keeping in Minnesota some 60 years ago, opened this shop to showcase their lines of award-winning gourmet products that they manufacture on-site and distribute nationally. Check out the signature flavored honeys, especially the spreadable honey creams that come in fruit flavors like blueberry and strawberry-rhubarb. Enjoy fresh fudge, preserves, syrups, and the old-fashioned candy counter. On the savory side, there are salsas, salad dressings, and barbeque sauces, some with honey. Pick up cookbooks, Laura Ingalls Wilder books, and published recollections of pioneers' lives. They make their own soaps with old-fashioned scents of cinnamon oatmeal, honeysuckle, lilac, and prairie spice, and greeting cards that slap current humor onto old-time advertisements. You can also find some of the Mercantile's products at the Laura Ingalls Wilder Museum gift shop in Walnut Grove.

This weekend is mostly about taking a pilgrimage to look for Laura. Standing by Plum Creek and gazing upon the open lands that still stretch out as they did in the 1870s, visitors are able to find a connection with one little girl who was a pioneer for all of us.

SPECIAL EVENTS

Wilder Pageant, second, third, and fourth weekends in July. Outdoor evening performances in Walnut Grove. Discover the joys and hardships of life on the prairie, and meet the townsfolk of Walnut Grove during Laura's day. For tickets call (888) 859-3102. Also save room for the special evening meal, Walnut

Grove Community Center, 311 Sixth Street, Walnut Grove. Home cooking from church and community groups.

Corn Day Celebration, Sleepy Eye, (507) 794-4731, www.sleepyeyechamber .com. Mid-August. Go on Friday for the free, hot buttered corn, entertainment, games, and flea market. Parade on Saturday.

Harvest on the Prairie, Jeffers Petroglyphs, Cottonwood County, (507) 628-5591. Three miles east of Highway 71 on County Road 10, then one mile south on County Road 2. Mid-September. Admissions, pre-registration, and payment required. Relax on a prairie bus tour, sample wild foods, satisfy cravings for real food at a bison supper (additional fee), and listen to a Native American tell of life on the prairie—before. It is said that farmwives saved this ancient site back in the 1960s.

Holmberg Orchard, 12697 325th Street, Vesta, (507) 762-3131, www.holmberg orchard.com. Autumn in the Country, late September. Jack-O-Lantern Jamboree, early October. Apple Butter Time, mid-October (they cook it outdoors over an open fire, weather permitting).

PLACES TO EAT

Mike's Café, 1501 East College Drive, Marshall, (507) 532-5477. Home-cooked meals, all homemade soups, pies.

Nellie's Café, Highway 14, Walnut Grove, (507) 859-2384. Home cooking with noontime specials. Ice cream.

PLACES TO STAY

AmericInn, 1406 E. Lyon Street, Marshall, (507) 537-9424. All rooms feature microwave and refrigerator, indoor pool/whirlpool, lobby fireplace, extended continental breakfast.

Sod House Bed and Breakfast, 12598 Magnolia Avenue, Sanborn, (507) 723-5138, www.sodhouse.org. Live as Laura did in a beautifully handcrafted soddy, with a sod roof atop the mud walls (white plaster inside) and flour mill beams. This place takes about two seconds to wrap you up in the nineteenth century: hand-sewn quilts, woodstove, floorboards, and a prairie that sings you to sleep. Only one party at a time can be accommodated, so the 10-acre prairie that starts right outside your door is all yours to enjoy once the daytime tourists return to the twenty-first century. Family and friends back home don't have to know that your pioneer moxie included air-conditioning; better to hold forth about the oil lamps, wood-burning stove, and prairie clothes. Full country breakfast cooked in the owner's farm kitchen and brought to you piping hot in an old-fashioned pail.

Triple L. Farm Bed and Breakfast, 1110 280th Street, Hendricks, (507) 275-3740. Accommodations in the 1890 farmhouse or the primitive bunkhouse for a pioneer experience. Four guestrooms available. Full or continental breakfast.

Valentine Inn Bed and Breakfast, 385 Emory Street, Tracy, (507) 629-3827.

Three-story 1902 Victorian with four guest rooms, private baths, A/C in each room, full breakfast. Two blocks off the Laura Ingalls Wilder Historic Highway.

15. IN HARMONY WITH THE AMISH

In 1974 a modern-day, old-fashioned migration occurred in the American Heartland. That year, Old Order Amish families from Ohio arrived in the Harmony and Canton areas of southeastern Minnesota. Why not follow them to this pretty little corner of the American Heartland? It is 50 miles or so southeast of Rochester and primarily in Fillmore County. On the new lands, the Amish re-settlers began to farm and establish themselves as a new community within the existing ones. Today the area's Amish total about one hundred families and represent the largest Amish settlement within the state. You are bound to see buggies along the roads; in fact, Highway 52 between Preston and Prosper is designated as the Amish Buggy Byway. Fascinated visitors enjoy professionally guided tours to the Amish farms and farm-based businesses, and views of farmers who may be planting or harvesting in the passing fields.

This weekend getaway also explores surrounding towns in the Root River Valley, and invites you to take a road trip outside of Harmony to experience shrines to canned lunchmeat and canned vegetables. These are the SPAM Museum in Austin, which is in Mower County, and the world's tallest Jolly Green Giant in Blue Earth, which is about halfway across Minnesota in Faribault County.

In Harmony

Let's start in Harmony, which is a couple of miles north of the Iowa border. In The Village Depot at The Village Green, **Amish Country Tours**, (507) 886-2303, www.shawcorp.com/amish, offers a choice of touring in their mini-bus or in your vehicle with a step-on guide. The mini-bus option is available to individual travelers, not just to groups. Learn about the purpose of the migration to Harmony, and how it was accomplished. **Michel's Amish Tours**, (800) 752-6474, also departs from Harmony, but only offers the "your vehicle, their guide" tour option. Leaving from Lanesboro, **Flaby's Amish Tours**, (800) 944-0099, whisks you about in their vans on either the Harmony/Canton route, or to the Amish community near Saint Charles. **R & M Amish Tours**, (507) 467-2128, www.rm amish.com, is also based in Lanesboro and it offers the option of the two routes. Lanesboro is about 14 miles north of Harmony.

A popular tour stop is **Austin's Angora Goats and Mohair Gift Shop**, RR 2, Harmony, (507) 886-6731. You can't miss Austin's, for no other farmer in the area has purple fences and purple picnic tables. It is not Amish, but it is a fun farm experience and only a mile east of town off Highway 52. But you don't have to be on a tour to join the other visitors who come to coo over the snowy-white goats.

The farm has an interesting origin. Back when her own kids were growing

Sign up for Amish Country Tours at the Village Green in the town of Harmony.

From inside the minibus

Myron Scheevel, owner of Amish Country Tours, sat in the depot one summer day and talked of how the Amish came to be in Harmony, Minnesota.

"It's supply and demand. If they've got a lot of teenagers growing up looking for wives and husbands and they aren't available in their community without being related, it's time to start moving some of these people on. They live in a community for so long and start running into blood-relation problems for marital purposes. So they will choose their scouts, two or three family leaders who will get on a bus, and just start going down the road and stopping and inquiring.

"In 1974, this group stopped at a coffee shop here and asked if there was land available. This happened to be the typical type of area they wanted: we have rolling land, streams, springs, wooded land, and this is all part of their lifestyle. Here they found small farms and old farms that people were ready to give up. So they had an opportunity to buy. Conditions of buildings mean nothing to them, because they can fix them up and build new. They put an ad in *The Budget,* which is the Amish newspaper, inviting people to join the new community, and it was only a matter of six or seven years that it grew to over a hundred families.

"I have a lot of people come back from touring and say, 'Gee, that's a neat way to live. I'd like to live that way.' And I say, 'Yeah, you would until about 7:00 tonight when you want to take a shower and you go get a bucket of water and heat it on the stove to wash. How many household items and switches do you touch a day? You don't even know.'"

---

up, Ada Austin could not afford to be a stay-at-home mom, but she always wished for the opportunity. Eventually, she and husband Jim started up the goat farm, and Ada decided to make her old stay-at-home dream come true for other area mothers. She puts some 15 of them to work handcrafting original products that feature the silky, white hair of her goats.

The products are lovely and not available elsewhere. Shop for roving, goat's milk soap, washable/breathable socks, dolls, clothing, buttons, musical instruments made from goat horns, and dog chews made from the hooves. Goat milk fudge and summer sausage are also available. So, you gotta ask, what's with all the purple? Austin will be tickled pink to tell you that it is all about being of a certain age and doing exactly what you want, especially if it is somewhat eccentric. And those stylish red hats for sale in the shop? They are just the thing for members of the Red Hat Society. Seems that when you don a red hat, ladies, nothing and nobody can get you down.

Back in town at The Village Green, a trio of dollhouse-cute shops offers foods and Amish-related gifts and books, and can be found just south of Fourth Street NW at Highway 52. **The Village Depot** (at The Village Green), where you can also arrange for Amish Country Tours, is located at 90 Second Street NW, (507) 886-2409, and has gourmet foods like soups, dip mixes, jams, jellies, salad dressings, trail mix, salsas, and honey. Feast your eyes on flavor-rich products like Double Berry Spread (all-fruit red raspberries and blueberries), pickled brussels sprouts, dilly beans, and raspberry-pecan honey butter. The **Village School Quilt Shop**, 92 Second Street, (507) 886-2409, has a large assortment of Amish-made quilts, as well as insightful books and cookbooks. The quilts are handcrafted by one woman at a time, mostly with 11 stitches or more per inch, and might take six months to sell—or 10 minutes. The **Village Sugar Plum House** is a tiny ice cream parlor and candy store. People come from all over to buy their Amish-made cashew crunch, which is a toffee with cashews. Continue south on Highway 52 (Main Avenue) for two blocks to **Kingsley Mercantile**, 2 Main Avenue, (507) 886-2323, where Norwegian *lefse*-making equipment is offered for sale among the hardware. Find farm toys and other playthings on the shelves of the **Harmony Toy Museum**, 30 Main Avenue South, (507) 867-3380. It is half a block south of Kingsley's. The **Amish Connection Store**, 103 Main Avenue, (507) 886-2979, carries Amish-made furniture on two levels.

Ready for an underground adventure? From Harmony, drive 2.5 miles south on Highway 139, then 2.5 miles west on County Road 30 and follow the signs to a cave that was, in a way, discovered by farm pigs. This is **Niagara Cave**, (507) 886-6606, (800) 837-6606, www.niagaracave.com, and a guided tour takes you to see its 60-foot waterfall, canyons, and gorges. But first listen to the story of the cave's discovery, at least as local legend has it. Seems the area around the cave entrance was once a farmer's pasture. One day in 1924, three of the farmer's little pigs disappeared. He sent a hired hand and some neighbor boys out to search. Eventually they discovered that the pigs had fallen into a sinkhole, so they lowered one of the boys down to see if the pigs could be rescued. Sure enough, the pigs were alive and well, so the rescuers hoisted them up using ropes. But they found more than pigs down there. Word got out about the discovery, and 10 years later, three young cavers from Decorah, Iowa, had developed the cave and opened it up for tours.

Around Harmony

To catch a glimpse of local history and stock up on foods that have some local flavor, head out to Rushford, about 31 miles from Harmony. Head east on Highway 44 to Highway 43, turn left, and proceed north to the Root River Valley, where the town lies at the junction with Highway 16. Rushford is a growing town that has a huge grain elevator, a Norwegian heritage, and an 1894 former flour mill

Ada Austin and her granddaughter admire a white kid at the farm that supplies products for Austin's Angora Goat and Mohair Gift Shop, Harmony.

that is privately owned and not open to the public, but it can be viewed from the street. **Litscher's Processing** 106 W. Park Street, (507) 864-7906, is popular with locals in need of fresh bratwursts, boneless chicken breasts, rib eyes, and T-bone steaks at reasonable prices. Find Norwegian potato soup mixes in the **IGA**, 400 South Mill Street, (507) 864-2878, and a world of Norwegian taste treats in **Norsland Lefse**, 303 South Elm Street, (800) 584-6777.

Driving 14 miles west on Highway 16, cross the bridge over the Root River into Whalan, population something like 94. Talk about quiet. Whalan is all tranquil streets and count-on-one-hand businesses. That's the way they like it, and so will you, especially from a window-side table at the homey **Aroma Pie Shoppe**, 618 Main Street, (507) 467-2623. Rhubarb, raspberry, lemon sour cream, blueberry cream cheese, blackberry cream cheese, and other delicious favorites are sold by the slice or whole, but never frozen. Many local fruits find their way into these popular pies.

Located a few pretty miles west of Whalan, Lanesboro is about as Colorado-cool of a town as you are likely to find in the American Heartland. With primary-colored kayaks, tubes, and canoes for rent, outfitters cater to those who love the Root River. They also rent mountain and touring bicycles, recumbents, tandems, other wheeled convolutions, and even a jaunty, out-on-the-town surrey. It is the perfect vehicle for four chatty friends to all talk at once and nod greetings to passersby as if from a sprightly carriage. All this pedal power came into vogue here because in the recent past, the DNR paved the way for recreational riding along a former railroad track. It is called the **Root River State Trail**, and it runs for 42 miles from Houston to Fountain, and another 12 miles from Preston to Harmony. You want scenery? How about working family farms, bluffs, wildlife, wild berries, and 61 bridges over water riffles? Everyone town-hops to revel in historic facades, quaint shops, little museums, sandwiches, ice cream, and pie. You should too.

But Lanesboro has more to offer. It has the **Amish Experience**, 105 Parkway Avenue, (507) 467-2992, which is located in the former R. R. Greer Dry Goods Store and carries locally handcrafted Amish furniture, quilts, and baskets, along with gourmet foods and other items. It is not unusual to see Amish folks resting their horses in town, or proffering produce in **Sylvan Park** off Parkway Avenue between Elmwood Street and Kirkwood Street East.

Historic sites about town include the hydroelectric plant that harnesses water power where a flour mill once operated, and several homes that had some association with local farming (Henry Ellestad House, circa 1916; Vickerman #1 House, circa 1893; Cady Hayes House, circa 1894). Located one and one-half miles southwest of Lanesboro, **Avian Acres' Wild Bird Supply and Petting Zoo**, Route 2, Box 5, Lanesboro, (507) 467-2996, (800) 967-BIRD, www.aawildbirdsupply.com, offers both a petting-zoo experience (admission) in a pretty, spacious setting, and feasts for your feathered friends back home. Quality feeds are specially mixed and bagged fresh weekly to suit the particular needs of individual backyards and their owners. Avian Acres can help you customize a bird-feeding system in an effort to attract more than sparrows, starlings, and squirrels. The shop carries all the structures a bird could possibly want, including a bed-and-breakfast unit. There are Amish-built, name-brand, and house-made bird feeders, nesting material dispensers, and bird houses to satisfy all your flights of fancy.

Continue driving west on Highway 16 to the junction of Highway 52 (which would take you south back into Harmony if you needed more Amish goodies or maybe one of those red hats from Austin's). But stay on Highway 16 and take it into Preston, for a total of eight miles from Lanesboro. This small, quiet town welcomes you with its 1890-something grain elevator that stored grains up until the 1980s, its easy Root River State Trail access, and its Italianate jailhouse that is so beautiful it became a bed and breakfast. Visit the un-touristy **Foremost Farms Cheese Store** at River and Saint Paul streets. Open Monday through Friday, the tiny shop of a great Midwestern dairy cooperative stocks real Minnesota cheese. Specialties of the refrigerator case—the varieties that out-of-towners demand—include Muenster, vintage Cheddar, and mozzarella string cheese. Think real cheddar cheese with orchard-fresh apples. That's a definite mmm. And at these prices, anyone can afford to load up the cooler for an old-fashioned country picnic at the next little wayside.

Preston also has two apple orchards. One is the **Preston Apple and Berry Farm**, 645 Highway 52/16, (507) 765-4486, where a jolly Hungarian import bakes three thousand pies each year. He is Joe Gosi, a friendly fellow with an undeniable twinkle in his eye and an easy manner that makes you want to sit awhile longer and have another slice of pie topped with Schwan's ice cream, or maybe try one of those apple turnovers. Before leaving, you could take home a whole fresh or frozen, baked-by-order fruit pie, pre-picked apples (almost 30 varieties sold seasonally), wild jams like huckleberry and gooseberry, interesting salsas and horseradishes, honey, sorghum, pecans, cheese, and Watkins products. For more information on Watkins, check out the **Watkins Museum and Store** in Winona (see below). Just north of Preston on County Road 17, **Pine Tree Apple Orchard**, (507) 765-2408, is an expansive spread up on a hill. Open August through November and offering wagon rides in October, Pine Tree Apple Orchard sweetens your weekend with apples, cider, baked goods, and apple-related gifts in a country atmosphere.

A little west of downtown Preston, visit Historic Forestville in **Forestville/Mystery Cave State Park**, County Road 118, (507) 765-2785 (Forestville), (507) 352-5111 (Park Office), (507) 937-3251 (Cave). Be sure to call ahead, then enjoy visiting this popular living history and pioneer agricultural interpretive site within the beautiful state park that also has a cave. Tour the 1850s general store that still has artifacts left behind in 1910 by Thomas Meighen.

Nowhere near Harmony

Ready to shift gears? There is no way to soft-pedal this transition, but it is just hard not to suggest a visit to the free **SPAM Museum**, 1937 SPAM Boulevard, Austin, (507) 437-5100, (800) LUV-SPAM. Geographically, Austin is kinda-sorta close enough to the Root River Valley, and as long as you are in the neighborhood, well, just stay on Highway 16 until it hooks up with I-90, and take the Austin exit, for a drive of about 48 miles west of Preston. In this its hometown, Hormel Foods Corporation has cooked up a feisty funhouse for its most famous food product. So make the pilgrimage to this 16,500-square-foot museum. It is worth the drive even if you are among those who turn up their noses. Just wait, they'll fix you. By the time you are extruded into the gift shop, you are jostling other visitors for SPAM-everything. Suddenly, you have to have a piece of SPAM. There you are grabbing cans of Turkey and Hickory Smoked SPAM Luncheon Meat, blue-and-yellow logo clothing, mugs, key chains, magnets, flying discs, pencils, cookbooks, and toys.

About a dozen Austin eateries feature SPAM Luncheon Meat specialties, like SPAM Jam Pizza at Green Mill, SPAM Fried Rice at Oriental Express, and SPAM and Eggs at Torge's Grille. Who knew?

Are you planning to head farther west on I-90? Well, even if not, you should take one giant step to Blue Earth (60 miles from Austin), which is the Minnesota town that gave us the world's tallest statue of the Jolly Green Giant. It was built here because of the local association with the company that started in 1903 as the Minnesota Valley Canning Company, and which became the Green Giant Company in 1950. At 55.5 feet tall and wearing size 78 boots, the giant gazes beatifically

The SPAM Museum, Austin.

out across the neat Minnesota farmlands that represent his famous valley. But you should see the giant in his biker leathers. He dons them annually in honor of the Sturgis crowd that, every year, rumbles westward across Minnesota in search of Hog Heaven. Vegetables are good for you and all that, but youngsters might be more pleased to know that Blue Earth also makes the claim for having given us the ice cream sandwich. Blue Earth is, admittedly, far outside the orbit of southeastern Minnesota's Amish country. Yet here you are, scoping out a giant man who presides over Early June Peas, and somehow, it seems perfectly normal. But think about this possibility for a moment. What if the Amish decide to migrate out to the Blue Earth area? *They* haven't seen the TV commercials or heard the jingle. Can you imagine them getting a load of the 55.5-foot green man wearing biker leathers?

And we think *they're* different.

SPECIAL EVENTS

Whalan Stand Still Parade, www.lanesboro.com/ssparade.html. Mid-May. For whatever reason, the parade does not move, but the ethnic foods will surely put a spring into your step. Foods like Irish whiskey oat cake, Bohemian nut bread, Russian tea cakes, French éclairs and cream puffs, Norwegian *sweetsoppa, rommegrøt, lefse, krumkaka,* and *rosettes.*

Antique Engine and Tractor Show, Spring Valley, www.bluffcountry.com/rr power.htm. Third weekend in July. The old-timers are out in force: Massey-Harris equipment, steam and gas engines, J. I. Case tractors, binders, threshers, saw and shingle mills, a corn sheller, a rock crusher. Enjoy the farmhouse, blacksmith, barber shop, country store, etc. Watch demonstrations of butter churning, fiber spinning, chair caning, and Scandinavian treats from a wood-burning stove. Eat up all the fun of a pancake and sausage breakfast, live musical entertainment, petting zoo, horse and pony pulls, tractor pulls, and chainsaw carving.

Forestville's Bread and Butter, Historic Forestville, Forestville State Park, between Preston and Spring Valley, (507) 352-5111. State park permit or daily admission required. Mid-August. Costumed staff mix and knead bread dough and bake it in a wood-fired oven as if it were a hundred years ago. Butter making and sampling are also featured. Return for Pickle It Weekend in late August, when costumed staff gather garden veggies and put them up for good eating through the winter.

Steam Engine Days, Mabel, (507) 493-5350. September. Catch the grain-threshing and wood-sawing action that lets the old equipment work off a little steam. Horse plowing demonstrations too.

PLACES TO EAT

Old Village Hall Restaurant and Pub, 111 Coffee Street, Lanesboro, (507) 467-2962, www.oldvillagehall.com. Fine Midwestern fare like grilled apple-smoked pork chop topped with apple cider sauce, pan-seared organic free-range chicken with mango port sauce, and grilled beef tenderloin with morel mushroom butter.

The Country Bread Basket Restaurant, 350 Main Avenue North, Harmony, (507) 886-6277. Go for the pies.

The Harmony House Restaurant, 57 Main Avenue North, Harmony, (507) 886-4612. Home-style cooking: roast beef and potatoes, homemade pies.

The Old Mill, adjacent to the Ramsey Golf Course at northeast edge of Austin, 54446 244th Street, (507) 437-2076, www.oldmill.net. 1872 flour mill has been a restaurant since 1949. Seafood, steaks, prime rib. SPAMBURGER served here. Saturdays are dinner-only.

PLACES TO STAY

Carrolton Country Inn, RR 2, Box 139, Lanesboro, (507) 467-2257, www.lanesboro.com. Down on the livestock farm, this country guesthouse features an upstairs balcony and downstairs porch, as well as charming features like a fireplace, dumbwaiter, and antiques. A/C, private and shared baths. Full breakfast.

Gourmet's Garden Bed and Breakfast, RR 1, Harmony, (507) 886-2971, www.gourmetsgardenbandb.com. Renovated 1890s farmhouse on 10 acres of organic farmland. Gourmet breakfast, cooking classes available.

Jailhouse Inn Bed and Breakfast, 109 Houston Street, Preston, (507) 765-2181, www.jailhouseinn.com. The story goes that prisoners once used dinner spoons to break out of this former jailhouse, but today's guests turn themselves in voluntarily and escape to antique décor and gourmet breakfasts served at restaurant-style tables. On a lazy afternoon, join the other jailhouse rockers on the big porch. Spend a night behind bars in the Cell Block suite.

Stone Mill Suites, 100 Beacon Street East, Lanesboro, (507) 467-8663, www .stonemillsuites.com. The whole place is an antique, having been built of local lime-stone about 1885, initially for cold storage of pond-cut ice. Later it was used for egg/poultry processing, and there is also a historic connection with a feed mill that can still be seen nearby. Your comfort is assured with microwaves and refriger-ators in every room, also some double whirlpools and fireplaces. The expanded continental breakfast includes French toast with fruits and whipped cream, and is self-serve within a leisurely two-hour window.

Sunnyside Cottage of Forestville, RR 2, Preston, (507) 765-3357, www.bluff country.com/Sunnyside.htm. Whole-cottage rental, 3 bedrooms, A/C. One-quar-ter mile from their 720-acre dairy/beef cattle farm where a variety of wildfowl keep things lively. Adjoins Forestville State Park. Inquire about the available farm tour.

The Country Lodge Motel, Highway 52 North, Harmony, (507) 886-2515. Former Rochester Dairy Creamery serves up a buffet breakfast for guests.

The Ice Haus Bed and Breakfast, 65150 220th Street, Dexter, (507) 584-0101, (888) ICE-HAUS, www.icehaus.com. Country home on 22-acre farm. Spacious rooms have private baths. Full breakfast. Ten miles east of Austin.

16. A IS FOR APPLE

Mississippi River bluff country bears much fruit along the 17-mile Apple Blos-som Scenic Drive, which connects with Highway 61 (the Great River Road) at both its north and south ends, and takes you from Houston County into Winona County. Why not plan a weekend getaway to a stretch of Minnesota that trips along with the Mississippi River and takes you on a fruitful journey through some serious scenery? You can do just the Apple Blossom Scenic Drive, or cover a wider range by driving deeper into Winona County and even continuing up to Wabasha County, which is home to Minnesota's largest apple orchard. So, from south to north, you may find yourself traversing Houston, Winona, and Wabasha coun-ties, which are all nestled in the far southeastern tip of Minnesota and edged with the blue ribbon that is the Mississippi River.

The apple orchards thrive in the well-drained highlands, along with the newest crop—view homes. Down below in La Crescent, which is still called the Apple Capital of Minnesota, there are roadside stands, a great little market, and the grand event called Applefest.

Apple Blossom Scenic Drive

Pick up **Apple Blossom Scenic Drive** (beginning as North Elm Street/County Road 29) in La Crescent, and start driving north. The road ascends toward the bluff tops and becomes County Road 29. Pull off the road at the Apple Blossom Over-look Park for a jaw-dropping vista of the Mississippi River Valley. Far below on the river, southbound barges transport grain and other precious cargo, and houseboats take families on journeys of discovery.

Back on the Drive, you will pass the trees of **Fruit Acres,** RR 2, (507) 895-4750, La Crescent, which is the largest orchard in the area and which supplies apples wholesale. Nearby is **Leidel's Apples,** 406 North Hill Street, La Crescent, (507) 895-4832. Leidel's started small in 1917 and today its orchardists tend six thousand trees across 60 acres. Leidel's operates a seasonal roadside stand in La Crescent, but it is also possible to buy direct at the orchard. Next up, **Hoch Orchard and Gardens,** 1222 W. 5th Street, La Crescent, (507) 474-1465, www.hochorchard.com, prides itself on sustainable agriculture and certification as an environmentally friendly and socially responsible food grower. During Applefest, Hoch Orchard welcomes visitors with tours of the orchard and packing line, as well as demonstrations of cider making and insight into their innovative farming practices.

The Drive becomes County Road 12 and officially continues northwest through Nodine, then north until it reconnects with Highway 61. But you can also cut east on County Road 12 to enjoy the stunning view of the apple trees at **Southwind Orchards,** 45440 County Road 12, Dakota. Stop in to Southwind in autumn to sample apples and discover which varieties appeal most to your taste; call (507) 643-6255. Go through Dakota, drop down to Dresbach, then zip south on I-90 and back into La Crescent.

The local apple crop starts pouring in to **Bauer's Market,** 221 North Second Street (Highway 14/61), La Crescent, (507) 895-4583, www.bauersmarket.com, around mid-July. Some of the names are as colorful as the fruits, and could be characters

A common scene in southeast Minnesota; here it's Southwind Orchards, Dakota.

out of an old western: Ida Red, Paula Red, Prime Red Jon, Whitney Crab, Williams Pride. Stock up on produce, seasonal cider and hand-dipped caramel apples, preserved foods, and apple-related supplies. How about cinnamon sticks, apple crisp mix (just add apples), and apple pie spice for your baking needs? And wouldn't mulling spices, added to a favorite beverage, warm up a chilly winter evening?

Also in La Crescent, visit **Hein Orchard**, 476 Highway 16 (south of the stoplights), La Crescent, (507) 895-4495. Pick up apples to eat and to cook with, as well as jams, jellies, honeys, caramel apples, and ciders to savor. About one-tenth of a mile south, visit **Leidel's Apple Stand**, 704 Highway 16, La Crescent, (507) 895-8221, which kicks off its season in early August with Oriole, Mantet, Quinty, Okabena, and Viking apples. Return later for Wealthy, an old variety that Leidel's says you can use for eating, pie baking, applesauce, apple butter, freezing, and canning. Additional varieties ripen throughout September, including the popular Honeycrisp, Gala, Jonathan, and Red Delicious. Keepsake hits the stand around mid-October, and it is so named because you will be eating these keepers in January. So if you like variety, you will find over 32 varieties through mid-November, and enjoy samples to help you decide. The stand also stocks jams, jellies, honey, red and brown apple syrup, maple syrup, sorghum syrup, fresh pasteurized cider, and seasonal veggies like homegrown sweet corn. Check to see if Leidel's is still running the guided bus tours, which include a swing through town and up to their orchard to see the pack house and to learn how apples are grown.

Bauer's Market, La Crescent, full of the bounty from local fields and orchards.

Branching Out

If you are hungry for even more local flavor and interesting sites, then before loop-ing back to La Crescent, drive north on Highway 14/61 instead of south on I-90. At County Road 7, go left to explore the six-story **Pickwick Mill**, 26421 County Road 7, Winona, (507) 457-0499, www.pickwickmill.org. Sitting on the banks of Big Trout Creek, Pickwick Mill was built of limestone in 1858 and still houses orig-inal machinery. According to the mill's Web site, when the mill was in its heyday, farm wagon traffic would back up for a mile as area wheat growers waited to unload their grain.

Backtrack to Highway 14/61 and continue north to Winona, which is 27 miles from La Crescent. Visit the **Watkins Museum and Store**, 150 Liberty Street, Winona, (507) 457-3300. Closed on Sundays, free admission. Learn all about those little bottles of vanilla, jars of spices, bottles of grapeseed oil, and liniments and tonics that are sold at county fairs and other venues in the company's orig-inal direct-sale tradition. Among the earliest settlers to Winona and surround-ing farmlands were immigrants from Poland, and for visitors who wish to learn more about the culture that brought kielbasa, pierogis, and similarly hearty fare to America, visit the **Polish Cultural Institute and Museum**, 102 Liberty Street, Winona, (507) 454-3431.

Would you drive 30 miles or so to visit a pie shop? Of course you would, so after getting your fill of Winona, why not take I-90 or Highway 14 to the west-ern border of Winona County? There, the **White Water Valley Orchard Pie Shop**, 24496 Highway 74 North, Saint Charles, (507) 932-4003, awaits your pleasure. Follow your nose one-half mile north of Saint Charles on Highway 74 leading to the White Water State Park. Pick up some of their made-fresh-daily apple pies and five kinds of apple butters and plum preserves.

So now, if the open road is still calling, you could continue north into Wabasha County and visit two apple orchards there. From Saint Charles, you could drive west on I-90, through Rochester, and north on Highway 52 and a little east on Highway 60 into Mazeppa, for a distance of about 45 miles. You are at the west-ern border of Wabasha County. The **Apple Ridge Orchard**, Route 1, Box 296, Mazeppa, (507) 843-3033, www.appleridgeorchard.com, is a fun autumn-time place with u-pick apples and pumpkins with tractor-pulled rides each weekend, a kids' corn maze, llamas, and barnyard critters. Take your pick of favorite apple varieties like Honeycrisp, Haralson, Honeygold, and Sweet Sixteen.

To visit the other orchard, from Mazeppa drive north on Highway 60, then northeast on Highway 63 to Highway 61 in Lake City. The **Pepin Heights Orchards Store**, on Highway 61, one and one-half miles south of town, (651) 345-2305, (800) 652-3779, www.pepinheights.com, is loaded with apples that are grown by the state's largest orchard. It is open seasonally, so go during the autumn for Hon-eycrisp, Haralson, Fireside, and other popular varieties. Shop for homemade pressed and sparkling ciders, caramel apples, and bakery goods. Also buy won-derful foods like maple syrup, honey, fruit butters, jams/jellies/preserves, and

Long-term growth

La Crescent's apple growing industry took root in 1857, when John S. Harris came to town and began to plant apple trees in the well-drained clay soil. This despite local wisdom that insisted the winters were too darn cold for this kind of farming. "John became the laughingstock of area farmers when he planted apple trees on the sunny slopes." But Harris's efforts bore fruit: "His descendants had the last laugh when the area became known as Minnesota's Apple Capital." (*History of Houston County*, compiled by The Houston County Historical Society, 1982)

At Fruit Acres, the area's largest orchard, orchardist Gordon Yates talks about the changing industry. "At one time, there were as many as 40 orchards, but it's gradually diminished over time," Yates observes. He says that three main reasons account for the change: economics, labor, and real estate development. "But," he adds, "we still have a considerable number of orchards operating here."

Yates estimates that today's annual yield is 300,000 to 400,000 bushels. He knows the region well, and what makes it so suitable. "They used to call it the Banana Belt because of the amount of water that is here, which makes the area warmer. The other things are the topography—cold air goes from the top to the bottom just like water. The soils we have are deep Dubuque loams, which give us a good, firm apple."

And even though Fruit Acres is strictly a wholesale operation, Yates said that consumers cannot go wrong when they come out and buy their apples from other La Crescent growers. "Direct," he said, "they're a thousand miles fresher." 🐝

domestic and imported cheeses. Open daily May through March, and autumn farm tours can be arranged by appointment.

If they've come at the right time, people leave the area with bushels of apples rolling around in their trunks and the cinnamon-tinged sweetness of apple pie a fresh memory. So it's easy to see why they can, in a way, return again and again, each time they take a bite of crisp, juicy apple, and whenever they serve an apple pie or crumbly cobbler of their own.

SPECIAL EVENTS

La Crosse Farmers' Market, Cameron Park, downtown La Crosse, Wisconsin, www.cameronparkmarket.com. Fridays during the growing season from 3:00 p.m. to dusk. Enjoy the shade of this tree-filled park that comes alive with the harvest, some of which has crossed the border from Minnesota.

La Crescent Applefest, La Crescent, (507) 895-2800, www.applefestusa.com. Celebrated each September since 1949, this gala weekend starts to rev up with pre-fest events in late August: Apple Annie Night, Queen Candidate Fashion Show, Applefest Demo Derby, and Apple Cobbler Golf Open. The big weekend, which starts on a Thursday afternoon in mid-September, offers bus tours of orchards and apple packing plants, apple displays and sampling, a chicken barbeque, a pancake breakfast, helicopter rides, and lots of other fun stuff.

Pickwick Mill Day, Winona, (507) 452-9658. Mid-September. Free mill tours, pancake breakfast, homemade pie and bake sale, arts and crafts, family entertainment.

Polish Apple Day or *Smaczne Jablka* **Day**, Winona, www.pickwickmill.org. Second Sunday in October. Start with a Polish meal at the 1894 Saint Stanislaus Kostka Catholic Church, 625 East Fourth Street. Eat apple pie and ice cream, caramel apples, and freshly pressed apple cider, learn traditional Polish dance steps, listen to live music, enjoy various games and family activities.

PLACES TO EAT

Apple on Main Tea Room and Gifts, 329 Main Street, La Crescent, (507) 895-1995. Step inside this cozy 1918 bungalow for morning pastries and coffee, daily-special lunches, and afternoon desserts. The gifts part includes gourmet foods on the order of mustards and honey butters.

La Crescent American Legion Club, 509 North Chestnut Street, La Crescent, (507) 895-4595. Lunch specials, Sunday evening grills. Steak fry third Saturday of each month. Breakfast buffet Sunday mornings. It is a good, old-fashioned American Legion hall—go!

The Old Barn Resort, three miles northeast of Preston off County Road 17, (800) 552-2512, www.barnresort.com. Casual bar and grill in open-air, two-story part of the barn. Ribs and pork smoked on-premises, also charbroiled steaks, burgers, chicken, and seafood. The resort is a campground and hostel.

PLACES TO STAY

Dancing Winds Farm Retreat and Goat Cheesery, 6863 County Road 12, Kenyon, (507) 789-6606. Stay on this 1856 Norwegian farmstead where you are welcome to learn all about the working dairy goat farm and Minnesota's first goat cheese plant. Relax in the private, two-story guesthouse's living room, and on the deck overlooking a pond. Make your own breakfast of farm fresh eggs, goat cheese of course, local jams, and fresh-baked goods. Cheese-making classes available.

Room to Roam, W656 Veraguth Drive, Fountain City, Wisconsin, (608) 687-8575. Just over the border in Wisconsin, there is a wonderful farm vacation experience that is not to be missed, by advance reservation. Kids and the young at heart will enjoy this fourth-generation family farm where they can feed cattle and calves, perhaps even witness the birth of a calf. Observe the seasonal planting, chopping,

Farther afield

The diversity of regional specialty farming in southeastern Minnesota is almost unbelievable. Here is a sampling of those that specialize in the hoof and fiber set, and whose farms are scattered across six of the region's counties, including two counties that are north of Rochester:

Dancing Winds Farm Retreat and Goat Cheesery, 6863 County #12 Boulevard, Kenyon, (507) 789-6606, call before coming. Goodhue County. Goat cheese plant, farm-stay retreat, educational farm tours by appointment only.

Ellison Sheep Farm, 15775 Highway 60 Boulevard, Zumbrota, (507) 732-5281, open by appointment. Goodhue County. Scheduled farm tours, classes, and demonstrations available. Icelandic, Shetland, and Finnish sheep to pet. Give a spinning wheel or weaving loom a whirl, and consider a purchase. Wool, yarn, kids' crafts, finished pieces.

Hill and Vale Farms, RR1, Box 152, Wyckoff, (507) 352-4441, call for hours. Fillmore County. Lamb cuts, washable lamb wool pelts, processed wool for crafts, ewe lambs for your flock. Farm tours by appointment.

Sheep Sorrel Farm, 31005 County 7 Boulevard, Vasa, (651) 258-4290, call ahead. Goodhue County. Sustainably raised pasture-fed lambs. Meat cuts, special-order tanned pelts. B&B accommodation available. 🐏

and picking of corn, as well as the baling of hay. Accommodations consist of three-plus bedrooms and a kitchen to do your own cooking. So this is how you keep 'em down on the farm.

Windom Park Bed and Breakfast, 369 West Broadway Street, Winona, (507) 457-9515, (866) 737-1719, www.windompark.com. This 1900 Colonial Revival welcomes guests with six rooms all with private baths, including Coach House loft rooms. Historic neighborhood, antiques, great room with a copper fireplace, Oriental carpets, across from Victorian park with gazebo and fountain. Walk to the Mississippi River and downtown. Full five-course breakfast served in the dining room.

Flaby's Amish Tours leave from Lanesboro.

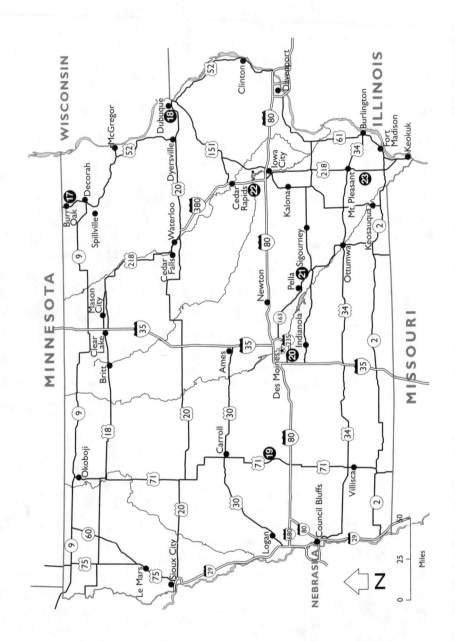

Iowa

Iowa's legendary agricultural heritage goes back to the days when Native Americans grew the "three sisters of life": squash, beans, and corn. Today Iowa is stronger than ever, one of the country's leading agricultural states. Indeed, the Hawkeye State keeps close watch over the quality of its famous beef and pork, which owes its goodness, in part, to the land's rich corn crop. But there are fascinating specialty markets thriving here as well. So let's take part in some great farm tours, agricultural museums, and events like the Iowa State Fair, when it seems as if the entire state empties out and gathers in Des Moines.

17. NORTHEAST IOWA'S FIELDS OF EXPERTISE

This section of the state showcases specialty agriculture like few other places in the Heartland—so much so that it has been designated a state Silos and Smokestacks National Heritage Area. Here growers are passionate about everything from ancient breeds of cattle to a variety of ground cherry that originated in Poland. Bring your appetite, because in addition to the growers offering un-sprayed this and free-range that, the Norwegians of Decorah will be whipping up specialties like *rullepølse*, a sandwich meat of beef flank rolled with seasonings, and a flavorful fruit compote called *søtsuppe*.

The tour is mostly about Winneshiek County, which shares a border with Minnesota, but the rolling hills of northeast Iowa are so pretty that you will most certainly want to see what's around the next bend. So let's start in Howard County, spend time in Winneshiek County, take a dip down into northeastern Fayette County, and see what there is to see due east in Clayton County.

Lidtke Mill

In Howard County, the first point of interest is **Lidtke Mill Historic Site**, 828 Lincoln Street, Lime Springs, www.howard-county.com, a couple of miles south of the Minnesota border. This is a quick stop, but worth it for mill buffs, and it is open on weekends from 1:00 to 4:00 p.m. From the town of Lime Springs, go north on County Road V36; the mill will appear on the banks of the Upper Iowa River. Construction of Lidtke Mill began in 1857 and was completed in 1860. Exactly one hundred years later, the mill ceased operation. But back in the 1870s, flour ground here was shipped as far away as Europe. The mill features working turbines and a period-furnished mill house.

In Cresco, about 16 miles south of Lime Springs on Highway 63 and east on Highway 9, visit **Peckview Dairy Goats**, 24296 95th Street, Cresco, (563) 547-3823.

The family's five-hundred-head dairy goat farm offers an opportunity to learn about an alternative farming operation and to shop for fresh goat cheese, homegrown meats, soaps, and lotions.

Winneshiek County

Now continue southeast for about 19 miles on Highway 9, crossing into Winneshiek County and heading into Decorah. The town drips with charm and character; even the Chamber of Commerce building has a history of being, among other things, a blacksmith shop, farm machinery store, bakery, and a tavern that bagged only groceries after Prohibition.

White trim looks like frosting on the red bricks of the main building that houses **Vesterheim Norwegian-American Museum**, 523 West Water Street, Decorah, (563) 382-9681, www.vesterheim.org. Take to heart the struggles and courage of the 800,000 Norwegians who immigrated to the New World during the decades of 1825 to 1930. Read the food- and farm-oriented chapters of these stalwart peoples' story. Find out that during emigration, the foods they survived on usually included dried and smoked fish and meat, cheese, flat bread, hulled grain, flour, potatoes, coffee, sugar, salt, and butter. Various cooking and baking exhibits interpret their culinary history. Walk through a life-size replica of an immigrant farmhouse that was constructed with wooden floorboards and walls. Upstairs, models from two historical periods show the changing face of the Norwegian-American farm.

Be sure to sign up for the guided tour of the 16 outbuildings, including the nineteenth-century farmhouse and the tiny gristmill that would have been sited directly over a stream in Norway. Explore the three-story limestone mill (this part is self-guided) that no longer grinds grain but houses an agricultural/industrial museum. The building itself, which is possibly the oldest building in Decorah, qualifies as a museum piece. It was built by nineteenth-century British settlers at this location, and water-powered until 1946. Wheat was ground until the 1890s wheat blight, followed by corn and buckwheat, then feeds. When the U.S. Army Corps of Engineers took flood control measures here and throughout downtown Decorah in the 1940s, the mill could no longer draw water. But the mill owner fought back, demanding that the city buy a diesel engine, and so it continued operation until the 1960s. A weigh scale is about all that is left of the mill's original workings, but you will discover a wealth of agricultural implements and explanations of their use on an early Norwegian-American farm.

Leaving the museum, you may wish to pick up fresh, local foods at convenient, in-town locations. The **Winneshiek Farmers' Market** appeals to every taste. It is also a chance to meet some of Decorah's passionate producers—a colorful cast. Shop the farmers' market on Saturday mornings for free-range eggs, hormone-free meats, honey creams, beeswax, orange cantaloupes, Iowa sweet corn, Norwegian baked goods, and more. Over at 915 Short Street, **K&S Foods**, (563) 382-8791, looks like an ordinary grocery store until you notice the strong emphasis on local, Iowa-made, and Midwestern products; Norwegian heritage foods like *lutefisk, lefse,* and cheeses; and grill-ready Deep Basted meats that undergo a tumbling process so that seasonings flavor the cuts through and through.

Then hit the **Oneota Community Food Co-op**, 415 West Water Street, Decorah, (563) 382-4666, for fun, healthy, minimally packaged foods to go. How about dried sour cherries, wild blueberry granola, or blue tortilla chips for the road? Discover *gjetost,* a goat cheese that Norwegians travel a long way to buy; *lefse,* a bakery treat made from potato flour; and breads from Waving Grains Bakery. For the grill, consider beef steaks from a farm where the cattle are pasture-fed and free of hormones, synthetic chemicals, and antibiotics. Thirsty? How about organic pop?

Now that you have freshened up and perhaps sat down to a wholesome Norwegian lunch, it is time to visit a few places in the surrounding countryside. Going north on Highway 52, the first stop is **Craft's at Bluffton Farm**, 2572 Village Road, Decorah, (563) 735-5533. You might say that this establishment is a place of biblical proportions that is guaranteed to have you seeing spots. That is because owners Marianne and Bob Norton raise Jacob sheep, a breed that got a mention in the Bible, and is therefore ancient but rare. It is also a breed that is uniquely spotted. The Jacob Sheep Breeders Association of Bozeman, Montana, reports that hand-spinners love the spotted wool, which is also a pleasure to work with, and that the meat is tasty and lean. While shopping for wool and yarn, enjoy the views of craggy limestone bluffs and the novelty of some 150 exotic sheep on these 50 acres.

Owners Marianne and Bob Norton with some Jacob sheep at their Craft's at Bluffton Farm, Decorah.

Blooms and barns at the Seed Savers Exchange, near Decorah.

Then it's on to another rare find, this one located on the way back to Decorah, about nine miles southeast of Craft's. It is **Seed Savers Exchange**, 3076 North Winn Road, Decorah, (563) 382-5990, www.seedsavers.org. Drive east, then southeast, then north on Highway 52 for about 7.5 miles north of downtown Decorah. Seed Savers Exchange is an acclaimed enterprise that preserves heirloom fruits and vegetables, native prairie plants, and even ancient White Park cattle. Thousands of members support the organization, and some even "grow out" the heirloom seeds in their own gardens for safekeeping of the genetic material and of the heirloom tradition. You can enjoy a visit on several levels. Seed Savers Exchange is a remarkable reinvention of a farm, a place of natural beauty, and a gorgeous source for garden ideas and products.

But there is another message here, one that may forever change the way you look at foods. You can read the message in the interpretive signs, but also look around, because it is there in every flower, every leaf, every Jimmy Nardello's Sweet Italian Frying Pepper. It is the message of how critical it is not to lose original genetic material to forces such as drought, global warming, pesticide-resistant insects, or hybridization, but instead to protect it for everyone's benefit. Signs point out that this is important to help protect the world's food supply, and to preserve characteristics of flavor and diversity. So go ahead and enjoy the diversity. Stroll through the Heritage Farm's organic Preservation Gardens, where spidery cleomes and willowy hollyhocks whisk you back to Grandma's backyard. Rare Russian and Eastern European plants grow here, alongside morning glories of the deepest purple. Over at the Historic Orchard, they tend apple trees of the nineteenth-century variety. Seven hundred varieties.

Just east of Decorah off Highway 9 is the **Siewer Springs State Trout Rearing Station**, 2321 Siewer Springs Road, Decorah, (563) 382-8324, a kind of feedlot for fish, except that the fattened trout are driven by truck for release into 17 clear, cold northeast Iowa streams where anglers can try their luck. Find it a little under two and one-half miles south of the food co-op. About 150,000 rainbow, 30,000 brown, and 30,000 brook trout are raised annually. Peer into the depths of the 24 concrete raceways, where the two- to four-inch fingerlings spend their time safely growing to lengths of 10 to 12 inches. Spring for food pellets that make the waters explode with tail-lashing turbulence. This entertainment alone is worth the price of, well, there is no admission.

It gets wilder. Shoot out to a fifth-generation dairy farm, located a little over six miles south of the trout station. Except that instead of cows, they have game birds and a hunting lodge that used to be the dairy barn. This is **Chase the Adventure**, 1838 Middle Calmar Road (County Road W38), Decorah, (563) 382-8012, www.chasetheadventure.com, a hunt and gun club that represents the dream of one farm family that decided to trade in their cows and milking machines for the sporting life. Visitors can sharpen marksmanship skills with skeet and trap, five-stand, and sporting clays. The old silos have been reinvented as lofty launch pads for some of the clays. All skill levels are welcome, and novices can enjoy expert safety training and coaching on techniques of proper stance and aim, holding of the gun, and timing of the shots. The family is busy restoring 500 acres of the farm to a pre-farm habitat that would have been typical for this area, including tens of thousands of trees like oaks, ashes, and wild plums, as well as prairie areas and ponds. For sportsmen, it is a lot of room to roam.

For a close-up look at advanced dairy farming practices in a region that boasts a high concentration of milk cows, drive 15 miles south from Decorah to visit **The Dairy Center** on Highway 150 south of Calmar. A project of Iowa State University Extension, Northeast Iowa Community College, and the Northeast Iowa Dairy Foundation, this gleaming facility provides state-of-the-art education to future farmers and is an exciting resource for the field trip crowd. But it is also a working dairy farm, open to anyone who wishes to take a free, self-guided tour or a close-up guided tour. Check out the numerous artifacts and displays from Monday through Friday, 8:00 a.m. to 4:30 p.m., and remember to take the whole family along. For information, call NICC at (800) 728-2256, ext. 341, or The Dairy Center at (866) 474-4692 x101.

Within The Dairy Center, the Iowa Dairy Story Museum showcases comprehensive displays of dairying, and there are teaching tools such as a Jersey cow sculpted by Norma Duffield Lyon. Affectionately known as Duffy, Lyon is the famous Iowa State Fair butter-cow lady, who sculpted this particular cow from plaster, not butter, so there is no danger of a meltdown. Watch Holstein, Jersey, Brown Swiss, and Ayrshire cows being milked every afternoon in the viewing area of the milking parlor. Play the Dairy Cart Quiz and see how many dairy cows are in your area of the United States. If you wish to see more of the working dairy itself, reservations can be made for a guided tour. Don plastic boots and watch the cows eat, chew their cud, and sleep in the comfortable free-stall area; and maybe a new calf has come into the world this day. In various areas, cows calve, eat, sleep, and observe visitors up-close. Outside, their feed is stored in horizontal bunkers, which are the silos of today. Two manure systems handle the high value organic matter (manure) that each cow produces daily. This outside barn tour must be arranged ahead of time and charges a small fee.

Fayette County

Continue south on Highway 150, cross into Fayette County, then take scenic County Road B40 southeast to sleepy little Clermont. For information on any of the sites in town, visit www.visitclermontia.org. Without touristy fanfare, this small town oozes Heartland history, and much of it is agricultural in nature. Starting north of the Turkey River, drive about a mile along Highway 18 (Mill Street) to the **European Rural Heritage Institute**, which takes you back some 50 to 75 years. It is open for special events during the warmer months. These include folk dances in the spring, a horse and tractor pull in July, and Cornfest in October. While enjoying the activities, you will see the renovated barn that houses agricultural displays, and the test plots where unusual varieties of corn,

The Dairy Center, Calmar.

Grinning from ear to ear at the Country Heritage Maize Maze, near Elgin.

peanuts, and cotton are being assessed. Back toward the river, the **Montauk Historic Governor's Home**, 26223 Harding Road, Clermont, (563) 423-7173, presides over Clermont like a benevolent elder. Iowa's 12th governor, who had been an agriculturalist, lived in this 1874 brick and limestone mansion. Guided tours are offered and admission is free. The residence's old creamery, icehouse, and barn are preserved for your inspection.

Downtown Clermont also has a historic tractor on display, as well as a blacksmith shop that still houses the tools and horseshoe products much as they were left when it closed in the early 1980s. At the river's edge, what is now the power plant was Clermont's flour mill from 1855 to 1909.

From Clermont, take County Road W51 almost 4.5 miles south to Elgin, and follow the signs east of town on County Road B64 to the **Country Heritage Maize Maze**, a four-acre funhouse through an Iowa corn field; visit www.silosand smokestacks.org. Nothing beats a corn maze when it comes to losing yourself in a farm immersion experience. This one throws in elements of education and competition, with quizzes that test your knowledge of field corn and the local land, stands of popcorn, broomcorn, Indian corn, and vintage farm equipment. Climb the bridge to sneak in a videotape of your children as they try to puzzle their way out of the confusion.

There is more to do nearby. The 327-acre **Gilbertson Conservation Education Area**, 22580 A Avenue, Elgin, (563) 426-5740, (five more miles of walking trails, in case you haven't had enough) features a nice petting zoo with friendly farm animals. Nearby, the **Connor Dummermuth Historical Building**, Elgin, contains farm and home antiques, along with vintage seed and feed sacks. The **Hart Dummermuth Historical House** depicts rural life in Iowa as it would have been during the 1890–1920 era.

Clayton County

Take County Road W55 south to Highway 56, cross over into Clayton County, and continue driving east to charming Elkader, a distance of about 16 miles from Elgin. Here the **George Maier Rural Heritage Center**, located in the City Park just off the Highway 13 bypass, 400 Mascara Road, Elkader, (563) 245-1849, first opened in 2003. This museum is great, representing the lifetime collection of George Maier, who for his own reasons sought to tell the story of life in the rural American Heartland. The quality and scope of this collection, which is appropriately housed in an old sales barn, makes it seem impossible to be the work of one man. But, by George, it is indeed that. Seems that throughout the decades, Maier just kept adding chapters of the rural-life story until finally he had a museum on his hands, and it was time to close the book.

There is plenty more American agricultural history to check out. From Elkader, take Highway 13 north to Highway 52, go a very short distance, then pick up Highway 18 into Froelich, which is a little over 14 miles from Elkader. Here in 1892 John Froelich built the first gasoline tractor. The Waterloo Gasoline Tractor Engine

Company was born, then snapped up by the John Deere Company in 1918. Visit the **Tractor and General Store Museum**: past the Historical Marker sign, turn onto Hickory Avenue, then turn right onto Froelich Road. Call (563) 536-2841 for information.

Or, if you go 7 miles southeast of Elkader (begin where the Highway 13 bypass meets County Road C1X, cross three bridges, right at the first gravel road), you come to the six-story limestone **Motor Mill Historic Site** along the Turkey River. In its day, this workhorse was the tallest pioneer mill in the American Heartland and a center of commerce for the settlement of Motor, which existed only from the early 1860s to the 1880s. The mill ground oats and rye for livestock feed, buckwheat for pancake flour, and wheat for bread and pastry flour. Farmers waiting to have their harvest processed found convenient lodging at the limestone inn. During a recent 80-year stretch, the site became part of a family dairy farm. Have a picnic, launch a canoe, hike the hills, mill around. There are no regularly scheduled tours, but you may be able to catch one of the periodic open houses or special events; call (563) 245-1516.

Northeast Iowa is a beautiful land of rolling green hills and well-kept farms. But there is also a wealth of country-style attractions that roll out the welcome mat for visitors and can make the difference between "just looking," and really experiencing the region with all of one's senses.

SPECIAL EVENTS

Mighty Howard County Fair, (563) 547-3400, Cresco, www.mightyhoward countyfair.com. Late June. 4-H and FFA competition, historical and wildlife exhibits, carnival midway, grandstand entertainment, food.

Heritage Days, Elkader, (563) 245-1516. Early October. Pioneer crafts and skills are demonstrated, over 50 in all, including blacksmithing, wood crafts, spinning, and basket-making. Buffalo chip throwing contests. Pioneer ancestry foods.

Heritage Farm Park Corn Fest, European Rural Heritage Institute, 26225 Harding Road, Clermont, www.clermontia.org. Early October. Demonstrations of historic farming practices in a country setting.

Scandinavian Food Fest, Vesterheim Norwegian-American Museum, 523 W. Water Street, Decorah, (563) 382-9681. Early October. Nosh on Nordic specialties, observe traditional-food preparation demonstrations, and collect recipes in charming, authentic museum buildings.

PLACES TO EAT

Dayton Norwegian House Café, 516 West Water Street, Decorah, (563) 382-9683. Classic Norwegian fare and more. Try open-faced sandwiches with choice of smoked capon and Gouda, gravlax with green onion and horseradish cream cheese, or shaved beef and cheddar. *Bierock* is sweetened baked yeast dough filled with grilled salmon, wild rice, and spinach, then topped with seasoned shrimp cream and kept company by veggies.

La Rana Bistro, 120 Washington Street, Decorah, (563) 382-3067. Urban eatery features local organic produce and creative dishes with the finest ingredients. Cabbage salad with Fuji apples and sweet white balsamic vinaigrette is refreshingly crisp on a hot summer day. The bacon on Bevan's BLT is applewood smoked, and dinner entrées include shellfish, fish, lamb, and beef choices.

Shanti Inc., 17455 Gunder Road, Elgin, (563) 864-9289. People swear by the magnificent Gunderburger and its companion fries.

Victorian Rose Restaurant, Hotel Winneshiek, 104 East Water Street, Decorah, (563) 382-4164, (800) 998-4164. Mmm, superb. Classic Caesar salad features romaine hearts and a Parmesan cigar. Seasonal veggies abound, and locally grown chestnuts pop up in wintertime. Don't miss dishes such as the grilled ostrich filet with lingonberry demi-glacé. Iowa pork tenderloin is coated in apricot curry glaze, then grilled and accompanied by basmati rice, strawberries, and crushed pistachios. Capon, sourced from a Decorah facility, is also on the menu.

PLACES TO STAY

Chase the Adventure, 1838 Middle Calmar Road (W38), Decorah, (563) 382-8012, www.chasetheadventure.com. Rustic digs in an 1889 dairy barn transformed into an outdoor sportsman's lodge on former family farm. A hay fork has been uniquely reinvented as a chandelier. Complete services available to game bird hunters and shooters on-site. Five rooms. Continental breakfast features homemade cinnamon rolls, and pheasant eggs may be offered seasonally.

Goshawk Farm Bed and Breakfast and Equestrian Training Center, 27596 Ironwood Road, Elkader, (563) 964-9321, www.goshawkfarm.com. Make yourself at home in this nineteenth-century farm cottage built of limestone. Farm-sized breakfast each morning. Equestrian training available.

Hotel Winneshiek, 104 East Water Street, Decorah, (563) 382-4164, www.hotelwinn.com. History of lodging on the site dates back to 1849 log cabin. Present hotel restored to turn-of-the-century glory with cherry millwork done by the same contractor that helped build the hotel back in 1905. Connecting opera house. Lovely, spacious rooms with thoughtful touches and continental breakfast.

House in the Woods, 217 Ellingson Bridge Drive, Decorah, (563) 546-7912. Farmhouse with pond, trout streams, and fire pit in secluded wooded area.

Hutchinson Family Farm Campground and B&B, 2299 Scenic River Road, Decorah, (563) 382-3054. Enjoy pure country on this working beef and quarter horse farm where your stay is in the cozy, relaxed B&B home (two guest rooms/ shared bath available), including full farmer's breakfast with a lot of local ingredients, or in the riverside campground. Learn something about barn restoration and walk the gravel road to the bridge over the Upper Iowa River, where you can kayak, fish, soak up the sunsets, and regret having to return home. Kayak and inner tube rentals available.

18. DUBUQUE COUNTY: WHEN FARMERS DREAM

Back in 1989, Universal Studios hit a homer with *Field of Dreams*. In the movie, neighboring farmers shook their heads as the central character, Ray Kinsella (Kevin Costner), cut a baseball diamond into his corn field. But as everyone knows, the Ghost Players really did come. And for their own sometimes inexplicable reasons, real people come too, all these years later, to the world's most famous farm field. This isn't heaven, it's Dyersville, Iowa. It is a place where lots of little dreams come true too, because Dyersville is also known as the Farm Toy Capital of the World. And some 27 miles to the east, another Dubuque County phenomenon lies in the ruins of a nineteenth-century farm. It is not a living history farm brought to life by costumed interpreters. Instead, it is a kind of ghost farm that leaves it up to your imagination to dream of what farming here must have been like.

And somewhere in between, Trappistine nuns are still stirring kettles of creamy caramel.

Where do you go to find all of this? To Dubuque County, which meets both the southwestern tip of Wisconsin and the northwestern tip of Illinois, and which is bordered on the east by the Mississippi River and on the west by vast and abundant corn fields.

Big Dreams

Farm field, baseball field, it's all the same in Dyersville. They built it; people come. They come in a steady stream of minivans and SUVs that are loaded up with kids, catcher's mitts, jerseys, salty snacks, lawn chairs, and fistfuls of cash. Men, women, girls, boys, it doesn't matter; everyone is out to have a catch, to walk in and out of the corn, to plunk down bills for T-shirts and assorted souvenirs like Dream Dirt, baseball-mitt key chains, videos, you know. After more than a decade, this faithfulness testifies to the power of the movies, but it also says something about the endurance of baseball. People want not only to stand in the field where Ray Kinsella first reconnected with Shoeless Joe, but they also want to swing a bat in the summer sun.

You don't even have to like baseball to sport a grin throughout the duration of the Ghost Players' performance, which comes courtesy of Left & Center Field of Dreams, on the last Sunday afternoon of each month from June through September. When it comes to baseball, this is a whole new ballgame, with the wisecracks and antics coming fast and furious and frequently at the expense of the crowd. These guys have been cultivating new fans since 1990, and it is clear they still love every minute of the play. You will too. Or, if you are in the mood for quieter reflection on baseball and the meaning of it all, visit Field of Dreams on a day when nothing special is scheduled. It is an entirely different experience then.

Unlike in the movie, this is not one farm but two, and the split is evident. On the right, Don and Becky Lansing own the part called the Field of Dreams Movie Site, which includes the picturesque white farmhouse, much of the infield, and a gift shop. On the left, Al and Rita Ameskamp own the part called Left & Center

This way to the Field of Dreams, Dyersville.

Field of Dreams, which includes left field and center field, that famous corn, a corn maze, and a gift shop. But the crowds that come to enjoy the world's most famous farm field do not care or do not seem to notice. Besides, everyone knows that baseball has divisions.

To go the distance to **Field of Dreams**, take the 294 exit off Highway 20, drive north on Highway 136, then follow the signs for 3.3 miles on County Road D21 to the field. Uh, fields. Take the road that belongs to Left & Center Field of Dreams, 29001 Lansing Road, Dyersville, (563) 875-6012, www.leftandcenterfod.com, or drive a few more feet and take the road that belongs to Field of Dreams Movie Site, 28963 Lansing Road, Dyersville, (563) 875-8404, www.fodmoviesite.com.

Little Dreams

Dyersville also fuels dreams that are forged of die-cast steel and painted in a rainbow of manufacturers' trademark colors—blue, red, orange, yellow, and green-and-yellow. These are little farm toys that are so finely detailed, and so intertwined with American agriculture, that the appeal is as strong for adults as it is for children. The toys even merit their own museum.

The **National Farm Toy Museum**, 1110 16th Avenue Court SE, Dyersville, (563) 875-2727, www.nationalfarmtoymuseum.com, displays some 30,000 farm toy collectibles. It is off the same exit as the Field of Dreams site, but in town and closer to Highway 20. The displays include farm equipment such as tractors and combines, as well as implements, trucks, and pedal cars. Kids love the idea of a museum that is dedicated to toys, but often it is their fathers who must be dragged out. So are they toys or not? Whether toy or valuable collectible, these museum artifacts are finely crafted and easy to like. Anyone who shares a love

or appreciation for American farming, for miniatures, for toys, will enjoy spending a few hours in the National Farm Toy Museum.

A museum visit begins with the first of many toy and collectible displays. Past
the life-size farmhouse porch and farm scene, a multi-media video points out that
farm toys are playthings, of course, but also agricultural timelines on wheels.
Miniature farm scenes provide an intriguing history lesson about the changing
look of the family farm from 1900 to the present day. View a segment of a 1950s
Ertl assembly line. View 1950s toy farms that were made of tin, enough logo trucks
to form a formidable convoy, scale models from foreign countries, and a "History of Grain Harvesting" exhibit that takes you all the way back to 5200 BC.

If it all inspires you to start or strengthen a collection, visit the museum gift
shop and the specialty retailers in and around Dyersville. Making farm toys in
these parts all started with Fred Ertl, Sr., who began manufacturing toy tractors
in the basement of his Dubuque home in 1945, and that was the beginning of the
Ertl Toy Company. With expansion came a move to Dyersville in 1959. Since then,
manufacturing has gone to China, but the company still maintains its **Racing
Champions Ertl Outlet Store** one block south of Highway 20 on Highway 136,
(563) 875-5613, www.rcertl.com. The **Farm Toy Outlet Store and Restoration
Center**, 1426 Ninth Street SE, Dyersville, (563) 875-8900, www.farmtoyoutlet.com,
works hard to bring the latest models onto its shelves, but also offers hard-to-find
pieces from private collections. Its Restoration Center and Parts Department
breathe new life into tired but beloved pieces.

Also visit the **Toy Collector Club/SpecCast Outlet**, 1235 16th Avenue SE,
Dyersville, (800) 452-3303, www.toycollectorclub.com. The **Plaza Antique Mall**,
1235 16th Avenue Court SE, Dyersville, (563) 875-8945, www.plaza-antique-
mall.com, is a stage set of antiques, including farm toys, behind a rescued theater
marquis. The **Toy Farmer Country Store**, 1161 16th Avenue Court SE, (563) 875-
8850, is a cute gift shop with some farm-themed decorating ideas. Got time for
one more? Thirty-five miles west of Dyersville, **Bossen Implement, Inc.**, 300 Washburn Avenue, Lamont, (563) 924-2880, www.bossenimp.com, gives the toy farmers of the world their own life-size dealership, with inventories of new and used
items, parts, and complete restoration services.

Imagining the Farm

Let's go find those farm ruins. From Dyersville, drive 27 easy miles east on Highway 20 to the bustling and architecturally rich river town of Dubuque. Your first
stop is the old **Junkermann farm site** located within the 1,380-acre Mines of
Spain State Recreation Area. They do not call it a ghost farm, but the presence
of the former farm is somehow haunting. That is because it was all here—a working farm, an apple orchard, a root cellar, a winery—and all that is left are the remnants of these things. It is just enough to intrigue, and not enough to complete
the picture.

In 1859, Otto Junkermann, a German immigrant and wholesale druggist practicing in Dubuque, bought land with his partner, Julius Haas, and began to build a farm the next year. Junkermann started with a stone cottage and an attached summer kitchen, and soon had a working farm that produced medicinal herbs for the business, along with grapes and apples. The partners never lived on the farm, instead hiring two caretakers to see to things. Eventually, Mr. Junkermann began building a grand estate, but died before anything but the stone foundation could be laid. That was in 1883, and two years later, everything was sold off. A succession of 12 farmers followed, until 1943, when Junkermann's granddaughter and her husband bought everything back.

Follow the trail map to visit the sites, which begin at the **E. B. Lyons Interpretive Center**, 8999 Bellevue Heights Road, Dubuque, (319) 556-0620, www.state.ia.us/parks or www.minesofspain.org, and lead you on a thought-provoking journey through a beautiful woodland. First up is the Old Apple Orchard, which was located near the parking lot and used to be replanted for interpretive purposes. Unfortunately, it is now completely overgrown. Descend a series of stairs past former farm fields and a garden that have been reclaimed by nature. Explore the tiny Pine Chapel that Junkermann built in 1861, and the vineyard terraces that stairstep down to the Farm Site to take advantage of the good air drainage. There was a farmhouse here, but it burned in 1943, and all that remains is the stone foundation, along with that of the 1860 barn.

The Root Cellar is perhaps the most intriguing structure, because it looks like a mysterious cave or a ruined castle cut into the limestone outcroppings. Here vegetables were stored and preserved, and in later years, meats were smoked. Junkermann would make wine from his grapes, and he used the stone-arch Wine Cellar to store the bottles. Looping back toward the parking lot, the trail passes a Surface Lead Mine and a Shaft Lead Mine, but that is harvesting of a different nature, and the surrounding Mines of Spain land has many more stories to tell.

When you are ready to return to the twenty-first century, have fun exploring Dubuque's exciting new riverfront. Enjoy the Mississippi Riverwalk, National Mississippi River Museum and Aquarium, and the Grand Harbor Resort and Water Park, with its playfully designed slide that sneaks right out of the building and back in again. Grab a bite to eat in Dubuque too.

This weekend involves baseball as it was never played before, and in the middle of a corn field, no less. A weekend of farm toys that are almost as much a part of the American agricultural scene as are their real-life counterparts. A weekend that includes a farm of the imagination in a city that is as old as Iowa itself, and as young as its exciting new riverfront.

SPECIAL EVENTS

Summer Farm Toy Show, Dyersville, (563) 875-2727, (563) 875-2311, www.nationalfarmtoymuseum.com. Early June. Farm and construction toys for sale, tractor parade, great food.

Old-Fashioned Ice Cream Social, Dubuque, (800) 226-3369. July 4. Mathias

Sweet devotion
IN DUBUQUE COUNTY

Just south of Dubuque, thirty Trappistine nuns live in a cloistered community according to guidelines set forth by the Order of Cistercians of the Strict Observance back in 1098. Their abbey is situated on a 550-acre, certified organic farm that grows corn, soybeans, and oats, as well as vegetables in the kitchen garden. Farming is integral to the lives of these sisters.

"Throughout the history of monasticism, monks and nuns have lived on farms. The land has a special place in our Cistercian Benedictine spirituality. Not only does it feed our bodies, but also refreshes the spirit. Stewardship of the land is extremely important to us," explained Sister Suzanne Mattiuzzo.

"Only in recent times have we developed other industries," she added.

Here in Iowa, this means candy making. Anyone who pops a chewy Trappistine Creamy Caramel into their mouth may think they have gone to heaven. Indeed, one devotee described the experience as a "mouth party." Flavor choices include Irish mint, Swiss mint, hazelnut meltaways, hand-decorated truffles (French chocolate, dairy cream), vanilla and chocolate caramels, dark chocolate-coated caramels, and others in a variety of packaging. "We have tried over the years to introduce new flavors of caramels, but vanilla and chocolate are still the favorite. When we are making candy for Christmas gifts, we experiment with different ingredients. One of my favorites was Black Forest Caramel—walnuts and dried cherries in chocolate caramel. It was great! So far it is not for sale," Sister Suzanne Mattiuzzo mused.

Every batch of Trappistine Creamy Caramels begins with fine ingredients like cream, butter, and corn syrup that are individually measured and cooked by a sister and an assistant. The cream is slowly added to the mixture through a large dripper, and once the batch has reached the correct temperature, it is poured out onto a long table to harden. Next, it is cut into slabs and fed into a wrapping machine, or cut into pieces and coated with chocolate. "The aromas really do fill the air—especially outside on a crisp autumn day," said Sister Suzanne Mattiuzzo.

Throw your own "mouth party" by popping into one of the shops of downtown Dubuque or down at the Riverfront. Order online at www.trappistine.com, or by calling (866) 556-3400. Rest assured that, back at the abbey where fields of corn, soybeans, and oats wave in the wind high

The Pine Chapel, part of the Junkermann farm site at the Mines of Spain, Dubuque.

up above the Mississippi River, the sisters are saying a prayer for you. That's right—they pray for each one of their customers. 🐾

———————◆•◆•◆———————

Ham House historic site comes alive with music, food, children's activities, home tour, and, of course, ice cream!

Deppe Threshing and Antique Day, Cletus Deppe Farm, Bellevue, (563) 872-4170. Fourth Sunday in August. When a twenty-first-century farm family and the neighbors decide to recreate an old-fashioned grain harvest, you are in for a rare treat. Some farmers bought equipment for the event, others dusted off antiques, and they all learned how to bring in the grain nineteenth-century style. Demonstrations of threshing, clover hulling, rock crushing, corn shredding. 70 exhibitors, lunch available.

Czipar's Annual Apple Festival, Czipar's Orchard, 8562 Highway 52 South, Dubuque, (563) 582-7476. Late September. Sample varieties of apples, enjoy fresh-pressed cider, caramel apples, arts and crafts, and a flea market.

Sorghumfest, St. Donatus, (563) 773-2496. Late September. Observe the making of sorghum as it begins in the field and ends in the jar. Harvest goods for sale.

National Farm Toy Show, Beckman High School and Commercial Club Park, Dyersville, (800) 533-8293. First full weekend of November. Buy, sell, trade, drool.

PLACES TO EAT

Breitbach's Country Dining, 563 Balltown Road, Dubuque, (563) 552-2220. Iowa's oldest eating and drinking establishment first opened in 1852 and today makes everything from scratch, including soups, salads, and pies. Stuff accumulates after more than 150 years, so look for curiosities like the outlaw James gang horse blanket, and the 1934 gypsy mural that bought the wily wanderers a two-week stay.

Country Junction Restaurant, 913 15th Avenue SE, Dyersville, (563) 875-7055. In tribute to the Midwestern farmer, the casual restaurant is housed in a barn/silo replica, albeit with some materials rescued from old Iowa farms, and farm-antique décor. Breakfast, lunch, dinner. Here's an unusual deal: anyone not ordering a country dinner can share in the family-style sides for a small price. Thick-cut and smoked Iowa pork chop, Iowa ham steak, more.

Potter's Mill, 300 Potter Drive, Bellevue, (563) 872-3838, www.pottersmill.net. Dine and dream within this quaint 1843 gristmill at the confluence of Big Mill Creek and the Mississippi River. Home-style lunch, dinner, Sunday brunch. Also overnight accommodations.

PLACES TO STAY

Steamboat William M. Black and Boat and Breakfast, docked at National Mississippi River Museum and Aquarium, 350 East Third Street, Dubuque, (563) 557-9545, www.mississippirivermuseum.com. Overnight in a stateroom, dine in the galley of this 1934 steamer.

19. DANISH VILLAGES AND A "GARST" GETAWAY

East of the windswept Loess Hills, rows of corn and soybeans undulate across west-central Iowa. Here and there, the roofs of old barns sag in the way of old couches, but with an unmistakable antique quality. This is the part of Iowa where, back in the 1860s, Danish immigrants came to farm, to erect tidy villages, to mix up batches of *æbleskiver*, and to stay forever. Today they represent America's largest concentration of Danes in a traditionally rural setting. Come for a taste of Danish culture and hospitality, and let the people tell you of the love story that brought a windmill from Denmark to Iowa. It is the story of an entire community's love for a shared heritage, and it happened long after the first settlers left their homeland.

The Danish Villages are located 85 miles west of Des Moines and about 60 miles northeast of Council Bluffs, Iowa and Omaha, Nebraska. Most of the tour happens a few short miles north of I-80. It features the Danish Villages of Elk Horn and Kimballton, but branches out to get a look at surrounding towns of related interest. All in all, the counties that you will be traveling through are Audubon, Carroll, Shelby, and Pottawattamie. There is no way to miss the Elk Horn exit off I-80. Just follow the billboards to Exit 54 and go 6 miles north on Highway 173.

Elk Horn

The **Danish Windmill**, (712) 764-7472, www.danishwindmill.com, was built on a Danish farm in 1848. In 1975, an Elk Horn farmer thought it would be great to have a real Danish windmill in his hometown, so, with massive community support, it was funded, shipped, and reassembled here in 1977. This despite challenges from U.S. Customs, overland trucking companies, and Danish carpenters who, it is reported, figured the American Danes could never put it back together again. It took a year, but these farmers, contractors, and other skilled workers (who had built lots of things but never a windmill) galvanized tractors, a boom truck, a crane, professional expertise, and volunteer sweat, and got the job done. Read the complete story in the book *Velkommen to The Danish Windmill*, available on-site.

The self-guided mill tour begins with a 15-minute video. Climb to the top of the structure, see the grinding stones, and watch the sails turn if the wind is up. Together weighing nearly 2,200 pounds, the grinding stones are made of agate and concrete. Only the top runner stone turns, while the bottom bedstone remains stationary, and the resultant friction grinds the grain to the desired texture. A pattern of grooves cut into the stones controls the movement of the grains. The mechanism is completely functional, but in order to meet current safety standards, the rye and wheat flour sold to visitors is stone-ground at the adjacent millhouse, using stainless steel equipment of modern make.

A block north of the windmill, Elk Horn Foodtown, which sits between Broadway and Washington streets, would be an ordinary small-town market except that it carries Danish meats, cheeses, and bread in addition to regular groceries. Take a left on Washington Street and go 4 blocks west to the **Danish Immigrant Museum**, 2212 Washington Street, Elk Horn, (712) 764-7001, www.dkmuseum.org. This national resource of Danish heritage in America sits tucked into a beautiful hillside on 33 acres that offer endless views of farmland. The half-timbered museum building represents just the start of an ambitious complex in which the buildings themselves help to tell the cultural story. Future plans call for a Danish-American heritage village and a Danish-American farmstead. The farm will be of a historic design wherein the barn, livestock, and crop storage quarters are connected to the home.

The museum has a wealth of cultural items on display. For instance, there is a little item called a meat box that was used in an early Danish community located in Minnesota. Apparently, the settlers had organized something called a meat ring, so that when livestock was butchered, each of the families that belonged to the meat ring got cuts for their meat boxes. They took turns taking the best cuts so that everyone got a fair share. It was not communal, but cooperative, in the very early days of refrigeration. Entertaining was planned around the meat ring schedule, so that the finest cuts could be served at the most important events in a family's life. The meat box before you is a small thing that sheds great light on the early American Heartland.

Kimballton

Three gorgeous miles north of Elk Horn on Highway 173 lies Kimballton, which has a miniature *bondehus* or Danish farm cottage, and the small but significant **General Store Museum and National Corn Husking Museum**. The two museums are housed together in the same building on the main street of town. Walk into the tiny storefront building and back to a time when women heated irons on the stovetop and got clothes their whitest with something called Blueing. View old farm toys, spinning wheels, milk cans, and butter boxes from the Crystal Springs Creamery of Kimballton. Learn about the candle test for eggs and the oyster shells for chickens.

The National Corn Husking Museum is even smaller than the General Store Museum, but it has a big story to tell. Once commonly done by hand, corn husking was an important skill for a farmer to have. That began to change in the 1930s with the arrival of picking machines. View a scale model of a husker, team, and wagon in a corn field, a full-size shovel board and scoop shovel, husking hooks and pegs, a hand corn sheller, contest books, and news clippings. But as you will discover, corn husking hasn't disappeared from the American farm scene.

Kimballton is where the official state Hand Corn Husking Contest has been held since 1991, and where several national contests have also taken place. Almost the whole town gets involved, with Danish breakfasts, dinners, a parade, food stands and the 10-, 20-, or 30-minute contests offered for various age and gender classes. Since the husking is done the old-fashioned way, by hand, the wagon that collects the husked corn is pulled by a team of horses, just as it used to be done all over the American Heartland. It is about the thwack of dry cobs against the

Danish Windmill, Elk Horn.

Demystifying Æbleskiver

Everyone in the Danish Villages knows about æbleskiver, but most outsiders need some enlightenment about this un-Americanized Danish delight. The translation is "apple turnover," says Clayton Jens Nielsen of the National Corn Husking Museum in Kimballton. "But I've never seen *æbleskiver* eaten with apples," he adds. Jan Paulsen, a former tour coordinator over at the windmill in Elk Horn, agrees the traditional Danish way is to put apple inside, but she doesn't see it done that way around here, either. And depending on whom you talk to, the pronunciation is ABBL-skeever or ABBL-skiver.

In the Danish Villages, they describe *æbleskiver* as light, round, and like pancakes. But there's a problem. Thinking pancakes, American Danes eat them for breakfast, on any morning they feel like pulling out the *æbleskiver* pan, whereas they will tell you that in Denmark, they are eaten for dessert, and only around Christmastime. How you eat them and what you eat them with is different, too. "The Danes take them in their hands and dip them in sugar, but I break them, and Calvin puts butter on them, but most don't. And then I use a little syrup and a little jam, but it's whatever a person wants to do," says Phyllis Hoegh, spooning on homemade wild raspberry jam during breakfast at the Our House Bed and Breakfast one summer morning.

Calvin Hoegh happily defends his non-traditional butter version. But he stands firm on the proper size and shape of an *æbleskiver*, which is not, he insists, that of a fried egg. After Phyllis mixes her special batter, Calvin fills each of the pan's round cups to the proper level and begins cooking. At the right moment, he deftly turns each *æbleskiver* over in its cup, so that it can finish cooking and achieve its distinctive round shape. "That's the way they're supposed to look," he says, done cooking.

Armed with these insider tips and the recipe below courtesy of the Hoeghs, you can try making *æbleskiver* at home, but you still need the unique *æbleskiver* pan. The windmill gift shop stocks non-stick and cast iron versions. To really get a sense of perspective, you can also see some antique pans on display at the Danish Immigrant Museum.

Æbleskiver

6 eggs, beaten until cream color
2$\frac{1}{2}$ cups buttermilk
$\frac{1}{2}$ teaspoon lemon flavoring
Beat together.

Add:
3 cups flour
2 tablespoons baking powder
³/₄ teaspoon baking soda
1¹/₂ teaspoon salt
3 tablespoons sugar
Beat again.

Cook in *æbleskiver* pan with a little oil in each cup. Turn frequently to get ball shape. Good luck and enjoy. You may divide eggs and beat whites and add last—maybe a little fluffier—but not necessary.
Recipe from Phyllis and Calvin Hoegh, Elk Horn, Iowa, courtesy "Our House" Æbleskiver 🐦

———— • — • ————

bang board, the occasional snort of patient horses, the swift movements of huskers, and the anticipation of the crowd.

Planting the Seeds Of Fun

For real rural recreation, nothing beats a visit to Garst Farm Resort in Coon Rapids. Coon Rapids is not designated as one of the area's Danish Villages, but it is only 42 miles from Kimballton, and **Garst Farm Resort**, 1390 Highway 141, Coon Rapids, (712) 684-2964, www.farmresort.com, is just too good to pass up. Garst Farm Resort is the family home of Roswell Garst (1898-1977), who was instrumental in the development and acceptance of hybrid corn, and who hosted Soviet Premier Nikita Khrushchev in 1959. Do everything under the sun—and the stars—on these 4,500 acres. No other Midwest farm-immersion experience can match this spread for sheer size and scope, but expect to drive on gravel and to respect the active farming operation. Decide what you want to do in advance, then make arrangements for your individually tailored visit. It is not an inclusive resort, so each organized activity is individually, and reasonably, priced.

Ready for some country fun? Here are some of the things you can do. Guided trail riding at Garst Farm Resort is popular for good reason. Even beginning riders will get an opportunity to feel some of the excitement of horseback riding, because outings include not just walking, but also trotting and cantering gaits. The Middle Raccoon River and private ponds supply canoeing and fishing pleasure, and you can even swim in the river at the River House Campground. When darkness falls in this region, it falls hard, for it is said to have the darkest nighttime skies in all of Iowa, because light pollution is kept to an absolute minimum. So on clear nights, the Astronomy Tour becomes an unforgettable experience. Getting around is easy on a John Deere Gator that you can rent to drive on dirt roads past ponds, cattle, a dance-hall barn, a Depression-era log cabin, restored prairies, and woodlands.

Garst Farm Resort, Coon Rapids.

Garst Farm Resort embraces conservation practices such as terracing on hillsides. Learn about this and other aspects of modern crop and cattle farming with a guided tour of this commercial operation. Or opt for the Alternative Agriculture Tour, which takes you to a separate, smaller operation where antique apples and honeybees thrive. Visit the gift shop in the basement of the Garst Home Farm to purchase frozen buffalo meat, a tub of the alternative farm's cinnamon creamed honey, and additional local goods. People who take an interest in the environment will enjoy turkey stalking and raptor experiences. And, if all of this is not enough, plan to just spend time in the country where you can reconnect with family and friends.

The best way to take it all in is to stay overnight on the property (see below for accommodation options), because then you can enjoy sunsets and full country breakfasts (included or optional, depending on your accommodation choice) that feature local, seasonal ingredients. Overnight guests may enjoy a history talk by Roswell and Elizabeth Garst's granddaughter, Liz Garst, who runs the resort on this working farm. They can also take a self-guided tour around the cattle-breeding buildings, where the rates of weight gain, ease of calving, and other statistics of the farm's thousand-head herd are monitored.

More Farms

There are a lot more rural-themed places to see around here. From Coon Rapids, you could go over to the **Farmstead Museum**, Swan Lake State Park, 22811 Swan Lake Drive, Carroll, (712) 792-4614. Carroll is 24 miles northwest of Coon Rapids, and the park is two miles south and one mile east of Carroll. Wander among the agricultural machinery and conservation displays in the old red barn, and commune with the petting-zoo critters.

Then you can head south on Highway 71 and west along Highway 141, a total of about 22 miles, to the **German Hausbarn, Leet-Hassler Farmstead, Hausbarn Restaurant and Konferenz Centre**, 12196 311th Street, Manning, (712) 655-3131. The thatched roof is the shining star of the Hausbarn, a brick structure that was actually built in Schleswig-Holstein, Germany in 1660, and reconstructed here in 1999. In a literal grassroots effort, the roof was made on-site by professional thatchers who came in from Germany, using reeds grown near the Baltic Sea. The roof's expected lifespan is an impressive 75 years. The Hausbarn, where seventeenth- and eighteenth-century German farmers shared living quarters with their animals, would have been called a *bauernhaus*, or farmer's house. The *herd*, a fireplace from which smoke rose through airways and filtered through the reeds, was used for cooking, smoking meat, and generating heat. In the living area, the family would have heated cherry pits or pebbles over the fire to put at the foot of their beds for warmth on cold nights. Don't miss the 1915 Leet-Hassler Farmstead just back of the Hausbarn, which includes a bungalow, carriage house, and six outbuildings. This farmstead is original to the site, and was once home to a fine Poland China hog operation that commanded $20,000 for a single boar in 1920.

From there, you might want to go back east on 141, then south on 71 for about 20 miles to Audubon. South of town, **Albert the Bull** pays tribute, in a big way, to the beef industry. Weighing in at 45 tons, Albert would be more than ready for market, except that his concrete-and-steel body is too tough for most tastes. Continue south to the small **Nathaniel Hamlin Museum and Park**, 1887 215th Street, Audubon, (712) 563-3780, a work in progress to which local farmers have donated 18 windmills. The brick house has a pioneer kitchen equipped with a wood-burning combination cook stove, cast iron utensils, and side pantry. The park's Corn Museum houses a corn husking display, especially in honor of two strapping brothers. It seems that in 1935 Elmer Carlson broke the world record for corn husking and was sent by President Harry Truman to Europe after World War II to teach modern agricultural practices to the farmers there, and his brother, Carl Carlson, was the Corn Husking Champion of 1936. The Machinery Building's 200-foot mural illustrates the movement of cattle from western plains to Iowa feedlots and eventually to the family table, and there are antique tractors, plows, cultivators, a grain drill, a reaper, and a treadmill to view. Continuing south on Highway 71 a mile south of Exira, you come to **Plow-in-the-Oak Park**, where it is said that before going off to serve in the Civil War, a farmer leaned his plow against a sapling and the tree simply grew around it. The plow is still there, but increasingly less visible.

By the way, the distance from Coon Rapids to Carroll to Manning to Audubon is about 65 miles.

From Exira, head south a few miles to I-80 and take that west to the Shelby exit. Cross the interstate to the south and follow the signs toward **Carstens 1880 Farmstead**, 32409 308th Street, Shelby, (712) 544-2404, www.thefarmstead.org.

Visit during Farm Days on the first weekend after Labor Day, on Sunday afternoons from June to August, or by appointment. This three-generation German family farm sits on 80 acres. It is very much a work in progress, a labor of love by an organization of area residents. The traditional yellow farmhouse (1888) is in the early stages of restoration, so do not expect to see an elegant Victorian parlor or a wealth of artifacts, but do appreciate the fact that furnishings are original, including a straw bed. That is something to consider. Beds have come a long way since they were made of straw. People usually cannot wait to get rid of an old and worn bed and replace it with a new one. For a family to keep a straw bed in the house as late as the 1970s is often what makes it possible for such an item to not only become a museum piece, but also to have a provenance, a tie to real life.

The blacksmith shop has a secret beer bottle cooler dug eight feet down in the floor. The chicken coop (1915) is so big it has windows on two levels, and the horse and dairy cattle barn dates back to 1888. Carstens Farmstead is so well documented (the family threw *nothing* away) that along with an old tractor is a memo from the office manager of the Avery Company. Dated July 18, 1923, and reprinted in the farmstead newspaper, it advises Mr. H. J. Carstens that the "second hand 12/25 Tractor you ordered recently was shipped from Omaha today on NOGN Car No. 746." But this is not just a quaint farm. Fifty acres of its cropland are leased out to a local farmer who keeps it productive in the present day. So as you study the artifacts and relax beneath the shade of old trees, you still get the feel of a working farm.

This is a weekend that celebrates folkways intrinsic to the Midwestern farmer, and those that set the Danish heritage apart from all others. It's a weekend of being among people who love to share their heritage with visitors, whether that heritage is Danish or agricultural or a little of both.

SPECIAL EVENTS

Tivoli Fest, Elk Horn, (800) 451-7960, www.elkhorniowa.com. Memorial Day weekend. Scandinavian folk dancing, mill and museum tours, Danish open-face sandwiches and desserts at the Town Hall, *æbleskiver* and *medisterpølse* (Danish version of pancakes and sausage) at the Fire Station.

Sigmon Threshing Bee, Arlin Sigmon Farm, 3825 Xavier Avenue, just southwest of Auburn, Carroll County, (712) 688-7782. Last Sunday of August. Traditional threshing bee and antique equipment power show.

Farm Days, Carstens 1880 Farmstead, 32409 308th Street, Shelby, (712) 544-2404. Weekend after Labor Day. Threshers' breakfasts, threshing, sawmilling, field demonstrations, sheep shearing, loom work, blacksmithing, corn shelling, straw baling, house tours, petting zoo, kid's tractor pull, pork barbeque, cake walk.

Manning German Hausbarn Oktoberfest, 12196 311th Street, Manning, (712) 655-3131. Early October. German dancing, music, food. Pick pumpkins and gourds from the pumpkin patch, enjoy horseback rides.

State Hand Corn Husking Contest and Festival, Kimballton, call (712) 773-2112

The historic Carstens 1880 Farmstead, Shelby.

(ask for Paul C. Christensen, Monday through Friday, 8:00 a.m. to 5:00 p.m.). Second full weekend in October. Saturday night banquet, Sunday morning Danish breakfast with *æbleskiver* and Danish sausage, community worship service, working machinery and equipment displays, pioneer craft demonstrations, food stands, and parade of horses, wagons and huskers.

PLACES TO EAT

Chatterbox Café, 120 North Division Street, Audubon, (712) 563-3428. 6:00 a.m. to 8:00 p.m. Monday through Saturday. Everyone's talking about the homemade tenderloins, homemade pie, daily specials.

Danish Inn, 4116 Main Street, Elk Horn, (712) 764-4251. Traditional Danish cuisine with beautiful, healthy open-face sandwiches.

Jacquelyn's Danish Bake Shoppe and Kaffe Hus, 4234 Main Street, Elk Horn, (712) 764-3100. Homemade lunch, Danish breads, kringle, pastries, fresh-ground coffee.

PLACES TO STAY

Garst Farm Resort, 1390 Highway 141, Coon Rapids, (712) 684-2964, www .farmresort.com. Individually priced activities include guided commercial-farm and alternative-agriculture tours, horseback riding, John Deere Gator rental (like a golf cart, but with oomph), fishing in any of 15 stocked ponds, canoeing, stargazing, and the list goes on. Stay in the Home Farm B&B, which has the look of the 1940s and includes a big farm breakfast featuring fresh, local ingredients, or choose among additional houses (including the Hollyhock Cottage, which

FIELD NOTES

Stopping off at a cattle feedlot

Monte Hoegh owns a cattle feedlot just outside of Elk Horn. His recipe for Iowa corn-fed beef starts each autumn with a trip to the ranchlands of South Dakota. There he buys some 600 head of 450– to 550–pound feeder cattle, mostly Black Angus, some Red Angus, as well as other breeds. He selects individuals with an experienced eye, looking, for instance, for the ability to gain weight by frame size.

Once back in Elk Horn, Hoegh, who's the nephew of Calvin Hoegh (he of local *æbleskiver* fame), starts the one-year-olds on a growing ration of corn silage (the whole plant, chopped), ground hay, and commercial feed with protein, minerals, and vitamins. On his 1,200 acres, Monte also grows the Iowa corn that the cattle enjoy. From October through March, he turns them out into the field to munch on grass and morsels that the combine didn't pick up, as well as nutritional supplements.

Now that the cattle weigh some 800 pounds, it is back to the feed yard for increased amounts of corn, along with other feeds. The cattle reach market weight of 1,200–1,400 pounds during the period of August through November. Buyers come to the farm, then Hoegh delivers the finished cattle to area packing plants.

The cycle is ended, but with autumn in the air, the new one is just beginning. And so it is time for Monte Hoegh to take that drive to the ranchlands of South Dakota again.

Note: not open to the public.

was originally built as a chicken coop) and camping.

Our House Bed and Breakfast, 2007 Washington Street, Elk Horn, (712) 764-4111. Relax at this cozy, in-town bungalow with beautiful wood built-ins, rocking chairs, and heartwarming comfort. Main floor guestroom with private bath. Phyllis and Calvin Hoegh, the Danish couple who may as well be your own grandparents, work magic with country hospitality and lots of food. Enjoy homemade *æbleskiver* (light, pancake-like balls) at breakfast with homemade preserves, and buy homegrown veggies from Calvin's garden.

Taylor Hill Lodge, 1667 Highway 71, Audubon, (712) 563-2248, www.thlodge. com. Remodeled English barn, six rooms, four full baths, fireplace, loft, outdoor patio, full breakfast. Former livestock and hay barn in the family for three generations.

20. COUNTRY IN THE CITY: THIS IS DES MOINES?

Des Moines is growing and reconstructing itself, yet not at the expense of its agricultural roots, for this capital city is careful not to plow the past under steel and glass. Urban culture dominates the scene, but you would be hard-pressed to find another city that devotes so much space and spirit to the farming way of life. Between Living History Farms and the Iowa State Fairgrounds, you are looking at a thousand acres, and as for spirit, it shines in the eyes of every blue-ribbon winner. Both geographically and symbolically, Des Moines is in the heart of the Heartland's great agricultural expanse.

Living History Farms

First, let's go down to the farm; actually, three of them in a single attraction. Located northwest of downtown Des Moines, the 600-acre **Living History Farms**, 2600 111th Street, Urbandale, (515) 278-5286, www.livinghistoryfarms.org, immerses you in the farms of three eras, along with a town, extensive Visitor Center services, and the newer agricultural exhibits. The advantage of depicting a three-hundred-year time span, from the years 1700 to 2000, is that visitors can discover how turning points profoundly changed the work of the farm. Costumed interpreters bring it all to life in the third person, and frequently invite you to try your hand at activities that are as new as they are old—crosscut sawing, oxen grooming, corn shelling.

Board the tractor ride that chugs along to the 1700 Ioway Indian farm. Sketched out here is a pre-settlement farm consisting of seasonal houses that have been authentically crafted of bark and twigs. The little farm is planted with the "three sisters of life," which are yellow squash, red beans, and blue corn. Learn about how these foods were harvested and dried before being cached underground until ready for use. Depending on what needs to be done during your visit, you may be taught the secret of braiding strips of corn husk into rope, help gather berries, or help make fry bread and jerky.

Take a woodland hike to the 1850 Pioneer Farm, where the experience of Midwestern farm life is much more settled, yet still a far cry from the present day. Oxen do the heavy fieldwork (along with the staff). Inside the log cabin, the farm wife may be cooking fragrant shepherd's pie over her open hearth. She might tell you how she uses sand to help draw moisture from vegetables that are drying in the root cellar. The farmer may tell you how he has built split rail fences and a wooden barn that is significantly smaller than later versions, because its purpose is to store tools and some crops rather than to house animals and heavy machinery. He grows corn, oats, and potatoes. The family keeps iridescent-green Cayuga ducks, chickens, and pointy-nosed hogs. Visitors can help churn butter, mow with a scythe, card wool, or do any number of other chores—there is no job shortage on an 1850 farm.

Go around the barn to the dawn of a new century at the 1900 Horse-Powered Farm with its signature wooden windmill, big red barn, assorted outbuildings, and

Jessemynn Kanis cooks up some shepherd's pie and potatoes at the 1850 Pioneer Farm exhibit, Living History Farms, Urbandale.

classic white farmhouse. Get a whiff of pork pie, ketchup making, or bread baking at the 1887 kitchen woodstove that is still used daily. You can even eat here, by reserving your seat at a family-style 1900 Farm Dinner. These special-event meals feature fried chicken, roast beef or ham roast, potatoes, side dishes, homemade rolls with churned butter and jams/jellies, beverages, and dessert. The dinners last about two and one-half hours, there is an additional fee, and participation is by advance reservation only. Here's an incentive to sign up early: the first party to make a reservation for a given date picks the meat choice. So make plans to sit down with the family and share a meal they will likely remember all their lives.

Outside, Percheron horses have taken over the work of oxen, since the tough virgin prairie has already been broken and is now easier to work. Corn, oats, and hay are the crops of choice. Keep those garden gloves on, because there is more work to be done, 1900-style. Try your hand at milking a cow, cultivating a field with a horse, loading manure, putting up hay, shocking or shoveling oats, making candy, preserving food, or whatever needs doing.

Grab a bite to eat at the 1875 Town of Walnut Hill, which depicts the interdependence between farmers and craftspeople such as blacksmiths and general store keepers. If the implement dealer tells you that red plow over there is actually a John Deere, he is not trying to hoodwink you. It is just that the legendary company did not adopt its trademark colors until 1908. Tour the rest of Walnut Hill's 17 structures, including the Beem Broom-maker Shop where crowds gather to watch old-fashioned broom making. Over in the blacksmith shop, you might hear the wise-guy smithy call out, "Whoa, watch your hind foot there!" to a little kid attempting to cross a rope barrier. The showpiece of Walnut Hill is the 1870 Flynn Farm Mansion, a gingerbread-encrusted brick beauty that is original to the site, along with its matching barn. Don't miss it.

Leading to the Henry A. Wallace Exhibit Center is the "Seeds of Change," a crop walk featuring varieties of crops that have grown in Iowa over the years. The center contains numerous exhibits showing agricultural innovations—particularly mechanized ones—that revolutionized farming over the past hundred years. The cement-walled, sod-roofed structure offers welcome relief with, ah, air-conditioning, restrooms, water fountains, and beverage machines. Join the farmers who sit enthralled before the John Deere sales films from the 1940s. Compare model farms that show how the traditional farmhouse has been replaced with a single-story ranch house, and how the open-slatted corn crib became the metal grain bin. Such changes are dramatically depicted in aerial photos of one Minnesota farm, photos that were shot over time in the 1950s, 1970s, and 1990s.

Discovering Des Moines

Who was Henry A. Wallace? Let's go to his grandfather's home, **The Wallace House**, to find out (open weekends by appointment). The restored 1882 Victorian home where Henry Wallace lived is located almost 10 miles east of the Living History Farms and very near downtown Des Moines. The address is 756 16th

Street (at Center Street), Des Moines, (515) 243-7063, www.wallace.org. Henry A. Wallace developed commercial hybrid seed corn in 1926 and later served as the U.S. Secretary of Agriculture. He was the grandson of Henry Wallace, who was a national leader in agriculture and conservation. Not to confuse you, but Henry Wallace (1836–1916) was the first of five Henry Wallaces, and the man who founded and edited the trade journal *Wallaces' Farmer*, which is still available. Exhibits include the Wallace Era of *Wallaces' Farmer*, a multimedia timeline of the life of Henry A. Wallace and a perennial garden of plant varieties that grew here when the various Wallaces were in residence. The house had gone through some rough times, and so it does not have original furnishings and even a fireplace had to be replaced. But two paintings on display were kindly donated back by Wallace family descendants.

Drive east through town and across the Des Moines River toward the gloriously gold-domed State Capitol building. Park free in the lot just to the west of the spectacular structure (take in a tour of the Capitol building while you are at it) and walk west to the **State Historical Society Museum**, 600 East Locust Street, Des Moines, (515) 281-5111, www.iowahistory.org. This place is first-rate, with extensive exhibits on two levels. There is plenty to take in, and the agricultural exhibits tell a great story. Kids can push a plow and heft a yoke, balancing the equivalent weight of two buckets filled with water, then consider what it would have been like to do so four times a day, 365 days a year, as some pioneer children did to help their families survive. Learn the history of grain that tapped into ready sources of power—Iowa's waterways—and made economic sense in the late 1800s. Turn a model waterwheel by hand to feel the force that water would have had to exert to move the heavy buhrstones, and view a portable mill that was first used on the Iowa River in 1877. The exhibit "A Few of Our Favorite Things: 100 Creations of the Twentieth Century" is a wonderful amalgamation of artifacts, including seed corn signs, seed sacks, and miniature sample sacks that Pioneer distributed to farmers in 1948 when promoting its revolutionary new hybrid corn. Still attached to one sample sack is a sales-pitch poem from "Garst and Thomas, Hybrid Corn Company, Coon Rapids, IA." Learn about the emergence of Iowa's soybean crop in the 1940s, and view little bits of history like the butter boxes labeled "Pride O' Langworthy, mfgd. by Farmers Mutual Co-op Creamery Co., Langworthy, IA."

Fair Skies Ahead

Feel the need for some really big fun? Expect fair skies ahead when the **Iowa State Fair** comes to town. This is it, the granddaddy event that inspired Rogers and Hammerstein's hit Broadway musical *State Fair*. It is held for 10 days each August on the Iowa State Fairgrounds, located east of downtown and 12 blocks east of I-235 at East 30th Street and University Avenue, Des Moines; call (515) 262-3111 or visit www.iowastatefair.org. Bang-for-your-buck admission and parking fees apply. Make plans for lodging far, far in advance, because every good room fills up fast. Expect to find more old-fashioned country fun than would seem possible in the city, from champion cows to those sculpted from butter. The Iowa State Fair has all the sights, sounds, and smells you would expect from one of the biggest parties around.

Just how big is this thing? It varies by year, but consider that in a recent year, there were an estimated 55,000 food, livestock, and other entries; $400,000 awarded in premiums; 12 major building and exhibit facilities; 80 rides, shows, and games; 400 acres of land (160 in campgrounds); 1,000,000 visitors; and the biggest Foods Department of any state fair. Throw yourself into the whirlwind and eat it all up, because Iowans have had over 150 years to perfect the show.

The Iowa State Fair shows off the Hawkeye State's agricultural know-how with everything from livestock judging to farm machinery exhibited across 20 acres. A good starting point is the John Deere Agriculture Building (1904), which sits on an angle right about in the middle of the fairgrounds (Rock Island and Grand avenues; yes, this thing has its own streets). Check the schedule for the free sweet corn feed that will be held outside. Inside, tables overflow with the year's finest vegetable, fruit, and grain entries, and once the ribbons have been awarded, see if you too can figure out why this plate of "Beans, Snap, edible stage, 12 specimens" edged out the one next to it. Catch a cooking demonstration. Pick up recipes and coloring booklets from the USDA and other exhibitors. Gape at this year's Duffy's Butter Cow. What's a butter cow? It's a fair icon, a sculpture of a cow rendered in butter.

Cut across Pella Plaza, where flags wave high above splashy water jets that cool everyone off, to the round Pavilion, and catch a livestock judging from a bleacher seat. Then it is on to the livestock barns: cattle, swine, sheep, youth cattle, and horse. Listen to what the judges have to say. "She's one of the longer-bodied ewes in this particular class, you certainly like her for that, she's really got a lot of elevation, and I think a great future ahead," summarizes one. Check the schedule for the Dairy Goat Celebrity Milking Contest, 4-H Market Swine Show, and other events. In the pens where well-scrubbed creatures like creamy-white Saanen dairy goats and wide-eyed Jersey cows sleep on straw, you will see makeshift beds where many of the young exhibitors also catch winks when they can. Dog lovers will especially enjoy the sheep dog trials, as border collies help their handlers to control the movements of sheep with laser eyes and precision timing. Pop into the 50,000-square-foot 4-H Exhibit Building to stroll past the young people's displays on everything from clothing construction to peach preservation. Don't be shy about asking questions of the exhibitors, because if you have never milked a goat in your life, this world might need a little explanation. Enjoy share-the-fun performances, participate in the working exhibits, and listen to the educational presentations on everything from pie making to showing model horses.

Ready for refreshment? The Iowa State Fair has every kind of food and drink you could want on a steamy summer day. Classic fair fare comes on a stick. So stuff yourself silly with Iowa Pork Chop on a Stick, Corn Dog on a Stick, Pickle on a

Stick, Cheese on a Stick, Chocolate-Covered Banana on a Stick, Fried Candy Bar on a Stick, Stick of Butter on a Stick (kidding). Keep your energy level high with hot and cold sandwiches, walking tacos, curly fries, fruit cups, and lemonade.

Before hitting those mad midway rides, why not see what's happening in Heritage Village? Pioneer Hall (1886) contains quiet exhibits such as a blacksmith shop, but shakes to the rafters when the Ladies' Husband Calling Contest gets underway. At the Hawkeye Gas Engine/Antique Tractor Display, steam engines cough and splutter like angry little things. Grandfather's Farm is the ultimate respite—quiet, tree-shaded, and just a little harder to find.

For a small fee and a bird's-eye view of the fair, board Sky Glider number 1 to the circa-1921 Ye Old Mill ride, then walk west on Grand Avenue to the Family Center, where you can buy the *State Fair Cookbook* and view the staggering variety of food entries that vie for coveted premiums in some 150 divisions— yeast breads, Iowa wines, pickles in 21 classes, bread pudding, ribs, honey, and muffins, jumbo. Living History Farms sponsors the Recipes & Remedies of Yesteryear contest with some 46 classes like Lard & Cracklings and Blackbird Pie. To win their Apple Paring contest, entrants must peel an apple before the eagle eye of a judge, and end up with one continuous peel. Get comfortable as you watch the judging of, say, comfort foods like chicken pot pies, meat loaves, and mashed potatoes and gravy.

The Great Iowa Harvest

Living History Farms and the Iowa State Fair are the biggies in Des Moines, but the city has yet more local flavor that is worth crowing about. How about a stop at the **Des Moines Farmers' Market?** You do not have to get up with the sun to find the day's freshest produce, coffee, and donuts, but you can if you wish, because the Des Moines Farmers' Market is open for business from 7:00 a.m. to 1:00 p.m. It spills across several blocks around Court Avenue and Fourth Street, west of the Des Moines River. So make plans to fit this source-direct shopping spree into your Des Moines getaway.

Have a hankering for Iowa sweet corn? Come and get it in late summer, when one vendor will even feed you on the spot, roasting up sunshine-yellow ears and supplying plenty of butter and salt. How about selecting some juicy, red tomatoes, green beans or Missouri peaches? Sample the likes of basil oil on Italian bread or piquant salsa on a cracker, and take home jars of honey and fruit preserves. Along with Cleverley Farms' (Mingo) heirloom veggies and garlic, you can pick up Niman Ranch pork cuts, which are the darling of local chefs and produced from humanely treated pigs. Enjoy live music and friendly chats with the farmers who grew all of this great food, and wouldn't that bunch of sunflowers brighten your afternoon picnic spread?

A great Iowa harvest is always in store at **Heart of Iowa Market Place,** 221 Fifth Street, West Des Moines, (515) 274-4692, www.heartofiowamarketplace.com. It's one of the great little shops of Historic Valley Junction, www.valleyjunction.com,

Freshly picked sweet corn at the Des Moines Farmers' Market, with the Polk County Courthouse in the background.

which is located southwest of downtown Des Moines in West Des Moines. To get there from I-235, take the 63rd Street or Eighth Street exit, go south, and follow the brown directional signs. Instead of chain stores, you will find independent proprietors; and instead of contrived buildings, you will enjoy turn-of-the-century storefronts with original charm intact. The Heart of Iowa Market Place shop loads its shelves with Iowa specialty foods like Trappistine Creamy Caramels (Dubuque), Maytag Blue Cheese (Newton), Regi's Cranberries (Des Moines), and Log Chain Honey and corn-shaped beeswax candles (Allerton). The store also stocks Prairieland Herbs' (Woodward) Darn Good Soap brand; some of the bars come in the shape of cows. You will also take delight in the Dessert Factory's (West Des Moines) brightly colored candy suckers that are shaped into pig's heads, tractors, and corn on the cob.

About a block down, **Kavanaugh Gallery**, 131 Fifth Street, West Des Moines, (515) 279-8682, represents artists from around the world and also from the regional American Heartland. Among the available works, you can find gorgeous farm landscapes to beautify your home and to always remind you of your weekend in Des Moines.

This weekend should prove that it's never hard to find the country in the city of Des Moines. From living history farms to a farmers' market to the state fair that they write songs about, this city has it all. And when people start craving that great Iowa beef, pork, and sweet corn, it will be waiting for them, right here in the heart of the Heartland.

SPECIAL EVENTS

Iowa Horse Fair, Iowa State Fairgrounds, 12 blocks east of I-235 at East 30th Street and University Avenue, Des Moines, April. Enjoy performances, demos, speakers, and the beauty of horses, from the American Bashkir Curly to the Welsh Pony. Thrill to one of the country's fastest-growing equestrian sports, cowboy mounted shooting. It is a rule-governed competition like any other, except it involves galloping, shooting (blanks), and 1800s garb.

At Living History Farms:

FARM TO FASHION. Early May. Wool, flax, and other fibers are spun into yarn, woven into cloth, and sewn into clothing. Take home a free bottle of sarsaparilla.

SHEAR ENTERTAINMENT. Early May. Horned Dorset and Border Leicester sheep are clipped by expert hands and organized by border collies.

BRINGING IN THE SHEAVES: OAT AND WHEAT HARVEST. Late July. Flails smash and threshers rumble as the oats are brought in from the field, and later used to feed the animals throughout the winter.

FARMSTEADING IN THE MIDWEST. Late August. How the first American farms were bought, supplied, and operated.

FALL HARVEST WEEKEND. Early October. Sample apple butter and other products of the Iowa harvest. Learn about the history of corn and take a horse-drawn wagon ride into the fields for demonstrations of machine-harvested corn as it would have been done from 1910 to 1950. Learn to pick corn by hand.

Wolf "Dessert" Train, Boone & Scenic Valley Railroad, 225 10th Street, Boone, (800) 626-0319, www.scenic-valleyrr.com. Weekends from Memorial Day Weekend to October 31, plus Memorial Day, July 4, Labor Day. Linger over dessert and coffee on a two and one-half hour, 22-mile roundtrip ride through the Des Moines River Valley. Reservations encouraged. Also four-course Dinner Train on Saturday evenings April through December 13. Reservations required.

PLACES TO EAT

Iowa Machine Shed, 11151 Hickman Road (I-80/35 at Hickman Road), exit 125, Urbandale, (515) 270-6818. At Living History Farms, and the farm-theme décor is beautifully done. Farm-style favorites on the lunch menu include double-roasted Iowa pork chop, Plowman's Meatloaf™, old-fashioned pot roast. Dinners include Parmesan Crusted America's Cut, which is a pork filet that is charbroiled and served over wild rice and beneath a Parmesan butter sauce.

Iowa Room Restaurant, Renaissance Savery Hotel, 401 Locust Street, Des Moines, (515) 244-2151. Savory Midwestern cuisine. Savery Salad combines Boston bibb lettuce with Maytag Blue Cheese, candied walnuts, Mandarin oranges, and cranberry vinaigrette. Iowa corn chowder is served in a golden-baked sourdough bread bowl and garnished with cheddar corn fritters and fresh chives. Dinner entrées served with Heartland bread basket including corn muffins with Iowa honey-butter. Bone-In Iowa rib chop is stuffed with apple-almond cornbread stuffing, seared on the grill, pan-roasted, and served with Regi's Cranberry Chutney.

Jesse's Embers Steaks and Seafood. Two locations: 50th & E. P. True Parkway, West Des Moines, (515) 225-9711; 3301 Ingersoll Avenue, Des Moines, (515) 255-6011. The flames are hot for open-pit grilled steaks, pork, baby-back ribs, and more.

Sage the Restaurant, 6587 University Avenue, Des Moines (Windsor Heights), (515) 255-7722, www.sagetherestaurant.com. Hand-picked ingredients form the basis for the finest of flavors, from Niman Ranch meats to Jamison Farm's lamb that is raised on a 210-acre farm.

PLACES TO STAY

Comfort Suites at Living History Farms, 11167 Hickman Road, Urbandale, (515) 276-1126. Farm décor including quilt-inspired hallway carpeting, barn-door coffee table, charming sign over the registration desk: "Rooms 50 Cents," paintings of beef cattle. Living History Farm Suite is a condo-size splurge with hot tub, kitchen, and sepia-tone photos depicting Living History Farms scenes. Continental breakfast.

The Country Connection, 9737 West 93rd Street South, Prairie City, (515) 994-2023. Turn-of-the-century farm home with full breakfast, bedtime snacks, and homemade ice cream.

Country Home/Whitaker Farm Bed and Breakfast, 11045 NE 82nd Avenue, Mitchellville, (515) 967-3184. Charming farmhouse on 20-acre farm. Full breakfast.

Countryside Inn, 1204 Guthrie Street (Exit 110 off I-80 at Highway 169), De Soto, (515) 834-9140. Sparkling-clean, cute, friendly, reasonable motel. About 22 miles west of Des Moines, but I-80 zips along so you are back in the action in no time.

The Grey Goose Bed and Breakfast, 1740 290th, Adel, (515) 833-2338. Renovated 1920 catalog farmhouse, wraparound porch, 40 acres with pond, near bike trail. Full breakfast.

The Renaissance Savery Hotel, 401 Locust Street, Des Moines, (515) 244-2151, www.renaissancehotels.com. U.S. Presidents have slept here, and if that is not reason enough to check in, know that this place drips with all the romance and class you would expect of a 1919-era historic hotel. But it has modern amenities too, like an indoor pool and spa, fitness center, and well-appointed rooms. Now, about that ghost. In 1928, Patrick J. Monihan opened a speakeasy on the third floor. It was, according to the hotel, the city's hottest gin joint. When police staged their last raid on the place in 1932, they found gallons of whiskey and slot machines, but no Patrick J. Monihan. Seems he evaporated and was never heard from in these parts again. Except that hotel employees have reported hearing jazz music on the third floor, even though today, the reincarnated Monihan's Speakeasy does its thing not on the third floor, but on the first. In a salute to bathtub gin but using only premium spirits, Monihan's trademark cocktail comes in a miniature bathtub that, once drained, goes home with you as a fond memory.

21. PRESERVING THE PAST NEAR OSKALOOSA

Oskaloosa, the population center of Mahaska County, bustles with the pace of a modern city, yet every time the town band plays from the magnificently restored 1912-era bandstand, the city's pioneer heart beats loud and clear in the present day. And what a classic venue this bandstand is for enjoying an ice cream cone in the good ol' summertime. You will find Oskaloosa 59 miles southeast of Des Moines and 18 miles southeast of Pella and its proud Dutch heritage.

Nelson Pioneer Farm

Just a few miles northeast of the Oskaloosa town square, the Nelson Pioneer Farm, 2294 Oxford Avenue, Oskaloosa, (641) 672-2989, www.nelsonpioneer.org, also revels in that spirit of the past. Here visitors are invited to experience Americana on a 30-acre complex that is part of the farm that still keeps 280 acres in crops. This was the Nelson family farm, the first and only American farm on this parcel. It was donated by the family to the Mahaska County Historical Society in 1958.

It all started when Daniel Nelson began farming here in 1844. When the Iowa land office opened on July 4, 1846, and set a six-month deadline for filing land

---

FIELD TO TABLE

Super zippy egg spread

6 hard-cooked eggs, diced
1 8-ounce package reduced-fat cream cheese
2 cups sharp cheddar cheese, shredded
1 1-ounce package dry ranch dressing mix
1 cup pecan pieces
1/2 cup red pepper, diced (green or yellow peppers may be used also)

In a large bowl, mix together cream cheese, cheddar cheese, ranch dressing mix, and hard-cooked eggs. Use your hands to form into two balls or one log and set aside.

Mix pecans and red pepper together in separate bowl. Roll each ball or log in the mixture until covered. Wrap with plastic wrap and refrigerate for at least 2 hours before serving. Serve with crackers.

Recipe reprinted by permission from the Iowa Egg Council. 🐓

---

claims, Nelson walked the 70 miles to the land office to file his claim. Jumping ahead to the 1950s, the last of the Nelson family to live here were siblings Roy and Lillian Nelson, neither of whom had married. It is said that after his sister's death, Roy could not bring himself to eat, and so died within a short time of her passing.

Restored to the 1850–1890 period, the Nelson Pioneer Farm is special for other reasons as well. It is big, with lots to see, and you go on your own, taking as much time as you want. The setting is completely rural, and all that you can see for miles around are other farms on their own rolling land. The setting enhances your experience even though it lies beyond the historical farm's boundaries. And, it preserves not only the agriculture of the Nelson family farm, but with over 20 village buildings, the entire region as well. You could easily spend half a day here, taking your time and perhaps refreshing yourself with a mid-tour lunch break. The staffer on hand will orient you to the complex, give you a map, and answer questions. From Oskaloosa, take Highway 63 north past William Penn University, then 2 miles east on County Road T65 (Glendale Road); closed Sundays and Mondays.

Start inside the Historical Society's on-site museum building that takes you deeper into the past than you might have expected to go on a farm visit. Look through the glass of the polished, old wooden cases, the kind many museums are tossing out as if old things have no place in a museum. There the vast collections of regional artifacts lead you back to a time when mastodons rumbled across Iowa, and when Indians shaped arrowheads of stone. Learn about the origins of the American corn crop, and that it was the Native Americans who taught the settlers how to make corn pone, crackling bread, mush, scrapple, ash cake, hoe cake, hominy, and hushpuppies.

A 1930 newspaper clipping documents the demolition of the 1855 Courier Mill, which once ground flour, corn, and feed, seven and one-half miles east of Oskaloosa on Highway 2. You can also learn the five steps needed to make a cornhusk doll. Downstairs, there are food-related artifacts like a water jug that was used to carry water to threshing crews hard at work on the Nelson farm. There is a detailed description of how cheese and butter were once made. There is a slew of crockery that once stored pioneer foods like vinegar, molasses, cider, and honey.

Exit the museum building and follow the brick path to the barn. Original to the farm, the barn was constructed of wooden pegs, which were preferred over nails because they would neither rust nor split the boards. Turns out they lasted long too. On display are a hand-cranked rope maker, a seed corn tester, harnesses and saddles, and a chair that was caned with corn husks that were twisted into a two-ply rope. Upstairs, learn about each month of the farmer's life, as it would

Inside the original barn at the Nelson Pioneer Farm, Oskaloosa.

have been lived on a farm like this. June, for example, brought on the necessity of doing a comparatively unknown chore. It was the mending of roads, which farmers accomplished by filling in holes and ruts, crowning for drainage, and clearing brush. By November, as another placard reads, the growing-season chores diminished, and so there was time for the harvest of wild game, the swapping of stories, and the barn dances. As you study the silent exhibits, can you imagine that on a cold November night, this very barn was alive with the dance—the swish of skirts, the music of a fiddle, the chance to fall in love?

Cross the street to the farmhouse, a two-story brick beauty where two generations of the Nelson family lived. Besides the barn, it is the only other original building on the farm. It stands complete with a hearth fireplace and a high chair that was first used by the Nelsons in the mid-1800s. Be sure to look through the second-floor hallway landing window, which is the only original glass remaining in the house, tiny bubbles and all. Exit onto the back porch, and see the summer kitchen and the meat house where preservation methods are explained in great detail.

Read the accounts of how local farmers and townspeople came to save the nineteenth-century village buildings that have become part of the farm. Stop by the wooden windmill, cupola, and mule cemetery. Mule cemetery? Sure enough. Remember Daniel Nelson? He owned two white mules that answered to the names of Becky and Jennie. Both of these creatures served in the U.S. Artillery during the Civil War, then returned to the farm until their deaths, when Nelson saw fit to erect headstones and a little picket fence. Finally, be sure to explore the two modern pole barns that house heavy equipment such as a grain drill, a hand corn sheller, and a peddler's wagon that saved the farmers a trip into town.

Rural Roots

Two more Oskaloosa area stops show off this historic town's rural roots. A little over four miles southeast of Nelson Pioneer Farm, **Tschetter's Red Barn/Antiques,** 2379 Highway 92 East, Oskaloosa, (641) 672-2795, is a rustic peg-and-beam craft barn offering dried flowers, wreaths/swags, and custom-built furniture. A little to the east, **Striegel Acres,** 2452 Plymouth Avenue, Oskaloosa, (641) 673-4043, raises ostriches and emus. Enjoy these inquisitive big birds and look for products like meat, emu oil, and decoratively etched eggshells.

When it comes to pioneer farming, breaking new ground is hardly a thing of the past. A brand new winery just opened in the area, and it is called **Tassel Ridge Winery,** 1681 220th Street, Leighton, (641) 672-1133, www.tasselridgewinery.com. You will find Tassel Ridge Winery just four miles northwest of Oskaloosa off Highway 163. A complimentary tour and tasting includes suggestions for wine selection, aging, and pairing with food. Beginning in the summer of 2005, the vineyard tour takes people out on the tractor-pulled Grape Mobile to see the vines and the process of developing a vineyard. Tassel Ridge is largely supplied by local grapes from the winery's Meadowcreek Vineyards.

For gorgeous country views and a visit to a pioneer gristmill, drive north on Highway 63, which becomes Highway 146, then go left on Highway 225 into little Lynnville, about 26 miles northwest of Oskaloosa. There the 1848 **Wagaman Mill** perches on the banks of the Skunk River. Find out why it was W. K. Wagaman who got his name above the door, although many enterprising settlers had come before. Learn about the Wagaman family's Red Bird and White Lion brands of flour, as well as Wheat Heart cereal. Catch a Sunday afternoon tour, but call ahead. Cross the pedestrian bridge to have a picnic lunch across the river, where a grill is just waiting to cook your Iowa beef, pork, and sweet corn.

Got time for another mill? In September and by advance arrangement only, you can visit **Maasdam Sorghum Mills**, 6495 East 132nd Street South, Lynnville. To arrange a tour, call (641) 594-4369 and check out www.maasdamsorghum.com. Sweet sorghum is most closely compared to molasses. It is thick, sweet syrup milled from the juice-rich stems of the sorghum plant, and you can use it to bake gingerbread (great with cream cheese) or classic gingerbread men. L. J. Maasdam started the mill in 1926, and it is still in the family. And although it has been updated, it is still powered by the steam engine they installed in 1945.

SPECIAL EVENTS

Southern Iowa Fair, Oskaloosa, (641) 673-7004, www.southerniowafair.com. Last week of July. Large county fair with antique machinery, 4-H/FFA and open class exhibits, traditional midway, food.

Sweet Corn Serenade, town square, Oskaloosa, (641) 672-2591, www.oskaloosa chamber.org. Early August. Live band music and home-style food: cheap, fresh, Iowa sweet corn, pork sandwiches, homemade pies.

National Tractor Pull, Southern Iowa Fairgrounds, Oskaloosa, (641) 673-7004. End of August.

Fall Festival, Nelson Pioneer Farm, Oskaloosa, (641) 672-2989, www.nelson pioneer.org. Third Saturday in September. Over 30 pioneer skills demonstrated, from butter churning and canning to blacksmithing and threshing. Gunnysack races, special exhibits, musical entertainment, spelling bee, petting zoo, farm and kiddie parade, country dinner (that's lunch to you) available.

PLACES TO EAT

Hunter's Café, 113 High Avenue West, Oskaloosa, (641) 673-9911. Tiny tea room back of a giftware shop. Lunch only, closed Sunday. Creative soups and sandwiches. The European cook uses farmers' market produce and eggs from happy (free-range) chickens, and whips up fresh chicken salads, meat loaf sandwiches, and apricot-peach-apple muffins.

Jaarsma Bakery, 210 A Avenue East, Oskaloosa, (641) 673-6415.

The Peppertree, 2274 Highway 63 North, Oskaloosa, (641) 673-9191.

McNeill Stone Mansion Bed and Breakfast, 1282 C Avenue East, Oskaloosa, (641) 673-4348, www.thestonemansion.com. Stunning Indiana-limestone palace with rooms that have electric fireplaces and cable, and are twice the size found at many B&Bs. Having rescued the mansion over the course of five years, the hosts convey its graciousness through lavish décor, evening dessert, and extensive common areas including solarium, library, and outdoor terrace. Full breakfast on weekends.

The Old Mill Riverside Inn, 202 East Street, Lynnville, (641) 527-2300, www.the oldmillinn.com. White dollhouse steps from the Wagaman Mill and the babble of the Skunk River. Pretty décor is balanced with the rustic look of the downstairs hunter's lounge. Private baths, cable, phones, queen or king beds. Full breakfast; Sunday breakfast buffet.

22. THE AMANAS AND A CZECH ENCLAVE

Savor history that comes served up with a German accent and communal-kitchen-size portions of hearty fare. Smell the pungency of sauerbraten, swirl a glass of whole-fruit wine, and view kitchens of days gone by. Do all of this in the Amana Colonies, a patchwork quilt of seven east-central Iowa villages that are located in Iowa County about 20 miles southwest of Cedar Rapids. Beginning in 1855, the Amana Colonies were stitched together by faith and the distance an ox-cart could go in a day. This is not a living history museum, but a place where people really live and continue to practice the best of their old arts.

A typically tranquil scene in the Amanas.

Make that places, for there are seven villages, six of them going by the name Amana. There are East Amana, West Amana, South Amana, and Middle Amana; High Amana is not sitting up on a hill, although that was the original plan. But then there is Amana, which should be self-explanatory until a helpful local says, "The Ronneburg Restaurant? Sure, that's over in Main." Yes, well, as it turns out, Main is short for Main Amana, which is really Amana, and which is mainly where the action is, and why they sometimes call it Main. Six down; one to go, and that is Homestead, which is not Homestead Amana because it was a regular town before it became an Amana in 1861.

The tour follows a clockwise direction around the loop formed roughly by Highways 151 and 6, and 220th Trail, for a total of about 20 miles. The trip starts in Amana, which is, well, the main Amana. You will enjoy visits to all of the villages' museums, as well as the shops that are quaint and charming, but uniquely reflective of the Amana culture. East Amana, which is located a hop-skip east of Amana, is not on the tour circuit. If you wish to go there, do so because it is one of the Amana Colonies—and for the peace that you will find there.

Amana

Get your bearings at the **Amana Colonies Visitors Center**, which is easy to find at the west end of Amana. This is the place to pick up brochures and essential information; call (319) 622-7622 or (800) 579-2294. Visit www.amana-colonies.org. Then visit all five of the Amana Heritage Society's museums, (319) 622-3567, www.amanaheritage.org, that are scattered throughout the colonies like colorful history books. Each one sheds light on a different aspect of the communal life.

We'll get to all those delicious shops and restaurants, but for now, start at the **Museum of Amana History**, 4310 220th Trail, Amana. Buy the punch pass that is good for the three nineteenth-century buildings here, as well as the Society's four other museums. Watch the introductory video, which provides a sometimes-poignant overview of the colonists' history, read the oral histories, read the thousand words in each old photograph. As you move through the museum, you will learn all about the unique, faith-based community that traces its origins to 1714 and immigrated here in 1855. Drawn by the farmland, they eventually bought 26,000 acres that are to this day farmed and protected by the Amana Society. The great advantage to visitors is that when hopping from village to village, all you see are fields and forests. No billboards, no neon signs.

Amana's historic specialty shops make new things in the old ways. The **Amana Meat Shop and Smokehouse**, 4513 F Street, Amana, (319) 622-7580, has been at it since 1855, updating throughout the decades. They do not give tours of the modern smoking operation that takes place at various stations and temperatures on the premises, but you can view their original smokehouse. Nibble on samples as you consider the vast array of smoked, double-smoked, and smokeless meats, including summer sausage, *pfefferwurst*, beef *thuringer*, ring bologna,

---

FIELD NOTES

Uncommon ground

Held in common and organized in the land-conserving German style, the landscape of the Amana Colonies looks nothing like a typical Midwestern farming community. Lanny Haldy, executive director of the Amana Heritage Society, calls it village-based farming, and points out that you will not see houses between the seven villages. Of the 26,000 acres, about 8,000 is cropland, 7,000 is hardwood forest, and 7,000 is in pasture for beef cattle. All the houses, along with the barns and outbuildings, are in town, along with the butcher shops, bakeries, dairy buildings, icehouses, wine cellars, and other harvest-processing facilities.

Note: the agricultural acreage is not open to the public 🐾

---

flavored bratwursts, flavored bacons, beef jerky, and sliced hams and turkeys. Lean, breaded pork tenderloins are tenderized twice, then battered with egg and coated with cracker crumbs. Corn-fed Amana beefsteaks and thick-cut Iowa chops would be perfect for the grill at the nearest park.

The **Chocolate Haus**, 4311 220th Trail, Amana, (319) 622-3025, blends fudge in a copper kettle. Go to **The Kitchen Sink**, 759 48th Avenue, Amana, (319) 622-3227 for gourmet kitchenware, coffee, tea, and spices.

The **Amana Woolen Mill**, 800 48th Avenue, Amana, (319) 622-3432, dates back to 1857 and is Iowa's only operating woolen mill. Here they weave wool, cotton, and acrylic blankets in traditional Nordic and Tartan patterns, delicate colors for babies, soft animals, sweaters, scarves, and more. At one point in the 1980s, this historic mill supplied the U.S. Army with 380,000 blankets, an order that kept the looms humming 24/7 for two years. Gone are the flour, calico, and other mills, although the six and one-half mile, 1860s Mill Race that once powered them continues to flow through town. (A mill race is the water channel that powers a mill's waterwheel.)

Something on the order of nine wineries lend a festive air and continue a winemaking tradition that dates back to communal days. Everyone helped, and everyone got some. The present-day wine makers emphasize fruit wines that go great with desserts like cherry cheesecake. But **Ackerman Winery**, 4406 220th Trail, Amana, (319) 622-3379, has some additional thoughts on that subject. Thinking beyond desserts, it suggests meal ideas like Elderberry Wine Slow-Cooked Beef Stew and Apricot Wine Marinated Chicken Breasts. Ackerman Winery makes rhubarb and dandelion wines from locally grown produce, berry wines like dry cranberry, Iowa honey wine, and red and white table wines ranging from dry to sweet. Take a quick, self-guided tour through the cellar to see the production, aging, and bottling facilities. Also in town, **Millstream Brewing Co.**, 835 48th Avenue, Amana, (319) 622-3672, invites visitors to view the brewing and bottling areas, and to taste a range of beers that are made from Midwest malted grains and cold-filtered the Old World way. Millstream Wheat is light and served with a slice of lemon. Schild Brau Amber is a rich, premium brew. Root beer and cream soda are available. Take a glass of your favorite out to the deck where people gather and polka music plays.

Homestead

Traveling clockwise through the colonies, take Highway 151 for 3 miles south to Homestead. But on the way, you may wish to take an interesting walk on the wooded Amana Colonies Nature Trail, which features a birds-eye view of a structure that was built into the Iowa River by Indians an estimated 250 years ago. Called the **Indian Dam**, this pre-settlement fish trap consists of glacial boulders that were placed to form a barrier in the water. When fish swam by, they were guided into a small area, caught, and moved to an adjoining holding pool. You can only see the Indian Dam, which is listed on the National Register of Historic Places, when the river is very low.

Two more Amana Heritage Society museums call Homestead home. These are the new **Homestead Store Museum**, 4430 V Street, Homestead, and the **Amana Community Church**, 4210 V Street, Homestead. The Homestead Store Museum takes an authentic general store that first opened in 1865, and turns it into a history lesson about commerce in communal Amana. A few early fixtures remain, like the painted tin ceiling, a cash register, shelves, and cases. Customers from surrounding communities would come to shop for groceries, dry goods, work clothing, tobacco, candy, fruits, vegetables, chicken feed, nutritional supplements for beef cattle, and other goods. The museum also interprets early commercial enterprises. Basket making was apparently specialized, with one style of basket specifically for the picking of apples, and another to contain rising dough. Learn too that the Amana Colonies' Homestead Farm was an early test site for Hi-Bred Seed Corn, which was being introduced by a company founded by Henry A. Wallace in 1926, a company that later became the Pioneer Seed Company.

Also in Homestead, the **Colony Country Store**, 3142 Highway 6 Trail, Homestead, (319) 622-3197, features Amana food products, wines, gifts, and a pastoral setting.

South Amana

Now it's on to South Amana, five miles west on Highway 6. There the **Communal Agriculture Museum**, 505 P Street, South Amana, is perfectly situated in a community where sometimes the loudest sound is the buzzing of bees among the old grapevines. It is just a good setting for an 1860 barn stuffed with agricultural artifacts that interpret not just farming, but communal farming. Learn why oxen helped power colony farms longer than on family farms. Learn about the role of blacksmiths and harness shops, and that in the 1890s, South Amana alone had 50 horses. Artifacts, photos, and signage tell the story of cow and sheep farming, ice harvesting, kitchen gardens, potato and onion fields, grain crops, and much more. It is important, somehow, that implements that were once so important, like an old seed corn grader, we cannot even identify today without help.

Next door, visit the **Mini-Americana Barn Museum**, Box 124, South Amana, (319) 622-3058, which is one family's endeavor and not on the punch card, so separate admission fees apply. It is housed in the last barn built by the colonists, which was back in 1913. For 15 years, retired farmer Henry Moore, now deceased, painstakingly handcrafted replicas of the buildings that existed in his lifetime and within the realm of his personal experience. These include gorgeous Amana miniatures, some of which are especially valuable because the real structures no longer exist. Enter the realm of tiny Iowa farmsteads, and the log structures of central Illinois' New Salem State Historic Site. Find out what did and did not go on in something called the hog powder house.

If you are looking for handmade beeswax candles from 1800s molds, you will find them at **The Granary Emporium**, 1603 Fourth Avenue, South Amana, (319) 622-6806. The building is an 1865 brick granary, agriculturally historic in its own right. Pop into **Schanz Furniture Refinishing Shop**, 2773 Highway 6 Trail, South Amana, (319) 622-3529 for miniature windmills and split-rail fences that make beautiful farm scene displays or toys for children.

West Amana

You will not find any museums in West Amana, which is three miles north of South Amana along the northwest curve of 220th Trail, but you will find some intriguing shops whose products are colony-inspired. You can't miss the giant rocking chair at the **Broom and Basket Shop**, 618 Eighth Avenue, West Amana, (319) 622-3315. The brooms are actually made from the field crop known as broomcorn. The shop grows a demonstration plot of it outside, so you can see that it resembles corn but tops out with long, feathery flower clusters. The shop's brochure explains that back in the day, brooms were a profitable colony product. As harvest neared, colonists walked through the fields to break over the broomcorn flower clusters in order for them to dry. Then they would return to cut them from the stalks and thresh them to separate the seeds for the next year's crop. Several weeks after harvest, the broomcorn was dry enough so broom making could begin. Today, the shop continues the tradition. Its trademark is the distinctively angled sideliner whisk broom.

High Amana

Drive another mile east on 220th Trail to High Amana. Built of sandstone, the 1857 **High Amana General Store**, 1308 G Street, High Amana, (319) 622-3232, sells local

Quaint Amana streetscape.

crafts like rag rugs that are woven on a third-generation loom, preserves, horse-radish jelly, corncob syrup, roasted field corn, old-fashioned candies from jars on the counter, farm animal statues, and spearmint-scented soap they cannot keep in stock. Indeed this emporium started out as a general store, selling generally every-thing. Today it feels like a museum, except that you can buy the artifacts.

Middle Amana

From High Amana, continue east for two and one-half miles on 220th Trail to Middle Amana and the fifth and final Amana Heritage Society museum. The **Communal Kitchen and Cooper Shop**, 1003 26th Avenue, Middle Amana, offers guided tours of the only intact communal-era kitchen (circa 1863) that is left over from the early days. It is preserved as it appeared in 1932 after being used to pre-pare a meal for the last time. A sample Tuesday menu from the bygone era reads "buckwheat cakes, syrup, and coffee for breakfast; cheese, apple butter, bread, and coffee for lunch; barley soup, potato dumpling, creamed chicken, coleslaw, and fruit pie for dinner; bread, jelly, fruit pie, and coffee for the second lunch; and potato salad, liver sausage, kidney beans, and tea for supper." There is a great hearth oven, and a highly resourceful ice chest that had a pipe leading to a basement trough, where water from melting ice would collect to help cool milk cans. At each of the colonies, the farms, gardens, orchards, vineyards, cheese makers, sausage makers, and bakers worked together to keep their communal kitchens stocked. Each vil-lage had several communal kitchens, and everyone ate together at their assigned one. The kitchen boss and her staff served 30 to 40 colonists at each meal, men at one table, women and youngsters at the other. Cookbooks are available for sale for your own kitchen creations.

So what happened to the other communal kitchens? Over in Amana, one of these has been appropriately transformed into the popular Ronneburg Restaurant. And here in Middle Amana, The Cloister Haus Bed and Breakfast keeps guests well fed every morning.

Also in Middle Amana, **Hahn's Original Hearth Oven Bakery**, 2510 J Street, Middle Amana, (319) 622-3439, keeps the circa-1860s hearth oven stoked for hard-crusted white, rye, and whole-wheat breads, fruit-filled streusels, and cinnamon rolls that have been known to disappear by 8:00 a.m. Also in town is a name you know but may not have connected with the colonies: Amana Refrigeration Products and Maytag Appliances. Originally called Amana Refrigeration, the company was founded right here in 1934.

Cedar Rapids

Cedar Rapids is a worthwhile cultural, ethnic, and historic stop about 20 miles northeast of the Amana Colonies. There, especially on 16th Avenue, you can get a taste of the city's Czech heritage, not the least of which is in the form of those fruit-filled cookies called *kolaches*. The **National Czech and Slovak Museum**, 30 16th Avenue SW, Cedar Rapids, (319) 362-8500, www.ncsml.org, is a big, beautiful tribute to an ethnic heritage that is perhaps not so familiar to many Americans, but certainly worth getting to know better for its warmth and charm. See the 1880s immigrant home where, as the museum suggests, you might imagine children clambering about while their mother prepares cabbage with a wooden cutter. Shop for beautifully decorated eggs in the gift shop.

Polehna's Meat Market, 96 16th Avenue SW, Cedar Rapids, (319) 378-9240, is located on the same street and has an antique smokehouse where logs of hickory and cherry wood, along with a half-full bottle of whiskey, flavor the meat. Take a short drive over to **Seminole Valley Farm Museum**, 1400 Seminole Valley Road NE, Seminole Valley Park, (319) 377-7740. This 1900-era farmstead has 10 artifact-filled buildings, including the farmhouse, barn, chicken house, implement and tool sheds, privy, smokehouse, summer kitchen, and Seminole Valley Farm Theater. By the way, the largest cereal mill in the world, Quaker Oats, has a plant in Cedar Rapids, shipping out box loads of cereal from the banks of the Cedar River.

Memories of the Amana Colonies are something that people carry with them for years, especially if they have played at the villages' festivals, eaten in their restaurants, and dreamed the night away in their guestrooms.

SPECIAL EVENTS

Maifest, Amana. First weekend in May. Enjoy a warm-time welcome with a candy making demo at the chocolate shop, hand-carding and spinning at the mill, live band, and prize trivia contest at the brewery, food sampling at the general store and sausage shop, barbeque sauce competition, wine walk, and lots more.

Houby Days, Czech Village, Cedar Rapids, (319) 362-8500, www.czechvilla-geofiowa.com. Mid-May. The mushroom is king at this springtime celebration. Czech it out.

Minneapolis-Moline Implement Reunion and Allis Chalmers Days, Homestead. Father's Day weekend. Antique tractors, farm equipment, demos, parade.

Amana Farm Fest, Festhalle Barn, Amana, (800) 579-2294. End of July. Tractor parade, agricultural displays, music, entertainment, food.

Amana Trail Ride, Amana Outdoor Convention Facility, Amana, (319) 462-2206, www.amanatrailride.com. Mid-September. Daily guided rides through over 2,000 acres of old logging trails, home-cooked meals, music, camping.

Honey Fest, Indian Creek Nature Center, 6665 Otis Road SE, Cedar Rapids, (319) 362-0664, www.indiancreeknaturecenter.org. Late September. Come celebrate one of nature's sweetest gifts with the honey trail, beeswax candle-dipping, games, crafts, and food.

PLACES TO EAT

Colony Inn Restaurant, 741 47th Avenue, Amana, (319) 622-6270. How about Amana cheddar bratwurst with Colony (grainy, eye-watering, wow!) Mustard, cold sauerkraut salad, apple strudel, and a Millstream German Pilsner? The building dates back to 1860 and was once the Amana Hotel with its own kitchen, garden, and dining rooms where travelers partook. It became the restaurant just three years after the end of communalism in 1932, and family-style dinners were served for fifty cents.

Ox Yoke Inn, 4420 220th Trail, Amana, (319) 622-3441. More good food and lots of it. Since 1940. Four dining rooms, gift nooks. The carryout menu includes grilled chicken salad, sides like pickled beets and onion rings. Inquire about packages with The Old Creamery Theatre.

The Ronneburg Restaurant, 4408 220th Trail, Amana, (319) 622-3641. Get this: the building is one of the original communal kitchens. The atmosphere is considerably warmer today, but the food is still real: sauerbraten with dumplings, schnitzels and *spaetzle*, Amana ham, steaks, fish, soups/salads/sandwiches.

PLACES TO STAY

Bábi's Bed and Breakfast, 2788 Highway 6 Trail, South Amana, (866) 752-5286. Relax in a pretty guesthouse room. The common area in the owners' 1915 farmhouse offers TV, games, and mornings with full breakfasts of pastries, breakfast meats, an egg dish or pancakes, fresh fruits, and juices. Mowed-path walking trails on the 10-acre property, country quiet.

Baeckerei B&B, 507 Q Street, South Amana, (319) 622-3597. Built as a communal bakery in 1860, this warm B&B offers a private bath, color TV and VCR, and a selection of free movies for each guestroom.

Colony Inn sauerkraut salad

You don't even have to like sauerkraut to love this recipe courtesy of the Colony Inn Restaurant, Amana (it is the only one they will give out).

1 quart sauerkraut
1 cup diced celery
$^1\!/_2$ onion, chopped (medium)
1 cup sugar
$^1\!/_2$ cup salad oil (Wesson Oil)
$^1\!/_4$ cup red and green peppers, chopped (for taste and color)

Mix all ingredients thoroughly. Let stand in refrigerator overnight. 🐾

Dusk to Dawn B&B, 2616 K Street, Middle Amana, (319) 622-3029. Soak in the outdoor hot tub beneath stars and a symphony of cricket-music. Quiet, comfortable, residential setting; hosts have a farming background. Yummy hot breakfasts that may feature egg omelets stuffed with crumbled bacon and topped with salsa.

Guest House Motel Motor Inn, 4712 220th Trail, Amana, (319) 622-3599. Request a room in the sandstone building that originally was a colony home for four families and their communal kitchen. Shopping and dining galore, steps from your door.

Loy's Farm Bed and Breakfast, 2077 KK Avenue, Marengo, (319) 642-7787. 2,500-acre corn and soybean farm with farm tours and pheasant hunting available. Grilled Iowa chop dinner available by special arrangement. Full breakfast with house-specialty sausage and corn meal waffles, homegrown farm produce, and homemade breads.

While in town, visit Pioneer Heritage Museum, 675 East South Street, Marengo, (319) 642-7018. Awaiting discovery at the museum are an 1861 log house, 1856 bachelor cabin from an Iowa farm, indoor reconstructed farmhouse, country store room, more.

The Cloister Haus Bed and Breakfast, 1117 26th Avenue, Middle Amana, (800) 996-6964. This circa-1893 former communal kitchen offers three guest-rooms with authentic colony antiques in a residential atmosphere. All rooms have private bath, TV, and A/C. Full breakfast features eggs, meat, bakery goods, juice, coffee, and tea.

23. RIVERSIDE MILLS AND THRESHERMEN SKILLS

There is something special about an old Midwestern river town. A sense of a place where even peeling paint and crumbling bricks are things of beauty. Where the waterway reflects everything that is happening in the sky. Where fish tends to turn up more on the restaurant menus. Van Buren County in southeastern Iowa has places like these, collectively called the Villages of Van Buren. These river towns were also mill towns, industriously taking advantage of the waterway at their doorsteps. They are located just north of the Missouri border and roughly 130 miles southwest of the Quad Cities. Some of the Villages of Van Buren have begun to catch the eye of artists and artisans, who are usually first to feel the pull.

Keosauqua

In the county seat of Keosauqua, the pull goes all the way back to 1840. Along with the farmers who initially came for fertile, inexpensive land, the enterprising millwrights and other craftsmen were among the first settlers in the area. The old **Farmer's Creamery** building on the corner of Dodge and First Streets can still be seen in town. As documented by the Van Buren County Historical Society and supplied by the Villages of Van Buren, Inc. office, its history gives insight into the way Midwestern creameries operated. First opened in 1927, the Farmer's Creamery processed farm-separated cream that was supplied by the local farmers. In its first week, the creamery made 50 tubs of butter. During the World War II years, the creamery began supplying whole milk, and it also sold dried skim milk and ice cream mix to regional Tastee Freeze outlets. Then, after its 36-year run, the old creamery closed, but if you look up above the roof at the east end of the building, you can still see the evaporator that was used to produce sweetened condensed milk.

Bentonsport

From Keosauqua, drive south on Highway 1, then east on County Road J40 (a total of about seven miles) to Bentonsport, population 50. The town is magical, with brick cottages, quaint shops, and white-gravel streets that will scrub away any lingering traces of the twenty-first century. Signs supply at-a-glance history lessons for each designated building. Once upon a time in Bentonsport, gristmills, woolen mills, and Iowa's first paper mill hummed with the pluck and enterprise of the American pioneer. Things are quieter today. All that is left of the 1843 **Hitchcock and Noble Flourmill** is its stone foundation. Signage preserves the memory of the mill, but what do you do with an old stone foundation? In Bentonsport, they thought the foundation looked like a garden wall, all crumbly and nostalgic, and so they kept its integrity while substituting flowers for flour. The site has become the domain of those who love history, those who love gardens, and those who love each other.

Wander across the nearby 1880s truss bridge, which is open only to foot and bicycle traffic, to the town of Vernon, which once had a nineteenth-century grist-mill. In 1851 the river washed around the mill and put it on its own island, so the building was moved, fixed, and put back into service. The owner, George C. Allender, then converted it into a woolen mill in 1857, and when the Civil War broke out, it was used to make blankets for the soldiers. All of this and more has been researched and documented by the owners of the Mason House Inn in *A History of Benton's Port, Iowa.*

Back in Bentonsport, walk into the 1853 Federal-style **Greef General Store**, (319) 592-3579. Head to the back where **Addie May Fudge**, 21964 Hawk Drive, Bentonsport, (same phone number) offers fantastic flavors of sweet-cream-and-butter fudge in quarter- to one-pound chunks. There are a lot of reasons to visit Addie May. Let's see, she's got fudge in flavors of butter pecan, chewy praline, cookie dough, cranberry, key lime, lemon chiffon, lemonade, mrtl-trtl, peppermint swirl, pumpkin pie, tiger butter, and lots more. Some of these are offered seasonally. Two doors west, the **Iron and Lace Shop** was created from salvaged barn wood.

Bonaparte

Four miles downriver along J40, the village of Bonaparte has similar nineteenth-century charm. Milling was also big here, and Bonaparte was in fact called Meek's

A view of Bonaparte from across the Des Moines River.

Mills until 1847. Bonaparte was also at the repeated mercy of the river's tendency to flood every half century or so. But the residents lived with it, because they could successfully harness the river's power in between those devastating episodes, especially for the Bonaparte Mills. Fortunately, the nineteenth-century gristmill and woolen mill still stand, and if you cut across the bridge to the opposite bank, you get a great view of these enduring structures. Today, the gristmill is the **Bonaparte Retreat Restaurant**, regionally renowned and proud of its roots. The owners report that back in the day, farmers from a hundred miles around sometimes had to wait for days on end to cross the river via ferry, in order to have their wagon-loads of grain processed at the mill. But they did what they had to do and no doubt used the time to catch up on the latest news and to shoot the breeze with fellow farmers.

Points Beyond
An unusual farm attraction exists about 15 miles southwest of Bonaparte near Cantril. The **Wickfield Farm Sales Pavilion** (located 2.5 miles east of Cantril) was built not as a barn, but as an impressive auction and lodging facility with rooms upstairs and a well-equipped kitchen and dining room in the basement. In the 1920s, the Wickfield Farm was known for purebred Hampshire hogs, and it was in the sales pavilion that they were presented to prospective customers. Distinctive for its round shape, four stories, dormer windows, and unusual construction materials, the pavilion is open to the public on scheduled Open House weekends (one a month May through October). These are the best times to visit, but if you are in the area on other dates, it is still worth pulling in to view the structure from the outside. In Cantril, **Dutchman's Store**, 103 Division Street, Cantril, (319) 397-2322, sells bulk foods, fresh local produce, candies from jars, fabrics, meats from local smokehouses and meat lockers. Closed on Sundays.

At this point you have two options. One is to head north on County Road V64 just outside Cantril toward Douds-Leandro. The second is to enjoy a bit of Amish country by continuing west on Highway 2 to Milton, and picking up County Road V56 north to County Road J40 to the tiny community of Lebanon. This little corner of the world is home to Old Order Amish families, who began settling in during the 1960s. Watch for signs of wash drying on the line, horse-drawn buggies, and a schoolhouse with a tetherball outside. If an Amish farm family has hung out a shingle advertising homemade candy, produce, and other products for sale, by all means pull in and buy direct from the source, except on Sundays, of course. Then head east a short distance on J40 to V64, where a quarter mile north on Fir Avenue—a good, old Iowa gravel road—you'll find the Red Barn Bistro, an interesting spot for lunch.

No matter what option you took, continue north on V64 through Douds-Leando, then east on Highway 16 and north on Highway 1 to Birmingham, where nineteenth-century enterprises included a saw and gristmill, and factories that churned out cheese, woolens, plows, and wagons. From Birmingham, take County

Road J16 east into Stockport, then go north on County Road W30 to **Morris Memorial Park**, 10938 Timber Road, Stockport, (319) 796-2148. This 60-acre park has a stocked pond and seven pioneer-settlement reconstructions that house artifacts from Van Buren County's agricultural history. A Utica huckster wagon, a hay stacker, and a glass-sided, horse-drawn hearse are among the items you will see here, but quite possibly nowhere else.

A Mount Pleasant Surprise

From Morris Memorial Park, it is about a 25-mile drive northeast to Henry County and **Midwest Old Threshers**, 405 East Threshers Road, Mount Pleasant, (319) 385-8937, www.oldthreshers.org. Here, you'll find an amalgamation of museums, trains, streetcars, and a carousel, and a five-day event, all dedicated to interpreting American agricultural history. The event is the Midwest Old Threshers Reunion, and if you decide to attend, it is best to plan well in advance, because crowds exceed 100,000. See museum pieces in motion, eat like a thresher, chew the fat with old thresher men, watch gunfights explode in the wild-west town of Snipe Run, and experience a pioneer settlement that is temporarily populated by local scouts and craftspeople. Settle in for the night at the on-site campground (no advance reservations available), area motels/B&Bs, or in the home of a local; call (319) 385-2577 to arrange a home stay.

The Heritage Museums of Midwest Old Threshers are extraordinary. Long rows of colorful, lovingly tended threshing machines and a host of other farm vehicles await inspection. Farm wives get their due with a thoughtful exhibit that commemorates their special contributions, including the astonishing volumes of food they had to bring to the table at threshing time. It is documented that Ada Mae Brinton once fed 20 men with her mashed potatoes, beef roast, gravy, ham loaf, baked kidney beans, creamed corn, homemade cottage cheese, dill pickles, plum jelly, homemade rolls with butter, two kinds of cake, homemade ice cream, iced tea, coffee, and cream. A replica of a 1915 family farmhouse brings home the lifestyles of the past. The recreated Peterson Farm Implement dealership calls to mind the year 1939.

You can also study the innards of a former Iowa gristmill, Marvin Mills, which operated under gasoline-engine power until 1947. Three cutaway floors of reconstructed posts and beams reveal a corn sheller, grinding stones, a fanning mill, and a flour sifter. There is also a sorghum press with its belt-driven rollers. Historically, Marvin Mills ground buckwheat flour, graham flour, and corn meal, but it is all a memory now. The exhibit of "Water: Too Little . . . Too Much" takes sophisticated looks at windmills and the land-drainage method of burying drainage tiles underground. "Electricity—Comes to the Farm" highlights rural electrification that forever changed the way farmers did chores. Housed in a simulated opera house, the Theatre Museum of Repertoire Americana (admission applies) may seem incongruous at this site, until you learn how important the traveling tent shows were to farmers who otherwise lacked ready sources of entertainment. The playhouse offers a limited performance schedule.

Food, and lots of it, fueled the men who did the arduous work of threshing. At the reunion, be sure to educate yourself on that aspect of agricultural history as well. Local churches, civic groups, grower associations, and farmers serve food hot and fresh as in the old days when threshers would eat legendary quantities to fuel the workload. Enjoy Iowa pork, beef, and elk; sweet corn and green beans; potatoes and pies. The Iowa Turkey Federation kicks in grilled turkey legs. A family farm serves hundreds of pounds of elk burgers as well as smoked dried elk. Others supply meatloaf, beef and noodles, walking tacos, baked potatoes, funnel cakes, pancakes, ice cream, and more. Don't forget to pick up the latest edition of the *Midwest Old Threshers Cookbook.*

Oh, just one more stop. It is the little **Swedish American Museum,** 107 Freeport Avenue, Swedesburg, (319) 254-2317, and it is a quick 10 miles north of Mount Pleasant, visible on your left from Highway 27, and free of charge. Enjoy the museum's distinctively ethnic Country Store, Huckster Building, Kaffestuga, gift shop, and Swedish heritage events.

This weekend includes poking around southeastern Iowa river towns, moving languidly through them just as the river does most years. And the drive up to Mount Pleasant reveals why the hard labor of threshing grain, as it was done in the old days, became such a part of the farm family's life that it came to merit a weeklong reunion event.

SPECIAL EVENTS

Morel Mushroom Festival, Bonaparte, (319) 592-3389. Early May. Seek and you shall probably find.

Swedish Pancake Breakfast, Swedesburg, (319) 254-2317. Early June.

Farmington Strawberry Festival, Farmington, (319) 878-3313. Second full weekend of June. Free strawberries and ice cream, quilt show, car show.

World's Expo of Antique Farm Equipment, Mount Pleasant, (319) 385-8937. Late June.

Van Buren County Barn Tour, (800) 868-7822, www.800-tourvbc.com. Fourth Saturday of June. County-wide barn tour including Amish barns. Tour guides on buses, owners' talks, lunch provided.

Douds Field Day, Douds, (641) 936-4687. Mid-July. Pancake breakfast, parade, children's games, sanctioned pedal pull, entertainment, flea market, food.

Midwest Old Threshers Reunion, Mount Pleasant, (319) 385-8937. Always the five days ending with Labor Day.

Forest Craft and Scenic Drive Festival, Keosauqua, (800) 868-7822. October. Lumberjack show, juried woodcraft show, buck skinners' camp, food.

PLACES TO EAT

Bonaparte Retreat Restaurant, 100 First Street, Bonaparte, (319) 592-3339. Diners enjoy good food against a backdrop of history that includes gristmill relics, a walnut back bar, and beams that measure two feet thick. This was actually the second mill built on the site, after the 1836 mill burned down. Steaks (filet, rib eye, New York strip, beef burger) are Iowa Prime or Top Choice and broiled. Dinners include soup, salad, potato, and pan-fried bread.

Harvest Family Restaurant, 1110 West Washington Street, Mount Pleasant, (319) 385-9820.

Red Barn Bistro, 21268 Fir Avenue, seven miles west of Keosauqua on J40, Keosauqua, (319) 293-6154. Friday and Saturday 5:00 to 9:00 p.m.; Sundays 11:00 a.m. to 2:00 p.m. Steaks, chops, salad bar, homemade bread, real mashed potatoes. Hand-cut Iowa steaks, fresh produce from Amish neighbors. "Big, bone-in, one-pound ham steak, not any of that chopped-up, pressed-back-together-to-make-it-look-like-ham," says owner Julie Campbell, who adds that it is too much for one person to eat, but if they cut it in half, it just wouldn't look right on the plate. Fish fry on Friday nights. Casual country atmosphere in a Dutch gambrel roof barn, views of barnyard critters in an outdoor pen.

PLACES TO STAY

Mason House Inn, 21982 Hawk Drive, Bentonsport, (319) 592-3133, www .masonhouseinn.com. Cookie jar in every room, steps to the river. Cozy rooms have magnificent carved-wood beds and private baths. The General Store Room is stocked with tins of goods that an 1850 homemaker would have needed. Full

The yellow soft-brick and white porches of the Mansion Inn, Keosauqua.

TABLE TALK:

The Red Barn Bistro

Julie Campbell makes no bones about the fact that at her country restaurant, the hand-cut steaks are marinated not for tenderness, but for flavor. It's all about quality.

"Because we buy good meat," she explains. So why do they buy Iowa beef, in particular? "Because we were farmers, and we know quality meat. It's the same reason we buy potatoes by the hundred-pound gunnysack, and we have an Army-issue potato peeler, and we serve real mashed potatoes on Sunday," she explains.

Campbell describes her menu at the Red Barn Bistro, which is located about seven miles west of Keosauqua, as good, basic, country food. When she starts talking about unbleached, high gluten flour in the wheat bread, though, it begins to sound suspiciously like gourmet. But then she turns the tables, and it's back to home-style. "Today we had pork loin with dressing, and I did a scalloped cabbage, which is as simple as simple can be, and if I'm going to be well known for anything, it will be that dumb cabbage," she laments with a certain resignation. 🐾

breakfast, at the hour of your choice, may include orange-yolk eggs courtesy of local free-range chickens, and local fresh fruits. Cool evenings may inspire lit fireplaces, popcorn, and apple cider.

The Mansion Inn, 500 Henry Street, Keosauqua, (319) 293-2511, www.mansion-inn.com. Original farmlands are gone, but legendary Southern hospitality starts at this northerly latitude, where guests feel welcome with a rare combination of grandeur and easy hospitality. Look for the curved wooden door beneath the grand staircase, and the haymaking scene in the stained glass window above it. Your gracious hosts offer beverages to enjoy on the five-columned front porch, the screened side porch, or the back porch. Guests of the upstairs suite get the balcony. Full breakfast in glorious dining room may include egg dish from farm-fresh eggs, sausages, fruit, French toast, sweet strudels, and other pastries.

Van Vorhies Haus, 601 West Monroe Street, Mount Pleasant, (319) 385-3935. Okay, it is mostly a retirement home, but when you need a nice, clean room during the Midwest Old Threshers Reunion (or any other time of the year), you are welcome to stay in the guest wing and enjoy the parlor's piano and fireplace and the three acres of fruit trees, gardens, and green space. The original part of the house was built in 1858. Breakfast may be available by special arrangement.

Old fashioned cleomes and hollyhocks at Seed Savers, Decorah.

IOWA

Rockford
Woodstock 12
Wauconda
Des Plaines
Oregon
Oak
Brook
Chicago
Lemont
Kankakee
Galesburg
Peoria
Bloomington
INDIANA
Champaign
Quincy
Springfield
Decatur
Arcola
Altamont
Alton
MISSOURI
Carbondale
Rosiclare
N
0   50   100
Miles
KENTUCKY
Metropolis

Illinois

Waving fields of soybeans and corn are central to Illinois' agricultural bounty, but wouldn't it be nice to see the occasional peach tree, or maybe a bison or llama ranch? As it turns out, you need not go farther than the Prairie State to see these things and indeed to reconnect with them. So if you get a craving to feast your eyes on a pizza farm or to gather 'round an old-fashioned weenie roast at a B&B farm, then save some weekends for Illinois. Oh, and have you ever thought about climbing a silo?

24. THE "NORTHWESTERN-MOST" CORNER

Jo Daviess County—it seems as if this entire northwestern-most corner of Illinois was tailor-made for a weekend in the country. It is a storybook setting of family farms that could be there just to enhance the beauty of the hills and valleys. The crown jewel of Jo Daviess County is Galena, a small town that slept through most of the twentieth century only to find that sleep is a good thing. Galena's excess of distinctive nineteenth-century architecture drips with charm from each red brick, and from every white shutter. Inside the little windows, you will see cozy shops and restaurants and inns, all of which work together to keep things oh-so-civilized.

To get oriented, know that Galena is 165 miles west of Chicago and 80 miles west of Rockford. Also know that Jo Daviess County meets up with Wisconsin at its northern edge, and with Iowa, and the Mississippi River, to the west.

Touring the Farms

Two organizations, both based in sleepy Elizabeth (15 miles southeast of Galena along Highway 20), have begun to offer two very different agricultural tours. First up during the growing season is the self-guided **Farm Tour**. About seven (number may vary from year to year) dairy, beef, crop, pig, and sheep farms are open throughout one Saturday in July. Your first stop, though, should be a telephone call to the Jo Daviess County Farm Bureau at (815) 858-2235. For additional information, call (877) 444-5850 or visit www.galena.org. Farmers talk about the history of their operation, current agricultural practices, and what it takes to be a farmer. They also offer fun and educational things for people of all ages to do, like milk a cow, hold a pig, pet critters, or ride on a tractor. The farmers may also provide samples of county-made agricultural products, excluding, of course, silk purses.

Return to the region in September, when the **Jo Daviess Conservation Foundation Farm Tour** kicks in with a hearty breakfast and guided bus jaunts. Start

A typical back road in Jo Daviess County.

the day with the Country Breakfast and Family Attractions experience. The breakfast is special, featuring scrambled eggs, French toast, and whole-hog sausage from Arnold's Farm in Elizabeth. Local 4-H'ers serve it up hot, and afterward, you can take in the educational agricultural exhibits, farmers' market, petting zoo, and new and antique farm equipment displays. Bus trips depart throughout the morning and last about three hours, and one of the great things is that you don't have to hear things like, "Weren't we supposed to turn left back there?" Both traditional (livestock, crops) and specialty (vineyard, Christmas trees, horses, etc.) farms are featured. Call (815) 858-9100 for information and advance registration, then look forward to a delightful day.

Going To Galena

Continuing on your own from Elizabeth, go northwest on Highway 20 for the most direct route and 15 miles to charming, historic Galena. Galena is a destination unto itself, and a great place to start is east of downtown across the Galena River at the Old Train Depot/Visitor's Information Center on Park Avenue. Park for free and pick up brochures and maps, including the Jo Daviess County Farm Bureau's Home Grown Directory, which lists a great variety of about 15 to 20 producers each year. To avoid disappointment, it is a good idea to call ahead to the places that interest you. Now walk across the pedestrian bridge to the heart of Galena.

Up on Bench Street, duck into the **Galena Jo Daviess County Historical**

Society and Museum, 211 South Bench Street, Galena, (815) 777-9129, www.galena historymuseum.org, which houses farm and cooking artifacts that were once used on farms of the region. View an 1870s corn planter that was yanked out of an 1852 barn, an 1831 ox yoke, a milking machine that was man-ufactured in Chicago, a cooper's bench and tools, a Galena brewery keg, a coun-ty fair booklet from 1860, and Galena pottery. On the historic home front, view handy-dandy gadgets like an 1886 washing machine from Galena, a waffle iron, an eggbeater, and a pancake griddle. These specimens represent only a small por-tion of the museum's exhibits, and you will want to view everything, including the original 1830s mine shaft. Intriguingly, it is believed that tunnels still go through the rocky hillside.

Galena's Kandy Kitchen, 100 North Main Street, Galena, (815) 777-0241, offers hand-dipped chocolates, bark, fudge, caramels, nut logs, and more tooth-some confections. But the shop also has an exceptionally fine pedigree, and owner George Paxton is carrying on the family tradition of candy making. Ever heard of "Chuckles" candy; you know, those fruit-flavored jellies that came pack-aged all in a row? Turns out Paxton's father invented them in the 1930s.

Galena River Wine and Cheese Shop, 420 South Main Street, Galena, (815) 777-9430, is a great stop for gourmet cheeses, meats, wines . . . the good life. Dur-ing various periods, the 1845 building housed wine and liquor wholesalers and three creameries. Today you can shop for some 170 wines, 120 cheeses, many of which are locally made, as well as specialty mustards, pastas, crackers, breads, preserves, dried fruits and nuts, chocolates, coffees, teas, and microbrews. A sig-nature line of gourmet products is available from Chef Ivo's Galena Canning Company, such as raspberry honey mustard dip, jalapeño and honey barbeque sauce, and fudge sauce. And when Chef Ivo himself is on the premises, you will want to be too.

Walk across the street to the grapevine-festooned retail store of the Galena Cellars Tasting Room and Gift Shop, 515 South Main Street, Galena, (815) 777-3330. Galena Cellars is a winery and vineyard that produces nearly 40 varieties of red, white, and fruit wines that are either estate-bottled or made from grapes grown elsewhere. The Main Street store is housed in an 1840s granary and con-venient for its in-town location.

While in Galena, take your pick of any number of cozy restaurants, and relax for a time at a little table by a window. It is the perfect vantage point for watch-ing the people parade pass by, and a great opportunity to savor delicious food.

Country Roads

Siblings Scott and Chris Lawlor own the in-town store as well as the Galena Cellars Vineyard and Winery, 4746 North Ford Road, Galena. It is easy to find; from Main Street, turn right onto Stagecoach Trail, drive 6 miles into the coun-tryside, and turn left at North Ford Road. Is it redundant, in Jo Daviess Coun-ty, to say the view from the vineyard is magnificent? Perhaps not, because when

Owner Scott Lawlor in the vineyard of Galena Cellars Winery, Galena.

you relax with a glass of wine on the sun-dappled deck, you can see clear to Iowa and Wisconsin. For a nominal fee, vineyard tours are offered at set times on weekend afternoons. Begin with an educational tasting, then proceed to the fermenting, blending, and bottling areas, before taking a glass of your favorite vintage out onto the deck. It could be one of the newer dry red zinfandels made from 50-year-old vines and aged in American oak barrels of Midwestern origin. The zinfandel hints of wild berries and black cherry. A bottle of the black raspberry framboise, which is a dessert wine with an intense raspberry flavor, would make an impressive hostess gift.

An on-farm shopping experience awaits at **Christmas in the Valley**, Valley View Farm, 4032 West Stagecoach Trail, Galena, (815) 777-9375. From the vineyard, return to Stagecoach Trail and follow the hillside drive down. Both the barn and oversized house of this century-old farmstead are packed to the rafters with gift items. In the house, shop for decorative chickens and roosters, cookie cutters, cookbooks, apple garlands, and gourmet foods such as pretzel dips and cheese ball mixes.

Here are some additional Home Grown Directory producers, all of which are located in the northern half of the county. It is a sampling; pick your own favorites. Keep in mind too that individual circumstances change, so please call ahead.

From W. Stagecoach Trail, drive south to **Cedardale Farm Flowers**, 2637 North

Cogan Lane, Galena, (815) 777-1771. Here you can buy the goods to fill your home with the natural beauty of dried-flower wreaths, swags, and centerpieces. On this large family farm, they not only create the arrangements but also grow, gather, and dry the materials. These include flowers, fruits, ornamental grasses, herbs, and vegetables. You are welcome to view the freeze-drying operation. It keeps flowers such as roses and peonies, and vegetables such as oranges and Brussels sprouts, looking fresh. In summer, wander among the production and display gardens.

On to the **Brown Barn Vegetable Stop**, 2807 North Elizabeth/Scales Mound Road, Scales Mound, (815) 777-6934. From Cedardale Farm Flowers, go back north on North Cogan Lane, right on West Guilford Road (becomes West Rawlins Road), and left on Elizabeth/Scales Mound Road for a total of 3 miles. When no one is around, settle up using their honor system. Haven't seen that in a while? It is a matter of trust, and it could only work in the country. On a seasonal basis, you are likely to find organic beets, broccoli, cabbage, cucumbers, onions, potatoes, sweet corn, tomatoes, sweet peppers, and squash.

There are plenty of other places you could visit throughout Jo Daviess County for fresh beef, produce, Christmas trees, and other fine agricultural products. If your plans call for a return to Galena and you happen to get a craving for fresh raspberries, visit **Murphy's Gardens**, 12550 West Norris Lane, Galena, (815) 777-4273. Murphy's Gardens is off Highway 20 and just close enough to Galena to be convenient, yet far enough away to give a country feel that comes courtesy of grazing horses and panoramic vistas. Murphy's Gardens is located just over four miles northwest of downtown Galena. There you can pick raspberries or buy them pre-picked, shop for flowering plants throughout the growing season, and find colorful squashes and funny gourds into autumn. Look for seasonal Concord grapes, apples, herbs, tomatoes, and peppers.

For farm-based fun with a little more kick to it, take a guided ATV tour with **Ehrler's Outdoor Adventures**, 11866 West Chetlain Lane, (815) 777-4852, www.charismaunlimited.com. Rides last from one hour to half a day, and special lunch and sunset adventures are available. Call ahead.

Some weekends are just meant to be perfect, and this could be one of them. From the traditional and specialty farms that offer you a chance to tour, to the little jar of pretzel dip to be found in Galena, to the dinner to be savored as evening settles into colors more complex than sky-blue, this trip provides the opportunity to be oh-so-civilized.

SPECIAL EVENTS

Echoes of the Past, at Oak Hill Farm, 8044 Gabel Lane (off Stagecoach Trail), Apple River, (815) 594-2348. Labor Day weekend. Beautiful 172-acre farm throws an old-fashioned party. Catch antique farm equipment demonstrations with draft horses, mules, and small engines. Wagon and carriage rides. Lunch stand with lemonade, grilled burgers and brats, homemade pickles and relishes,

---

FIELD TO TABLE

Pesto from the kitchen
OF MURPHY'S GARDENS

3 cups fresh basil leaves
4 cloves garlic (more or less if you like)
³/₄ cup grated Parmesan cheese (canned works fine)
½ cup olive oil
¼ cup pine nuts or walnuts
½ cup chopped fresh parsley (optional)
1 fresh tomato (optional)

Combine basil, garlic, parsley, nuts, and tomato in food processor. Blend until well chopped. Add Parmesan and olive oil and process again until well blended. Delicious over cooked pasta—hot or cold.
Recipe courtesy of Lori Murphy, owner, Murphy's Gardens.

---

and blue-ribbon pies available. Donations accepted.

Ladies, don your hats, grab your girlfriends/sisters/mothers, and sashay out to **Ladies Getaway in Galena** in mid-September. Get your bearings and post messages at the historic DeSoto House Hotel, 230 South Main Street, then do the free stuff all over town: mini-manicures, decorating how-to's, demos of all kinds, gift certificate drawings, tea/cheese/wine tastings. Enjoy special sales and accommodations packages, and by all means win the hat contest. Call (815) 777-9050, visit www.galenachamber.com/ladiesgetaway.htm.

Old Market Days, Old Market House, 123 North Commerce Street, Galena, (815) 777-3310. End of September. Ladies in turn-of-the-century costume demonstrate heritage skills and sell baked goods, produce, jams/jellies, honey, candy, and cutlery. This is a homemakers' association benefit, so for goodness' sake, support the gals who still know how to bake pies.

Harvest Hoedown, Derinda Farm Antique Market, 8585 South Derinda, Elizabeth, (888) 202-1200. Early October. Fiddle music, square dances, local farm produce, farm education programs in Old Derinda School, children's farm games, butter making, ice cream making. Antiques available in restored farm buildings.

Tea and Tarts with America's Great Ladies, DeSoto House Hotel, 230 South Main Street, Galena, (800) 343-6562. Recurring Series. Lively dramatic interpretations with elegant teas on selected Saturday afternoons. Reservations/tickets. The actress, Lucy Miele, lives in a pre-Civil War farmhouse.

PLACES TO EAT

Fried Green Tomatoes, 1301 Irish Hollow Road, Galena, (815) 777-3938, www.friedgreen.com. This acclaimed Italian restaurant/steakhouse occupies a brick building that was part of the nineteenth century, 80-acre county poor farm. Able-bodied residents helped raise crops and livestock to support themselves and pay debts, but that is all in the past. Dinner only, not cheap but the freshest foods, and they bake your bread fresh with a golden, parmesan-crusted top.

The Great Galena Cookery, The Artists' Annex, 412 Spring Street, B, Galena, (815) 777-1556. Real Food Midwest American Style is just one of the dinners you could learn how to whip up, and then eat, as a student in the evening cooking class.

PLACES TO STAY

Charisma Country Cottage, 11866 West Chetlain Lane, Galena, (815) 777-4852, www.charismaunlimited.com. This richly appointed cottage is all yours on a working family farm. Whirlpool, fireplace, TV/VCR. No breakfast.

Cloran Mansion, 1237 Franklin Street, Galena, (815) 777-0583, www.cloran mansion.com. Italianate Victorian was built in 1880 and today welcomes guests with four rooms with fireplaces and double whirlpools, a suite, and a 530-square-foot cottage. Adjacent to a 239-acre working farm.

Galena Cellars Vineyard Guest House and Guest Suite, North Ford Road, Galena, (815) 777-3330, (800)-397-WINE, www.galenacellars.com. Two-bedroom farmhouse, or one-bedroom suite above the tasting room. No breakfast.

Peaceful Pines, 9033 East Canyon Road, Apple River, (815) 745-2536, www.peacefulpines.net. Beneath towering trees, the only sounds disturbing the peace are wild turkeys, hoot owls, and other critters that feel just as at home on this 19-acre farmette as you will. Imagine the privacy and relaxation of a spacious cottage set just far enough apart from the owners' home, and where you are the only guest. Screened porch, air-conditioned, full kitchen with a fridge the size you left back home, TV, deck, stars included. No breakfast.

Pine Hollow Inn, 4700 North Council Hill Road, Galena, (815) 777-1071. Breathe the freshest possible air on this 120-acre Christmas tree farm. Four suites, one guest room, country décor, microwave and refrigerator available, full breakfast.

25. ROCK RIVER VALLEY

A few counties west of Chicagoland, things begin to settle down among green hills and a lazy waterway. This beautiful region, fancifully known as both the Rock River Valley and Blackhawk Waterways, contains Carroll, Whiteside, Lee, and Ogle counties. Among all the green of the Rock River Valley, you will find a bison ranch, a windmill, a gristmill, and a First Thanksgiving Dinner presided over by a descendant of the Pilgrims. And it was in the Rock River Valley, way

---

FARTHER AFIELD

A cup of sand

HERE'S A LITTLE STORY BEHIND THE FULTON WINDMILL TOLD BY MILLER RON VENEMA.

"One of the things that they would like to add [to the windmill] is what would be called a tax house, just another building that would be associated with the mill. [It would be authentic because in Holland] when people brought their grain in [to be ground], they had to pay the tax on it. Being economical, some Dutchmen would claim that their grain was going to be for cattle feed rather than for human consumption. So there would be less tax on it. They could say the animals were going to eat it, then take it home and eat it themselves. [But] the tax man, he got wise to them, so he'd throw a cup of sand in. So you could tell the poor ones from the rich ones by the length of their teeth. I had one visitor that had been over to Holland, and he told that story, so I assume there's a certain amount of truth to it."

---

back in 1837, that John Deere first showed farmers how his self-scouring steel plow could cut through the prairie like butter.

Going Dutch

We will get to all of it, but let's start at the western edge, in Whiteside County. To help get an idea of exactly where this weekend will take you, know that the Whiteside County community of Sterling is located about 55 miles northeast of Moline, and that Dixon, which is in Lee County, is about 60 miles southwest of Rockford.

A few years ago, the people of Fulton commissioned a windmill for their quiet little village on the banks of the Mississippi River. It was to be a tourist attraction and a kind of exclamation point for their Dutch heritage. And so they found a builder in the Netherlands and had their new, traditional-style windmill shipped across the Atlantic. They even sent locals abroad to learn how to maneuver and care for the sails, and how to grind grain into flour that they could sell. Today visitors come from all over to tour **De Immigrant**, which is the name a local schoolgirl gave to the windmill. Climb up inside the various levels to see how it all works. Up at the top where the sails connect to the 25-ton cap, sheep fat lubricates the wooden beams, and beeswax lubricates the brake wheel cogs in the traditional way. To experience it all for yourself, drive into town on Highway 84 or Highway 30, to 10th Avenue and First Street. Call (815) 589-4545 or visit www.cityoffulton.us.

But De Immigrant is not Fulton's only windmill, for wistful little windmill replicas have decorated people's lawns for years. And Fulton's newest mill turns out another kind of product. It is the **Fulton Fiber Mill**, 1007 Fourth Street, Fulton, (815) 589-9963. It opened in 2002 to produce rovings and batts for hand-spinners, and wool yarns and fibers that are collected from an assortment of critters. These include alpacas and even dogs that love a good brushing. Finished clothes are also available.

Back At the Ranch

The twin cities of Sterling and Rock Falls are population centers of the Rock River Valley. From Fulton, Sterling is about 27 miles to the east via Highway 30. While in town, get locally raised certified Angus beef at the **Sauk Valley Angus Country Store**, 8681 Hickory Hills Road, Sterling, (815) 622-0002.

Just outside of Sterling, you can see where the buffalo roam and the deer and the other animals play at **Chief Shikshak Northwest Bison Ranch**, 23637 Quinn Road, Sterling, (815) 336-2145. When he initially bought the land, local dentist Dr. Charles Lyon wanted a place for off-roading. Somehow that became a working ranch with bison, red deer, a game bird hatchery, and room enough

Mammoth residents of the Chief Shikshak Northwest Bison Ranch, Sterling.

for visitors. Call ahead to make arrangements for what you would like to do on a weekend visit; fees apply. Schedule a hayrack ride, or cut your teeth on a Hummer tour that includes three camel-hump hills that the vehicle eats for lunch. You might enjoy an interpretive presentation of items that were hand-crafted by Native Americans from bison hooves and hides. Or simply take a hike and visit with the animals. Before leaving, buy a couple of frozen low-fat bison or venison steaks to put in your cooler and to throw on a grill at home or at one of the Rock River Valley's many beautiful parks.

Now it's time to head north on Highway 40 into Carroll County. Just past the line, you may wish to saddle up at **Eagle Point Horseback Riding Farm**, 5399 Maple Road, Milledgeville, (815) 225-7473. Call for availability of mounts on weekends. Children must be at least five to trail-ride, but adult riders can lead younger ones around the farm for free.

Milling Around

From the stable, let's cut over to Lee County, specifically Franklin Grove, and—more specifically—the **Franklin Creek Gristmill and Interpretive Center**, 1893 Twist Road, Franklin Grove, (815) 456-2718, www.franklingroveil.org/grstml. htm. You get there by driving east on Milledgeville Road to Polo, then south on Highway 26 to Dixon and east on Highway 38 to Franklin Grove. Turn north on Daysville Road, go 2 blocks, and turn left on Old Mill Road. Follow the signs for 2.5 miles, turn right onto aptly named Twist Road, and go another quarter-mile; the entire trip is about 30 miles.

Now we have arrived at the peaceful little mill that reconstructs the original 1847 structure. Surrounding it is the Franklin Creek State Natural Area that covers 664 acres of natural springs, prairies, hardwood forests, reclaimed farmlands, and scenic bedrock outcroppings. Water from the mill pond powers the water-wheel, activating gears and pulleys to turn the runner stone and grind the corn-meal. Watch the process on the last Saturday of the month and take home a bag of cornmeal.

Turning Points

You are not far from the site where John Deere, a young blacksmith from Ver-mont, forged a legendary plow and made quite a name for himself and all of his descendants. To reach the **John Deere Historic Site**, 8393 South Main Street, Grand Detour, (815) 652-4551, you will have to snake back into Franklin Grove, then go back through Dixon and northeast on Highway 2 along the beautiful Rock River for a total of almost seven and one-half miles. But it is worth the effort, because the site recreates a key point in the history of modern agriculture. Tell the ones in the back seat to stop yawning; they haven't met the blacksmith yet.

The idyllic atmosphere of the John Deere Historic Site is worlds away from the twenty-first-century displays of power back at Deere & Company World Headquarters in Moline. The story unfolds within the Archeology Exhibit,

The blacksmith shop at the John Deere Historic Site, Grand Detour.

where you take in a video and simulated conversations while studying the actual site of Deere's blacksmith shop that is laid out at your feet. Nearby, a replica of the original shop comes alive as a convivial, professional blacksmith demonstrates how iron (today they typically use steel) is forged into graceful shapes that are also practical products. Fire and sparks supply the drama; the anvil and tools make it happen; and the fast-talking smithy's spirited patter grabs your attention. He might, for example, tell you that if you had brought your horse in for shoeing, you would have had the most important job at the shop—swatting the flies to help keep the horse still.

Resume the pretty drive on Highway 2, then east on Highway 72 into Byron, crossing the Rock River to the **Byron Heritage Farm Museum**, 7993 North River Road, Byron, (815) 234-8535. You are now about 21 miles northeast of Grand Detour, and back in Ogle County, which you cut through earlier on the way to the Franklin Creek Gristmill. A work in progress, the rescued 1847 farmstead is a quick stop at a busy crossroads. The quiet of the country is nowhere near, but you cannot help but be glad that the locals saved the farm. One building displays a row of furnished period rooms like life-size dioramas. Pick up the black telephone receivers and listen to the recordings that interpret each room; one of these describes what the family would have eaten, including hotcakes and pork at sunrise. Wander through the farmstead's red barns and outbuildings. Learn how the family would have looked to trees to help supplement their diet. The honey locust, for example, kept children happily chewing the sweet pulp from the long seedpods (this is not a recommendation). The most giggle-inducing artifacts, though, are those that have been dredged up from the 1930s/40s family privy. Archeologists everywhere have discovered that the privy is a prime portal into the past. On display at this particular portal are lots of glass bottles, which told the diggers that this family could afford to toss them out instead of reusing them.

Meandering through the highways and byways of the Rock River Valley gives travelers a sense of its agricultural heritage. It is a great heritage indeed, for when John Deere first cut the prairie like butter, he also planted the seeds of change that were the turning point for modern farming methods. But the tour also gives visitors the chance to meet those who want the prairie back, and who are in fact bringing it back in spades, at places like Chief Shikshak Northwest Bison Ranch and the Franklin Creek State Natural Area. Finally, it's intriguing to note the presence of two mills, both new and both powered by traditional forces, namely wind and water.

SPECIAL EVENTS

Fulton Dutch Days, Fulton, (815) 589-2616. First weekend in May. Everyone in town goes Dutch at this ethnic heritage celebration.

Heritage Tractor Adventure along the I & M Canal, (815) 727-2323, www.heritagetractoradventure.com. Mid-June. Max Armstrong of WGN Radio in Chicago rides in this three-day parade along with numerous other tractor buffs, down the length of the I & M Canal Path.

Franklin Grove Summer Harvest Festival, in and around the town and south on Whitney Road, Franklin Grove, (815) 456-3030. Early August. Old-fashioned threshing event with antique tractors and farm machinery. Draft horse jamboree and working blacksmith at Chaplin Creek Historic Village.

Two-Cylinder Days, John Deere Historic Site, 8393 South Main Street, Grand Detour, (815) 652-4551. Early August. It's a tractor thing.

Blue Goose Run/Haunted Halloween Maze, 14609 Blue Goose Road, Sterling, (815) 772-7200, www.bluegooserun.com. End of August through October. Ten-acre maze, pick your own popcorn and Indian corn, hayrack rides, bonfires, giant chess/checkers set, corn crib banquet hall.

Corny Events Cornfield MAiZE, 17505 Polo Road, Sterling, (815) 632-0899. End of August through October. Seven-acre maze with chance to test your knowledge of agriculture. Soybean maze too. Live farm animals.

Franklin Creek Preservation Area Pork Event, 1893 Twist Road, Franklin Grove, (815) 456-2718. September. Corn grinding demos at the mill, covered wagon tours, and plenty of pork.

Farm Visit Day, Ogle County, (815) 732-2191. Mid-September.

First Thanksgiving Dinner, Heritage Center, Lanark, (815) 493-2307, (866) 493-2307. Second Saturday of November. Join Norman Standish, a descendant

FIELD NOTES

Blue Moon Llamas

Chris Armstrong does not bother with an umbrella as some 60 soggy llamas mill about the barnyard one rainy morning. One llama mama hums
to her wobbly baby, called a cria, while another female resorts to spitting
as an exuberant male chases her. But most just want to nibble the grain
from Armstrong's hands.

This is Blue Moon Llamas in Byron, Illinois. It is a specialty breeding
farm on 14 country acres, with plenty of room for miniature horses,
goats, cats, dogs, and a young family. Armstrong says the llamas have
always taken special care around her children, gingerly stepping around
any who took a tumble or just plain got underfoot.

This is no ordinary llama farm. It actually has a strong community
service component. Armstrong explains. "We also take our llamas to
nursing homes and schools, and we run a summer camp here with the
Lutheran Outdoor Ministry Center. For the week, the campers each get
their own llama to learn about it, groom it, and build an obstacle course
to train it. They also learn to felt, spin, and dye the wool."

Blue Moon Llamas has also started an informal program whereby
people can spend time with the llamas in various ways. 🐾

Chris Armstrong with daughter Lauren and members of the herd at Blue Moon Llamas, Byron.

of the Pilgrim Myles Standish, for an authentic recreation of America's earliest feast. It is a tasteful history lesson, and the subject is roast turkey with dressing, cucumber soup, cottage potatoes, cranberry relish, scalloped onions in a cream and cheddar sauce, cornmeal rolls, and succotash, which is a blend of sweet corn and beans.

PLACES TO EAT

Candlelight Inn, 2905 North Locust Street, Sterling, (815) 625-2600. Try their signature Chicken George, sliced chicken breasts dipped in batter and fried. Down home, wood-paneled atmosphere in a converted barn.

Colonial Rose Inn and Restaurant, 8230 South Green Street, Grand Detour, (815) 652-4422, www.colonialroseinn.com. Fine dining in nineteenth-century bed and breakfast. Entrées may include hickory smoked pork chops (smoked on premises) with maple-pecan bourbon glaze, seared salmon with balsamic lemon sauce, grilled Black Angus filet mignon with béarnaise.

Log Cabin Restaurant, Dinner Theatre, both at White Pines Inn, White Pines Forest State Park, 6712 West Pines Road, Mount Morris, (815) 946-3817. Corn Husker's Sunday buffet, both breakfast and dinner seatings. Dinner theater matinee and evening performances.

PLACES TO STAY

Country Inn and Suites, 2106 1st Avenue (Highway 40), Rock Falls, (815) 625-3200. Continental breakfast, indoor pool/whirlpool, fitness center, game room.

Country Palmer House, 17035 Elizabeth Road, Mount Carroll, (815) 244-2343. Circa-1911 home on a farm. Full country breakfast including seasonal fruits and vegetables from the farm garden. Outdoor spa.

Evergreen Farm Inn, 10003 West Coffman Road, Forreston, (815) 938-2198. Join the big, comfy, 1917 farmhouse in its fragrant, green nest. A 225-acre crop farm, this one's been in the family since 1845; the owner recalls big, harvest-time thresher meals that her mother presided over in the dining room. Sit on the porch with cats and enjoy the view of the Amish-restored windmill. Spend the evening pond-side at Marshmallow Retreat, the perfect place for a weenie roast. Lose count of the stars. Full breakfast.

The Standish House Bed and Breakfast, 540 West Carroll Street, Lanark, (815) 493-2307, (866) 493-2307. Enjoy the peaceful, small-town setting and the hosts' passion for local and American history. Local farm tours can be arranged.

26. COUNTRY IN THE CITY: THIS IS CHICAGO?

More commerce than corn and more skyscraper than silo, Chicagoland still makes room for real working farms that dig deep into a past that is almost, but not quite, paved over. These are the living history farms, and the area has a surprising number of first-rate examples. Here the costumed interpreters roll up frayed sleeves and cut wood to build new outbuildings, scenting the air with sawdust, muck out horse stalls, rinse dinner dishes in soapy tubs outside, and don protective mesh to pull honeycombs out of clean, white hives. Instead of just telling you, they show you what life was like and sometimes, they invite you to shell peas. Here too, you can scoop up handfuls of hay and inhale deeply of the sweet, green fragrance. It takes you back a century. And, maybe more importantly, it takes you back to your own childhood summers. These rustic getaways can be found in nearby suburbs, and all can be reached from downtown. Depending on traffic, you will get there eventually.

Still Farming in the Northwest 'Burbs

The first farm on our list is located in one of the unlikeliest places for an agricultural attraction that you can imagine: a few miles from the monolithic Woodfield Shopping Center in northwest suburban Schaumburg. Located on Plum Grove Road south of Schaumburg Road, the Volkening Heritage Farm is where the sights, sounds, and smells of a real farmyard transport all of your senses to the 1880s. And on this farm, chickens need feeding, vegetables need tending, and sheep need to be sheared. Enjoy weekend events like "From Hoghouse to Smokehouse," when you can help grind and press pork for sausage; or "Christmas in the Valley," with crafts, horse-drawn hayrides, holiday treats, and chores to warm you up; or "Wake Up and Work on the Farm," which happens very early (farmers get up early, you know) on selected summer weekend mornings (advance registration and fee required). During "Wake Up and Work on the Farm," you will do chores like gather eggs, fix fences, and milk the cow, but also eat, eat, eat a hearty farm breakfast. And somewhere inside the surrounding Spring Valley Nature Sanctuary, you can see remnants of a 1920s peony farm. So come join the fun at **Volkening Heritage Farm at Spring Valley**, 201 South Plum Grove Road (1/4 mile south of Schaumburg Road), Schaumburg, (847) 985-2100, www.parkfun.com/spv.

Still Farming in the Western 'Burbs

Now it is time to head south on I-290 to I-355, then west on Route 64 to **Kline Creek Farm at Timber Ridge Forest Preserve**, 1N600 County Farm Road (between North Avenue and Geneva Road), Winfield, (630) 876-5900, www.dupageforest.com/EDUCATION/klinecreek.html. At this point, you are in the far western suburbs, about 20 miles southwest of Schaumburg. Suddenly it is 1890-something, and you are walking alongside several hundred acres of cropland. Cross the footbridge and hurry over to the farmhouse as a bell clangs— calling you not to supper but to your tour of the Victorian farmhouse that is painted the color of fresh cream. Generations of a DuPage County farm family lived and worked here, and prospered enough to have a fancy parlor with a pump organ and lace curtains that pooled with pointed excess upon the floor.

Tour the outbuildings on your own. Stick your head inside the brick smokehouse, which is Kline Creek Farm's oldest building, to smell an ashy century and a half of meat preservation. Poke around the barn where swallows swoop above the heads of livestock, just as they would have a hundred years ago. Learn how the windmill, pump house, and milk house kept the farm's liquid lifelines (water and milk) flowing. Up the dusty road a piece, watch as the apiary hums with the busyness of some 800,000 resident honeybees. You can buy their finished product at the new visitor center that also has exhibits. Year-round, there is always activity at Kline Creek Farm, including the canning of heirloom vegetables in summer. Expect special events like maple sugaring, sheep shearing, and even funerary customs. But Kline Creek Farm is not just for show. Livestock that is not kept to expand the herd is sold at auction to local farmers, or sent to market. Eggs are not only used in cooking demonstrations, but also shipped to a nearby wildlife rehabilitation center. Grain is marketed and known for its excellence. So go—this is the real thing.

For another authentic farm experience, follow Highway 38 westward for about 20 miles to **Garfield Farm Museum**, 3N016 Garfield Road (just north of 38), LaFox, (630) 584-8485, www.garfieldfarm.org. Far west suburban LaFox is a small town that recently awoke to the sounds of bulldozers and builders. The rooftops are sprouting like corn, but Garfield Farm is not budging from its 374 acres. Indeed, it is listed on the National Register of Historic Sites. That's good news, because it is a treasure complete with artifacts like two thousand documents from the nineteenth century and a surviving native prairie.

In 1846 the Garfield family built a brick inn to accommodate teamsters hauling grain to hungry Chicago markets, as well as weary stagecoach passengers. The inn's three stories feature five bedrooms, a taproom, ballroom, and other rooms in which the travelers could comfortably wash away the trail dust. Additional buildings that you can see include the 1842 hay barn, 1860s buggy shed, 1890s granary, and 1906 dairy barn. All of this is very much in the process of being restored, so your access is limited to guided tours and special events. But what events! Here is the lineup: Rare Breeds Show in mid-May, Antique Tool Show and Heirloom Garden Show in August, Harvest Days in October, Candlelight at the Inn during December, and prairie walks from May to September.

South of the farm, pick up I-88 and head east now to I-294 south and exit at Ogden Avenue for an amazing glimpse into old-fashioned grain processing. You are going to **Graue Mill and Museum**, York and Spring Roads (a quarter mile north of Ogden Avenue), Oak Brook, (630) 655-2090, www.grauemill.org. For 60 years beginning in 1852, three generations of the Graue family ground grain into meal and flour at this handsome, brick-and-timber gristmill. Today Graue Mill shares the banks of Salt Creek with pricey homes and the 222 acres of Fullersburg Woods. Begin your tour on the first floor, where a white-aproned miller cranks out a bucket of yellow cornmeal in mere seconds. Do not be fooled by that massive waterwheel outside; it still turns, but the miller's grinding stones use electrical power. Still, the cornmeal is wonderfully free of preservatives with its germ intact, and you can buy sacks of it to take home.

Upstairs in what used to be the granary, there are spinning wheels, butter churns, and volunteer interpreters who bring the old equipment to life for you with expert demonstrations and informative patter. And listen to the words of Dorothy Graue, who in 1989 recounted her childhood experiences at "Uncle Walt's mill." As she recalled, "We liked to chew raw wheat kernels. If you chew them long enough, and don't swallow any, the wad will turn into a glutenous mass that you can pull and stretch like gum."

Be Your Own Farmhand

If you prefer a more hands-on rural experience, you can harvest your own fruits and vegetables at scenic u-pick farms and country markets that are scattered farther afield but worth the drive. One is **Royal Oak Farm Orchard**, 15908 Hebron Road, Harvard, (815) 648-4141, www.royaloakfarmorchard.com. Closed on Sundays. Here in far northwest Harvard, 20 varieties of apples grow on 10,000 trees that pay homage to one 240-year-old oak. Like a hug from a big family, gourds of every stripe and bump welcome you onto the porch of the Country Store. Buy bagged apples by the peck, or find out what varieties you can pick yourself on any given day. Go in early September for Jonamac, Ozark Gold, and McIntosh. Expect Cortlands mid-month, and stake your claim for Goldrush in October. Beyond apples, you can also pick raspberries in July, peaches in August, and pumpkins and gourds in October. A handcrafted playland, petting zoo, and pony rides entertain children and adults alike. The Country Kitchen restaurant serves up hot, home-style entrées, and the bakery offers take-home apple treats. Stock up on regional cookbooks in the country store.

Still have a hankering for the great outdoors? Then head over to **Richardson Farm**, 9407 Richardson Road, Spring Grove, (815) 675-9729, www.richardson farm.com. Drive east on Highway 173 to Richmond (stop there for old-fashioned shopping, including honey from an in-store beehive), then continue east, making a right onto Richardson Road. Now into its sixth generation of Richardsons, this inventive farm sprawls over 450 acres and two farmsteads. Fifty-thousand Christmas trees scent the air, and you can cut your own after Thanksgiving. But during the crisp, golden days of autumn, nothing beats an invigorating chase through the 20-acre corn maze. Try a midnight run with help from your flashlight and any beams the moon cares to throw down.

Fair Weather

Starting in July, the Chicagoland county fair season kicks in with tractor pulls, big name entertainment, good eatin', crazy midway rides, and prize livestock. The **Sandwich Fair**, (815) 786-2389, www.sandwichfair.com, celebrates not sandwiches but the agriculture of DeKalb County. Everyone calls it the Sandwich Fair because it's in Sandwich, Illinois, which is about 60 miles southwest of downtown Chicago, and worth the drive if you are in town in mid-September.

This is one of the greatest county fairs around.

Other Chicagoland events, not as big as the county fairs but true to their locales, include the **Big Rock Plowing Match** in May (since 1895), the **Saint Charles Scarecrow Festival** in October, (800) 777-4373, and **Harvard Milk Days** in May/June, (815) 943-4614. In September, Chicago's grand Garfield Park Conservatory, 300 North Central Park Avenue, Chicago, (312) 746-5100, www .garfieldconservatory.org, hosts a **County Fair** of sorts. They don't call it the Cook County Fair, but they do offer a variety of events that would be typical of a county fair. These include pony rides, a petting zoo, harvest competitions, garden demonstrations, and food booths. Careful, though. The conservatory's west side location is known as a high-crime area.

Country-in-the-City

Don't let the fact that Chicago is the nation's third largest city lead you to believe that it offers nothing but skyscrapers and expressways. Five miles north of downtown, yet still in the heart of the city, the multi-million-dollar brownstones of tony Lincoln Park form an unlikely backdrop for the silver silo, barns, and waving corn plants of a farm. But there it is, in this city neighborhood, and it is called **Farm in the Zoo**. This newly reopened and much beloved feature of **Lincoln Park Zoo** now offers interactive experiences like cow milking, keeper talks, butter churning, a weather station, and a working farmhouse kitchen where visitors learn about those legendary farm breakfasts. Farmers-for-the-day explore the various barns, the crop plot, the farmhouse, and its adjacent chicken and rabbit yards, and even a tiny shop that sells toy farm animals and machinery. So be sure to visit the Lincoln Park Zoo, 2200 North Cannon Drive (at Lake Shore Drive and Fullerton Parkway), Lincoln Park, (312) 742-2000, www.lpzoo.com.

But one farm in the city is not enough for a city like Chicago. Over at **Brookfield Zoo**, 3300 Golf Road, Brookfield, (708) 485-0263, (800) 201-0784, www .brookfieldzoo.org, they have their share of resident farmyard critters, barns, and special programs as well. Brookfield is actually not a city neighborhood but a suburb; get it? Here the farm setting is called the Children's Zoo, and a small additional fee applies. In the Big Barn, you and your little ones can watch milking demonstrations and chicks hatching out of their eggs. The barn is also where you can learn how to make your own butter.

Watching Chicago's great grain markets in action is a part of agriculture that you can only experience here. It was way back in 1848 that the United States' first grain futures exchange was established as the **Board of Trade**, 141 West Jackson Blvd., Chicago, (312) 435-3590, www.cbot.com. Closed to visitors since terrorist attacks of 2001; check for current accessibility. Also located downtown, the **Chicago Mercantile Exchange**, 30 South Wacker Drive, Fourth Floor, Chicago, (800) 331-3332, www.cme.com, also has a long history, and you can learn about it, as well as the current advanced operation, on an exciting

Brookfield Zoo's Children's Zoo, Brookfield. Photo Courtesy Brookfield Zoo.

weekday visit.

Everyone who visits Chicago wants Chicago-style pizza, but the American Heartland's largest city dishes out way more local flavor than you can stuff into a crust. Local chefs who helped to pioneer the concept of regional foods as the basis for exquisite cuisine have attained national celebrity status. It is no surprise, then, that they insist on Midwestern and world ingredients from the best growers. Also on Chicago's plate is neighborhood fare, which is frequently ethnic in nature, just as its colorful neighborhoods are. So go, eat up, and enjoy yourself.

From the powerful grain markets in the Loop to the outlying living history farms, and with the immigrant tradition that guarantees you can always find something extraordinary to eat, Chicago is a great place to find the country in the city.

PLACES TO EAT

CHICAGO

Café Selmarie, 4729 North Lincoln Avenue, Chicago, (773) 989-5595, www .cafeselmarie.com. Quiet spot popular with locals. American cuisine with French and Italian influences. Lunch sandwiches and entrées. Try warm marinated goat cheese with mixed organic greens and grilled country Italian bread. Or Amish half chicken with creamy polenta, roasted shallots, and Italian parsley salad.

erwin, 2925 North Halsted Street, Chicago, (773) 528-7200, www.erwincafe .com. Opened in 1994, this acclaimed spot features what it terms Urban Heartland cuisine in a fine dining atmosphere. Brunch and dinner. There is a definite farmers' market freshness at work here, with plenty of northern-Midwest ingredients putting in an appearance.

WEST

The Milk Pail, 14N630 Highway 25, East Dundee, (847) 742-5040, www.the milkpail.com. Located on a 30-acre wooded site since 1939. Sandwiches, lots of entrée choices including sage-stuffed Cornish hen, homemade meatloaf, and honey pecan chicken. Also French Country Market, 1870s farmhouse to tour, and entertainment options.

SOUTH

White Fence Farm, 11700 Joliet Road, Lemont, (630) 739-1720, www.white fencefarm.com/chicago. Modestly billed as the "World's Greatest Chicken," it is fried to perfection and served up family style. Try the half chicken with down-home sides like corn fritters and a baked potato with homemade gravy. Secret-recipe breading is milled exclusively for White Fence Farm. It would not be a farm without animals, so be sure to visit the on-site petting zoo. A family favorite since the 1920s.

PLACES TO STAY

NORTH

Sweet Basil Hill Farm Bed and Breakfast Inn, 15937 West Washington Street, Gurnee, (847) 244-3333, www.sweetbasilhill.com. Over seven wooded acres with orchard, veggie garden, and llamas. Hot spiced cider, lemonade, cookies, etc. each evening plus continental breakfast. Three guestrooms plus guest cottage.

The Richmond Inn, 10314 East Street, Richmond, (815) 678-2505, www.the richmondinn.com. 1893 Italianate Painted Lady that does not show her age. Three-course, chef-prepared gourmet breakfast. Optional cooking classes. Four guestrooms.

NORTHWEST AND WEST

Oscar Swan Country Inn, 1800 West State Street, Geneva, (630) 232-0173, www.oscarswan.com. Relax in this turn-of-the-century inn on eight acres of beautiful land that even has a barn dating back to 1836. The history of the place includes a gentleman's farm and country estate. Seven private baths, one shared.

Victorian Rose Garden Bed and Breakfast, 314 Washington Street, Algonquin, (847) 854-9667, (888) 854-9667, www.sleepandeat.com. 1886 Victorian once owned by a cheese maker and farmer. Four guestrooms, private baths. Great wraparound porch, full breakfast including hot entrée, breakfast meat, fresh or baked fruit.

FIELD NOTES

Kinnikinnick farm

After 30 years of in-state politics and at the Chicago Board of Trade, David Cleverdon became a specialty grower of organic produce. The way he tells it, this was the logical next step. "I love the risk involved because of the weather, and the intensity of it all. There is no greater high than somebody saying, 'The last time I had arugula like this was in Italy.' It's like a comic getting a laugh," he explains.

Cleverdon's Kinnikinnick Farm in Caledonia, east of Rockford, specializes in healthy, leafy produce like baby greens, chicories, and Italian cooking greens that Cleverdon says you can buy in Chicago— or in Tuscany. He imports the seeds of yet-undiscovered greens, like *spigiarello* and *bietina*, from the Old Country. And then there are the beets that get their flavor from the heavy clay soil. "We grow awesome beets. In some ways, I wish we didn't, because it's time- and labor-consuming," Cleverdon laments, adding that once a chef tastes a Kinnikinnick Farm beet, it's sold.

The prize produce makes appearances each year at the Evanston Farmers' Market, Chicago Green City Market, and some of the city's finest restaurants, including North Pond, Blackbird, and Fortunato.

In the late 1980s, Kinnikinnick Farm rose from the detritus of an abandoned farm. The messy transformation started with three weekends of hands-and-knees clearing before any of the Cleverdon family members could even mow grass without blowing a tire. But buying the farm was not just about business. It was neutral ground where a blended family could get along and grow together.

The Cleverdons sold the first of their *abbondanza* in 1994. They have been reaping the rewards ever since.

Note: Not open to the public. 🐾

---

27. WEST-CENTRAL ILLINOIS: RECALLING THE AGRARIAN PAST

In 1846, charismatic religious leader Erik Jansson led a group of Swedish dissidents to the remote, rich farmland of west-central Illinois, and called it Bishop Hill. The group's faith-centered, agrarian communal living lasted for 15 years and peaked at an estimated one thousand individuals. Today the community of Bishop Hill is a remarkable State Historic Site complete with original buildings and Swedish-American restaurants and shops. Bishop Hill is located in Henry County. As long as you are in Henry County, you may wish to take a round barn tour and indulge in Illinois pork sandwiches at Kewanee's Hog Capital of the World Festival. Make time too to learn more of the John Deere story in nearby Moline, which is one of the Quad Cities and located in the county of Rock Island.

Bishop Hill
First, let's go back in time to the nineteenth century when the founders of Bishop Hill—named for Jansson's birthplace of Biskopskulla, Sweden—walked 160 miles from Chicago to settle here on 40 acres. They went on to erect 20 buildings, own over 10,000 acres of land with several thousand acres under cultivation, and sell agricultural products at a profit on the open market. Learn facts like these at the **State of Illinois Bishop Hill Museum**, 304 South Bishop Hill Street, Bishop Hill, (309) 927-3345.

From an agricultural perspective, find out about the growing of flax and the milling of grain, and the 14- to 16-hour workdays that the settlers endured. You can get a glimpse into these lives from the original folk art paintings by Olof Krans, who lived in Bishop Hill beginning in 1850. Most riveting are the stern, determined faces of the colonists, but you can also see how the people farmed and the clothes they wore in the fields. One painting depicts orderly rows of men cutting golden wheat with scythes, while the women followed in their wake, tying the stalks into bundles.

Go north to the 1854 Steeple Building, which is across from tranquil, historic Bishop Hill Park. Inside is the **Steeple Building Museum**, with comprehensive exhibits on the Janssonites and their determined leader. A handful of the artifacts are household items that the colonists had crafted by hand, and you can get a great understanding of the arduous work involved in processing flax. After your exploration of the collections and historic interpretation, browse the gift store for Swedish heritage and farm-related books.

The Bishop Hill buildings listed below provide some specific insight into the colony's farming or food practices. The descriptions, historic information, and numbering system are taken from the handy-dandy Official Walking Tour brochure/map, which is published by the Bishop Hill Heritage Association. Buildings that are not open to the public are privately owned and viewable from the street. Starting from the Steeple Building Museum, you could take a counter-clockwise turn through town to see all of these.

The **Red House** (#25), 1855, was relocated from its original outpost site adjacent to the colony's farm fields, and it was inhabited during the busiest periods of the growing season. It is the only outpost left out of five, and while it is not open for tours, you can appreciate the logic of its existence and location, given the fact that the community members had 12,000 to 14,000 acres to tend. The **Eric Krans House** (#3), 1848, is not open either, but notable for the fact that it was built without a kitchen, since communal dining took place in Big Brick, and a home kitchen was simply unnecessary. The nearby **Blacksmith Shop** (#4), 1857, houses **Windy Corner Farm**, (309) 927-3033, where decorative items are sold. These are special for being handcrafted from natural materials like dried flowers and grains, poultry feathers and eggs. The nearby **Poppy Barn** (#5), 1882, post-dates the colony era, but was built on the colony farm and moved into town in 1979. Today it is a cheerful shop where baskets, herbs, and botanicals are offered for sale. Two blocks north is the **Dairy Building** (#24), 1854, which the colonists built and used for dairy processing, storage, and living. In 1853, a visitor reported observing 40 to 50 young girls milking an estimated 200 cows in a half-hour timeframe. In yet another display of efficiency, the girls lived on the second floor, never far away from their bovine charges.

Look to the north where the Edwards River flows. There the **Gristmill** (#27), 1847, once supplied flour to the colony. But the river's waterpower quickly proved to be unreliable, so colonists built a steam-driven mill in 1850. The Gristmill's use as a granary continued until 1949, when it was demolished. Back in town, view the **Boys' Dormitory** (#7), 1847, which housed the Ox Boys whose job it was to work farm fields and tend livestock. It is not open to the public. Next up are three more gone-but-not-forgotten sites. Imagine the fragrant aromas and bustle of the **Bakery and Brewery** (#29), 1853, where all of the cooking occurred for the hardworking people. Here, too, kitchen staff baked bread and brewed beer. Once done, it was all wheeled on carts to the dining room of Big Brick, which was located just to the west. **Big Brick** (#28), 1848-1851, was the big communal residence with a full basement where one thousand people could eat at one sitting. Once located in what is now a baseball field near the park, the Bakery and Brewery was demolished in 1961, and Big Brick burned in 1928. Somewhat to the west is the site of a former colony orchard. From the road just north, you can view the **Meat Storage House** (#22), 1851, from the street, as it is privately owned and not open to the public. This brick structure was once part of a complex of barns, an icehouse, a slaughterhouse, a smokehouse, and livestock pens, and here meat was salted for preservation.

Walk south behind the park to the **Colony Hotel** (#13), which was first built in 1852 and is open for tours today. The kitchen is on the first floor. The attic of the **Apartment House and Privy** (#14), 1855, still has poles that were built to store hardtack and seed corn. The **Colony Store** (#16), 1853, is fun because you can shop where the colonists did, at the same counters, and mostly for Scandinavian merchandise and food. The long wooden bar displays lingonberry and wild cloudberry preserves, fish-shaped candies, herring, *Bond Ost* (a creamy yellow cheese), pancake mixes, beets, pickles, cucumbers, red cabbage, cookies, and you-name-it of Swedish origin. Carved and colorful Dalahorse statues stand patiently in neat rows along the store shelves. These carvings are true to the traditional Dalahorse design that originated deep in the forests of Sweden. You will pretty much see it in any shop that sells Swedish wares. It is thought that horses were such a popular subject for Swedish woodcarvers because of the animals' great value to the family and its farm. Speaking of horses, colonists once stabled their own horses in the **Olson Barn** (#12), 1856–60. It is the only barn left from that era, and it was moved to this site in 1982. Finally, the **Krusbo House** (#21), 1855, was a center for cheese production. It is not open to the public.

The **Henry County Historical Museum**, 202 South Park Street, Bishop Hill, (309) 927-3528, focuses not on the famous town that unfolds at its feet, but on the history of the entire county. It is a small museum located just south of the Olson Barn. One room is devoted exclusively to agricultural history. Unusual items on display are a horsehair coat, an open carriage, and farm implements like a centrifugal cream separator.

Bishop Hill stages events throughout the year, but it is during late September at **Jordbruksdagarna—Agriculture Days**—that visitors can help crank the broomcorn scraper; take home sorghum, apples, and produce; make corn husk dolls; listen to music; and sample Colony Stew. Next time you're in Biskopskulla, Sweden, you could attend the Midsummer Eve party with its Bishop Hill theme and museum. It is a great tribute to those who immigrated here from the homeland all those years ago. It signals to their descendants that the connection will always be there. To get to Biskopskulla, first walk 160 miles to Chicago . . .

Make time while in Bishop Hill to sample Swedish cuisine, a legacy of colony days. But now, as you leave Bishop Hill and drive almost 19 miles northeast, you are in for another kind of treat when you visit the **Johnson-Sauk Trail State Park**, 27500 North 1200 Avenue, Kewanee, (309) 853-5589. The park features the unique **Ryan's Round Barn**, which is available for tours, but you have to

Jams and jellies galore at the Colony Store in Bishop Hill.

call ahead to schedule an appointment. This 1910 barn is one of the largest of its kind in the country, standing over 80 feet tall, with an 85-foot diameter and a 16-foot silo within.

Moline

Bishop Hill is about 50 miles from Moline, one of the Quad Cities in neighboring Rock Island County. The thing about Moline is that it is home to Deere & Company World Headquarters, where the legendary agricultural company's story continues to play out. So as long as you are this close, why not go? The John Deere Commons, sited on River Drive between 12th and 19th streets, is an exciting, free-admission complex consisting of the John Deere Pavilion, the John Deere Store, and the John Deere Collectors Center.

If it sounds like a departure from idyllic Bishop Hill, it is, but there is a murky connection. According to historians Carolyn Anderson Wilson and J. Hiram Wilson, in 1851, two men from the Deere Plow Works in Moline visited Bishop Hill. No information is available on how this visit may have affected plowing in the colony, and it is known that the colonists made their own farm implements. But it establishes that there was communication with the famous manufacturing company, which was, in 1851, just getting off the ground.

Start your tour in the **John Deere Pavilion**, 1400 River Drive, Moline, (309) 765-1000, www.johndeerepavilion.com, where the latest combine contrasts wildly with the oldest vintage tractor, although both come wrapped in the same yellow and green. For those who have spent a lifetime in the fields, no candy store could be sweeter. And you can tell who they are. They come in wearing feed caps and with an unmistakable gleam in the eye, a reflection of a feeling for the equipment that could only have been built up over time and row by row. You see the hunkering down of the old timers who seem willing to talk torque and transmissions until the sun goes down. For little kids who love big rigs, it is a chance to climb into cabs that may as well be in the sky. And for anyone who wants to learn how a one-man blacksmith shop became the world's leading producer of agricultural equipment, it is a living, breathing history lesson. Interactive exhibits simulate a factory tour to explain how tractors and combines are built and what they do. Children find answers to questions about how their food gets from the field to the kitchen table. Historic photos and words create an agricultural timeline. Peeking into the future of a planet packed with people, a 40-inch touch-screen display reveals how much fruit, grain, and eggs will be needed to feed them all.

Also visit two Deere family mansions located within a stone's throw from one another and less than a mile (but uphill) from the Pavilion. Even if you were not in town on a Deere hunt, a tour of the two Deere family mansions would make your heart race a little. The **Deere-Wiman House**, 817 11th Avenue, Moline, and the **Butterworth Center**, 1105 Eighth Street, Moline, (309) 765-7971, showcase Victorian lifestyles made possible by the invention of the right

A study in contrasts at the John Deere Pavilion, Moline.

plow at the right time. Guided tours are by donation at set times on Sunday afternoons in July and August, or by appointment if it can be arranged.

Got some downtime? Check out these other Quad Cities attractions: **The Family Museum of Arts and Science,** 2900 Learning Campus Drive (next to the library on 18th Street), Bettendorf, IA, (563) 344-4106. Among many other things, explore early and current farm life and the effects of weather on agriculture. Kids can drive a combine, touch a tornado, and make a cloud ring. **Hauberg Indian Museum,** at Black Hawk State Historic Site, Highway 5, 1510 46th Avenue (Blackhawk Road), Rock Island, (309) 788-9536. Peer into dioramas to learn about maple syrup bottling in spring, the summer corn harvest, and other seasonal activities of the Sauk and Mesquakie Indians during pre-settlement times. In Quad Cities grocery stores, look for Boetje's Stone-Ground Dutch Mustard. Locals swear by it and probably know how to pronounce it too. And, of course, you will want to make time for a nice lunch or dinner in this town that still maintains strong ties to the surrounding farming community.

This tour gives people a glimpse into a rare rural lifestyle that was extraordinary in its day and would be almost impossible to imagine in the present day, if not for the preservation of Bishop Hill. They can also see the thread of the John Deere story as it continues to play out in Moline and the world. The trip provides other delights: eating regional favorites like pork sandwiches and lingonberries, along with the Quad Cities' own brand of ice cream. The region is a fascinating part of Illinois and, perhaps, reveals something about the folks who help keep it that way.

SPECIAL EVENTS

Strawberry Days, Teresa's Tasty Produce, 12420 County Road 5, Atkinson, (309) 936-7792. June. U-pick or pre-picked, kiddie train, straw bale bowling, pedal cars, corn maze, lunch stand. Return in July for Sweet Corn Roast, and in October for Halloween Happenings.

Hog Capital of the World Festival, Kewanee, (309) 852-2175. August/September. Grand-scale pork chop barbecue.

PLACES TO EAT

P. L. Johnson Dining Room, 110 West Bjorkland Street, Bishop Hill, (309) 927-3885. Swedish-American fare in rustic, 1896 former hardware store of P. L. Johnson, who, among other things, was once a farmer. Swedish meatballs always, Swedish potato sausage on Sundays, also Swedish Sampler Platter with sweet-sour cabbage, meatballs, potato sausage, herring, cheese. Try a pork chop sandwich or barbeque ribs that will please the local producers as much as you.

The Filling Station, 303 North Bishop Hill Street, Bishop Hill, (309) 927-3355. Fill up and catch up on the latest gossip from the fields.

The Red Oak, 106 Bishop Hill Street, Bishop Hill, (309) 927-3539. Try *köttbullar* with lingonberries, Swedish meatballs in lingonberry cream sauce served over mashed potatoes; The Stockholm open-faced sandwich of sliced turkey breast, mustard sauce, lingonberries, and dill weed; or a salad with lingonberry vinaigrette. *Välsmakande!* Yellow, blue, and orange décor is a cheery setting for lunch or a card game of the local bridge club. Frozen fruit pies to bake at home.

The inside scoop on the Quad Cities is that the folks here have a special way with ice cream. **Lagomarcino's,** 1422 5th Avenue, Moline, (309) 764-1814, is a turn-of-the-century ice cream parlor dripping with hot fudge sundaes, hand-dipped chocolates, sponge candy, filled chocolate eggs, and old-fashioned fixtures. In 1927, J. F. "Grandpa" McCullough and his son, Alex, opened their first ice cream store in Davenport, on the Iowa side. But the people of Illinois will forgive them for that, because it was in Illinois that the entrepreneurs first successfully taste tested soft-serve ice cream, and where they opened the world's first **Dairy Queen.** Today even Iowa has Dairy Queens. Finally, you don't grow up in the Quad Cities without knowing about **Whitey's Ice Cream,** www.whiteysicecream.com. This family enterprise has many QC shops; ask and someone will happily point. It was at Whitey's that candy bar shakes and chocolate chip cookie dough ice cream first came to America.

Belgian Museum of the Quad Cities, a.k.a., Center for Belgian Culture, 712 18th Avenue, Moline, (309) 762-0167, www.belgianmuseumquadcities.org. Belgian Waffle Breakfast first Saturday morning of each month and Memorial Day.

Five, 1624 5th Avenue, Moline, (309) 764-5555. Urban industrial décor with oversized u-shaped banquettes, creative seafood and meat entrees, crème brûlée sampler dessert. S'mores for two dessert with flaming sterno is fun and messy and turns heads with its campfire smell.

PLACES TO STAY

Radisson on John Deere Commons, 1415 River Drive, Moline, (309) 764-6715. Convenient to John Deere attractions, classic furnishings with lots of wood, indoor pool and whirlpool, fitness center, deluxe continental breakfast in the John Deere Room.

The Colony Hospital Bed and Breakfast, 110 North Olson Street, Bishop Hill, (309) 927-3506, www.bishophilllodging.com. This 1855 colony construction underwent a little surgery to transform it from hospital to hospitality. Today the prescribed treatment is continental breakfast with juices, assorted Swedish scones, muffins, and homemade bread, rocking chairs, in-room TV/VCRs, and original wide plank flooring.

The Olde Brick House Inn, 502 North High Street, Port Byron, (309) 523-3236. About 20 miles north of Moline, but the thing is, Cyrus McCormick, who invented the reaper, once owned this 1855 Greek Revival as a summer home. Watch the Mississippi roll by, watch wildlife in the forested acres.

28. FROM "SIRUP" TO NUTS IN MCLEAN COUNTY

Consistently in the top three among Illinois corn-producing counties, McLean County is an Illinois agricultural hub with a good crop of farm attractions to explore. At the heart of it all is Bloomington-Normal, a twin-city metropolis that, as you will see, has some of the nuttiest attractions around. Bloomington is situated in north-central Illinois, conveniently close to Peoria (40 miles), Decatur (46 miles), and Champaign (52 miles). The route for this tour goes more or less clockwise around western and northern McLean County, before dropping down into Bloomington-Normal. But it also dips into some surrounding counties, where more unique attractions await discovery.

Start your adventure in Atlanta, located 25 miles from Bloomington-Normal and just off I-55 in Logan County. Here the **J. H. Hawes Grain Elevator Museum**, 301 Southwest Second Street, (217) 648-2056, offers a rare opportunity to tour a grain elevator. Built in 1904, this wooden workhorse was rescued and restored, and is now pursuing a teaching career for anyone who wants a glimpse inside the workings of a real Midwestern grain elevator. It is located in downtown Atlanta and open for tours June through August on Sunday afternoons.

Next up is **Funks Grove Pure Maple Sirup**, 5257 Old Highway 66, Shirley, (309) 874-3360. From Atlanta, you could take Highway 66 or I-55 north to this sugar bush, which is 15 miles south of Bloomington. When daytime temperatures begin to rise around the end of February, and the sap begins to run up inside the maple trees, Funks Grove springs into action. It is harvest time, and visitors are invited to find out how real maple syrup (or "sirup" as the Funks folks spell it) is made; call ahead to see what is happening on any given day, because they are at the mercy of the weather. Buy the finished product along with pure maple cream, which is boiled longer and therefore becomes thicker and spreadable.

FIELD NOTES

It's not a typo

Inside the shop of the Funks Grove Maple Sirup camp hangs a poster that explains why the Funks spell *sirup* with an i. Debby Funk, working the counter one day, says, sure, you can take a picture of the sign, everyone does, although she can't think why.

So, for those whose duty it is to point out typographical errors, the Funk family says that this time, they are barking up the wrong tree. And they are—the 11th edition of *Merriam-Webster's Collegiate Dictionary* lists *sirup* as another form of *syrup*. (We're not sure how Funk and Wagnalls stands on the issue.)

But there is more confusion ahead. Even though the spelling of the product is funky, one would think it is safe to assume that Funks Grove Pure Maple Sirup is in Funks Grove, Illinois. So why does the brochure say Shirley, Illinois? Surely that's a typo? Wrong again. It is just that Funks Grove the town doesn't have a post office. You're not from around here, are you?

But even if you spell it right and you don't end up wandering around in Shirley, you cannot always get a bottle of Funks Grove Pure Maple Sirup. Others may already have already snapped it all up. The golden-brown liquid is so rich and thick, that it is generally all sold and sweetening someone else's short stack by August.

Historically, and according to Webster, "sirup" was the preferred spelling when referring to the product made by boiling sap. "Syrup" with a "y", however, was defined as the end product of adding sugar to fruit juice. Though the "i" spelling is no longer commonly used, the United States Department of Agriculture and Canada also still use it when referring to pure maple sirup. Hazel Funk Holmes, whose trust continues to preserve and protect this timber for maple sirup production, insisted on the "i" spelling during her lifetime. It's another tradition that will continue at Funk's Grove.

Isaac Funk (1797–1865) started it all in 1824 when he settled in the area. Along with his brothers, Isaac was among the first pioneers to settle in central Illinois. By trade, he was a farmer, cattleman, and legislator who began making maple syrup with his sons, just for family use. By 1891, grandson Arthur Funk started selling the family's liquid gold for $1 a gallon. Subsequent Funks kept it up, tweaking as they went.

Twenty miles west of Bloomington and two miles east of Mackinaw in Tazewell County, the **Lavender Creek Farm**, 32379 Highway 9, Mackinaw, (309) 359-5555, www.lavendercreekfarm.com, represents the only commercial lavender farm in the American Heartland. While not on the scale of lavender farms in France, it is a rare glimpse into this specialized type of farming. Each spring, the owners anxiously await the renewal of the farm's organically grown acres of French hybrid lavender plants that look like purple foothills in a miniature landscape. Harvest Fest is June through August (closed Sundays). For a small fee, you can stroll about the exotic plantings and linger on a garden bench to enjoy the beauty and the peace of the 10-acre farm and surrounding countryside. You can also pick your own fresh lavender, or buy live lavender plants for planting in your own garden, dried bundles for room and closet fresheners, or just the flowers for culinary creations.

If you were not familiar with the scent of lavender before, you may never forget it after visiting the shop. They make gorgeous lavender soaps, some swirled with shades of purple, others uncolored but packing a lavender punch. Dry skin

A purple river of lavender plants at Lavender Creek Farm, Mackinaw.

eats up the Body Butter, which is a rich, creamy, head-to-toe lotion. Sip a cup of lavender tea sweetened with honey, and maybe a chunk of lavender fudge.

Leaving the lavender farm, you can go barnstorming at **Conklin's Barn II Dinner Theatre**, Goodfield, (309) 965-2545, www.mtco.com/~barn2, which is located north of Lavender Creek Farm and 30 minutes northwest of Bloomington in Woodford County on I-74. Live stage performances inside the 1940-era barn include comedies, musicals, and mysteries that have entertained audiences since 1975. Built of solid oak, the barn sits on a farmstead site that dates back to 1857. The barn's onetime cattle show ring is now the downstairs dining area.

So now it is time to get a little nutty in Bloomington-Normal. First up is the **Beer Nuts, Inc. Outlet Shoppe** at the Sale Barn, 2027 South Main Street, Highway 51 South, Bloomington, (309) 829-8091, www.beernuts.com. Livestock used to be traded in this large, white barn. The Beer Nuts operation started at a different location in 1937, when the E.G. Shirk family bought a small Bloomington confectionery that came with a recipe for glazed peanuts. They were called Redskins for the red-colored skins that were retained as part of the finished product. So much for the confectionery's other treats—by 1953, the family had sold off their Caramel Crisp Shop and focused on making the original Redskins and marketing them under the brand name of Beer Nuts. The name came about as a result of the nuts' overwhelming popularity in local taverns, and by 1960, they were available to munchers everywhere. The company is still independently owned, with headquarters and production happening only in Bloomington.

Watch a video on the company's history and in-depth information on peanut growing. The peanuts are shipped in to the factory from southern states like Georgia, Alabama, and Virginia, whereas the almonds come from California and the cashews are imported from India, Mozambique, and Tanzania. For friends and family who are nuts about sports, you can buy nut mixes that are prepared in the special Beer Nuts way and stuffed into a Beer Nuts cooler. It is just the thing for crunch time. Try samples of the different flavors.

Things are about to get nuttier, because you are only three miles away from a rare opportunity to go silo climbing. Huh? Let's put it this way. What do you do with a grain elevator that is built like the Rock of Gibraltar but has outlived its usefulness and looms over everything? You climb the beast (after dumping the leftover grain and evicting the wildlife).

Yes, it's probably a stretch to call silo climbing an agricultural experience. But the folks at **Upper Limits Rock Climbing Gym and Pro Shop**, 1304 West Washington Street, Bloomington, (309) 829-8255, www.upperlimits.com, look at things a little differently than farmers do. Upper Limits is the first of its kind, a bit of extreme adventure on the Illinois prairie, and one of the largest climbing facilities in the country. The climbing area totals 20,000 square feet with five 65-foot silos that feel edgy and oddly urban for what was an agricultural structure. The beast's original character remains intact, with a raw grit and somewhat damp mustiness just waiting to be conquered. You can climb at Upper Limits even if you have never climbed before, although the outdoor rappelling and ice-fall climbing are only for the experts. You can be any age, from a toddler to a senior, but you don't have to be in top physical shape. After taking a class or demonstrating proficiency, you can climb 65 feet up the insides of the silos, using hand- and foot-holds drilled into the concrete walls.

Come back down to earth at the **McLean County Museum of History**, 200 North Main Street, Bloomington, (309) 827-0428, www.mchistory.org. It is located in Bloomington's historic downtown somewhat south of Illinois State and Illinois Wesleyan universities. From Upper Limits, it is almost a two-mile drive to the east. The museum's Farming Gallery offers insight into central Illinois agriculture. Here you can trace the development of McLean County farming beginning with the breakup and draining of the prairie. In the Pioneer Neighborhood, children can don pioneer clothing, carry water, and plow a field.

Near I-55 and Highway 24 in the town of Chenoa, which is about 30 miles northeast of the museum, you can tour the 1855 **Matthew T. Scott Home**, 227 North First Street, Chenoa, (815) 945-4555. Scott was a central Illinois agriculturalist who made a fortune developing over 45,000 acres of farmland. Tours are available by appointment and on Sundays from 2:00 to 4:00 p.m. only.

From "sirup" to nuts, this weekend jaunt through McLean County is a great way to take in the local flavor. Who would have thought that an old grain elevator would make a world-class climbing gym? That the same tour would include sedate visits to a lavender farm and a barn-based dinner theater? All of this—and more—goes to show that although they sure grow a lot of corn in McLean County, that is not all they do on the farms.

SPECIAL EVENTS

Grand Village of the Kickapoo Park Powwow, LeRoy, (309) 962-2700, (309) 962-4106. End of May/Early June. Members of the Kickapoo nation gather again at the site of their grand village in McLean County. Enjoy the color and tradition of live performances, art, and great food.

McLean County Fair/4-H Show, Interstate Center, 2301 West Market Street, Bloomington, www.mcleancountyfair.org. Early August. Don't miss the county fair with the largest 4-H fair in the country, featuring over 1,100 project exhibits.

Sweet Blues/Sweet Corn Festival, Downtown Normal, (309) 454-9557. End of August. Sure it's corny, but that's the point, and you won't turn your nose up as 16 tons of sweet corn roll off the steam engine. Lend an ear as great blues music wafts through the air along with the quintessentially Midwestern aroma of hot, buttered sweet corn. Captain Cornelius of the Illinois Corn Marketing Board always puts in an appearance.

Harvest Bloom Festival, Downtown Bloomington, (309) 829-9599. Early September.

Fair skies ahead

A Fair to Remember: The Proud Tradition of the McLean County 4-H Fair, published by the McLean County Extension Service Foundation, is one of those lovingly chronicled souvenir fair books that make you long for Americana, only to discover that for some people, it really does exist. According to the book, America's first agricultural fair happened in 1810, back east in Pittsfield, Massachusetts. The concept caught on in McLean County in 1852, and by 1923 the locale was holding its first 4-H fair, appropriately enough, on a farm. The book reports that on an August afternoon some three miles west of Bloomington, 30 boys and girls exhibited livestock, vegetables, and sewing projects. You can still attend the McLean County Fair/4-H Show with its agricultural exhibits, funnel cakes and corn dogs, and activities like a family farm contest and a horse pulling contest. And put some Americana into your own life. 🏃

PLACES TO EAT

Michael's Restaurant, 110 West Washington Street, Bloomington, (309) 820-1330. This popular spot across from the McLean County Museum of History is responsible for the savory smells wafting about. Salads, burgers, sandwiches, pastas, and entrées, all reasonably priced, fill the lunch menu. Stuffed with mushrooms, mozzarella, and feta, Michael's Burger is a half-pounder topped with lettuce and tomato. Come on, you can climb it off at Upper Limits.

PLACES TO STAY

Burr House, 210 East Chestnut Street, Bloomington, (309) 828-7686, (800) 449-4182. Civil War-era home features five guestrooms (four with private baths) and a brick terrace that overlooks a historic park. The full breakfast can be made vegetarian upon request.

Davis Manor, 1001 East Jefferson Street, Bloomington, (309) 829-7703. The original owner was a wealthy cattleman, and today you can choose from three guestrooms (one with private bath). Hot tub available upon request.

Vrooman Mansion, 701 East Taylor Street, Bloomington, (309) 828-8816, (877) 346-6488, www.vroomanmansion.com. Southeast of downtown, this 1869, 13,600-square-foot mansion has four floors and five guestrooms (three have private baths). Full gourmet breakfast. Abraham Lincoln didn't sleep here, but spoke in the southeast gardens.

29. AN AMISH FAITH IN FARMING

The Amish settlement areas of east-central Illinois represent the largest in the state and the fourth largest in North America. The families here consist of over 4,200 Old Order Amish who first arrived in 1865 and settled across Coles, Douglas, Moultrie, and Piatt counties, in communities like Arcola, Arthur, Atwood, Cadwell, Chesterville, Cooks Mills, Lovington, and Sullivan. Find yourself in Illinois Amish country just a few miles west of I-57. Arthur, which is home to the most Amish, is about 45 miles south of Champaign and 30 miles east of Decatur.

Stop in the towns and see the attractions, of course, but also drive the quiet back roads. You will not have to look for the trademark black buggies—they are everywhere. Once you know what to look for, it is easy to tell which farms are Amish-owned: about 80 to 100 acres in size, bicycles and buggies instead of cars and tractors, laundry and quilts on the line, windmills, horses, a jumble of houses on each farm, and, of course, the people themselves. You may see bonneted tots driving their own ponies from the seat of a miniature cart. You may see draft horses shaking blond manes as they lumber through the fields, their enormous power often entrusted to little hands, for Amish children are vital contributors to the work of the family farm. The farmers raise hogs, cattle, poultry, and goats, and they grow wheat, oats, clover, and corn. Vegetable gardens and orchards are common sights. Look for hand-lettered signs that advertise honey, produce, eggs, and other farm-grown foods for sale, and by all means pull in to purchase some of the goodies direct from the source. Amish cottage businesses include bulk food stores, buggy and harness shops, blacksmiths, a meat packing plant, and a feed mill. Finally, what you have heard about Amish buggies being slow is true relative to cars, but you don't hear enough about the silent grace of the horses that pull them. So rather than clip-clopping by in a stodgy, methodical manner, the sleek, dark beauties whisk silently by with smooth, long-legged gaits. Many have retired from the racetrack. Anyone can tell they still like to run.

Sullivan

Let's start in Sullivan, in Moultrie County. It is the southwestern-most stop on this tour, although all of the Amish communities are within an easy drive of one another. What you are looking for in Sullivan is **The Old School**, 208 West Jackson Street, Sullivan, (217) 728-3166. This stop is not exactly an educational experience, but a smart choice for anyone in search of Amish foods and furniture. Poke around the multi-level brick building with its handsome stone trim, because you will discover unusual items like the Mrs. Yoder's Kitchen line of cheeses, jams, and jellies. Plenty of cheese samples are available to help you decide among the variety of flavors. Sit down to a lavish spread at the Amish-Style Buffet, where they are cooking for lunch and dinner six days a week (never on Sunday). The hearty, healthy buffet items use Amish and Mennonite recipes, and fresh-never-frozen chicken, shrimp, walleye, roast beef, real mashed potatoes, fresh vegetables, home-baked bread, and more. The buffet includes a salad bar and a dessert bar. Enjoy the breakfast buffet every Saturday morning. Some of the home décor items available at The Old School have a farm theme. A figurine of a rooster declares "I rule the roost." Next to him, though, is a hen that clears up any misunderstanding with her own declaration of, "I rule the rooster." Push the chef's caps on the heads of this cocky pair to hear them cock-a-doodle-doo and cackle.

New as of 2004, Sullivan has begun to host the Spores 'n More Spring Fling. It is an event that celebrates the wonderful mushroom. Call (217) 728-4223 for current information.

Arcola

Let's head northeast into Arcola, on Highway 133 less than a mile west of I-57 in Douglas County. For preserved food items and kitchen gadgets, try the **Cook's Collection**, which is located in the **Arcola Emporium**, 201 East Main Street, Arcola, (217) 268-4866. Look for specialty cookbooks (even Aunt Bea of Mayberry peddles hers here) and preserved food items at the **Rockome Store**, 117 East Main Street, Arcola, (217) 268-3841; you can't miss its huge white balcony railing out front. On the weekend after Labor Day, the Broom Corn Festival, (800) 336-5456, sweeps into town with broom-making demonstrations, broom factory tours, and the National Broom Sweeping Contest. Arcola was, up until recently, a corn-broom-making capital.

The **Illinois Amish Interpretive Center**, 111 South Locust Street, Arcola, (217) 268-3599, is the place to go for answers to all your questions about the Amish way of life—history, religious beliefs, farming, and home life. Learn about farming practices that were once not so different from those used by the general American farm population. View the century-old buggy. Learn that when Amish families sit down to eat in their own homes, the father typically sits at the head of the table, boys sit on a bench against a wall, and women and girls, who do the serving, take their places where they will have easy access to the kitchen. See typical rooms inside an Amish home, including a table set for a wedding feast, and children's toys like miniature farm animals.

Need to get even closer to the Amish? You can easily arrange a tour at the Interpretive Center, but you have to do so by reservation either at the center or by calling (888) 45AMISH before you leave home. Options include the Amish Country Tour, where a step-on guide provides insight into the passing farm-scape; the Meal in an Amish Home experience, which allows you to enjoy food prepared and served by an Amish hostess in her home; the Afternoon Frolic, which is like paying a social call to an Amish farm wife; the Amish Home Tour; the Amish Farm Tour; and the Combo Home/Farm Tour. Since such tours are geared for groups, the Center will arrange for you to tour with others, but you drive your own car to get to the given farm. Whichever tour you choose, it will undoubtedly be thought-provoking.

Located in the country four miles southwest of downtown Arcola, **Rockome**

Gardens, 125 North County Road 425E, Arcola, (217) 268-4106, www.rockome .com, was a farm before it evolved into this 15-acre complex that includes resident farm animals. Children enjoy riding a horse that powers a buzz saw, then having the sawed wood personalized inside the blacksmith shop. Climb up some 50 stairs to the Lookout Tower in the Big Red Barn, then back down one level to view a musty lineup of treadle sewing machines. Continue down one more level to view the displays of period rooms and an Amish recipe for apple butter that calls for seven bushels of apples and 80 pounds of sugar. View horse-drawn farm machinery at the Dutch Barn, which was moved in from a nearby farm. Visit the gristmill where vintage equipment still grinds corn that you can buy in souvenir bags and bake into warm, fragrant corn bread. Pick up fresh bread, cookies, cinnamon rolls, and apple butter at the Bagdad Bakery. Tour the two-story building that is furnished as a 1950s Amish home. The on-site family-style restaurant features Amish-style cooking (comfort food and lots of it) from 11:00 a.m. to 7:00 p.m. when the gardens are open. Brace yourself for the abundance of fried chicken and one other meat, mashed potatoes and creamy gravy, noodles or bread dressing, vegetables, salad, warm bread and apple butter-topped biscuits, and dessert. Make plans to attend special events like the Farm Toy Tractor Show (August), Amish Farm Market Days (August), and the Horse Farming Festival (September and October).

Chesterville

Chesterville is located midway between Arcola and Arthur. From Rockome Gardens, go north on County Road 425 E, then turn left onto Highway 133 to **Dutch Valley Meats**, 376 East State Highway 133, Chesterville, (217) 543-3354. Amish women wearing prayer caps will take your order for fresh and smoked meats such as maple sausage and sugar-cured bacon. You can also buy homemade noodles, cheeses, spices, and condiments. Breathe in the intense fragrances of smoked meats and enjoy rubbing elbows with both Amish and English shoppers who are all in search of the finest, freshest flavors.

Arthur

Arthur is Illinois' largest Amish settlement and therefore offers great opportunities for back-roads exploring. If you happen to pass by a farm where a lot of buggies or maybe the church service wagon is parked, you can bet there is plenty of cooking going on inside. Amish women frequently cook for crowds, and often have two gas-powered stoves and refrigerators to handle the volume. On regular days, lunch is the biggest meal, and soups are often served for supper. If you go back south of Highway 133, visit **Beachy's Bulk Foods**, 259 North County Road 200E, Arthur, for interesting and low-priced items like whole grains, sweet cream buttermilk, flax seeds, and uncommon jams: gooseberry, elderberry, blackberry, blueberry, black raspberry, and cranberry. Fresh pies every Saturday! **Miller's Dry Goods**, 175 East County Road 50 North, Arthur, is similarly fun to explore with its fabric bolts and gas lighting. Find Miller's two miles east and about three and one-half miles south of town.

In-town Arthur is notable for quaint shops such as the **Country Spice Shoppe**, 110 North Vine Street, Arthur, (217) 543-3664. Where else can you find a grain grinder to process your own whole grains? Take a refreshing, nostalgic swig of Green River at **Dick's Pharmacy**, 118 South Vine Street, Arthur, (217) 543-2913. Try the special-recipe peanut butter spread at **Country Cheese and More**, 205 South Vine Street, Arthur, (217) 543-3544. Even the wood, antique, and fabric shops of Arthur manage to find some shelf space for Amish-made jams and jellies. Strolling around town with your ice cream cone or quarter-pound of fudge, you will likely notice over 28 hitch racks where patient horses await the return of their Amish masters.

Arthur boasts a variety of special events. Soak up the atmosphere, support worthy causes, and eat, eat, eat at Amish and Mennonite benefits and haystack suppers. The Farmers' Market begins in early July and lasts through September or the end of the growing season for both Amish and English farmers. It happens every Saturday morning at the Gazebo Parking Lot, corner of Vine and Progress, and is your chance to pick a peck of pickled peppers. The **Freedom Tractor Pull** in late June puts real tractors, not just hot rods, to the test in Jurgens Park; (217) 543-2242. The **Moultrie-Douglas County Fair** happens every summer in mid-July, and is located within walking distance just south of downtown. Enjoy junior livestock shows, agricultural product exhibits, tractor pulls, horse shows, and much more country fun. Although these days the cheese is no longer made here, the **Amish Country Cheese Festival** still happens every Labor Day weekend. A highlight is the Free Cheese Giveaway, with slices cut from a 300-pound wheel and served with crackers. Also relish the cheese-eating contest, the National Cheese Curling Contest, children's games, a kiddie tractor pull, craft vendors, and more down-home fun. Call (800) 72AMISH or visit www.arthurcheesefestival .com for upcoming dates.

Atwood

From Arthur, drive six miles north on Vine Street and cross Highway 36 into Atwood, where you can spend some time at the **Harris Agricultural Museum**, 202 West Locust Avenue, Atwood, (217) 578-2231, www.harrisagmuseum@harris companies.com. From Highway 36, go north into Atwood on Main Street, left on Magnolia Street, left on Illinois Street, and right on Locust Avenue. Call ahead to schedule your visit, because the Harris family runs the museum on the side. It is still a work in progress, but they will happily show you around and bring the array of artifacts to life. The idea is not just to display the machinery and tools, but also to restore them to working condition, which makes the museum that much more meaningful. What started as a retirement project is remarkable for its insight into a man's passion for agricultural history, and for the fact that many people can walk through today and not even know what most of the items were used for. The museum does not have an Amish focus, but the story it tells of central Illinois farm life includes the Amish farmers. You will find a direct link in the 1920s McCormick binder that had been used by an Amish farmer to cut and bundle grain in the field. A highlight is the 1919 Model T Ford grain/dump truck restored to gleaming, green-black perfection. View replicas of an early grain elevator office, a blacksmith shop, and a 1920s farm kitchen with gadgets like a chicken de-beaker (which removed part of the beak to prevent pecking of other chickens) and a cider press.

Another reason to visit Atwood is the **Apple Dumpling Festival** that is held every summer in August. Hot apple dumplings with homemade ice cream. (217) 578-2734. Finally, those who like a good barn tour will not mind the 25-mile drive north to the **Piatt County Museum**, Monticello, (217) 762-4731. Every October, the museum hosts the **Barn Tour and Historic Sites Tour**.

Tuscola

A nine-mile drive east from Atwood on Highway 36 gets you into Tuscola and a "shopportunity" on a grand scale along I-57. Look for bargains, not buggies, and all the fast-food joints you thought you left behind at home. Just west of I-57 on 36, there is a football-field-sized red barn that is stuffed to the rafters with all things country. This is not a historic, Amish-built barn, but a shopper's paradise called the **Amishland Red Barn Buffet**, 1304 Tuscola Boulevard (Highway 36 and I-57), Tuscola, (217) 253-9022. Shop for a variety of items including Amish-made furniture as well as crafts and antiques. The barn also houses an Amish bakery and a cheese shop. The 400-seat buffet is great, with all the tastes and smells of a busy home kitchen, yet with none of the work. If you have driven down I-57 before, you will very likely notice that something is missing from the scene. Alas, the big, beautiful, fiberglass Holstein cow is no longer munching a bale of hay out front. She has moved on to greener pastures and is reportedly enjoying her new home.

Downtown Tuscola is all sleepy small town. From Amishland, drive a mile west on 36 and take a right at the last Tuscola stoplight, which is Main Street leading into downtown. About a block down and on your left is the **Douglas County Museum**, 700 South Main Street, Tuscola, (217) 253-2535. The farming exhibit is on display every other year in odd-numbered years (but call ahead, as this may change). The tractors, about a dozen in all, fill up the floor with green John Deeres, blue Fords, and some unrestored models that lost their paint long ago. Glass display cases showcase agricultural tools and "household widgets and gadgets from the farm wife's toolbox."

At the tail end of every August, Tuscola hosts its **Old-Fashioned Bluegrass Harvest Fest** downtown, and if you like bluegrass music and down-home food, call (800) 441-9111.

Those roaming about Illinois Amish country doubtlessly feel that they have been in good hands. Hands that still know how to preserve fruits and vegetables,

An old seed sack on display at the Douglas County Museum, Tuscola.

drive a horse and buggy, and raise a barn. Hands that have always had faith in farming. Hands that know, too, how to welcome a visitor.

PLACES TO EAT

Amishland Red Barn Buffet, 1304 Tuscola Boulevard (Highway 36 and I-57), Tuscola, (217) 253-9022. Hearty, home-style food in a warm country atmosphere. Some of the cooks are Amish, and the vast offerings include real mashed potatoes, beef and noodles, country-style green beans, and Amish-baked breads.

Dutch Kitchen Restaurant, Locust and Main Streets, Arcola, (217) 268-3518. Fried chicken, Dutch sausage, warm breads with Yoder's Apple Butter, and shoo-fly pie. Breakfast, lunch, and dinner.

Dutch Oven Restaurant, 116 East Illinois Street, Arthur, (217) 543-2213. Daily buffet, homemade Amish pies, soup, and salad bar.

Flesor's Candy Kitchen, 101 West Sale Street, Tuscola, (217) 253-3753, www .flesorscandy.com. This local family institution re-opened to much local acclaim in 2004 with some original furnishings. Sandwiches, daily specials. Their own homemade chocolates available by the pound. Soda fountain drinks, phosphates, milk shakes, malts, banana splits, freshly squeezed lemonade.

Yoder's Kitchen, Highway 133 east of Arthur, (217) 543-2714,

Sun setting over the veranda of the Heart and Home B&B, Arthur.

www.yoderskitchen.com. Amish/Mennonite home-style cooking with broasted chicken, inch-thick pork chop, lunch and dinner buffets, pies, cinnamon rolls. All smoked meats are locally prepared by Dutch Valley Meats. Vast buffets. Bakery and gift shop.

PLACES TO STAY

Breakfast in the Country Bed and Breakfast, 1750 East State Highway 133, Hindsboro, (217) 346-2739. Quiet country home, full country breakfast, sheep and llamas nearby.

Heart & Home Bed and Breakfast, 137 East Illinois Street, Arthur, (217) 543-2910. In the heart of Illinois Amish country, you can stay conveniently in town and enjoy a full breakfast with homemade treats like fresh fruit compote and sticky buns. Breakfast is the time, too, to learn about the 1906 Victorian home and your hosts' Mennonite/Amish upbringings. Enjoy an afternoon snack that may be lemon squares baked with juice from a relative's Florida orchard. Evenings, as doves coo in the treetops and horses' hooves clip-clop by, the setting sun takes one last look at the wrap-around porch before slipping off to warm other parts of the world. Three bedrooms, private baths.

Little House on the Prairie Bed and Breakfast, RR 2, Patterson Road, Sullivan, (217) 728-4727. Stay in the 1894 Queen Anne farmhouse surrounded by acres of woodlands, gardens, and an in-ground outdoor pool. Full breakfast with the house-specialty Heavenly Bananas, choice of eggs, omelets, French toast, Belgian waffles, bacon. Late afternoon cup of tea or glass of wine.

30. SOUTHWEST SURPRISES

This tour rambles through five counties and features an abundance of beautiful sights along the way—some wrapped in thick-cut bacon, some dripping with Bavarian cream and strawberries, and still others hand-picked from vines and aged in oak barrels. You are in southwestern Illinois, where a string of small towns has little to do with arches either golden or silver. At every turn, good tastes, warm hospitality, and a few surprises will delight you. Select the sites that appeal most, and save the rest for another weekend, because it is a lot to digest. The tour leads you through Jersey, Madison, Saint Clair, Monroe, and Randolph counties. To get an idea of the general location, find Saint Louis on a map, and look to the north, east, and south of it in the state of Illinois.

A Pizza Farm?

Let's start the tour from the north in Jersey County. There you will find one of the most unusual farm experiences around—a pizza farm! The concept started in California, and now the good old Midwest has its first one too. **R Pizza Farm**, 25873 State Highway 3, Dow, (618) 466-5950, is a full half-acre of pizza immersion on an organic vegetable farm. Open by reservation only. Pizza lovers of all

---

FARTHER AFIELD

Horse progress days

Horse Progress Days is a summertime event that travels throughout several states, and is expected to be back in Illinois sometime around 2006 or 2007. It is a rare opportunity to watch horse-powered farm equipment demonstrated in the field. The purpose is to show farmers who use this stuff—the Amish, of course—how well the latest models work. Where else but in an Amish community could you hope to find an event like this in the twenty-first century, not to learn about the past, but to experience it today. Living history farms are great, but this is for real. You do not have to be a potential buyer to go and watch as muscular draft horses pull manure spreaders, tillage equipment, market garden equipment, lawn mowers, haying equipment, logging equipment, and more. 🐎

---

ages enjoy walking around the pizza ingredient beds and interpretive exhibits that teach all about what it takes to make a great pizza. Planted in the beds are wheat, tomatoes, green peppers, onions, and herbs, and the remaining sections (slices!) top off the experience with information on cheese and meat production. Round out your farm experience by visiting with the farm animals, shopping for Amish crafts, preserves, and other country goods, and stopping by the kitchen for a slice of organic pizza.

Now drive almost 50 miles southeast into Madison County, where you can visit **Mills Apple Farm**, 11477 Pocahontas Road (north of I-70 and east of I-55 between Marine and Grantfork), Marine, (618) 887-4732, www.millsapple farm.com. Pick your own apples and peaches, take home scratch pies, and while away the hours with farm animals and seasonal wagon rides.

If, for whatever reason, you have a need to see a giant bottle of catsup, then by all means drive by the water tower of the old Brooks Catsup Plant in Collinsville. Since 1949, it has been no ordinary water tower, but the **World's Largest Catsup Bottle**. From Mills Apple Farm, it is almost 21 miles to the southwest; I-70 will get you there in about a half hour. The address is 800 South Morrison Avenue, Collinsville, and for advance information, visit www.catsup bottle.com. This roadside wonder soars 170 feet into the skies of southwestern Illinois, and it could very well be the Best Reason in the World to stop for a hamburger and fries.

But on to a treasure considered so significant to human history that it is a

World Heritage Site, ranking right up there with the pyramids of Egypt, the Great Wall of China and the Taj Mahal in India. This is the **Cahokia Mounds State Historic Site**, 30 Ramey Drive, Collinsville, (618) 346-5160, www.cahokia mounds.com. From the catsup bottle, it is less than six miles west. Cahokia Mounds is an ancient anachronism caught up amid a tangle of interstates. According to the Cahokia Mounds Museum Society and the Illinois Historic Preservation Agency, it preserves the remains of what is known to be the only prehistoric Indian city north of Mexico. It is 2,200 acres of open space with 69 of the original 120 mounds preserved. The mounds were primary features of the city that first appeared about AD 700, but that was gradually abandoned after 1300 AD. The earliest residents depended not only on wild food sources, but also on cultivated corn and some seed-bearing crops like sunflower and lambs-quarter. It is also known that after about 850 to 900 AD, hunting and gathering continued, but agriculture became more important, and fields of corn and squash yielded a large surplus. Archeologists have found evidence too of garden plots that would have been planted near the homes. The structure called Woodhenge was the city's sun calendar system and used to mark agricultural and ceremonial cycles.

The Empire of Eckert

Once you get onto I-255 going south, merge onto Highway 15 and head into Belleville (Saint Clair County). Here multiple generations of the Eckert family keep visitors healthy and happy—as they have since 1837. There are three **Eckert's Country Store and Farms** locations. Belleville Farm is the classic u-pick. Millstadt Fun Farm, in Millstadt, is all about entertainment, with country music performances, pig races, the orchard wagon train, a 70-foot subterranean mine shaft slide, haunted hayrides, and bonfire sites. The scenic location of Grafton Farm, north of Saint Louis in Jersey County on the Great River Road, sets the stage for a more serene experience, with September events like Salute to the American Farmer and the Great River Road Fish Fry-Off. Combined, the three farms cover some 2,000 acres and represent the country's largest u-pick orchard. Assorted Eckert's live and work on the farms, so the family feeling is everywhere.

Take a 21-mile drive southeast from Cahokia Mounds to the first of the three, **Belleville Farm**, 951 South Green Mount Road, Belleville, (618) 233-0513, www.eckerts.com. It throws open its doors in March and does not close again until December, after the Christmas-tree-cutting is finished. It is not just local fruits that you get here, it is also local information, for during Fruit Tree Weekend in mid-March, the Eckert experts teach how to grow your own little orchard. Sign up for the Cooking with Asparagus Class that enhances culinary skills in early May. Or choose to attend the Memorial Day Weekend Festival, when tractor-pulled hay wagons haul you and your strawberry-picking boxes out to the fields for memorable springtime fun. Old hands and women who know their stains might

GRANDMA ELLA'S
Apple-cranberry relish

The Eckert's have a lot of family and friends to feed. Fortunately, they keep plenty of apples, peaches, strawberries, and pumpkins on hand, and they've gathered plenty of recipes in the *Eckert Family Cook Book*. Here's one of them.

2 apples, pared and cored
12 ounces fresh cranberries
1 quartered and seeded orange, with rind
1 cup sugar

Grind fruit using a food processor or blender; add sugar and mix well. Chill and serve.
Recipe courtesy of Eckert's Inc.

advise you, however, not to wear your best clothes, or at least to don something that is already red. Return to Eckert's for the Creating Jams and Jellies Class (end of June), Wine Making Seminar (early July), Super Salsas Class (early August), and just keep returning, because the fun never seems to end.

If the thought of home-baked, deep purple blackberry pie topped with snow-white vanilla ice cream is enough to get you out on the roads of southwestern Illinois, then visit Eckert's any time from mid-June to July. That's when the berries burst forth, and when you should be there to pick them, or at least to pick them up from the farm's Country Store. Also look for white asparagus and pickling and canning supplies. Go for peaches in July and August, apples in September to mid-October, and pumpkins in October.

Eckert's fruits are delicious, but what they do with them in the bakeries is sinful. How about wild berry pie (blackberry, raspberry, blueberry), Extraordinary Strawberry Stollen (almond shortbread, Bavarian cream, glazed strawberries), caramel apple walnut pie, chocolate-covered cherry pie, or a sugar-free choice? Also shop for honey, condiments, and jams and jellies (Damson plum, Dutch apple, peach). Now about the peanut squares. Let's just say that before certain tour buses pull into the Eckert's parking lot, the marketing director has to call up the baker to make sure the kitchen whips up extra batches of these sticky-sweet cakes. Eckert's Country Restaurant, where chicken—pot pie, tenders, fried, grilled, pulled, with dumplings—is a house favorite. Take fried

Scrumptious strawberry bread at Eckert's Country Store, Belleville.

chicken to go with a package of those peanut squares for a lip-smacking road-side picnic somewhere along the way. Or dine in at the restaurant with menu items like fried chicken, the Farmhandwich, or pork loin slow-roasted with apples and cinnamon.

Belleville and Beyond

Let's move on to another unique spot in Belleville. The **Labor and Industry Museum**, 123 North Church Street, Belleville, (618) 222-9430 opened in 2002. From Eckert's, go south onto Highway 13/15, get onto Highway 159, exit onto East Main Street, and turn left onto North Church Street; it is about a four-mile drive northwest of the farm. Learn about Belleville's trademark cast-iron stove industry that helped put the town on the industrial map after the Civil War, indeed earning it the nickname "Stove Capital of the World." The museum has 26 stoves that were made in Belleville from 1881 to 1940, many exhibiting beautiful craftsmanship and even elegance and grace, with tapered legs and polished fittings. Other artifacts that once served the food and farming industries of their day are on display, including a hand-fashioned apple picker, fruit jars, and a 1930 product catalog that customers used to place orders for sugar cane milling equipment, evaporators, and furnaces. By the way, the company that today makes Jelly Belly candies was founded in Belleville in 1868.

On to miniature Maeystown, which is in Monroe County and about 30 miles

Owner David Braswell admires the goodies at the Corner George Inn Sweet Shoppe, Maeystown.

southwest of the stove museum. The gateway to Maeystown is a nineteenth-century stone arch bridge. Maeystown is so cute—uh, historic—that they put the whole darn thing on the National Register. There are about 60 stone, wood, and brick structures in this old German settlement that was founded in order to serve area farmers, and that only about 150 people call home today. The large, white stone building past the bridge and to your right is **Zeitinger's Stone Mill,** which houses a visitor center and museum. It operated as a flour mill for only three years due to inadequate water pressure, but it has this pedigree, nonetheless. The **Corner George Inn Sweet Shoppe,** (618) 458-6660, is a big name for a small shop that satisfies the biggest sweet tooth with hand-dipped ice cream, bakery treats like marble squares, magic bars, and breads like strawberry, cherry-pecan, and banana.

Leaving Maeystown behind, drive southeast along the Mississippi River on Bluff Road, and to Chester, which puts you in Randolph County and about 37 miles southeast of Maeystown. Chester has a very special relationship with spinach. It is not that the iron-rich, deep green leaves are grown in abundance down here. It is that in 1929, Chester resident Elzie Segar created the world's most famous spinach-eater, Popeye the Sailor Man. Segar's comic characterization of a fellow who got his strength from tipping up a can of spinach became an American icon. For who in America has not witnessed the instantaneous musculature of Popeye's anchor-tattooed forearms, and beheld the power of spinach? Pay homage at **The Popeye Museum/Spinach Can Collectibles,** 1001 State Street, Chester, (618) 826-4567. View vintage merchandise that first became available in 1931, and shop for contemporary collectibles. The building itself is pertinent, because when Segar was young, it was an opera house, and Segar worked there as a projectionist.

When you make southwest Illinois a weekend destination, you're in for some surprises. Like the ancient city where agriculture was practiced long ago, the hometown of Popeye, and the family farms that indulge visitors with fresh country air and rich treats. And who can forget something like the World's Largest Catsup Bottle?

SPECIAL EVENTS

Sheep and Craft Festival, Monroe County Fairgrounds, Waterloo, www.urban ext.uiuc.edu. April.

Popeye Picnic, Chester, (618) 826-2721. September.

Colonial Cuisine, Martin-Boismenue State Historic Site, Prairie du Port, (618) 332-1782. November.

German heritage events in Maeystown: Saint John Church Fastnacht, German pancake and sausage dinner, Tuesday before Ash Wednesday; Oktoberfest, second Sunday in October. Call (618) 458-6660.

PLACES TO EAT

Dreamland Palace Restaurant, 3043 Highway 156, Foster Pond, (618) 939-9922. Famous for traditional German cuisine, German music playing in Tudor-style restaurant. Locals dream about the mile-high pie.

Eschys Bar and Restaurant, 1026 Main Street, Maeystown, (618) 458-6425. Even if you can't pronounce it, you can appreciate their fresh chicken.

Addy's Smoke Pit, 404 Belt Line Road, Collinsville, (618) 344-4950. Barbeque, pulled pork sandwiches.

PLACES TO STAY

Bilbrey Farms Bed and Breakfast and Exotic Animal Farm, 8724 Pin Oak Road, Edwardsville, (618) 692-1950. The estate sprawls across 65 acres and is home to some 60 creatures, many of which are pet-able, so you could easily spend more than eating and sleeping time here. Enjoy other exceptional amenities like the private theater, lake for fishing or swimming, adults-only tanning bed. Full breakfast served outdoors among the macaws or inside the large kitchen. Two-night stay required.

Corner George Inn, Main and Mill Streets, Maeystown, (618) 458-6660, www.cornergeorgeinn.com. Lots of options here in quaint, restored structures. How about bunking down in the Summer Kitchen, which is a guest cottage that once upon a time served as kitchen, bakery, and smokehouse? Breakfast is served upstairs in the 600-square-foot ballroom, where the host might be persuaded to give the pump organ a go.

A Civil War era white stone building across the street from the Corner George Inn, Maeystown.

Sausage-wrapped eggs

At the Corner George Inn in tiny Maeystown, food is always on the table in the morning. Innkeeper David Braswell shares this breakfast recipe based on an old Scottish dish.

2 boiled eggs
1/2 pound of pork sausage

Wrap peeled boiled eggs in pork sausage until the egg is completely covered. Bake at 400 degrees for 40 minutes or until browned. Makes 2 sausage-wrapped eggs.
Recipe courtesy of the Corner George Inn Bed and Breakfast 🐖

Econo Lodge, 1409 West Highway 50, O'Fallon, (618) 628-8895. Exceptionally stylish property at budget prices. Continental breakfast.
Timmerman House Bed and Breakfast, 6130 Old Highway 50, Breese, (618) 228-7068, (888) 328-7068. Stay in this 1947 farmhouse on one hundred acres of farmland. Make advance arrangements for the special family dairy farm tour. Full breakfast.

31. SOUTHERNMOST TRAILS

Turns out that the rolling hills of southern Illinois are perfect for growing more than spectacular scenery. Try sun-ripened apples, peaches, and distinctly Illinois-grown grapes. In Union County, they have trails—driving tours, actually—for these and other fine fruits mapped out all over the place, including vineyards and wineries. And get the inside story on the local barns too, in all of their shapes, sizes, and creative uses in a new day and age.

There are many ways to approach these trails, depending on interests, seasonality, and special events. First, of course, you will want to get the trail maps from www.shawneeheartland.com/maps.html, or call (800) 248-4373. The Wine Trail is entirely north of Anna, Illinois, while the Orchard Trail has only one stop south of Anna, and the Barn Trail is pretty much half north and half south. There are points where the trails overlap, so you may wish to combine stops as you go. The trails are comparatively new, so directional signage is not always what it could be, and don't expect any posted help along the Barn Trail. By nature, the trails' stopping points are scattered along winding back roads that twist and turn throughout the countryside. This means the drives are scenic, but as anywhere, they can also be more confusing than city streets, so take your time and don't fling maps out the window.

This tour takes you to far southern Illinois, an area that is so far south it borders Kentucky and Missouri rather than Iowa and Indiana. The nearest big city is Saint Louis, and that is about 150 miles northwest of Anna, which will serve as a point of orientation in Union County.

Getting Started

On the way toward the trails of Union County, you might want to visit the **Saline Creek Pioneer Village and Museum,** 1600 South Feazel Street, Harrisburg, (618) 253-7342.

Although it is a quick stop, it is a peaceful setting and a farm experience unlike any other. The main feature here is the **Poor House,** where Saline County's indigent residents went to live beginning in 1877. You can tour the building along with the pioneer homesteads that have been outfitted with cider presses, spinning wheels, and similar artifacts that were once mainstays of area life. The Poor House was built on the Poor Farm, which encompassed the surrounding lands. The idea was that with a place to live and 175 acres of farmland to tend, the poor would work to earn their own keep. Sadly, they didn't, so successions of other unfortunates were moved in: orphans, prisoners, the mentally ill. Twice the county threw up its hands and considered demolishing the whole thing, but it wasn't until the 1950s that the farm ceased operation.

From Harrisburg, head south on Highway 145 into Pope County and the **Shawnee National Forest,** most of which is reforested farmland, so its history is forever linked with agriculture. It is 277,831 acres in size. An area called Millstone Bluff was named for the millstone that early European settlers dug out to meet the needs of pioneer mills. The broken remains of one of these millstone relics are on display, and others are just out there in the woods. The thousand-year-old Mississippian Indian Village perches at the very top of Millstone Bluff; it is about a 15-minute hike up. The Indians were farmers, although they would have planted their crops at points farther down from the bluff-top elevation. Call the Vienna Ranger District, (618) 658-2111.

In Vienna (for heaven's sake, don't pronounce it that way; say VYE-enna, and kind of stretch it out, maybe dip it in honey), pick up Highway 146 heading west through Johnson County and drive 8 miles to the Union County border. The **Trail of Tears Welcome Center and King Neptune Memorial,** is the next stop. It is a rest stop, but also the final resting place for King Neptune, who wasn't royalty, but was associated with riches. He was a pig, raised on a farm up near West Frankfort at the beginning of World War II. You don't hear much about King Neptune, but his inadvertent contribution to the war effort was amazing. It all started when he was auctioned off at a victory-money-raising drive. He was given to Don Lingle, a Navy recruiter from Anna, who toured the state with him. Finally, Lingle

At the Saline Creek Pioneer Village and Museum in Harrisburg, a former poor house now contains exhibit rooms with local artifacts.

auctioned him off for the second time. But this auction, an effort to sell war bonds, stipulated that the highest bidder could keep the pig for just one minute before returning him to be re-auctioned at a future event. King Neptune apparently became so popular that a total of $19 million was collected in this way. Etched with flowers, his cracked tombstone reads: "King Neptune 1941–1950 buried here. King Neptune famous Navy mascot pig auctioned for $19,000,000 in War Bonds 1942–1946 to help make a free world."

The Wine Trail

Ready to hit the trails? Let's start with the Shawnee Hills Wine Trail, which features something on the order of five distinctive wineries/vineyards, eight bed and breakfasts, and the Giant City State Park Lodge. Talk about romance. The winding trail will help you unwind as you gad about from point to point. You can easily make a day of it—and definitely a night. You will be traveling through Union County, where they currently grow more grapes than anywhere else in Illinois. Here and throughout the state's southern region, the environment is perfect for this sort of thing: rolling hills, loamy soil, long, sunny summers. Not bad for traveling, either.

Continue west on Highway 146 toward Anna. Go north on Highway 51 (not Old 51), then right onto CR-8/Wing Hill Road to **Winghill Vineyard and Winery**, 5100 Wing Hill Road, Cobden, (618) 893-9463. You could also have stopped short of Anna and hopped north on I-57, taken exit 36 west on Lick Creek

Road, then right on Hall Church Road to Wing Hill Road. Either way, you will enjoy free tasting and tours. Winghill produces a range of dry reds and whites from estate-grown French hybrids. There are also interesting fruit wines. Red in color and semi-dry, Hallsberry Blue is made from local blueberries.

Owl Creek Vineyard, 2655 Water Valley Road, Cobden, (618) 893-2557, is to be found a bit north on the trail. From the intersection of Wing Hill Road and Highway 51, go north on Highway 51, then 2.5 miles east on Water Valley Road. The wine list includes reds like the dry, full-bodied Owl's Leap that is blended from Chambourcin and Norton grapes, a blush, and whites and dessert wines. Enjoy the distinct raspberry taste of framboise, which is fortified with grape spirits. Late-harvest Zengeist is interesting not only for its honey and pear flavors, but also because proceeds from its sale benefit the two injured barn owls for which it was named, and which are cared for by Owls of Illinois. Special events at Owl Creek Vineyard include the grape stomp in June. Compete by advance registration or just enjoy the merriment and the live music.

Swing back down into little Cobden and west on Poplar Street, which turns into Aldridge Road, to the intersection with Highway 127. Visit the newer **Inheritance Valley Vineyards**, 5490 State Highway 127 North, Cobden, (618) 893-6141. First planted in 1997, the fruits of these vines made their commercial production debut in 2002. Inheritance Valley opened for business the next year, and today sells wines made with seven varieties of grapes and in a range from dry to sweet. They also sell fresh table grapes that would be great for a simple dessert with sliced cheese.

At this point, you are two miles south of Alto Pass. Continue on through to its quaint downtown, where you pick up Highway 127 to one of the region's largest commercial growers, **Alto Vineyards**, 8515 State Highway 127 North, Alto Pass, (618) 893-4898, www.altovineyards.net. It is southern Illinois' oldest winery, and their product comes with an Italian accent on flavor. Alto Vineyards reports an increasing interest in their dry reds, such as Chancellor, Chambourcin with its black cherry and plum finish, and rich, complex Rosso Classico. Try whites that range from dry to intensely sweet, light blushes, and hearty ports. The sweet wines still sell the best, like Heartland Blush, which is a product of Concord grapes. Special events feature good food, good music, and good wine.

To get to our next stop, Von Jakob Vineyard, continue north on Highway 127 into sleepy Pomona. You will know you are in Pomona when you see the Pomona General Store with its bygone-era character and a certain crumbliness. This old building is not open to the public, but you can appreciate its charm from the road. Turn left onto Sadler Road. Soon you will see grape vines marching on both sides of the road and perhaps hear the wail of the blues, and you know you have found **Von Jakob Vineyard**, 1309 Sadler Road, Pomona, (618) 893-4500, www.vonjakobvineyard.com. The owner's ancestry comes into play with Tudor-style architecture and some emphasis on German-style wines.

Grapevines at Owl Creek Vineyard, along the Shawnee Hills Wine Trail near Cobden.

Honey Blush is a semi-sweet mead that combines Concord grapes with honey. In 2003, they offered a dry, estate-bottled Cabernet Sauvignon, the first that was grown, produced, and commercially released by any Illinois vineyard. Enjoy lots and lots of events, or just sit and watch grape picking and other vineyard activities as they occur throughout the seasons.

Continue on Sadler Road until it ends at Hickory Ridge Road, where you snake north to **Pomona Winery**, 2865 Hickory Ridge Road, Pomona, (618) 893-2623; altogether it's five and one-half miles north of Von Jakob. Let the undulating wall of Egyptian brick lead you to the rustic tasting room and the wooden deck, where you can relax, glass in hand, among the forest trees. Pomona Winery specializes in wines made from Illinois fruits that are grown within a 50-mile radius; some actually come from orchards that you will visit along the Orchard Trail. Whole, fresh apples, peaches, blueberries, and strawberries go into the wines, and the end results range from dry to sweet, so that you can enjoy them with meals as well as with or for dessert. Orchard Spice is the bestseller. It mixes the spicy-sweet flavors of apple pie, and it is heartily recommended for winter-evening enjoyment as a mulled wine. Strawberry Dessert is described as "screaming strawberries," and pairs well with dark chocolate or cheesecake.

It is not on the Wine Trail, but **Limestone Creek Winery**, 1250 State Highway 127 South, Jonesboro, (618) 534-9049, is a pleasant country stop one mile south of town. You will find Jonesboro just a little over a mile southwest of Anna. Learn about the small batch whites, reds, and dessert wines that are all carefully crafted by someone who loves to focus on making wine and teaching visitors about it over generous offerings of food. Time permitting, you may be able to enjoy a short lecture and walk through the winemaking areas.

The Orchard Trail

The Orchard Trail rambles north for three stops in Jackson County and four in Union County. The Jackson County stops are: **Mileur Orchard**, **Gammer Orchards**, and **Lipe Orchards**. Again beginning near Anna, you could make **Boyd Orchards**, 675 Sadler Road, Anna, (618) 833-5533, www.boydorchards.com, your first stop, provided it is autumn. Kids especially love the Barn Full of Fun with its 40-foot slide, sandbox, rope swing, giant blackboard, pumpkin house, petting zoo, and hayrides. Shop for freshly harvested produce, preserved products, cookbooks, and fall decorations. Special events include the Apple Festival, the Harvest Moon Celebration, and the Pumpkin Festival.

Drive north to Cobden, where refrigerated rail cars were first designed by a local fruit grower in the 1860s. Well, technically, he created a special compartment that kept his strawberries cold using ice, but someone had to get this ball rolling to ensure that the southern Illinois fruits could arrive fresh and sweet in the hungry Chicago market. Visit **Flamm Orchards**, 8760 Old Highway 51 North (not U.S. Highway 51), Coben, (618) 893-4241. The busy, fifth-generation Flamm family planted its first 117 acres in 1888, and now operates one of the state's largest peach orchards. They also grow apples and vegetables across two thousand acres. The Country Market offers fruit pie fillings, spiced fruits, honey, sorghum, chunky applesauce, pickled sweet tiny beets, and more preserved foods, along with fresh strawberries in May, peaches in July and August, and apples from September through November. How about a sweet treat from the Fruit and Cream Stand? As you spoon up in-season strawberry shortcake, peach cobbler, apple pie, or apple dumpling piled high with whipped cream, imagine the early days on this farm, when members of the Flamm family worked hard to build their business, but also found time for square dancing, ice skating, and hickory-nut hunts. They still find time for fun today, and so will you, especially at the fall festival in October.

Lipe Orchards lies to the north on Highway 51, but if you are sticking to Union County, head back south to Alto Pass, and make a stop at **Rendleman Orchards Farm Market**, 9680 Highway 127 North, Alto Pass, (618) 893-2771, www.rendlemanorchards.com. Rendleman's is another of the state's largest peach orchards. The Rendlemans have been at it since 1873, and now tend 800 acres.

The Barn Trail

The Barn Trail identifies eight historic barns of dramatically varying styles and innovative uses. At all but two of the barns, visitors are invited to enjoy down-to-earth shopping, dining, or lodging experiences in the kind of rugged environments that cannot be duplicated. Starting at the southern end, visit the 345-acre **Trail of Tears Lodge and Sports Resort**, 1575 Fair City Road, Jonesboro, (618)

Rendleman Orchards Farm Market, Alto Pass.

They do potatoes 14 ways at the Potato Barn restaurant and gift shop in Anna.

833-8697, www.trailoftears.com. The barn dates back to the 1930s and was remodeled in 1988 to house a restaurant and seven guest rooms. Go in April for guided morel mushroom hunts, recipes, cooking demonstrations, and seminars (part of a two-night lodging package), or at other times for outdoor sports.

The next three barns are in Dongola. **Fragrant Fields,** including the **Mule Barn Café,** 102 South Garden Street, Dongola, (618) 827-3677, www. fragrant fields.com, is about 17 miles from the lodge. The 150-year-old poplar and oak barn is big, white, and easy to find right in town. It was originally built to house mules that were sold to loggers, farmers, and the U.S. Army. But that was long ago, and today on warm afternoons, visitors linger over homemade lunch and lemonade with a sprig of fresh mint in an open area that overlooks the garden center. **Red's Barn and Greenhouse** ("She's Red, I'm Ed."), 915 Body Barn Road, Dongola, (618) 827-4575, lies in a quiet country setting a little to the north. Take Old Highway 51 north and turn left onto Body Barn Road. This 1890s barn was built with pegs instead of nails, and what once housed hay for livestock now houses a small selection of perennials and annuals. To reach the **James Cyrus Eddleman Barn,** 3520 Saint John Road, drive west on Body Barn Road, and continue west on Saint John Road. View this handsome 1918 barn from the road, as it is a private residence and not open to the public.

Proceeding north on 127, take Highway 146 to **The Potato Barn**, 169 East Vienna Street, Anna, (618) 833-7827, and you have come eight miles from the last barn. This busy, happy place is a trail highlight that serves up a great story and local-approved meals. No wonder. Put a schoolteacher, a baker, and their daughters to work on an old barn, and you are in for a treat. Soak up the rich history over dinner, including fresh-daily bread and a steaming side of potatoes. Back in 1921, Ralph Goddard opened up his barn to area sweet potato growers, who would store their harvests on the way to market. On the walls of the loft upstairs, the farmers' designated storage areas still bear their names, although this area is not open to the public. The current owners insisted on keeping this visual record and others that await your discovery, and they also display authentic artifacts, even down to softly faded quilts and overalls. Remarkably, they did not just preserve the beauty of the barn, but also the memory of the people who worked there. In the 1930s and 1940s, the Goddards also bought and sold cream, eggs, feed, and seed, and even some of the old egg crates are on display. Today there are rooms to explore and a gift shop that offers a nice selection of the local winemakers' vintages.

To view **The Walton Farm** from the road at 165 Lick Creek Road, Anna, head east on Highway 146, then left onto Lick Creek Road for a total of a little more than a mile. You may see the sheep outside of this 1860s Pennsylvania-style bank barn. Its mortise-and-tenon construction features 50-foot beams of white oak that once grew on the property. Go north on Highway 51 for about 6 miles to **Shawnee Hills Barn and Antiques**, 290 Water Valley Road, Cobden, (618) 893-2211, www.shawneehillbb.com. Talk about innovation. In this nineteenth-century barn, you can poke around in search of antiques, shop for stained glass, and visit the blacksmith shop. Need more reasons to go? How about hiking the trails, exploring the cave, fishing the ponds, and staying the night?

Another eight miles brings you to the last stop on the Barn Trail, and it's a peach. The three-story barn at **Hedman Orchards and Vineyards**, 560 Chestnut Street, Alto Pass, (618) 893-4923, www.peachbarn.com, was built in 1947 of oak cut from the property. Hedman Orchards also qualifies for a spot on the Orchard Trail because it sells peaches, nectarines, and grapes right out of the barn, and recently cleared some space for The Peach Barn Café. They even have old fruit equipment on display in the old barn. To get here from Shawnee Hill Barn and Antiques, you could take Water Valley Road, cross Highway 51 and pick up Bell Hill Road into Cobden. By now you should be able to find your own way, but here's some help. Take Aldridge Road west out of town to Highway 127, then go north toward Alto Pass, crossing Bald Knob Bridge (don't you love these names?) to the orchard.

Need more to do? In mid-August, do the **Cobden Peach Festival**, (800) 248-4373, or the Union County Fair, Anna Fairgrounds, (618) 833-6311.

Following one or all of the trails or selected segments of each affords travelers the pleasure of tasting new wines, eating the ripest of fruits, and enjoying country hospitality as it is dispensed within the timeless confines of antique barns. It must be said that, once again, the people of the American Heartland

FIELD NOTES

Through the grapevine

Southern Illinois, especially around Union County, is the leading grape-growing region for the state. Over at Owl Creek Vineyard, Karen Hand says the soils, drainage, and climate contribute to the vintners' success. She points out that the hybrid and native varieties do the best, because temperatures below 20 degrees can kill the *vinifera* vines. She adds that making wines from Illinois grapes is something the vineyard believes in.

"We believe in what's called *terroir*, and that means the wines reflect the climate, the temperature, the soil of the region. We're not trying to be the same as California. It's just like in Europe; French wines are different than Italian wines, and even in France you have all these different regions," she explains.

The Illinois wine industry is enjoying a sudden resurgence of interest among producers. It has the kind of possibilities that characterize a young industry trying to prove itself in the judging world. And the word is getting out among people who like wines and are very much interested in discovering new, local favorites. As for people who like to travel, the value of discovering things needs no explanation. ⁂

have offered some great reasons to hit the trail.

PLACES TO EAT

Northwest Passage and Root Beer Saloon, Main Street, Alto Pass, (618) 893-1634. It is the one with the pretty petunias outside and the wackiness inside: a giant statue of King Tut, incoming stuffed geese, a replica of a New York hotel fallen on hard times, and spices for sale. Drink it all in with five kinds of old-fashioned draft root beer from all over the American Heartland; catch the bounty of seafood fests like the Bayou Boogie Boil and the New England Clam Bake and Cheese Lovers Weekend; and browse among 200 seasonings, 130 coffees, and 100 hot sauces.

Peach Barn Café, 560 Chestnut Street, Alto Pass, (618) 893-4923, www.peach barn.com. Authentic Swedish cuisine on weekends. July through September.

The Potato Barn, 169 East Vienna Street, Anna, (618) 833-7827. Roll up your sleeves and start right in on salads, soups, subs, and sandwiches for lunch, or comfort-food dinners like fried fish, roast beef, and meat loaf. Potatoes, of course, also interesting vegetable sides like corn casserole and cooked apples. All breads home-baked.

The Mule Barn Café, 102 South Garden Street, Dongola, (618) 827-3677. Salads, sandwiches, and that mint lemonade. Take home rosemary bread, cranberry vinaigrette dressing, and mint lemonade.

PLACES TO STAY

Kite Hill Bed and Breakfast, 119 Kite Hill Road, Murphysboro, (618) 684-5072. Rural, 30-acre estate with five-acre vineyard and fishing pond. New country home with three guest rooms, private baths.

Morris Acres, 1645 Tunnel Hill Road, Tunnel Hill, (618) 658-4022. A farm experience on 40 acres with tractor and wagon rides, horses, chickens, goats, bloodhounds. Fishing equipment available free of charge for use in farm ponds. Full breakfast or check off your preferred menu items.

Peach Barn Bed and Breakfast, 560 Chestnut Street, Alto Pass, (618) 893-4923, www.peachbarn.com. Single suite with private bath, massage tub, DVD, refrigerator, private deck.

Shawnee Hills Bed and Breakfast, 290 Water Valley Road, Cobden, (618) 893-2211, www.shawneehillbb.com. Three rooms, private baths, full or continental breakfast. Caving, bird watching, fishing on property.

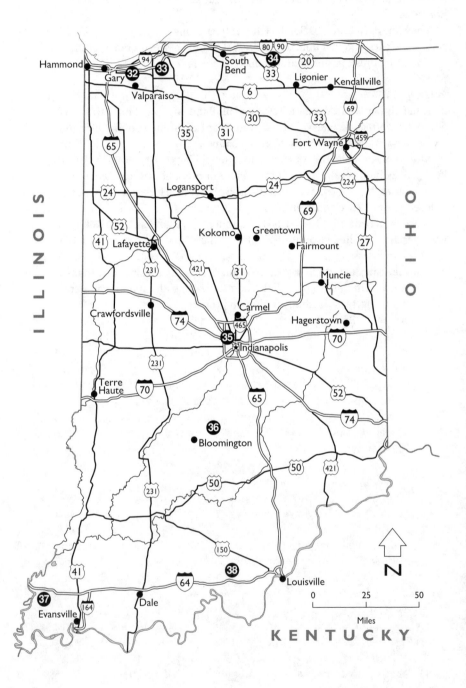

Indiana

Hoosier hospitality is deeply rooted in the fields and small towns and cities of Indiana. This weekend, why not get a taste of it? Way up north, you could take in the steamy fragrance of a hot ham and bean soup in Amish country. Down south, why not enjoy the friendly patter of a miller who demonstrates how kernels of corn become cornmeal inside a pioneer gristmill? And when you go to Indianapolis, you will like the way the city takes center stage by mixing a little urban style in with its own rural side.

32. A LITTLE INLAND FROM THE SANDY SHORE

Where sand meets surf at the far northwest tip of Indiana, people come to play. Here in Porter County, dunelands decorate the shoreline of Lake Michigan like frosting on a cake. Swim, have sun-baked summer fun, and never mind the occasional steel mill. But when it comes to farms and foods, venture a little inland to the smattering of old farms and young wineries.

You will encounter plenty of places named some version of port. It can get a little confusing, so here is an attempt to sort out the ports. The county is called Porter. Porter is also a town. Portage is Porter County's largest city and home to Portage Marina and Indiana's International Port, but neither Old Porter Road nor Portage Avenue, both of which run through Portage, will get you there. The county is actually short one port: mercifully, what was Portersville is now Valparaiso. The town of LaPorte is not in Porter County at all, but in neighboring LaPorte County, but that is another tour. There, that should clear it up. By the way, Valparaiso seems to have a thing for popcorn and is located about 55 miles southeast of downtown Chicago.

Just before you get to Porter County, you could make a few stops in Lake County, which sits just to the west and a little closer to Chicago. From I-80 and I-94, take exit 15A, or from I-90 (tollway) take exit 21. The **County Line Orchard**, 200 S. County Line Road, Hobart, (219) 947-4477, www.countylineorchard.com, is a great family place and the closest u-pick apple orchard to downtown Chicago. They are open from late August through October with pumpkins, a corn maze, and country foods such as fresh-baked apple pie, warm apple cinnamon donuts, fudge, caramel apples, cider, and lunches on the weekends. At The Kid's Farm, little ones get a little excited watching chicks hatch, goats climb, and pigs, sheep, chickens, donkeys, llamas, emus, peacocks, and zebu frolic, or whatever it is zebu do. About half a mile southwest, **Deep River County Park and Woods Historic Gristmill**, 9410 Old Lincoln Highway, Hobart, (219) 947-1958, (800) GRISTMILL, demonstrates cornmeal-grinding on the weekends.

The Baillys and the Chellbergs

About 18 miles northeast of the mill, there is a great living history farm, the **Chell-berg Farm and Bailly Homestead**, on Mineral Springs Road between Highways 12 and 20, Porter, (219) 926-7561, www.nps.gov/indu. At this faithfully restored site, the story of two northwest Indiana families is told across two different time periods. The Bailly Homestead was the home and workplace of a fur trader who settled here in 1822. Half a century later, in 1872, Anders and Johanna Kjellberg left Sweden to settle in this growing Swedish community. They bought their first 40 acres from a Bailly descendant. The family thrived. Three generations grew cash crops, raised livestock, and celebrated Swedish traditions here, until Anders' grandson sold it to the National Park Service in 1972—150 years after the story began. Today, sustainable agriculture, such as rotation of corn, sorghum, spelt (winter wheat), and hay crops, is practiced. Pumpkins mature just in time for the special Halloween event.

Follow the woodland path through the trees to the maple sugar house where today, as it was in the 1930s, maple tree sap is boiled down into sweet syrup. The red brick farmhouse dates back to 1885, and tours of various rooms include the kitchen with its hand pump and wood-burning stove. On weekends, volunteers still prepare meals on the same wood-burning stove that the Chellbergs used so long ago. Outbuildings are also open for your inspection, such as the granary that was constructed with square-cut nails, the pump house and windmill, the corn crib, and the 1890s chicken house. Resident chickens enjoy life with their spacious indoor shelter and outdoor yard that is perfect for scratching and pecking

The main house of the Chellberg Farm, near Porter, looks much like it did when it was built in 1885.

in the dirt. The nearby barn, which was built before 1885, houses Belgian draft horses, sheep, lambs, and goats, as well as little birds that fly in and out on their own schedules. Just beyond, a few pigs root around in a marvelously mucky pen. You might come upon an occasional cat going about its version of farm chores.

The Chellberg Farm really comes alive during the **Duneland Harvest Festival,** which is held each autumn in mid-September (minimal parking fee, free admission—a real old-fashioned bargain). See husks of corn become sturdy dolls. Watch the steam rise as apples are cooked over an open flame. Discover how soap can be made from rendered sheep fat. Watch a horse go around and around in order to power the sorghum press. Admire the steely gaze of border collies as they partner with handlers to successfully herd sheep. You can buy some of the finished products at a nearby stand, but the demonstration area is all about learning.

Food is everywhere. Load up on fresh produce at the small farmers' market that is appropriately set up near the kitchen garden. Pick up a jar of Indiana sorghum. Savor hearty treats that are offered exclusively by local non-profits. How about bean and ham soup, Swedish potato sausages, roasted corn, apple brown betty, popcorn, and cider for lunch and snacks to enjoy throughout your day in the fresh fall air?

Neighboring Farms

After the Chellberg-Bailly experience, how about visiting the **Alton Goin Countryside Museum,** 5250 East Highway 6, Portage, (219) 762-8349, www.ci.portage.in. us, where historical artifacts are displayed inside a late-1800s farmhouse. Another small farm experience can be had nearby at **Sunset Hill Farm County Park,** which is run by Porter County, (219) 465-3586. See lots of large, old farm buildings still undergoing restoration and packed with hay wagons, tractors, and implements. Chicago businessman Colonel Robert Heffron Murray bought the farm in 1934, adding acreage until it reached its present size of 235 acres. Sunset Hill was a dairy farm that began selling milk to surrounding residents in 1939 for 30 cents a gallon. This was the cream-topped raw stuff, which was marketable until 1954, when pasteurization forever changed all that. Milk production topped out at four hundred gallons a day in 1970, the same year that sales to the public ceased. Eight years later, the dairy farm closed and became county property.

Be sure to visit the nearby **Anderson's Orchard and Winery,** 430 East Highway 6, Valparaiso, (219) 464-4936, www.andersonsvineyard.com. Located about four miles east of Sunset Hill Farm County Park on Highway 6, this 45-acre boutique winery offers fresh apples but has also evolved in recent years into a true Indiana vineyard with some estate-bottled wines. The first of these became available in 2003. Tastings are free; ask to try their newer No Name Red, a full-bodied, dry oak-aged red that is produced on-site from the Frontenac grape, which was first hybridized by the University of Minnesota. They are referring to it as Indiana's Midwestern Merlot. Other dry wines include Proprietor's Select Chardonnay and Marechel Foch, which is slightly spicy and acidic. Blackberry, red raspberry, and rhubarb wines are very popular. Anderson's takes advantage of proximity to the lake and excellent air drainage due to the elevation of this particular site. Anderson's has a great country market that is stuffed with jams, beeswax, fresh produce, baked goods, winemaking supplies, and imported steins and crystal. Fruit trees are seasonally sold to budding orchardists, and they are always in high demand.

Also visit **Dune Ridge Winery**, which opened in 1998 and is located back in Porter on Highway 20 at 1240 Beam Street, Porter, www.dune ridgewinery.com. From I-94, take Exit 22B; from I-80/90 (Indiana Toll Road), exit at State Road 49. Or, from Anderson's Orchard and Winery, it is about a 13-mile drive (take Highway 6 west, merge onto State Road 49, then I-94, then Highway 20 via Exit 22B). Many of Dune Ridge's grapes come from Michigan. Try, for example, the Seyval Blanc Semi-dry with peach and apricot flavors, or the Cabernet Sauvignon Semi-dry with a blackberry aroma and chocolate undertones.

In addition to the homesteads and farms and wineries, visitors should try to find time to do the dunes. It is a sandy, beachy environment that can be enjoyed most times of the year, but especially in summer. But when it comes to farms and foods, it is also worth driving a little inland from the sandy shore.

SPECIAL EVENTS

Gaelic Festival, Sunset Hill Farm County Park, on Meridian Road south of Highway 6, between Chesterton and Valparaiso, (219) 465-3586, www.porterco .org. June. All things Irish and Scottish, including food, dancing, live ballads and pub songs, tractor-drawn wagon rides through the farm, pony rides, beer garden.

Porter County Fair, Porter County Expo Center and Fairgrounds, 215 East Division Road, off Indiana 49, Valparaiso, www.portercofair.org. July. Rodeo, 4-H exhibits.

Valparaiso Popcorn Fest, downtown Valparaiso, (219) 464-8332, www.popcorn fest.org. September. Join in honoring Orville Redenbacher and marvel at popcorn floats (averaging 200 to 300 pounds of popcorn per float) in the popcorn parade (a total of about 1,562,500 popcorn kernels float by; someone's counting).

PLACES TO EAT

Lucrezia Café and Catering, 428 South Calumet Road (corner of Porter Avenue and South Calumet Road), Chesterton, (219) 926-5829, www.lucreziacafe.com. Northern Italian fare. Fettuccine salmon combines fresh salmon and scallions in a lemon dill cream sauce. Roasted lamb shank is served with roasted potatoes, onions, and natural juices. Specialty coffees.

Strongbow Inn, 2405 East Highway 30, Valparaiso, (219) 531-0162, www.strong bowinn.com. History of the site includes a pre-Civil War farmhouse, turkey farm, and roadside turkey restaurant—all gone but still in the family's memory bank. Today's fine-dining restaurant features traditional turkey dinners and continental cuisine.

The Port Drive-In, 419 North Calumet Avenue, Chesterton, (219) 926-3500.

FIELD NOTES

David Lundstrom talks
ABOUT HIS ORCHARD

On an unexpectedly cold Mother's Day, it is raining sideways in northern Indiana, so instead of tending his vines, David Lundstrom of Anderson's Orchard and Winery in Valparaiso, is talking about them.

"I've got the greatest lifestyle in the world," says Lundstrom. "But it's not like I sit around all day with a glass of wine in my hand, watching my vineyards grow," he adds, shattering the good-life image like a dropped glass.

Lundstrom discovered his intense love of agriculture right out of high school, so instead of following his father into the steelworks, he began selling Christmas trees. When Anderson's Orchard went up for sale, Lundstrom and his wife, Kathy, bought it and eventually began planting the vines. Today, he says he couldn't afford not to have the vineyard. "We take the base product and transform it into something that has a great deal of value. The processing is where the value comes in," he explains.

It turns out Lundstrom's family was among the early Swedish settlers in the area, and they would have been contemporaries of the Chellbergs, another family that we've come across on this tour. His great-grandfather was one of the founders of the town of Miller, which was a Swedish community that later became Gary. His grandmother was its first postmistress.

"So we have a lot of background in this area," he says with the conviction of a man who knows the value of good, strong roots.

Homemade root beer, chili dogs. Warm-weather local favorite.

Wagner's Ribs, 361 Wagner Road, Porter, (219) 926-7614. House specialty is pork ribs.

PLACES TO STAY

Dunes Shore Inn, 33 Lakeshore County Road, Beverly Shores, (219) 879-9029. Ten rooms, six with private bath, full breakfast. One block to Lake Michigan. Casual atmosphere with outdoor patio, grill, picnic area, and screened gazebo.

Spring House Inn, 303 North Mineral Springs Road, Porter, (219) 929-4600, www.springhouseinn.com. Fifty oversized rooms. Lodge amenities, B&B charm.

Sitting porch on every floor. Deluxe fireside continental breakfast features make-your-own waffles with toppings. Ask for a room facing the woods, where you can step out onto your private balcony and feel as if you are in a tree house—but with all the comforts just inside your door. Indoor swim area with gas fireplace, pool, and huge whirlpool. Couldn't be closer to the Chellberg Farm.

The Inn at Aberdeen, 3158 South State Road 2, Valparaiso, (219) 465-3753, www.innataberdeen.com. Stately, historic home underwent extensive renovation to bring it up to B&B standards of authenticity and comfort. In the past, the home was called Timberlake Farm, where dairy cattle and thoroughbred horses were raised. The Timberlake Suites guestrooms reflect this piece of history. In the mid-nineteenth-century, the original owners planted 150 apple trees. Enjoy access to the nearby and newly built community swimming pool. The full breakfasts are special, starting with a parfait, sweetbreads, and muffins, and continuing with a hot item such as Belgian waffles, stuffed French toast, or quiche.

33. BLUEBERRIES AND OTHER LOCAL COLOR

So what's a few sticky, blueberry-juice-stained fingers when the third-largest Great Lake laps at the shoreline just minutes away from the orchards?

Imagine a summer day spent picking blueberries direct from the bushes in the morning and then, when the sun peaks in the sky, piling everyone back into the car and making a beeline for the beach, where you can enjoy a casual lunch and refreshing swim. Do it in LaPorte County, where blue sky, blue water, blue highways, and blueberries come together for one delicious weekend.

LaPorte County is in northwest Indiana, east of Porter County, west of South Bend and sharing a border with Michigan.

Blueberries

Get into a blue mood just south of the Michigan border, where you can take your pick of several blueberry farms. Delicious and easy things you can do with blueberries include mixing them into vanilla yogurt, dropping them into a cereal bowl, topping a cheesecake, or baking a pie. Three blueberry farms are conveniently clustered just south of the Michigan border. Closest to the state line is **Blueberry Dune Farm**, 10352 North State Road 39, LaPorte, (219) 324-6335. Wooded trails, wetlands, and picnic spots add a touch of nature to your picking experience. Grab one of the white pails and drive back to the fields. You could also plan to catch the annual Blues Fest that rocks the house in the restored barn. Open July to September.

At **Blueberries of Indiana**, 2388 West 1000 North, LaPorte, (219) 326-8686, they have been tending blueberry bushes since 1948 (although some plantings go back to 1936), just about one and one-half miles southeast of the Blueberry Dune Farm. The owner says more people are beginning to freeze the berries to have them available year-round for their antioxidant properties. Spending part of a day among

---

Blueberries of Indiana

Charles M. "Mike" Mainland, second-generation owner of Blueberries of Indiana, has a few ideas for enjoying your time spent picking blueberries in the orchard. He recommends bringing insect repellant, because although mosquitoes are usually not a problem, they can be after it rains. Mornings come with dew, so waterproof shoes are a good idea. Or bring a second pair. Pickers have been known to kick off their shoes entirely, but Mainland does not recommend it. Add sunscreen, a hat, and bottled water (no glass).

When picking, select berries that are plump, firm, and dark blue with a silvery bloom (this is Mother Nature being protective). Hold the berry cluster in your hand and gently roll the fruit with your thumb. The ones that are ready to fall, will.

Now, what do you do with the bounty? Blueberries are easy to freeze, and they keep well for up to a year. Mainland suggests two simple approaches to do this successfully. A) To freeze before washing, fill desired containers, seal, and freeze. When ready to use, remove desired amount (berries will pour freely) and wash before they thaw. B) To wash before freezing, wash, then drain excess water. Freeze on paper-towel-lined cookie sheet before transferring to desired sealed container. 🐜

---

the immaculate rows of bushes, none so high or low that you have to stretch or bend, is satisfying on these 20 acres. Open approximately July 10 to Labor Day. **Stateline Blueberries**, 9957 North Frontage Road, Michigan City, (219) 874-7721, www.statelineblueberries.com, offers a convenient yet rural setting for picking 10 varieties across 35 acres. It is located 16.5 miles southwest of Blueberries of Indiana. Stateline Blueberries provides picnic tables for relaxation, and also sells jams, honey, and maple syrup. The picking season generally goes from the last week of June to the middle of August.

Other Local Color

Beyond blueberries, the local harvest is a riot of color and texture and flavor that gives you a reason to get outdoors and celebrate each season. First, call the Fruit and Vegetable Hotline at (800) 572-3740 or (800) 572-3740, and order a picking brochure from the LaPorte County Convention and Visitors Bureau. Here is a sampling of places to visit on a small loop that ends in downtown LaPorte. Not

FIELD TO TABLE

Blueberry dump cake

This recipe is the all-time favorite of the folks at Blueberries of Indiana. They say it's tasty—and easy.

2 cups blueberries sweetened to taste
1 small can crushed pineapple (include half of the juice)
1 box yellow or pineapple cake mix
$1/2$ cup broken pecans
$1^1/2$ sticks butter or margarine, melted

Put berries in a greased baking pan, approximately 6 x 11 inches and cover with pineapple. Pour on dry cake mix and scatter pecans on top. Drip melted butter over the surface. Bake approx. 1 hour at 350 degrees. Serve topped with ice cream or whipped cream.
From the recipe collection of Blueberries of Indiana. 🐾

all of them will be open at the same time of the year.

Located south of downtown LaPorte and one-third mile east of Highway 35 is **Burek Farm,** 0381 East 400 South, LaPorte, (219) 393-5080. Pull in at the sign, park near the house, and start your search for fresh, seasonal produce. Jean Burek (coincidentally, the surname means "beet" in Polish) and her son, Ed, run the farm, which does the bulk of its business in commercial grains. Shop seasonally for hand-picked asparagus, broccoli, cabbage, green beans, peppers, strawberries (u-pick available toward the middle or end of June), sweet corn, tomatoes, and zucchini. The fall harvest brings cauliflower, pumpkins, and Indian corn.

Head south on Highway 35, then west on Highway 6 to **Huber Farms,** 4600 West U.S. Highway 6, Union Mills, (219) 393-5080. Huber Farms is about seven miles southwest of Burek Farm. In season, pick blueberries and pick up honey. In the mood for crisp asparagus in the springtime? Then continue west on 6 and turn right on Highway 421 to **Coulter's Farm Produce,** 5433 South U.S. Highway 421, Westville, (219) 785-2406. Here you can get out in the field and snap your own spears direct from the sandy soil. Or, for a little more money per pound, buy a couple of pre-picked bags and be on your merry way. But first, also look for ruby-red rhubarb stalks and homemade rhubarb jam. Return in summer for sweet corn and melons, and pick pumpkins in October.

Go north on Highway 421, cross I-80/90, and turn left on County Road 100

North for a total of about eight miles from Coulter's Farm Produce toward **Rosey's Berry Farm**, 1066 North 1150 West, Michigan City, (219) 874-2981. Another springtime treat, strawberries, await your winter-weary taste buds. Rosey's grows them organically, but you can only get them from late May to June.

To visit **Radke Orchards**, 8999 West 200 North, Michigan City, (219) 879-4185, drive back on 100 North to Highway 421 and go north to County Road 200 North, where you will turn right. You will have to wait until mid-September for this one, because it is all about apples. Radke Orchards is just under four miles from Rosey's Berry Farm.

Continue east on 200 North, and turn left onto Wozniak Road for a distance of just over a mile to **Miller's Orchard**, 2134 North Wozniak Road, Michigan City, (219) 874-6060. Look for apples, cider, Concord grapes, gourds, melons, pears, pumpkins, squash, sweet corn, tomatoes, and more fresh produce in season.

Pavolka Fruit Farm, 1776 North Wozniak Road, Michigan City, (219) 874-6056, sits less than one-half mile to the south. Pavolka packs so much variety into 40 acres that, if you come for apples, you may leave with a trunkful of peaches, pears, and plums. Not to mention asparagus spears, blackberries, cherries, and various nuts. Feel free to ask questions about older fruit varieties, which the owner extols for their superior taste and keeping qualities, but if you have any doubts about that, check out the five hundred or so county fair ribbons that she won through the years. With so many varieties of fruits available in one place, you may wish to ask for assistance in selecting some of each to learn about their taste differences and best uses. Here you will find Sheep's Nose, Winter Banana, and Yellow Transparent apples, and a sugar pear tree that has been bearing fruit for some one hundred years. You might also see turkeys, chickens, and other critters hanging around the farm. Open late June through February.

In and Around LaPorte

The Garwood family has been growing apples, peaches, and other produce in these parts since 1831, and is now into its sixth generation on some 350 acres. Located just over three and one-half miles southeast of Pavolka Fruit Farm at 5911 West 50 South, LaPorte (Pinola), (219) 362-4385, **Garwood Orchard** offers a thoroughly country experience, including rows and rows of preserved fruits and vegetables, fresh pies, cookbooks, and other home-style treats inside the great market. How about a hand-dipped caramel apple that has been rolled in a specialty topping such as toffee? Or cider from one of the last cider mills in these parts? Pick raspberries, pumpkins, and apples like Honeycrisp, Cameo, Golden and Red Delicious, Braeburn, and Fuji. In season, the back rooms hum with the intensity of packing for the wholesale market, as wholesale represents fully 90 percent of the crop. But the real excitement occurs during special events that feature live bands. Special events include Watermelon Toss, Apple Fest, and Antique Tractor Fest. The market is open daily July to December, but u-pick apples and pumpkins are available only on weekends from September through October.

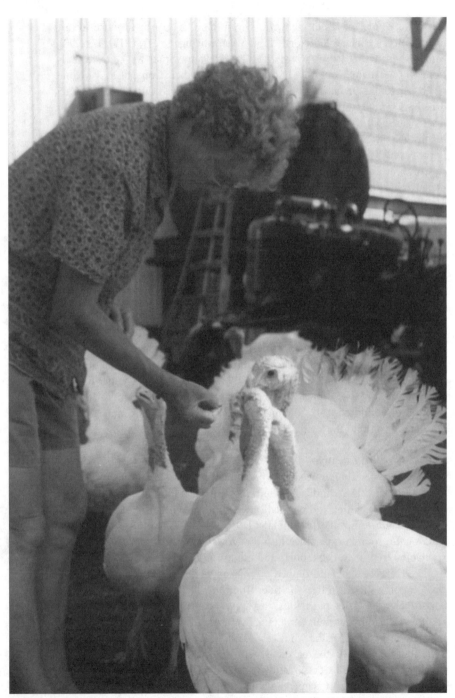

Dorothy Pavolka treats her turkeys to a taste of Italian prunes at the Pavolka Fruit Farm, Michigan City.

●

FIELD NOTES

Dorothy's best picks

After a lifetime of growing prize-winning fruit, Dorothy Pavolka has some great picking tips to share:

Be picky. You want to be discerning and not pick just anything that is within reach. Consider each fruit before you pick it. You are not supposed to be in a rush doing this sort of thing, anyway.

Don't pick unripe fruit. You will not be able to do anything with it.

Pick it up. The tendency for children especially is to grab the apple and pull down. Dorothy says this is very hard on the tree, especially if you come away with leaves and all. Instead, pick the apple up, and it will snap off with the stem, but not with half the tree.

And finally, don't climb the trees! 🐾

●

About six and one-half miles east in busy little LaPorte, the Garwoods also run the convenient **Garwood Farm Market**, 206 Lincolnway, LaPorte , (219) 362-4381. Old photos line the walls of the market to tell the story of the family's century of farm operations. You can buy backyard-sized packages of the same seeds that the Garwoods use to plant their highly successful bean and sweet corn crops. Open year-round.

Downtown LaPorte has some irresistibly quaint shops. At 816 Jefferson Avenue, scoop up some of **Temple News Agency's** newspapers and vividly colored ice creams, and soak up the early 1900s atmosphere beneath the painted tin ceiling that somehow fits in with the Internet café thing. The telephone number (219) 362-2676. **The Cookery**, 810 Lincolnway, LaPorte , (219) 325-3663, offers name-brand cookware, gourmet goodies, and cooking classes for all those veggies you have been picking. And **Crust and Crumble Homestyle Bakers**, 706 Jefferson Avenue, LaPorte , (219) 362-3344, serves up small-batch ethnic breads, cinnamon rolls, and bagels.

The **LaPorte County Historical Society Museum**, LaPorte County Complex, 809 State Street, LaPorte , (219) 326-6808, ext. 276, is free and open Tuesday through Saturday. Exhibits related to farms and foods include the General Store Display with its checkerboard ready for play, Pioneer Cooking with utensils that county pioneers bought in the 1830s and 1840s, agricultural items such as a cream separator, and a 1920s kitchen where visitors can learn about early ice preservation methods.

But one museum display tells a sinister story of the past. In 1900, Norwegian immigrant Belle Gunness collected $8,000 on her late husband's life insurance policy. That was in Chicago. Two years later, she and her second husband were farming in LaPorte . A coffee grinder that fell on his head killed him, and she again collected. Next, she began advertising in Norwegian-language newspapers, "Widow, with mortgaged farm, seeks marriage. Triflers need not apply." Many men responded, but it seemed that when the suitors would leave the farm, they always left at night. A niece got suspicious but then, according to Gunness, left for college in California. Andrew Helgelein was the last man to answer one of the ads. Gunness persuaded him to sell everything he had before joining her in LaPorte with the proceeds that totaled $3,000.

In early 1908, the farmhouse burned. What they found buried on the farm was shocking: the bodies of Helgelein and the niece, as well as at least 12 other people, although some estimated that Gunness had buried 40 men on the farm. A hired hand was charged with murder and arson, but only convicted of arson. He later died in prison, but claimed that Gunness had escaped. For years people reported sightings of Belle Gunness across the country. She was never found.

But most of LaPorte 's farming history is thoroughly respectable. For starters, the Advance-Rumely Company was LaPorte 's largest employer by 1869, when it was manufacturing the first kerosene-powered farm machinery, a type of equipment that helped to impact agriculture on a global scale. Then there is the uniquely nine-sided Door Prairie Barn that was built in 1878 and is located off Highway 35 South. And finally, scenes of the popular movie *Prancer* (1989) were filmed in the northeast part of LaPorte County, on County Road 700 North, just off Fail Road. Prancer is, as everyone knows, one of Santa Claus's reindeer, and in the movie, the daughter of an orchardist finds a reindeer. The movie's director, John D. Hancock, grew up on the Hancock Fruit Farm in LaPorte .

Savor more local flavor at the **LaPorte County Fair** each July at 2581 West State Road 2, (219) 362-2647, for livestock shows, 4-H exhibits, harness racing, and more country fun. The fair is, by the way, where Dorothy Pavolka won her ribbons all those years ago. Over in historic downtown Rolling Prairie, northeast of LaPorte , the **Olde Farmers Fest** takes you back in time during late August with tractor parades, a petting zoo, old-time demonstrations, a farmers' market, and more old-fashioned fun; visit www.rollingprairie.org. On Labor Day weekend, hop aboard the **Steam and Power Show at Hesston Steam Museum**, east of 39 and west of Basswood Road on 1000 North, LaPorte , (219) 872-5055. Ride steam trains and a steamboat on 155 acres. Check out antique tractors, gas engines, the sawmill, and the blacksmith shop.

During this Heartland weekend, if you have been seen around LaPorte County with a little peach juice dribbling down your chin, or the stain of blueberries on your fingers, no explanations are needed.

PLACES TO EAT

B & J's Café, 607 Lincolnway, LaPorte , (219) 362-3474. Authentic 1940s atmosphere with swing music and movie memories. Family breakfasts and lunches for over 75 years.

Dockside Café, Washington Park Marina, Michigan City, (219) 871-0645. Casual waterfront eatery that will happily pack your beachside lunch for you.

Sophie's Kitchen, 3051 Willowcreek Road, Portage, (219) 764-3631. Polish-American home-style cooking includes pierogis (potato, kraut, cheese, prune, or fruit), soups, and other traditional fare. Blueberries are likely to turn up in your breakfast pancakes and oatmeal.

PLACES TO STAY

Arbor Hill Inn, 263 West Johnson Road, LaPorte , (219) 362-9200, www.arbor hillinn.com. Enjoy privacy at the 1910 Greek Revival Colonial or the Guest House after taking an evening stroll along little Pine Lake (it is a short drive to the public park) from which the town once harvested up to 100,000 tons of ice each winter. Relax in spacious rooms among rich woods and fabrics. Enjoy days-gone-by elegance with appointments like fireplaces, TV/VCRs, hot tubs, full breakfasts, and tree-shaded porches. Twelve rooms/suites.

Creekwood Inn, Highway 20/35 at I-94, Michigan City, (800) 400-1981. Tuck yourself into this English country home on 33 wooded acres that have jogging and ski trails and creek fishing opportunities. Thirteen large, air-conditioned guest rooms, some with fireplaces, others with French doors opening to private terraces. Most rates include continental breakfast with homemade breads, fresh fruit, and cereal.

Tryon Farm Bed and Breakfast, 1400 Tryon Road, Michigan City, (219) 879-3618, www.tryonfarmguesthouse.com. The 1986 farmhouse of this onetime Indiana dairy farm has recently been opened for the pleasure of guests. The surrounding land is being transformed into a conservation community where folks who love the natural world wouldn't have it any other way. Enjoy the goats and chickens, hiking trails, and nearby beaches.

34. AMISH COUNTRY: WHERE EVERYTHING IS JUST PLAIN GOOD

An Amish living history farm is just the beginning of a great weekend in Indiana Amish Country. There are so many entertaining and educational ways to learn all about this culture that is a world away from our own, yet exists so peaceably within it. And the food! It is home-style, all right, and it keeps on coming in piping-hot platters and steaming bowls. And Amish women excel at pie-baking. Follow your nose to far north-central Indiana, east of South Bend and just this side of the Michigan border. Elkhart, which will be the starting point, is located about 15 miles east of South Bend.

With an eye toward farms and foods, you can easily tour Indiana Amish Country on your own, keeping in mind that many places are closed on Sundays. For a nominal, refundable fee, the **Elkhart County Visitors Center** will supply you with

FIELD TO TABLE

Buckwheat pancakes

from Bonneyville Mill

2$\frac{1}{2}$ cups buckwheat flour
2$\frac{1}{2}$ cups milk
1 tablespoon oil
2 tablespoons sugar
2 tablespoons molasses
1$\frac{1}{2}$ tablespoons baking powder
$\frac{1}{2}$ teaspoon salt
1 egg, beaten

Combine all of the ingredients in a large mixing bowl. Beat until well blended. Spoon batter on lightly greased hot griddle. Turn the pancakes when bubbles begin to retain their holes. Serve with syrup and butter.
Recipe courtesy Elkhart County Parks.

their Amish and Mennonite Heritage driving tour on cassette or CD; stop in at 219 Caravan Drive, Elkhart, off Indiana Toll Road Exit 92. Call (800) 860-5949. Their Heritage Trail route leads you across 90 miles of town and country. You could opt for a step-on guide from Elkhart-based **Down the Road Tours**, (574) 266-0048. Or call Shipshewana-based **Buggy Lane Tours**, (877) 825-5474, for buggy rides, farm visits, and Amish home meals.

Down by the Old Millstream

A fine first stop just south of State Road 120 and about 15 miles east of the Visitor Center is **Bonneyville Mill**, 53373 County Road 131, Bristol, (574) 535-6458. The Little Elkhart River still powers this historic gristmill that has ground out flour for over 150 years and continues to do so to the delight of visitors. Today the mill is quaint; in the mid-1830s, it was Edward Bonney's ambition, with its innovative horizontal waterwheel that generated greater power than traditional vertical waterwheels. For decades the mill continued to serve local farmers and merchants, and by the 1930s, it was supplying hydroelectric power, livestock feed, and "Famous Buckwheat Pancake Flour."

The 233 acres of Bonneyville Mill Park provide grassy picnic areas with benches, shelters, and grills, along with about five miles of trails, low waterfalls, a mill pond, and goslings in spring. Take a mill tour to learn, among other things, that explosions were of great concern to early American milling operations because airborne flour dust could be ignited, but that millers took precautions as they were able. See what the various grains look like before they are ground. Not all restored historic mills grind flour, but this one still does it using the waterpower method. The miller sets the grinding process in motion by opening up an underwater turbine to let water flow through. The old equipment bangs with the rhythm of a passing train. Don't pass up the opportunity to buy sacks of Bonneyville Mill flour ground from rye, wheat, buckwheat, cornmeal, and cracked wheat (miller's tip: add cracked wheat to refined flours for heartier bread).

Let's Eat

Continue just over 6 miles southeast on County Road 8 to Middlebury, where **Das Dutchman Essenhaus**, 240 U.S. Highway 20, (574) 825-9471, (800) 455-9471, www.essenhaus.com, represents a mecca for anyone who loves to shop and eat. This bustling complex does everything in a big way, and with an eye toward country style. Here they love to cook, serving eight thousand people on a busy day in the Amish Country Kitchen restaurant, both family-style and off the menu. A day's record for pies is 1,834. Together, the restaurant and Essenhaus Bakery eat up 120 gallons of apple butter in one week. The homemade noodles never stop coming.

At the Bonneyville Mill in Bristol, a miller grinds corn to various levels of refinement.

The Essenhaus Village Shops are housed in former farm buildings.

Three miles east of Middlebury on County Road 250 North in LaGrange County (County Road 16 in Elkhart County), **Deutsch Kase Haus**, 11275 West County Road 250 North, Middlebury, (574) 825-9511, is a cheese and gift barn that also draws crowds. You might see the tour bus set clutching armloads of cheese, flavored licorice, jars of beets, Amish dolls, cookbooks, and whatever else the shop sells. All of the cheeses are made of milk from Amish farms in this area and in southern Michigan. On these farms, the cows are still milked by hand. To ensure freshness and safety, the milk is water-cooled prior to delivery the next morning, where it is immediately cooled and pasteurized before the cheese making begins.

"Shopshewana"

Continue east on County Road 250 North before turning right on State Road 5 into Shipshewana, which is about nine miles from Middlebury. This shopping destination attracts both the Amish and the English (that's you, to them). Yoder seems to own everything, but as it turns out there are many, many Yoders in Shipshewana. You are likely to see so many buggies that you won't even bother to crane your neck anymore. You will be shopping right alongside so many Amish dressed in plain clothes that it actually begins to seem ordinary. But some of the merchandise is definitely extraordinary. Need a sheep, a cream separator, or a bolt of calico? No problem. Any of these goods are likely to be available at the **Shipshewana Auction**. It includes the trademark **Flea Market** (Tuesday, Wednesday), the **Livestock Auction** (Wednesday), the **Horse and Pony Auction** (Friday), and the **Antique and Miscellaneous Auction** (Wednesday). Go even if you aren't in the market for a new cow.

Hearty, home-style foods are easy to find in Shipshewana. Try **Yoder's Meat Shoppe**, 365 State Road 5, next to the Auction Barn, (260) 768-4715, www.yoders meatshoppe.com for hickory-smoked bacon, 17 varieties of jerky and beef sticks, and locally produced foods. Or **E & S Sales**, one quarter-mile north of Highway 20 on State Road 5, for a tremendous variety of bulk foods at gleefully low prices. Pick up snacks for the road, including green cheese.

Take a guided tour through **Menno-Hof**, the Mennonite-Amish Visitors Center, 510 South Van Buren Street, Shipshewana, (260) 768-4117, www.mennohof.org. Inside the center's immaculate farm buildings, you will learn about the history of the Anabaptist movement from its beginnings in 1525, with key events unforgettably recreated in dioramas that depict a dungeon, a harbormaster's shack, and a seventeenth-century sailing ship. Other exhibits help you to understand Amish cultural practices and attitudes toward singing, peace, humor, and other ways of life. The Tornado Theater dramatically showcases the famous Amish tradition of helping neighbors after disaster strikes.

For more uniquely Amish food, head south on State Road 5, turn right onto Highway 20, then go one and one-quarter miles south to **Country Lane Bakery**, 59162 County Road 43, Middlebury, (574) 825-7918. This home-based Amish bakery is always ready with fresh breads, cinnamon rolls, pies, and sweet rolls. Pick up County Road 26 back to State Road 5, then drive a short distance south to **Yoder Popcorn**, 7680 West 200 South, Topeka, (260) 768-4051, www.yoderpopcorn.com. It is a farm that grows almost 400 acres of popcorn and sells it in amazing variety, along with accompaniments, at the on-site Country Popcorn Shoppe. The smell of fresh-popped corn alone is worth a visit, but you are also welcome to enjoy a free sample. What a great place to learn about different popcorn varieties such as the tiny Yoder Lady Finger. Discover other extraordinary country operations such as **Maple Lane Wildlife Farm**, 7410 West 700 South, Topeka, (260) 593-2248 for self-guided tours and children's pony cart rides. Up in the northwest corner of LaGrange County, visit **Greenfield Mills**, 1050 East 7560 North, Howe, (260) 367-2394; tours are available by appointment only. It is one of the region's oldest working grain mills, and some local restaurants proudly serve baked goods made with its flour.

What's to See in Nappanee?

Let's get to Nappanee, which is about 30 miles southwest of Topeka (and about 16 miles south of Elkhart) and home to the famous **Amish Acres**, 1600 West Market Street (Highway 6), Nappanee, (574) 773-4188, (800) 800-4942, www.amish acres.com. Sitting on 80 acres and utterly neat and clean, Amish Acres is part living history farm, part entertainment, great food, shopping, and lodging, all centered on an Amish theme. Take the guided House and Farm Tour to see the main house, grossdaadi haus (grandparent house), windmill, food drying house, brick bake oven, smokehouse, root cellar, lye kiln for soap-making, and many more structures. This actually used to be a working Amish farm. The story is told that it was in the 1870s, around the time the village of Nappanee was established, that Amish pioneer Christian Stahly bought the property for his son, Moses. Three generations of related Amish families subsequently lived on what came to be known as the Stahly-Nissley-Kuhns Farm, until it was sold to the current owners in 1968 to be reinvented as Amish Acres. Read the complete story, including the account of a genuine cattle roundup, in the book that has been written about Amish Acres and is available on-site.

Expect to see plenty of farm animals, including horses, pigs, goats, cows, chickens, doves, and pigeons, in and around the barns and outbuildings. See the Schwietzer bank barn that was built in 1876 of timber cut on the farm, and which accommodates many of the resident animals with stables, milking stalls, a corn crib, and a wagon shed. Experience other aspects of farm life too. Watch as skilled artisans hand-stitch quilts, make lye soap and brooms, press cider, and weave rugs. Take the Farm Wagon Ride Tour out to the pond and the historic village buildings that have been moved in to the site. At the mint still, Amish farmers would produce spearmint and peppermint oils by cooking the leaves in steam, then distilling the oil. Note the lime-based whitewash on the trunks of the fruit trees—it helps to deter insects that have a taste for Sheep's Nose or Rusty Coat apples; two old varieties that still grow at Amish Acres.

After touring, you should be hungry enough to tackle Amish Acres' family-style Threshers' Dinner. Be forewarned that the fragrant bowls of hearty food seem to never stop coming out of the barn-based restaurant kitchen. Everything is well-seasoned, including ham and bean soup, beef noodles, lean beef tips, fried chicken, ham and turkey slices (two meat entrees per table), mashed potatoes with butter, green beans, sweet and sour cabbage salad, fresh veggies, stuffing, and pie, as if that is not enough. Take in a Saturday evening performance at the Round Barn Theatre. With rollicking humor and respect for two disparate worlds, *Plain and Fancy* is the classic favorite that tells the engaging story of a clash of cultures—Amish and English. Enjoy lovely singing voices, high energy, humor, and a darn good tale. The round barn itself was in use since 1911 before being dismantled, moved, and reconstructed here in 1992.

It would be hard to leave Amish Acres without visiting the cute shops for souvenir gifts, meats, noodles, condiments, Indiana black walnut fudge, and other local treats. Consider taking home a jar of the ham and bean soup, the same stuff that you enjoyed at the Threshers' Dinner. Or pick up a copy of the Amish Acres cookbook that includes the soup recipe and hundreds of others. Ask about having a shoo-fly pie shipped. You could also sign up for the Countryside Tour (their van) that highlights active Amish businesses that would be historic in most American communities but are essential here: a blacksmith, buggy and harness shops, sawmill and sorghum mills, a mint still.

Well, there it is—a taste of Indiana Amish Country that is just plain good.

A view of the Mint Still, once used to distill spearmint and peppermint oils, at Amish Acres, Nappanee.

FROM FARM TO FIELD

Oatmeal pancakes

FROM AMISH ACRES

1 1/2 cups quick oats
1 teaspoon salt
1 teaspoon baking soda
3/4 cup whole wheat flour
2 cups buttermilk
2 eggs, beaten
1 tablespoon maple syrup

Soak oatmeal in buttermilk a short time, add beaten eggs, add rest of ingredients.

Recipe courtesy Amish Acres, Nappanee, Indiana 🐎

Make that a big helping, from the hearty food to the heartfelt hospitality. There's no doubt that you will feel a little of the magic of this culture of faith and farming that has settled quite naturally into the Midwestern landscape.

SPECIAL EVENTS

Day on the Farm Tour, (574) 533-0554. September dates, across Elkhart County. Open-house showcases of farming, fun family activities, animal petting, hands-on demonstrations, and tours.

Elkhart County 4-H Fair, Goshen, (574) 533-FAIR. July. Foods, animal shows, midway, more.

Millersburg Farmers Days, Millersburg, (574) 642-3976. August. Hometown festival celebrates the American farmer. Tractor pull, sack races, parade, more.

PLACES TO EAT

Bread and Chocolate, 133 South Main Street, Goshen, (574) 534-3053. A distinctly un-Amish café where plain takes a backseat to fancy. Popular breads include honey wheat and granola. Chocolate cheesecakes, tortes, and peach bourbon pies round out the gourmet offerings. Late-1800s building with exposed brick walls and tin ceiling.

County Seat Café, 124 West Jefferson Street, Goshen, (574) 534-1348. Local-approved Amish cooking and a casual atmosphere.

Fern's Country Foods, 7970 West 400 South, Topeka, (260) 593-2222,

(888) 838-2837. While you wait for a table, grab a cup of coffee and observe as Amish women prepare noodle dough, eventually draping sheets of it on wooden racks, where it dries with the aid of big fans. Afterward, a machine cuts the sheets of dough into strips—noodles. Still waiting? Browse among the oodles of noodles for sale, including yolk-free, spinach, garlic-parsley, tomato-basil, and different widths, along with canned meats and condiments such as raspberry-rhubarb jam. Still? You can always ask to share a table and consider it a chance to make new friends, whether they be English or Amish.

Olympia Candy Kitchen, 136 North Main Street, Goshen, (574) 533-5040. Chocolate-covered cherries for lunch? Maybe, but you could start with a burger or sandwich and something cold from the old-fashioned soda fountain. Since 1912.

PLACES TO STAY

Meadows Inn B&B, 12013 Highway 20, Middlebury, (574) 825-3913, (888) 868-3913. It was an active Amish farmstead until 1997, and today welcomes guests with pleasing furnishings that have retained some of the simplicity that is a hallmark of the Amish way of life.

Ol' Barn Bed and Breakfast, 63469 County Road 33, Goshen, (574) 642-3222. Century-old restored barn home, whirlpools, separate entrance, full breakfast, nine acres of woods/crops.

The Inn at Amish Acres, 1234 West Market Street, Nappanee, (574) 773-2011, (800) 800-4942, ext 3. Sparkling-clean on-site lodging with complimentary continental breakfast and outdoor pool. Somewhat lower rates at charming, farm-themed **The Nappanee Inn**, located one-half mile west on Highway 6. Complimentary continental breakfast in The Milk Parlor; call (574) 773-5999.

35. COUNTRY IN THE CITY: THIS IS INDIANAPOLIS?

The town made famous by its fast track also runs in slower lanes, so visitors in search of food and farming attractions will always be able to refuel at farmers' markets, orchards, the state's oldest winery, an everlasting flower farm, the Indiana State Fair, and the Vintage Indiana Wine and Food Festival. And about 25 minutes northeast of the downtown high-rises, a spunky living history farm even puts visitors up for the night—ah, chamber pots provided. This is Indianapolis?

Located in Marion County and literally in the heart of Indiana, Indianapolis is the state's capital city. Besides sporting the affectionate nickname of Indy, Indianapolis is also called the Crossroads of America, since more interstates and U.S. highways converge here than in any other metro area of the country. It is hard *not* to get to Indy.

Model Farm

The age-old question of how you are going to keep them down on the farm is best answered at **Conner Prairie Living History Museum**, 13400 Allisonville

FARTHER AFIELD
Finding the farms

Of Swiss-German origins, the Old Order Amish first came to northern Indiana in the early 1840s. This was about 150 years after the founding of the Amish faith, which itself represented a split from the Mennonite movement. You will not have any trouble finding their farms, considering this is one of the largest Amish communities in the country. Here they raise corn, buckwheat, soybeans, vegetables, fruits, and dairy cows, largely without modern-powered farm machinery. They do not use gasoline tractors, due to cost and soil compaction, but gasoline-fueled push mowers are commonly seen.

To identify the Amish farms, look for these signs as you drive by on the beautiful back roads: wash and quilts hanging on clotheslines, windmills, horses (solid draft horses plus sleek carriage horses), bicycles, multiple homes, telephone booths, barefoot children hitching ponies to miniature carts, and the absence of cars.

Of course, you could also look for the most rewarding signs, the hand-lettered ones that hang from fence posts and read, "Brown Eggs," "Honey," and "Pies Today." 🐾

Road, Fishers, (317) 776-6006, (800) 966-1836, www.connerprairie.org. Northeast of the city, I-465 will get you there, a distance of about 23 miles from downtown. Conner Prairie has 1,400 acres of all the historic charm you would expect, and all the unexpected theatricality of a live performance. That is because life at the farm, in the village, and on the estate, is interpreted in the first person. So when a young lady in the parlor at Zimmerman Farm proudly tells you about the lace curtains her mother recently ordered from the Montgomery Ward catalog, don't gape and gently explain to the dear child that the retail giant is out of business. In this world, it's 1886.

Interpreters are not detachedly demonstrating tasks as though on display. They are more inclined to ask if you would like to pick up that hoe and help dig the potatoes. Your child might be asked to go fetch a bucket of water, and you can be sure he will never forget the weight of that bucket, nor the care needed to keep the water from sloshing out.

It will not take long to adjust. The real question becomes, will you want to go back to the twenty-first century? For a while at least, you will not have to. So start your journey in the year 1816, when the Lenape Indian Camp is busy growing

A costumed interpreter cuts grass the old-fashioned way at Conner Prairie in Fishers.

corn, squash, and beans. Be sure too, to take the nature trail past a beautiful crop field to the flatboat exhibit at the White River. Next in line is the 1836 Prairietown, where a water-powered gristmill has recently been added, and then it is on to Liberty Corner. In this town, the Zimmerman Farm, a Quaker Meeting House, and barns set the stage for 1886. The Conner Estate features what is believed to be the first brick home built in central Indiana (1823). You are invited to knock on the door and see what's cooking in the kitchen. The various periods and places are populated by generations of the Zimmerman family.

The lineup of events at Conner Prairie is staggering. In a single day, you could take in a morning sheep-shearing demonstration, watch the baking of spicy pudding and savory pies at mid-day, then join a lecture on designing and planting your own dye garden in the afternoon. Events follow the seasons. Each September, the Country Fair features special guest appearances, pie judging contests, historic livestock breeds, a pioneer tool show, an antique tractor parade, a cornet band, and games like hoop and stick. Or go whole hog and brave electricity-free living during Weekend on the Farm. It is an authentic immersion experience where you become a nineteenth-century farmer, cooking and doing chores with the guidance and encouragement of staff members. Sign up for Taste of the Past—it is all about eating the nineteenth-century-style foods you see being prepared in the historic areas. Reservation requirements and additional fees apply.

Take time to explore the vast visitor center with its walk-through exhibits, a gift shop where you can buy Indiana-made products, and heirloom vegetable and flower seeds that are harvested from Conner Prairie plants. At the Persimmons restaurant, Indiana ingredients help to flavor the menu. PastPort is a hands-on discovery area where children can actively engage in seasonal activities such as milking a cow, carding wool, churning butter, making a fence, walking on stilts, roping a bed, working with pioneer tools, and building a miniature log cabin.

It is time to head southward for a mix of adventures in the heart of Indy. Here is a quick orientation of the roadways. Downtown Indianapolis is the hub from which Interstates 65, 69, 70, and 74 radiate spokelike to 465, which encircles the city like a wheel. As in many major cities, the core streets move one-way, so watch for the signs. Monument Circle is right smack in the middle, with Meridian Street and Market Street bisecting it north–south and east–west respectively.

Doing the Town
Got kids along? Then don't miss a visit to the world's largest children's museum. It is **The Children's Museum of Indianapolis**, 3000 North Meridian Street, Indianapolis, (317) 334-3322, (800) 208-KIDS, www.childrensmuseum.org. To get there from Conner Prairie, get someone else to drive. Just kidding; it is pretty easy: turn right onto Allisonville Road toward East 132nd Street, right on East

A tulip tree in bloom near Conner Prairie's Quaker Meeting House.

Fall Creek Parkway North Drive/State Road 37 South, another right on East 38th Street/State Road 37 South, then left onto Meridian Street (Highway 31), heading south toward downtown. It is a drive of almost 15 miles. One of the many, many exhibits you will enjoy exploring at The Children's Museum of Indianapolis is the newer Biotechnology Learning Center. This focal point teaches the history and science of biotechnology as it will impact the plants we grow and the foods we eat.

Now let's visit another great museum, this one geared for all ages. The **Indiana State Museum**, 650 West Washington Street, Indianapolis, (317) 232-1637, www.indianamuseum.org, opened in 2002 and offers three floors of great exhibits and some tidbits of food fun. From the children's museum, continue south on Meridian Street, loop halfway around the soaring Monument Circle memorial (it is a roundabout), then pick up Meridian again at its southern end. A right on Washington Street, a drive of a few blocks, and you are there. Take comfort with a bowl of famous Chicken Velvet Soup and other time-tested dishes in the recreated L. S. Ayres Tea Room. The original tearoom became an Indiana icon after almost 100 years of service within the downtown location of the L. S. Ayres & Co. department store (still alive and kicking inside the malls of Indianapolis). Also in the museum, a recreated log cabin is the scene for endurance tests from churning butter to gathering firewood to lugging water. Learn about Indiana's agricultural heritage through artifacts ranging from hand tools to machinery. Find out why pioneers settled in Indiana, and how their work pretty much changed everything. Find out about food companies that got their start in Indiana. You will probably recognize many of the names.

Get a taste of vintage Indiana at **Easley Winery**, 205 North College Avenue, Indianapolis, (317) 636-4516. It is just about one and one-half miles east of the Indiana State Museum. This family-owned winery is conveniently located downtown on property that was once farmland belonging to the first governor of Indiana. Easley Winery offers free wine tastings and guided weekend tours, sales seven days a week, and two thousand-plus wine and grape-related items for sale. These include home accessories, glasses, and racks. Legendary Hoosier hospitality bubbles over at Easley Winery, and it is not hard to get someone talking about the favorite subject. They even sell fresh grape juice for home winemakers (arrange an order in advance). For a nominal fee and by reservation, a Saturday afternoon home winemaking class would add a touch of education and delight to your Indy visit.

This weekend involves running in Indianapolis' slower lanes, a far cry from the need-for-speed Indianapolis Motor Speedway. But it's a bit ironic that the owners of that most famous of racetracks made their family fortune on—get this—baking soda! The brand is Clabber Girl Baking Powder, and you can visit the company museum at Ninth and Wabash avenues in Terre Haute, but that's another weekend.

SPECIAL EVENTS

Vintage Indiana Wine and Food Festival, Military Park, White River State Park, 801 W. Washington Street, Indianapolis, (800) 832-WINE, www.vintageindiana. com. June. Feast your senses on glass and bottle sales of over one hundred award-winning Indiana wines, dishes prepared by local chefs, food and wine pairing sessions, and live music.

Fourth of July Ice Cream Social, President Benjamin Harrison Home, 1230 N. Delaware Street, Indianapolis, (317) 631-1888. You know when.

Throw yourself into the hoopla of the **Indiana State Fair** each August at the Indiana State Fairgrounds, 1202 East 38th Street, Indianapolis, (317) 927-7500, www.indianastatefair.com. The current crop of the state's finest farm animals compete, including the five hundred or so entries from the 4-H crowd. In the Home and Family Arts Building, they do daily cooking demonstrations, while in the Marsh Ag/Hort Building, you are likely to see prize-winning fruits and vegetables. Enjoy interactive agricultural displays in the Pioneer Our Land Pavilion. Sink your teeth into rib eye sandwiches from the Indiana Beef Cattle Association, pork burgers and butterfly chops from the Indiana Pork Producers, lamb kabobs from the Indiana Sheep Breeders Association, and turkey legs from the Indiana State Poultry Association.

Bean Supper, Scottish Rite Cathedral, 650 N. Meridian Street, Indianapolis, (317) 262-3100. September.

PLACES TO EAT

Circle City Bar and Grille, Indianapolis Marriott Downtown, 350 West Maryland Street, Indianapolis, (317) 822-3500. Upscale American grill with a farm connection: try the Indiana duck that has been raised on a specialized farm. Lunch entrees include home-style meatloaf, create your own panini, grilled burger, and more.

Indianapolis City Market, 222 East Market Street, Indianapolis, (317) 634-9266. Built in 1886 to provide covered space for fresh meat and produce sales, it is the city's enduring food-source landmark. Choose quick, something-for-everyone sandwiches, some ethnically spiced, from a variety of vendors. Spice shops upstairs, also fresh produce every Wednesday at the Farmers' Market.

Rathskeller Restaurant, The Athenaeum Building, 401 East Michigan Street, Indianapolis, (317) 636-0396. Traditional German cuisine and 40 European beers. Old-world ambience and live music four nights a week in Victorian-era Lockerbie neighborhood. Since 1894.

PLACES TO STAY

Country Gables Bed and Breakfast, 9302 Indiana 334, Zionsville, (317) 873-5382, www.countrygables.com. This late-1800s Victorian farmhouse has acreage, wrap-around porches, and full breakfasts.

The Frederick-Talbott Inn at the Prairie, 13805 Allisonville Road, Fishers,

(317) 578-3600, www.fredericktalbottinn.com. Ideally nestled across the street from Conner Prairie, this green B&B is a former farm that today coexists with a subdivision. The original farmhouse, barn, and milk house still stand. All rooms are decorated in fresh colors; one has pencil-thin green striped wallpaper and pink accents for a peppermint candy effect. Ladies who quilt sometimes come to stitch on the premises and only add to the charm.

Yellow Rose Inn, 1441 North Delaware Street, Indianapolis, (317) 636-7673, www .yellowroseinn.com. Pamper yourself silly amid early nineteenth-century antiques and twenty-first-century amenities. The 1898 yellow Georgian Colonial in the perked-up Old Northside neighborhood has soaring columns, a 1,200-square-foot rooftop deck with outdoor hot tub, and a third-floor ballroom suite with deep purple sheers cascading over one bed and a curved, white-oak bench overlooking the antique pool table. Now about your morning orange juice: when they say fresh-squeezed, they mean it. Full gourmet breakfast.

Walk two blocks south to tour the President Benjamin Harrison Home, 1230 North Delaware Street, Indianapolis, (317) 631-1888, with its reconstructed carriage house known as the "old red barn."

36. FRIED BISCUITS AND APPLE BUTTER IN BROWN COUNTY

If you're hungry, head for the hills of Brown County, where even place-names— Lake Lemon, Bean Blossom, Gnaw Bone—set you to thinking of food. Nashville is at the heart of it all. Nashville restaurants tend to feature hearty, honest cooking within preserved historic settings. They are easy to find and close together, and your biggest problem will probably be making choices.

The region is close to Indianapolis, just over 60 miles south, but here people drawl and call you honey. Instead of hills and valleys, they have hills and hollers. Chinked log cabins add a mountain-home feel. The occasional Confederate flag flutters by. But all of this can be discussed over fried biscuits and baked apple butter, because in Brown County, they love to feed you.

Let's Eat

In Nashville, let's begin our food adventure with **Hobnob Corner,** 17 Main Street West, (812) 988-4114, where worn floorboards wear no fine finish—just the testament of countless shoe heels. This lines-out-the-door restaurant first opened in 1873 as a dry goods, grocery, and sundry store. It eventually became Miller's Drugs, and today, dusty medicine bottles—Eye Bath, Castor Oil—rest museumlike in wooden display cases. Hobnob Corner is casual and comfortable, creaky and crowded. Even waitresses from other restaurants will steer you to the bread pudding dessert.

Across Van Buren Street, the **Nashville House Dining Room,** 15 S. Van Buren Street, (812) 988-4554, hands around hot fried biscuits and homemade baked

Nashville House fried biscuits

1 quart milk
$^1/_4$ cup sugar
$2^2/_3$ packages dry yeast or $^1/_6$ cup yeast
$^1/_2$ cup lard or shortening
6 teaspoons salt
7–9 cups flour

Add yeast to warm water. Add other ingredients and let dough rise. Work into biscuits and drop into hot fat.

This recipe will make about seven dozen biscuits. They can be frozen individually and stored in plastic bags. When you work them up, don't let the biscuits rise too high. The fat should be slightly hotter than 350 degrees. If fat should be too hot, the biscuits will be soggy in the center.

Permission granted by Andy Rogers, Brown County, Indiana. 🏃

apple butter that you can dollop on as thickly as you want. Choose from traditional southern Indiana foods. Pre-Civil War Nashville House has been hospitable to hungry and sleepy travelers since 1859. Back then it was Brown County's first hostelry, and it served everyone from loggers to the area's legendary artists. The current building dates to 1948, as the earlier structure was lost to fire in 1943. Browse the Old Country Store for cast-iron cookware, sassafras concentrate, parched corn, and other items they might need to teach you how to use.

You may also want to try **The Ordinary**, a block south at 61 S. Van Buren Street, (812) 988-6166, which, as locals know, is anything but. The wild game sandwich blankets turkey and pheasant beneath melted Swiss cheese. A vegetarian sandwich, served open face with melted cheese, is piled high with mushrooms and green peppers in a hearty tomato sauce. The restaurant's name harkens back to Colonial days when "The Ordinary" was a place where people gathered to drink and socialize. Rose tablecloths beautify the room with its wood furnishings and stone fireplace adorned with local color.

And one more block south on Van Buren at Franklin, 105 S. Van Buren Street, Nashville, follow the flower-framed path into **Artists Colony Inn and Restaurant**, (812) 988-0600, where outdoor seating is available on the genteel porch, and dishes are named for the artists who founded the Brown County art colony. The vegetable stir-fry, with your choice of beef, chicken, or vegetarian, is well seasoned and bursting with vegetables such as crisp-tender carrots, green peppers, broccoli, and

Food shops vie for customers along Main Street in Nashville.

cauliflower over a bed of rice, some of it wild. Try hand-cut steaks, chicken, or marinated tuna. A side order of coleslaw has finely grated cabbage, carrots, and broccoli in a secret dressing that the owners intend to keep that way.

Several miles south of the bustling downtown, **The Story Inn**, 6404 South State Road 135, Nashville, (812) 988-2273, serves gourmet fare in an authentic mid-nineteenth-century general store that went from being a trading hub in the early 1900s to a ghost town relic in the 1970s. As the story goes, this boomtown went bust when opportunities for timber harvest dwindled and any prospect of development ended with the creation of the state park. From Nashville, take State Road 46 East/135 South for 3.5 miles, then turn right on 135 South and continue driving 9.5 miles. You can also stay overnight at the inn.

Some visitors throw themselves into the Nashville shopping scene, while others get that pained look. For these folks especially, Nashville has some surprises in store. How about shops that make their own candy or ice cream? **The Candy Dish**, 61 West Main Street, Nashville, dishes out all the homemade fudge, freshly roasted nuts, and peanut brittle you can eat. Walk to **Miller's Ice Cream House** next door at 61 Main Street West, where the ice cream is whipped up in a wooden tub freezer and flavored with fresh fruit or hand-chopped luxury chocolate chips. Ever heard of Apple Butter Ice Cream? You have now, and it's made here from real apple butter cooked down at **The Harvest Preserve** next door. There was some confusion on a sign, and people just kept asking for it. Helpless to stop the trend, the shop decided it would be easier to make Apple Butter Ice Cream instead of explaining that it didn't exist.

The Art of Farming

Back in the early 1900s, six major art colonies were founded throughout America. One of these was in Brown County, where artists from all over arrived to draw inspiration from the rugged landscape and the country hospitality. According to the Brown County Convention and Visitors Bureau and the T. C. Steele State Historic Site brochure (Andrea Smith, "T. C. Steele at the House of the Singing Winds: Brown County, Indiana Historic Painting Sites Walk"), T.C. Steele was one artist who came and stayed, with his wife, Selma, for these same reasons. Steele acquired an abandoned farm where he began to paint Impressionist landscapes. He planted flowers and fruit trees, and if he needed weeds for a foreground, he would plant them too. Steele was not a wealthy man, but he went ahead and bought a second farm expressly for the views it supplied. It is said that neighboring subsistence farmers harbored suspicions of this man who made his living by painting his farmland instead of cultivating it. However, the Steeles did sell fruit that they grew in order to raise some cash. Yet the story goes that some of these same farmer neighbors welcomed opportunities to satisfy their curiosity during Sunday afternoon visits when Selma Steele served lemonade and cookies, or when she hosted picnics or light teas.

Today, one of the most unique farm experiences you can have is at the Steeles' former farm. It's become the 211-acre **T. C. Steele State Historic Site**, 4220 T. C. Steele Road, Nashville, (812) 988-2785, www.state.in.us/ism/sites/steele. It is located nine miles southwest of downtown. Take the self-guided walking tour to the same sites the artist chose, and try to view the land through his eyes.

Finally, share a little of your own artistic expression as you kick up your heels at **Mike's Music and Dance Barn**, 2277 State Road 46 West, Nashville, (812) 988-8636, www.mikesmusicdancebarn.com, which is located four miles southwest of Nashville. It's country music and dancing in a smoke- and alcohol-free environment, so folks of all ages can enjoy the pure atmosphere of the old-fashioned barn dance. Pizza, chili, hot dogs, and the like will take the edge off your appetite, pardner.

Brown County is an area that likes to keep it southern style.

PLACES TO STAY

5th Generation Farm Bed and Breakfast, 4564 North Bear Wallow Road, Nashville, (812) 988-7553. A Nashville address but five miles out on 40 acres. Stay in a reproduction farmhouse where the Schrougham family grew tobacco, milked cows, churned butter, and raised lots of little Schroughams since 1848. Trish Schrougham opened the B&B after buying it from her aunt and rescuing what she could—the stone foundation—and incorporating it into the present charming home. No animals, but you can hike in the woods on the property and explore the stocked pond. Enjoy homey country décor, two porches, flowers, beautiful views of hills, black-night sleeping, and full farm breakfasts that may be eggs, sausage gravy and biscuits, and potatoes.

Brown County Cabins, various locations near Nashville, (812) 873-6608, www. mygasthof.com. Breakfasts with vegetables and herbs from their garden, prepared to your specifications, when and where you wish to enjoy them. A typical menu: scones, poached pear, Dutch apple dish, thick maple-cured bacon, fried potatoes, biscuits and gravy.

The Seasons Lodge and Conference Center, 560 State Road 46 East (one-quarter mile east of downtown), Nashville, (812) 988-2284, www.seasonslodge.com. Ask for an upper room overlooking the hills, because it also includes a view of a farm field where cows graze scenically. The Seasons's rustic décor fits the area's historic emphasis on log cabins. Take the enclosed walkway to the indoor pool, which sits apart with glass walls for an outdoor feeling.

37. IN HARMONY IN NEW HARMONY

Beginning in 1814, a celibate religious commune called the Harmonie Society thrived in far southwestern Indiana with landholdings totaling 20,000 acres, a tidy brick town, and economic success that visitors of the day couldn't help but admire. They sold it all at a profit in January 1825 and went back east. But that was not the end of communal living in New Harmony. The buyer was Robert Owen, an industrialist and social theorist with societal dreams of his own, and so the focus shifted from spirituality to intellectualism. New Harmony is located in Posey County, the farthest southwest you can go in Indiana. It is 195 miles southwest of Indianapolis and 26 miles northwest of Evansville.

Especially around the historic buildings, New Harmony is a walking town, although you may have to share sidewalk space with some enthusiastic garden plants. So park the car in the visitor lot at the **Atheneum/Visitors Center,** 401 N. Arthur Street (just north of State Road 66), New Harmony, (812) 682-4474, (800) 231-2168, and buy tickets for the tours. They are self-paced, and costumed guides await your arrival at each site. Just outside of the visitor center, note the wooden fence that marks where a Harmonist orchard once thrived.

For insight into the Harmonists' food and farm ways, pay special attention to the following tour sites. In one of the **West Street Log Cabins,** which are from the time period but not of Harmonist origin, your guide will tell about rope making. The Harmonists grew hemp for this purpose, and the process consisted of drying and twisting the fibers. You might even walk away with a sample of rope that the guide assembles with the aid of an ingenious hand-powered device. Finished candles, lye soap, and loofahs, made from dried gourds of the type that the Harmonists would have grown, are also discussed. A typical Harmonist day is described as starting at 5:00 a.m. with the milking of cows, fulfillment of textile orders, tending of fields, and performance of other chores on a rotating basis.

The **Rapp Granary-David Dale Owen Laboratory** is privately owned and not on the tour, but you can walk by and appreciate that this five-story storage bin was the largest granary in America when the Harmonists built it in 1818. It is located on Granary Street near the West Street Cabins. Two years after the Owen experiment began in 1825, it became a storehouse of knowledge rather than grains. That was when Robert Owen's son, who later served as a U.S. Government geologist, decided to use it for his laboratory. Subsequently it became a woolen mill, flour mill, and pork packing plant. Restoration plans include offering tours when the facility is otherwise not in use, and providing exhibits on German heritage and geology.

Behind the Lenz House on North Street near the Atheneum/Visitors Center, the **Communal Bake Oven** is big enough to walk inside. It is a 1980 reconstruction that represents one of several such ovens that were scattered—in an orderly fashion, of course—throughout the community. Women were assigned the use of a given oven one day a week, which allowed all of them an opportunity to provide good things for their own families to eat.

Community House No. 2 was home to 40 to 60 single adults. This circa-1822 brick dormitory is at 420 Main Street just east of the granary, and it was originally one of four Community Houses. You can see the kitchen with its hearth-style brick fireplace and fire pit, along with examples of Dutch biscuits, which, however good they sound, were components of the building's insulation and therefore not edible. Long after the Harmonists left, a teahouse was opened within the building in the 1930s.

A grape arbor leads you into the **Salomon Wolf House,** which is located another block east at 601 Granary Street. Instead of traditional furnishings, an automated spinning diorama, "Panorama of New Harmony in 1824," sheds light on the Harmonist way of life. The narrative is taken directly from diary entries of people who visited the community during its heyday. Their writings draw you back in time to the horse-powered cotton mill, to a lavish dinner where wine flowed, and to the homes where people gathered to sing. Then, as you look down on the model of the town, evening falls, and the tiny lights of New Harmony cut through a wilderness that is no longer there.

The **Working Men's Institute,** 407 West Tavern Street, New Harmony, (812) 682-4806, is a great resource for visitors with its free museum and library. Yes, there is a farming connection in the museum. No, it is not for everyone. You see, on display is an eight-legged calf that was born in the early 1900s. The library was a library at this location since 1838, and it was built courtesy of Robert Owen's partner. Here you can learn that the society's farming operations included field crops, livestock, orchards, and vineyards. Indeed, one of the reasons that George Rapp and the Harmonists first came to the region was to purchase lots of good agricultural land for a low price. Here is how one observer in 1883 described the spirit of harvest time:

When the grain was ready to be cut, the band numbering 20 musicians with a great variety of instruments, would play in the public square early in the morning, and by 4 o'clock the harvesters, to the number of 200 or more, would assemble with their reap-hooks [sickles] in hand, and march out with the band to the field. At 6 a.m. a light breakfast would be brought to them, and another meal at 10 a.m. and still another at 3 p.m. In this way a field of wheat of 70 acres or more would be cut and shocked by 6 o'clock in the afternoon, when they would be escorted by the band back to their homes.

Also in the collection of The Working Men's Institute is an account of how, within only three years of arriving from Pennsylvania, an estimated 300 Harmonist families already had 200 acres of wheat, smaller parcels of rye, barley, oats, and grass, and 500 acres of pastureland to their name. Livestock included cattle, hogs, and a flock of 1,500 merino sheep. Additional library sources report that they planted orchards of apple, peach, pear, cherry, and quince trees, bushes bearing currants and gooseberries, and plenty of grapevines. Peach oil, as extracted from the kernel inside the stone, was described as a discovery in 1818, and school-boys were given the task of processing it. Individual homes had abundant kitchen gardens with vegetables and herbs. Keep digging; there's more. The exceptional industriousness of these German farmers meant they could market foodstuffs and eat well besides. Individual households did their own cooking. Initially, they made use of the evenly spaced public ovens. Ginger cookies were considered a specialty. Harmonist Gertrude Rapp described this recipe for round scalloped ginger cookies: one gallon molasses, one pound lard, six ounces of ginger, four ounces of soda, eight ounces of water, enough flour to make stiff dough.

Plan your visit to new Harmony around festivities like these: **Heritage Week** in April for nineteenth-century crafts and industries; **Kunstfest** in September for German food, music, and a craft event; **Scots in Harmony**, in October, for Scottish heritage games, foods, and exhibitions.

All of this earnest touring will certainly earn traveling folks a good meal, and they need to look no farther than the quaint Victorian main street to find one to suit their taste.

PLACES TO EAT

Cooper House Kitchen and Catering Co., 610 Church Street, New Harmony, (812) 682-3607. Try the Java Tenderloin. Lunch, dinner.

Red Geranium Restaurant, 508 North Street, New Harmony, (812) 682-4431. A Sunday-drive favorite offering classics like pecan chicken breast alongside updated entrees that emphasize fresh ingredients. Look for Midwest regional asparagus, beef, whitefish, and other foods that may be seasoned with chives, lemon basil, or whatever other herb-garden snippet caught the chef's eye earlier in the day. Try Wabaschwein, a fruity, light-bodied white from Terre Vin in Parke County, which is made from grapes grown at Red Geranium Enterprises' in-town vineyard, or a margarita rimmed with geranium-red salt. The Shaker lemon pie is dense, intense, and reportedly not above biting back.

Yellow Tavern, 521 Church Street, New Harmony, (812) 682-3303. Sandwiches, pizza, shrimp, pork chops, steak. Must be 21 to enter.

PLACES TO STAY

Living Legacy Farmstead Bed and Breakfast, 3759 North 900 Boulevard, Mount Carmel, IL, (618) 298-2476, (877) 548-3276. Cross the state line for a stay at this not-for-profit, 10-acre German family farmstead dating back to the 1870s. Explore the smokehouse, corn crib, feed house, and other outbuildings, along with the orchard, vegetable/herb/flower gardens, and pastures. Full country breakfast. About 25 miles from New Harmony; cross the toll bridge on 14, go north in Illinois on State Road 1 to Mount Carmel.

The New Harmony Inn, 504 North Street, (812) 682-4491. Boutique inn whose design echoes the community buildings where single Harmonists dwelled. Walk to historic sites.

The Wright Place Bed and Breakfast, 515 South Arthur Street, (812) 682-3453. Stay in a saltbox-style home on property where Harmonists once tended an orchard. Common areas include a library and music room with a grand piano, fireplace, and garden views. Walk to historic sites.

38. MILLING AROUND IN SOUTHERN INDIANA

Being in a northern state does not stop the folks of southern Indiana from being in a southern state of mind. You will feel it in the warm hospitality and taste it in the cheese grits and persimmon pudding. Get ready for a southern Indiana weekend adventure that takes you from a limestone museum to two pioneer gristmills that draw life from cave water, and a huge piece of agricultural equipment that few people have ever heard of. For the visitor who wants to take home something special from the hills of southern Indiana, there is nothing like the stone-ground cornmeal direct from the source.

The tour takes you to the counties of Lawrence, Orange, Crawford, and Harrison. You will find this region, which is yet another unique pocket of the American Heartland, in the far south-central part of Indiana. The tour begins 75 miles south of Indianapolis, in Bedford, and goes deeper south from there, almost clear on down to the Kentucky border.

Limestone

A visit to the **Land of Limestone Museum,** Oakland City University-Bedford Campus, 405 I Street, Bedford, (812) 275-7637, (800) 798-0769, www.limestone country.com, sheds light on the great natural resource that has earned Lawrence County the nickname of Limestone Capital of the World. You will learn that Indiana Limestone was first quarried here on a small scale in 1827, and today graces most

---

Field to table

Eat like a Harmonist, with hearty fare from easy, German-influenced recipes from the *Harmonist Cookbook*, published by the Southern Indiana Gas and Electric Company, Evansville, Indiana, 1989. It is really just a booklet, but across these 12 pages, you can get through a typical Harmonist day and pick up food tidbits along the way, such as: "Each Harmonist family had a cow, brought to its owner's gate each morning and evening. At other times, the cows were kept in the woods, tended by a herdsman." The first recipe will really send you back 200 years.

Smierkase
1 quart sour milk
1 quart warm water
Sweet or sour cream
Salt and pepper

Heat sour milk to lukewarm. Pour into cheesecloth bag. Pour warm water over this and let it drain. Can repeat 1 or 2 times. Tie bag and let drip until whey is all drained off. Serve with either sweet or sour cream, add salt and pepper, and season to taste. For seasoning, can add $2^1/2$ teaspoon finely chopped onion, 1 teaspoon finely chopped chives, a speck of garlic powder, or $1/4$ teaspoon caraway seed. About 4 servings.

If you cannot get past the first ingredient and do not know where to get a cheesecloth bag, this next recipe for sausage loaf should pose less of a challenge. It does not specify to remove any existing sausage skin, but it makes sense to do so.

Sausage Loaf
1 pound sausage
2 cups mashed potatoes
1 medium onion, minced
1 egg, beaten
1 teaspoon salt
$1/8$ teaspoon pepper
$1/2$ teaspoon poultry seasoning

Mix all ingredients together. Turn mixture onto wax paper and shape into a loaf, roll in rolled oats so that all loaf is covered. Slip loaf from wax paper into a loaf pan. Bake at 350 degrees for 1 hour. 8 to 10 servings. Finally, throw the kids a curve ball with the next one.

Peach Leather
Peel very ripe peaches, mash, and roll out on a flat platter. Cover with netting and set in a hot sun to dry. When completely dry, cut into strips and store. Food was often dried on the roof. This is eaten like candy.
Recipes courtesy Vectren Corporation, Evansville, Indiana. 🦌

---

of the country's great buildings, such as the Empire State Building, the Pentagon, and the National Archives. But in the interests of this weekend, you will also learn that the gristmill called Spring Mill, which you will visit on this tour, was built of Indiana limestone.

Let's move on. A few miles south, you come upon **Applacres**, State Road 37 South (just south of the Highway 50 junction), Bedford, (812) 279-9721. Applacres offers orchard-grown apples, peaches, apple cider, caramel apples, apple butter, jams, jellies, popcorn, Amish baked goods, and spices. Drive about another half-mile south on 37 to **Carousel Winery**, 8987 State Road 37 South, Bedford, (812) 277-9750. Watch through an observation window as they make fresh batches of the award-winning wines, shop for cheeses to go with your selection, and take note of the hand-carved limestone bar.

Sleepy Spring Mill
Continue south on State Road 37 toward Mitchell and turn left onto State Road 60 toward **Spring Mill State Park**, State Road 60 East, Mitchell, (812) 849-4129, (877) 9SPRING, www.in.gov/dnr/parklake/parks/springmill.html. Inside this heavily wooded, 1,319-acre park, there is a Pioneer Village that traces its beginnings to 1814. As you walk the quiet paths past Mill Creek, which rushes out of Hamer Cave much as it always has, it is not hard to imagine living and working here as the pioneers did. It is estimated that in 1850, the population of the village was about one hundred. Or perhaps it is easier to imagine yourself as one of the owners of the village. These were enterprising men who came in succession and added buildings to house new business ventures that they hoped would turn a profit.

Often they did, especially from the distillery, which was originally built in 1823 and restored in 1932. But it was not only people who benefited from the distillery. The pigs that were allowed to roam freely about the village got their fill of the mash that was a by-product of distillation. The restored summer kitchen would have been the scene for cooking, soap making, and other domestic chores. The spring house, which is largely original and dates from 1840, had an opening where spring water entered to keep milk, butter, and other perishables cool while being safely stored inside. Altogether there are 20 log buildings to explore, including the Granny White House, mill office, blacksmith shop, and general store/post office.

The three-story 1817 **Spring Mill** that you see today is the magnificent result of the reconstruction project that began in the late 1920s, and that ultimately saved the village from vanishing forever. A distinctive feature is the wooden log flume that shoots back out toward the mouth of the cave to divert some of the water that flows out from there. The flume is a long, horizontal plane that is supported high overhead by restored limestone piers. The waterwheel is of a design called overshot, which means the water flows across the top and sends the wheel to spinning from there. Then the water reaches the millrace, which takes it on a little ride back to the main creek. From April through October, the miller grinds corn, and you definitely should spring for several two-pound bags of the cornmeal. It is a connection to the mill's early days, when farmers would arrive in horse-drawn wagons loaded with grain from the fields, and wait, sometimes for days during peak times, for their harvests to be processed.

Drive south on State Road 37 to Harrison County, parts of which are actually south of Kentucky. In Leavenworth, on State Road 62 and located 60 miles south of Bedford, be sure to check out **Stephenson's General Store and Museum**, 618 West Plaza Drive, Leavenworth, (812) 739-4242. Here you can buy loose nails and marbles, frozen persimmon pulp (for bread and pudding), bottled sorghum (great for gingerbread in a pan or gingerbread cupcakes), cherry butter, and other preserves. Continue east on State Road 62. Keep an eye out, because somewhere along the way and on your left, there is a Mail Pouch Tobacco barn.

The Haypress

But we are on our way to the woods, specifically to O'Bannon Woods State Park, which begins two miles east of Leavenworth and is part of the 26,000-acre Harrison-Crawford State Forest. Much of this had been unproductive and abandoned farmland before the state reclaimed it. Along a section of hiking trail, the Homestead Shelter marks the foundation of an 1860s farmstead home. Stay on State Road 62, turn onto 462 (it only goes south), and continue to the parking for the **Homestead and Haypress.** Call (812) 738-8232.

Haypress? What's a haypress? You are about to find out that it represents a rare piece of agricultural history, being one of only seven known to exist in the country, and the only one that operates for the public. The one they have here, which is called the Leavenworth-Lang-Cole Haypress, looms large inside the cavernous barn that has sheltered it since the beginning. Built of wood in 1850, the highly specialized haypress rises from the barn floor and up 40 feet through the hayloft. Both the haypress and its barn were donated by a private individual, moved from the banks of the Ohio River, and painstakingly reconstructed at this DNR site. Amish craftsmen were brought in to help with the reconstruction.

So, what does a haypress do? On scheduled Saturdays across three seasons of the year, visitors are invited to gather on the first level of the barn to watch as

The base of the Leavenworth-Lang-Cole Haypress at O'Bannon Woods State Park.

the haypress performs its single, Herculean task with the help of an ox, an animal that is itself something of an anachronism. What you see is two stories of operation. Up on the second story, workers are busy forking loose hay into a compartment of the haypress. At ground level, the ox walks around and around, pulling a rope that has a 500-pound weight attached to it in the middle of the haypress. When the weight drops, it smashes the loose hay six to seven times to make one bale that ends up weighing 300 to 500 pounds.

Back in the day, the fresh bales would have been shipped by flatboat down the Ohio River, destined for urban markets that had large numbers of livestock doing all kinds of work, but no places to grow hay to feed them. The hay needed to be brought in to the cities, but transporting it loose was hardly efficient. In this region, the haypress solved that problem throughout the latter half of the nineteenth century, and was then supplanted by the steam-powered baling machine. What happens to the bales of hay today? Why, they feed the ox, of course, who lives in the barn and spends nice days in the adjacent yard. The barn also houses related exhibits, and a video is available for viewing. The haypress is a newer attraction, its singular action having been first demonstrated to visitors in 2003. Call (812) 738-8232, or visit www.crawfordcountyindiana.com/recreation/wyandottewoods.php.

The Deep South

On to Corydon (pronounced around these parts as "COR-din"), which was Indiana's first state capital and is located 70 miles southeast of Bedford. Over at the **Zimmerman Art Glass Factory**, 395 Valley Road, Corydon, (812) 738-2206, two brothers demonstrate a pre-colonial method of glass sculpting. Watch as they fashion over one hundred items including sparkling fruit—fat pumpkins, peaches, pears—without the use of molds. Eight miles east of Corydon, taste fine wines that are produced from grapes of the Ohio Valley Appellation, which is the country's first such designated prime growing region. This is **Turtle Run Winery**, 940 Saint Peters Church Road NE, Corydon, (812) 952-2650, (866) 288-7853, www.turtlerunwinery.com, where visitors enjoy both tours and free tastings of barrel-aged dry wines and other dry and semi-sweet wines. The winery also invites folks to enjoy a picnic lunch "somewhere" on their 74-acre farm.

Let's shift gears and go even deeper south to another historic gristmill. From Corydon, take State Road 135 south to **Squire Boone Caverns and Village**, 100 Squire Boone Road SW, Mauckport, (812) 732-4382, (888) 934-1804, www.squire boonecaverns.com. It was here in 1804 that Squire Boone, brother of the legendary Daniel Boone, built a gristmill that looks like a smaller version of Spring Mill, except that it is built of logs that are chinked in between. As you might expect, the mill that you see today is a reconstruction. The water flume that diverts water

The gristmill and waterwheel at Squire Boone Caverns, Mauckport.

from Squire Boone Caverns sends it to the top of the mill's overshot waterwheel. Inside the log mill, the miller adjusts two wooden levers to control the velocity of the waterwheel, which connects to the hopper by means of a shaft and belt system beneath the floorboards. Corn kernels that have been placed into the hopper drop down to the grinding stones and emerge below as ground corn.

You can see the water that powers the mill as it moves through Squire Boone Caverns. It is a dramatic sight hidden beneath the seemingly ordinary hill just back of the gristmill. Visitors purchase cave tour tickets in the gift shop off the parking lot, then go on an hour-long journey through this vast, underground sculpture park. Throughout the tour, the guide shines a light on cave formations, many of which are whimsically named after favorite foods. These include the Fried Eggs, Bacon, Birthday Cake, and hollow Soda Straws. One formation resembles an old-fashioned soda fountain, its row of stalagmites just waiting for a pull from the soda jerk. And throughout it all, the water alternately rushes like mad, pools like glass before its own dam, and drips inexorably in an amazing display of force, just as it did when Squire Boone built his mill.

As you stroll among the various log buildings that arc around the parking lot, you can catch demonstrations of pioneer activities. Here costumed interpreters make soap, dip candles, and bake fresh bread. Outside of the soap-making cabin there is a lye-leaching barrel with an interpretive sign that explains how pioneers made soap from lye, tallow, and water. Before they made the soap they had to make the lye. After saving ashes from the fireplace and the wood stove, they blended it with straw, and dumped this into the lye-leaching barrel. They poured hot water over it, waited a day, then collected the thick liquid acid called lye. Read about the egg test that determined whether the lye was of the proper strength for soap making. Who knows this stuff anymore?

Visitors can buy cornmeal that is actually ground at a modern mill in Indiana, but specially packaged under the 1804 brand name into souvenir sacks at the **Squire Boone Caverns Welcome Center and Candy Factory**. Find this rustic building at a separate location right off State Road 135, three miles from the mill. You may have seen it as you drove in. The collection of baking mixes includes speckled white grits and oatmeal molasses cookie mix. The shop makes Popz & Nutz, which is a happy indulgence of popcorn, almonds, macadamia nuts, walnuts, white chocolate, toffee, and milk chocolate. The shop also makes fudge on-site, with flavors like cookies & cream, rum raisin, maple nut, and butter pecan. Other tempting sweets include pastel lollipops that are soft and coiled like a rope, taffies, rock candies, and chocolate cow pies and buffalo chips.

There is nothing like spending time in places where time has stood still, places that have become symbols of the early America, from a time when farmers drove horses that pulled wagons to bring the freshly-harvested grain to the mill. Places where, still today, you can shop for loose marbles or oatmeal molasses cookie mix. And places where a piece of agricultural equipment that requires an ox to make it work, still has meaning for people today.

FARTHER AFIELD

Byways of bygone days

Fanning out from the main tour, you may also find yourself near some of these sites that are of related interest.

North of Bedford in Needmore, you can look down into the Empire Quarry, out of which the Empire State Building was sculpted. Somewhere in the area, there is the tiny town of Popcorn. With one house and one church left, Popcorn is a kernel of its former self. Speaking of kernels, KFC's famous Colonel Harlan Sanders was born and raised (mostly) in Scott County, which is two counties east of Lawrence County, and north of Louisville.

Back at the Avoca Fish Hatchery (off State Road 54/58 in Avoca), which you can tour, the site manager's home is not open to the public, but it was once the home of Joseph Hamer, who once operated a mill here, and whose brothers owned and operated Spring Mill from 1831 to 1881.

A little northeast of Salem near State Roads 135 and 56, John Williams worked a farm that he willed to be held in trust for the education of African Americans. Williams was an African American and former slave who had been given his freedom. Tragically, he was murdered in 1863. But his farm is still being used for the purpose he intended.

And down at the Kentucky border on the Ohio River, the town of Cannelton still has its great old Cannelton Cotton Mill, which operated continuously from 1851 to 1954 and was, in its day, the largest industrial building in the entire state. It has been converted into apartments. 🐾

Special Events

Special Events at Spring Mill State Park, Mitchell, (812) 849-4129, www.in.gov/dnr/parklake/parks/springmill.html. Antique Tractor and Engine Show *and* Outdoor Cooking Day and Cornmeal Recipe Contest, early April. Pioneer Living History Stroll, mid-June. Pioneer Heritage Days, early August.

Haypress Demonstration Dates, O'Bannon Woods State Park, Harrison-Crawford State Forest, (812) 738-8234. Generally over the big holiday weekends: Memorial Day, Fourth of July, Labor Day, and one in the autumn.

Herb Cooking and Learning Class, Apple Valley Greenhouse, 145 Rocky Meadow Road, New Salisbury, (812) 366-3377, www.apple-valley.com. Definitely out in the country, off Exit 105 from I-64, three miles north of Corydon. Register in advance, limited seating. Classes in May, June (July and August are too blasted-hot, says owner Margaret Speaker), September, October. They grow just about everything themselves from seed or cuttings that utilize over 30,000 square feet of greenhouse space. Poinsettias, bedding plants in spring, very large selection and variety of perennials and herbs, vegetable plants such as tomatoes, peppers, cabbage, broccoli, melons, cauliflower, collards, and spinach.

Farm Machinery Show, Lawrence County Fairgrounds, Bedford, www.limestonecountry.com. April, May, September, October. Old-fashioned displays, children's games and pedal tractor pull, entertainment, crafts, food.

4-H Fair. Lawrence County 4-H Fairgrounds, Highway 50, four miles southwest of Bedford, www.limestonecountry.com. July.

Harrison County Chicken Festival, Harrison County Fairgrounds, Corydon, www.tourindiana.com. September. Enjoy regional Kentuckiana music, family fun and, of course, chicken dinners.

Persimmon Festival, Mitchell, www.mitchell-indiana.org/persimmon.htm. Last full week of September. The persimmon is a native tree from which people strain the fruit to create a pulp that is then used for baking puddings and breads.

Places to Eat

Emery's Ice Cream, 112 West Walnut Street, Corydon, (812) 738-6047, www.amishalvin.com. This old-fashioned soda fountain is housed in an 1860s cottage and makes its sodas the old-fashioned way, with recipes from the 1950s. A member of the National Association of Soda Jerks, based in Omaha, Nebraska, owner Kevin Paul has endless recipes for chocolate sodas, and each one requires high-quality ice cream and highly carbonated water. "This is just not an ice cream shop to me, it's taking it to a level of bringing back the magic of what a soda shop is," Paul says. Put some of this magic into your own day.

Magdalena's Restaurant and Gourmet Gift Shop, 103 East Chestnut Street, Corydon, 47112, (812) 738-8075, www.magdalenas.com. Lunch, dinner. Any restaurant that lists desserts first, then makes desserts like hot apple dumpling and bumbleberry pie, has your best interests in mind. Or you could start with an appetizer like creamy spinach dip that is served hot with grilled bread, before moving on to wild raspberry chicken salad, a variety of grilled chickens or pastas, burgers, and steaks. The seafood selection includes honey mustard salmon, in which a flaky fillet gets dipped into a mixture of whole-grain mustard, garlic, honey, and olive oil, and served with rice pilaf and steamed vegetables.

Old Mill Café, 641 West Main Street, Mitchell, (812) 849-9350. Hometown atmosphere, country-style food, breakfast served all day, at least until 2:00 p.m., when they close.

Stoll's Restaurant, 1801 Plaza Drive (behind Stone City Mall), Bedford, (812) 279-8150. Old-fashioned Amish recipes are on the table at breakfast, lunch, and dinner. Buffets, too. Also homemade pies and bakery goods.

———— • ———— • ————

FIELD TO TABLE

From the Kintner House

Relatives coming to stay? Feed a crowd of 10 to 12 houseguests with these delicious breakfast recipes courtesy of the Kintner House Inn, Corydon, which has been keeping travelers well-fed since the 1800s.

Ham and Egg Puff
6 slightly beaten eggs
2 cups milk
1 teaspoon dry mustard
2 cups browned and drained diced ham or pork sausage
1 cup Bisquick
1 cup shredded Cheddar cheese
1 teaspoon dried oregano leaves

Mix ingredients, cover and refrigerate overnight. Uncover and bake at 350 degrees in a 2-quart casserole dish for 1 hour or until brown on top.

Sausage Cheese Grits
1 cup grits
4 cups water
2 cups shredded Cheddar cheese
2 eggs and milk, beaten to make 1 cup
1 teaspoon salt (optional)
1 teaspoon garlic salt
2 cups browned and drained sausage

Cook grits with water in a saucepan until thick. Stir in cheese until melted. Add egg and milk mixture. Stir in garlic salt. Place sausage in a greased casserole and pour grits mixture over it. Bake at 350 degrees for 1 hour. 🐾

———— • ———— • ————

Places to Stay

Big Locust Farm, 3295 West County Road 25 South, Paoli, (812) 723-4856. Enjoy the 60 acres including woodlands and a fish pond. The property has been in the family since the 1930s, but the house is of the 1990s vintage, so modern amenities are yours to enjoy. Three guestrooms, sitting room with TV. Breakfasts tend toward the hearty and healthy variety.

Kintner House Inn, 101 South Capitol Avenue, Corydon, (812) 738-2020, www.kintnerhouse.com. There is room at the inn that sprawls with 15 guest rooms, each with private bath, high ceilings, and antique furnishings. Third-floor rooms feature country décor. Breakfast is a beautiful affair with southern-style hot dishes, mixed fruit, and various kinds of home-baked breads, and the long dining table invites conversation. Most B&Bs specify a 4:00 p.m. check-in; this one welcomes you after 1:00 p.m. and, even after you check out, allows use of the porch, parlor, and reception-area restrooms as you do downtown Corydon. Now that's Hoosier Hospitality.

Spring Mill Inn, Highway 60 East, Mitchell, (812) 849-4081, (877) 9SPRING, www.springmillinn.com. This 1930s Civilian Conservation Corps lodge was built of Indiana limestone and welcomes travelers with a rustic fireplace, swimming pool, game room (table tennis, board games, much-loved classic books), beautiful and fire-lit dining room that does marvelous things with Spring Mill cornmeal. Take a woodland walk to the Pioneer Village and other park sites. Buy jams, jellies, mustards, and salad dressings at the inn.

The Leavenworth Inn, State Road 62, Leavenworth, (812) 739-2120, (888) 739-2120, www.leavenworthinn.com. This pristine, late-nineteenth-century home commands a magnificent view of the Ohio River and green hills far below. It was originally called Forest Grove Farm, and, shortly after the turn of the century, already had the B&B idea down pat: the current owners found an old letter that enticed guests with milk from the farm's Jersey cows and vegetables from its garden. Those amenities are a thing of the past, but today's guests are delighted with beautiful furnishings, antiques, private baths, in-room telephone, TV and VCR, central A/C, exercise room, videos, walnut-paneled library. Complimentary fresh-baked cookies, coffee, tea, orange juice. Guests enjoy a complimentary breakfast served at The Overlook Restaurant within walking distance of the inn.

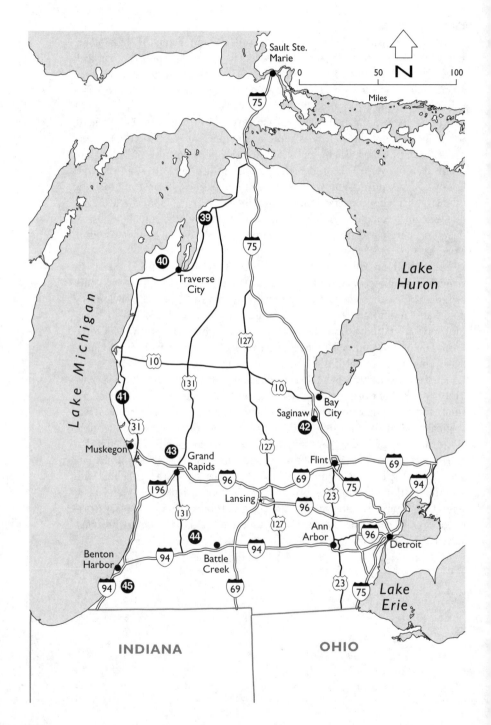

Michigan

From cherry orchards to sugar farms, Michigan is a sweet destination for agricultural touring. In Michigan, agri-tourism can mean almost anything you can imagine. There are little museums devoted entirely to the state's experience of farming, there is a huge tribute to cereal, there are a growing number of wineries and vineyards, and there is even a place to learn about celery farming as it was practiced by Dutch immigrants. Put it all together, and the weekend possibilities are almost endless, for when it comes to agriculture, Michigan specializes in diversity. Get a head start at www.michigan.gov/mda.

39. NORTHWESTERN MICHIGAN: THE VARIETY PAK

When it comes to agriculture and local foods, the growers in Michigan's far northwestern counties—Emmet, Charlevoix, Antrim—find their own independent niches, and then pursue them with a passion in the beautiful environment they call home.

The First Nibbles

If you are with the crowd that is making a beeline for Mackinac Island, why not consider exiting off I-75 a little sooner and planning to spend the weekend on the far northwestern shore?

Gaylord, which got its start as a lumbering and farming community, is a good place to exit and begin the exploration. Find Gaylord-made Albie's Famous Pasties at local supermarkets. From Gaylord, go north on I-75 to County Road C-48, and west to Boyne Falls, which every summer stages a Polish Festival in a carnival atmosphere. Or go west on Highway 32 and north on Highway 131 to Boyne Falls.

Drive northwest on Highway 75 (which is a state highway and separate from I-75) and pick up Lakeshore Road at pretty Boyne City, which is six miles from Boyne Falls, and which has cute shops, eateries, and inns on Lake Charlevoix. Beyond Boyne City, Lakeshore Road wraps tightly around the south shore of the lake to give you a long look at its clear blue beauty. A few miles ahead, the road sort of tapers off and then disintegrates into gravel, but if the Ironton Ferry is running (check in Boyne City before you make the drive), you are in luck. It is a scream, because just two minutes and a few bucks later, you and your car are back on dry land and on to the speedier Highway 66. There is an easier route, but this one is more colorful.

It is almost better not to have advance warning of **Castle Farms**, (231) 237-0884, www.castlefarms.com, because it is such an extraordinary sight. But knowing about this place ahead of time, you can schedule a tour, which is available on Sundays and Wednesdays at 2:00 p.m. The history of Castle Farms is as dramatic as its appearance. When Albert and Anna Loeb built it in 1918, it was part of a 1,600-acre model farm and the realization of a dream. Albert Loeb, who was the acting president of Sears, Roebuck & Co. at the time, wanted to demonstrate that prize livestock could be successfully raised using the latest farm equipment available through the Sears Catalog. He opened his castle to the public as a place where they could view the operation, buy cheese and ice cream, and even catch a baseball game. During this golden period, the farm employed 90 people.

Harvesting Fun in Charlevoix

Drive another two miles to Charlevoix with its water, water everywhere setting. You are never far from water here, for the community is surrounded by Lake Michigan, the Pine River Channel, Round Lake, and Lake Charlevoix. On these waterways, visitors can choose from a variety of experiences from serene to adventurous. Sailboats love Lake Charlevoix, and Sunshine Charters, (231) 547-0266, is pleased to take you out on Round Lake for a couple of hours aboard its sun-yellow, 45-foot cutter-rigged ketch. Or cruise 32 miles to Lake Michigan's Beaver Island courtesy of the **Beaver Island Boat Company**, (231) 547-2311, (888) 446-4095, www.bibco.com. They have put together an effortless package that includes a narrated island tour and lunch. While on the island, visit the Marine Museum that is housed in an authentic net shed dating from 1906; for information, call (231) 448-2254 or check out www.beaverisland.net/history.

Another great place to get a taste of local waters is **John Cross Fisheries**, 209 Belvedere Avenue, Charlevoix, (231) 547-2532, where boatloads of Great Lakes whitefish, lake trout, perch, herring, walleye, and smoked fish fill the market's cases, along with assorted shellfishes from distant waters. John Cross Fisheries is easily found in town and at the water's edge. Now into its third generation of commercial fishing, the family's secret-recipe whitefish dips and sausages have a way of making people drive five hundred miles for another fix. The family did all its own fishing until the 1970s.

Kellie Sutherland, a third-generation family member, remembers playing in the walk-in ice bins as a child, but never being allowed out on a fishing boat because tradition deemed it to be bad luck. Despite this restriction, she loves everything about the fish market, from filleting to smoking to long hours. She has lots of ideas for fish-friendly cooking ingredients, suggesting that you season yours with ingredients like Parmesan cheese, Italian bread crumbs, lemon, butter, dill, freshly-chopped garlic, tomatoes and capers, fresh herbs, or Italian dressing for flavor plus moisture. Local restaurants that offer John Cross Fisheries products proudly advertise the fact.

Find the perfect pairing of wine and gourmet condiments at **Esperance**, 12853 Highway 31 North, Charlevoix, (231) 237-9300, which is located two and one-half miles northeast of John Cross Fisheries, or a mile north of the Pine River Channel bridge. As you explore downtown Charlevoix, one piece of history that you

Lindsay Blechel and Kellie Sutherland, at the John Cross Fisheries, Charlevoix, with fresh salmon, smoked whitefish, and condiments.

might learn about is the old Argo Mill that once ground flour on the spot where the popular Weathervane Restaurant feeds visitors today. Stop into the lobby of the Edgewater Inn just across the channel to buy souvenir flour sacks that are imprinted with the old mill's logo. The sacks are empty and would make great wall art in a country kitchen.

To the South

Drive 10 miles south from Charlevoix to **Friske Orchards**, 10743 North U.S. Highway 31 at Atwood, Ellsworth, (231) 599-2604, www.friske.com. Michigan's lakeside fruit orchards thin out dramatically this far north, but that tendency has not discouraged three generations of the Friske family from growing great cherries and apples, or baking them into luscious treats that make customers swoon. This much-loved local landmark is a family affair that is big on seasonal strawberries, cherries, raspberries, peaches, and nectarines, and apples and cider. The Orchard Café serves luncheon fare such as cherry and apple brats, sandwiches, homemade soups, and fruit pies. Shop the Old World Bakery for moist, European-style cherry coffee cakes, their crumbly tops drizzled with icing, as well as donuts packed with the goodness of cherry, cider, or pumpkin fillings. The General Store sells wooden cherry magnets and John Deere collectibles, and the Country Haus gift shop and barnyard animals round out the day. It is all closed on Sundays, though.

Continue another 7 miles south along Highway 31 to the plant of **Brownwood**

Children's playground at Friske Orchards, Ellsworth.

Acres, 4819 U.S. Highway 31, Eastport, (231) 599-3101, (877) 591-3101, www
.brownwoodacres.com. This storehouse of tart cherry products also carries an
extensive line of gourmet specialties like wild blueberry juice concentrate from
Canada, northern Michigan blossom honey, Famous Kream Mustard (a little sweet,
a little heat, totally addictive, and first introduced in 1945 along with cherry butter), cherry barbecue sauce (sweet and sour with a fillip of spiciness), and cranberry salsa (whole cranberries, no tomatoes). Brownwood Acres had its origins in
the sugar-rationing days of World War II, when the family started raising bees for
honey. To get to Brownwood Acres' separate location that is all about cute shops—
a tiny pioneer homestead in the fragrant pines—go north on Highway 31, right
on Highway 88, right on East Torch Lake Drive for 3.5 miles, and look for the sign
on your right.

Far northwestern Michigan is not a big farming region, but you've got to
admit it would be tough to find a farm castle like that anywhere else in the American Heartland. Some of the region's resident families are big on producing foods
that make it memorable. Given the range of what is available, it is not likely that
you will remember the area for one particular food, unless, of course, that whitefish sausage begins to call your name sometime in the future.

SPECIAL EVENTS

Boyne Falls Polish Festival, Boyne Falls, (231) 582-6222. Early August. Since
1975, this event has been celebrating its community's heritage in a big way. Polka

tent, Polish music, food booths (kielbasa and sauerkraut, pierogis, *golombki*), and Polish Mass on Sunday. Also enjoy the all-American fun of a rodeo, log and timber show, pony/horse pulls, horseshoe tournament, carnival, more.

Harvest Festival, Friske Orchards, 10743 North U.S. Highway 31 at Atwood, Ellsworth, (231) 599-2604, www.friske.com. Early October (Saturday only). Antique tractor show, country/bluegrass/gospel, wagon rides, u-pick apples, Miss Apple and Miss Pumpkin, children's activities. Other Friske events: Strawberry Social (end of June), Cherry Jubilee (mid-July).

Charlevoix's Apple Fest, downtown Charlevoix at East Park overlooking Round Lake, (231) 547-2101, www.charlevoix.org. Mid-October. Area growers bring the orchards to town with 30 varieties of apples, some rare. Food booths feature apple treats, Northern Michigan Antique Flywheelers exhibit, pony rides, horse-drawn carriage rides, petting farm, entertainment, craft show.

PLACES TO EAT

Legs Inn, 6425 Lake Shore Drive, Cross Village, (231) 526-2281, www.legsinn .com. Sample Polish cuisine like *zurek* soup with sausage, hardboiled eggs, and potatoes in meat stock, kielbasa platter, whitefish polonaise with sautéed mushrooms and onions, *nalesnik* dessert, a crepe filled with lemon-flavored farmer cheese or apples. Live music and dancing, rustic/exotic décor to say the least, gift shop blends offerings of Polish and Native American culture, lake views, rustic housekeeping

A country store at the pioneer community run by Brownwood Acres, near Eastport.

cottages with private sandy beach. Oh, and the name? Look up to the ceiling and the row of inverted stove legs.

Schlang's Bavarian Inn, 3917 South Old Highway 27, Gaylord, (989) 732-9288. Steamed mussel appetizer (24 mussels in white wine and garlic butter), Grafer Special (homemade potato salad with melted Swiss, served hot with fried egg and toast), *kessler ripchen* (home-smoked chops with red cabbage), knockwurst (beef sausage with homemade sauerkraut), northern walleye, house specialty pork chops.

Stafford's Weathervane Restaurant, at the bridge, downtown Charlevoix, (231) 547-4311. Chilled cherry yogurt soup blends tart and sweet Michigan cherries with yogurt, brandy, and rum—yum! Oak-planked Lake Superior whitefish with duchesse potatoes and Parmesan tomato crown, remoulade sauce and lemon. Other fish, steak, and chicken choices, too. Former site of the Argo Mill.

The Villager Pub, 427 Bridge Street, Charlevoix, (231) 547-6925. Retro atmosphere featuring Great Lakes whitefish and chips, half-pound chopped steak burger, daily specials (served until sold out) including all-you-can-eat whitefish on Fridays after 5:00 p.m.

PLACES TO STAY

Edgewater Inn, 100 Michigan Avenue, Charlevoix, (231) 547-6044, (800) 748-0424, www.edgewater-charlevoix.com. Condominium rooms mean space and amenities, like fully equipped kitchens/kitchenettes in which to grill your John Cross Fisheries finds. It is so worth it to get a harbor/channel-front condo with a balcony, from which you can sip a Michigan vintage and watch the bridge make way for boats as seabirds search for supper. Indoor/outdoor pool with sundeck, sauna, and hot tub, Charly's Restaurant.

House on the Hill Bed and Breakfast Inn, 9661 Lake Street, Ellsworth, (231) 588-6304, www.thehouseonthehill.com. Modernized and enlarged farmhouse on the Chain O' Lakes with 53 woodland acres and lakefront property. Hiking, canoeing, kayaking. Seven guestrooms with private baths. Full breakfasts, evening social hour.

Rohn House and Farm, 10950 Rogers Road, Burt Lake, (231) 548-3652, (888) 895-7411, www.freeway.net/~rohnhous. Newer home/design studio on secluded 63-acre farm. Three guestrooms with private baths. Full breakfast.

40. CHERRY RED IN THE TRAVERSE AREA

In northwestern Michigan, the greater Traverse region will have you seeing red. Red, as in a splash of barn paint and the crimson of an evening sky. Red, as in the legions of cherry trees that yield half of Michigan's tart Montmorency cherry harvest. All the reds of cherry salsas, sauces, mustards, and dessert toppings. The ruby-red of a dry merlot and the truer red of cherry wine. And wouldn't you look good taking in all the colors and flavors of the region from the seat of a red-hot roadster?

Cherry orchards, gourmet food producers, vineyards; they are all here, along with chefs who love to play with the local harvest, innkeepers who invite you to stay, and special events that celebrate it all. The vineyards, which grow about half of the state's grape crop, are doing it largely with European-style *vinifera* grapes such as Chardonnay and Pinot Noir. Successfully growing these traditionally warmer-climate varietals makes for a true point of distinction in the American Heartland, but so does the range of cherry wines and brandies. So starting from the eastern end, point your car (the red one) north on Highway 37 and take the drive up the skinny Old Mission Peninsula. As a side note, tooling around the peninsulas (there are two here) feels like island hopping because they are awash in so much water, but the bonus is that they remain conveniently attached to the mainland.

Among the Purple Vines

The handful of vineyards on Old Mission welcomes visitors to their tasting rooms, and the occasional tour is available. **Peninsula Cellars**, 11480 Center Road (Highway 37), Traverse City, (231) 223-4050, www.peninsulacellars.com, considers its products to be "regionally expressive," which is good news for those in search of a cherry table wine or a cherry dessert wine. It is about eight miles to Peninsula Cellars from Traverse City. Next up, the pioneering **Château Grand Traverse**, 12239 Center Road, Traverse City, (231) 223-7355, www.cgtwines.com, loves to give free guided tours. Sample their thoughtful range of cherry-based offerings, including cherry wine, cherry Riesling, spice cherry wine, cherry wine sangria, and cherry ginseng wine. Theirs was the first all-*vinifera* vineyard in Michigan, and is today the oldest and largest vineyard on the peninsula. As long as you are in the neighborhood, also visit **Walt & Susan's Old Barn**, 2513 Nelson Road, Traverse City, (231) 223-4123, for vintage gas pumps and other antiques. And mosey on into **Old Mission General Store**, 18250 Mission Road, (about 17 miles north of town), Traverse City, (231) 223-4310, for pickles in barrels, sandwiches, ice cream, and generally rickety charm. Need an idea for a great picnic spot? A great place to swim? The proprietors are happy to make suggestions, and you can even sit down to a game of checkers or hang around the potbelly stove. Stick around and visit the rest of the Old Mission wineries, or stop at **Elzer Farms**, 12654 Center Road, Traverse City (231) 223-9292, before you leave the Old Mission Peninsula. From the general store, it is almost seven miles south. Elzer Farms offers u-pick cherries in July, along with a cornucopia of other seasonal fruits and cherry products.

For the ultimate in relaxation, backtrack south on Highway 37 to bustling Traverse City, and drive five miles northeast to **Grand Traverse Resort and Spa**, 100 Grand Traverse Village Boulevard, Acme, (231) 938-2100, (800) 748-0303, www .grandtraverseresort.com. You will not believe what they have on the services menu: a signature line of cherry treatments that will utterly surround you in the essence of the fruit. Now you can not only taste the Michigan cherry, but you can also breathe it in, bathe in it, and absorb it through the pores of your skin.

About seven miles east of Traverse City, **Amon Orchards**, 8066 U.S. Highway 31 North, Acme, (231) 938-9160, (800) 937-1644, www.amonorchards.com, offers orchard tours during Cherry Festival and on October weekends, as well as farm animals to see and original cherry products to savor. Back in Traverse City, **Grand Traverse Heritage Center**, 322 Sixth Street, Traverse City, (231) 995-0313, is a free-admission exhibition of railroad, lumber, pioneer, maritime, and Native American history (closed on Sundays). If you drive south on M-37/US-31, then follow US-31 to CR 633 going south for a total of 22 miles from Traverse City, you can detour to **The Ole Farm Museum**, 11459 Pavlis Road (three and one-half miles northwest of Buckley), Buckley, (231) 269-3672. Enjoy a guided tour through the grounds and outbuildings that house over three thousand antiques including farm tools and a horse-drawn hearse.

Round the bottom of West Grand Traverse Bay and take Highway 22 up the east face of the Leelanau Peninsula, home to over a dozen wineries and a number of specialty food producers. To follow the **Leelanau Peninsula Wine Trail**, first visit www.lpwines.com. Following is a sampling of Leelanau Peninsula vineyards.

The elegant **Ciccone Vineyard**, 10343 East Hilltop Road, Suttons Bay, (231) 271-5551, www.cicconevineyards.com, is located 12 miles from Traverse City, and puts an Italian accent on the cherry by marrying it with select grapes. Cherricetto is a cherry/dolcetto blend, and Cherri-Noir combines cherry with Pinot Noir. **Black Star Farms**, 10844 East Revold Road, Suttons Bay, (231) 271-4970, www.blackstarfarms.com, is polo-and-khaki agriculture located 12 miles north of Traverse City. Black Star Farms is what happens when successful business executives look around for something to do, settle on agriculture in a destination region, and proceed to do things in a big way. People who love great wines and inventive brandies will feel right at home, as will those who understand the importance of keeping local agricultural traditions from being plowed under the latest subdivision. Their cherry offerings include a fruity, semi-dry blush, Sirius Cherry Dessert Wine, and Spirit of Cherry Eau de Vie, which is a fruit brandy with subtle cherry flavors and robust but balanced alcohol. Thirty to 40 pounds of cherries are required to make a single bottle. It is of a type that Europeans would serve as a gesture of hospitality. Don't miss the educational signboards that tell of the different stages needed to bring the wines to bottling. Have a look through the observation window to watch the Swiss-style artisan cheese making.

One of Leelanau Peninsula's northernmost wineries is **Leelanau Cellars**, 12683 East Tatch Road, Omena, (231) 386-5201, www.leelanaucellars.com. To get there, continue north on Highway 22; Omena is 10 miles north of Black Star Farms. Stroll through Leelanau Cellars' vineyards to take in the sweeping view that the grapes enjoy, and take a tour of the production process to learn all about this large operation. They also do a Michigan cherry and other fruit wines. While you are out enjoying the fruits of the vines and the beautiful views, stop into **Stone House Bread**, 407 South Main Street, Leland, (231) 256-2577, (800) 256-2577, for regionally famous sourdough, organic, and whole grain loaves. To visit **Chateau Fontaine**

The elegant Black Star Farms, Suttons Bay.

Vineyards and Winery, 2290 South French Road, Lake Leelanau, (231) 256-0000, www.chateaufontaine.com, which lies six miles to the south of Leland on a former potato farm and cow pasture, you could take any number of routes and make vineyard stops along the way. Enjoy Chateau Fontaine's views of the countryside as you sip the cherry wine that is made from three varieties of the region's famous fruit.

The Culinary Cherry

Here in the Cherry Capital, a certain contingent of the region's entrepreneurs is thinking way outside the pie and elevating the cherry to gourmet status. Not to mention helping to keep Michigan in cherry trees.

Let's begin our search six miles west of Traverse City at **Carp River Trading Co.**, 6005 East Traverse Highway, Traverse City, (800) 526-9876. From Traverse City, take Highway 72 west for 4.5 miles and look for it on your right. The folks here know where the cherry belongs—up on a pedestal. That is why they make dessert toppings like Raspberry and Cherry Foster, which blends the two fruits with raspberry Chambord and dark Jamaican rum. There's a lot more excitement in Carp River's spirited cupboard. How about Marion Blackberry and Cherry Foster with Remy Martin cognac, Peach and Cherry Foster with Grand Marnier liqueur, or Blueberry and Cherry Foster with Courvoisier cognac? Carp River also concocts liqueur-free mustards, salsas, and grilling sauces, including Ultimate Cherry Salsa with 60 percent cherries and cilantro, lemon, onions, and jalapeño

Showing off some of the bounty at the Carp River Trading Company, near Traverse City.

peppers, Ultimate Cherry Grilling Sauce, cherry Italian vinaigrette, and wild horse-radish mustard. And what cheesecake wouldn't benefit from a silky cloak of Chocolate Cherry Pecan-Dine, which is infused with Disarrano amaretto and but-tered, roasted pecan halves? Fortunately, you can get this stuff in heftier sizes than are typical for gourmet products, because you will most certainly be needing them. And like makers of fine wines, the folks here pay attention to nuances of the nose, mouthfeel, and finish of their products.

The next stop is in Cedar, which is almost eight miles northwest of Carp River and 13 miles northwest of Traverse City. There, Pleva's Meats, www.plevas.com, had the bright idea of putting cherries into its specialty meats and into its hard-wood-smoked sausages, with the result that they've received national media attention for the flavor boost and the fat reduction. Visit their two locations, both in Cedar: **Ray Pleva's Products, Inc.**, 9101 South Lake Shore Drive, Cedar, (231) 228-5980, and **Pleva's Meats**, 8974 South Kasson Street, Cedar, (231) 228-5000. Look for cherry pecan pork sausage, Italian cherry brats, turkey cherry sticks, and cherry-cured bacon.

The cherry rules at **Cherry Republic**, 6026 South Lake Street, Glen Arbor, (231) 334-3150, (800) 206-6949, www.cherryrepublic.com. Glen Arbor is 16 miles west and north of Cedar, at Highway 22. Listing just a handful of the products, there is homemade cherry ice cream in 12 cherry flavors, Cherry Italiana oil and vinegar dressing, Kaboom! Kick'en Hot Sauce, cherry wine jelly, and wild cherry tea. On the snacky side, there are dried cherries (great in salads), Rain Orchard Crunch (save the orchards!), Boomchunka Cookies, and Cherry Sour Balls. They even sell a fruit bowl that is specially handcrafted from native cherry wood. And isn't the tart Montmorency cherry the perfect companion for a coating of dark chocolate? But why let your taste buds have all the fun? Please your other senses with a purchase of black cherry candles or cherry almond oatmeal soap. You can also eat lunch in this little kingdom, as they serve cherry hot dogs, cherry chicken salad, and cherry couscous. If you have not done a really old-fashioned summer thing lately, then buy a sack of chocolate-covered cherry pits, let them melt in your mouth, then launch them to add your own score to Cherry Republic's leader board.

More Local Flavor
One of the American Heartland's most remarkable farm preservation sites is located within the beautiful boundaries of the Sleeping Bear Dunes National Lakeshore, which is located at the western edge of the Leelanau Peninsula. Listed on the National Register of Historic Places since 1997, the **Port Oneida Rural Historic District** is an old farming community that has become a cultural icon on the three thousand acres that it sprawls across. Some of the settlers' farms are privately owned, others partially or wholly owned by the National Park Service. Call (231) 326-5134 or stop in the Visitor Center in Empire, just south of the lakeshore on Highway 22.

Remember the old saying that life is just a bowl of cherries? Well, if you don't believe that's true, come see what's playing tonight at the **Cherry Bowl Drive-In Theatre**, 9812 Honor Highway, Honor, (231) 325-3413. It is located 19 miles south of Cherry Republic. The theatre's own Cherry Bowl Diner offers fresh broasted chicken, hand-tossed pizza, and popcorn that's still made in the 1953 popper, and still comes with lots of hot, melt-y butter.

Even a short stay in the Traverse City area will lead you to grapes growing atop the sun-kissed hills and world-class wines that hold their own against those of California. Be sure to try the cherry wines too, and see for yourself that they are not necessarily of the sweet variety. Note the popularity of the culinary cherry, which adds gourmet sophistication to foods from sausages to ice creams. And be sure to let them make a fuss over you at the spa and discover the joys of the therapy cherry.

Special Events
National Cherry Festival, most events downtown Traverse City and the Open Space at corner of Grandview Parkway and Union Street, (231) 947-4230. Early July. There's room for a couple more as the cherry capital rolls out the red carpet for its favorite fruit. Cherry-pie-eating contest, three parades, headliner entertainment, fireworks over the bay, air shows, bingo tent, Native American Pow-Wow, arts and crafts, midway rides.

Mac and Cheese Cook-off, Old Mission Peninsula wineries, (800) 969-4009.

November. Participants buy a souvenir wine glass and savor the cheese cuisine and wines at each of the peninsula's wineries.

PLACES TO EAT

Good Harbor Grill, 6584 Western Avenue, Glen Arbor, (231) 334-3555. Local produce, fresh whitefish, meats, vegetarian fare.

Grand Traverse Dinner Train, departs from Traverse City Railway Station, 642 Railroad Place, Traverse City, (231) 933-3768. Five-course gourmet dinners, 60 miles of scenic Boardman River Valley, bygone-era elegance. Advance ticket purchase required.

Hattie's, 111 Saint Joseph Avenue, Suttons Bay, (231) 271-6222, www.hatties .com. Dinner only. Morel mushroom ravioli, local produce, fish.

Windows Restaurant, 7677 West Bayshore Drive, Traverse City, (231) 941-0100. Long list of Michigan vintages, seasonal fare prepared to order.

PLACES TO STAY

Aspen House, 1353 North Manitou Trail West, Leland, (231) 256-9724, (800) 762-7736, www.aspenhouseleland.com. Restored 1800s farmhouse showcases European atmosphere with down comforters and grand rooms. Breakfast, evening dessert.

Bed and Breakfast Inn at Black Star Farms, 10844 East Revold Road, Suttons Bay, (231) 271-4970, www.blackstarfarms.com. An agricultural destination of the most civilized sort. Learn about winemaking and cheese making as sleek horses train in the fine art of dressage. Full gourmet breakfast, afternoon refreshments (summertime iced tea or lemonade, autumn cider, winter spiced cherry wine), and evening reception featuring Black Star Farms' own fruit brandies, grappas, and dessert wines.

Chateau Chantal Winery and B&B, 15900 Rue de Vin, Old Mission Peninsula, (800) 969-4009, www.chateauchantal.com. Breathtaking views and a recent expansion make this 65-acre estate, which sits on a former cherry orchard, even more in demand. Cherry eau de vie and cherry liqueur.

Country Hermitage Bed and Breakfast, 7710 U.S. Highway 31 North, Williamsburg, (231) 938-5930, www.countryhermitage.com. Dollhouse that is really a farmhouse dating back to 1883 on, get this, a working, four-hundred-acre cherry orchard. Bay views from every room, two rooms with fireplace and jet tub. Full breakfast.

Grey Hare Inn Vineyard Bed and Breakfast, 1994 Carroll Road, Old Mission Peninsula, (231) 947-2214, (800) 873-0652, www.greyhareinn.com, The circa-1998 winery and inn captures the look of an old stone farmhouse, except that it pampers guests with vineyard views and wine-related cuisine. The Grange de Bois, or Barnwood Suite, borrows decorating panache from a French farmhouse. The inn offers u-pick French-American hybrid grapes, which are priced by the pound. Also Boat and Breakfast.

Field notes

In a remote woodland near the small town of Honor, a remarkable company creates gourmet foods that have become the darling of specialty shops and restaurateurs. This is Food for Thought, the realm of wine- and herb-infused preserves like cherry cabernet, wild blueberry merlot, strawberry basil, and blueberry lavender that can pair beautifully with pound cakes, cheesecakes and bries, whitefish, chicken, and pheasant, not to mention your breakfast bagel.

"You can take the blackberry Syrah and put it in a sauté pan and do a reduction with a little bit of balsamic vinegar or something and use it as a glaze over roast duck," suggests Timothy Young, founder and president. "One of the most popular things we serve at food shows is, we take our wild blueberry merlot, bake it over brie, and serve it on some nice sourdough or whole wheat bread. That's a real easy thing to make that tastes wonderful," says Young.

Food for Thought also harvests wild mushrooms and wild leeks for infused dipping oils and vinegars, or whatever fancy is currently being perfected in the kitchen. When asked to suggest a pairing for whitefish, Young suggests starting with the wild leek relish. "I've actually made tartar sauce out of it by mixing in a bit of mustard and mayonnaise. You've got something harvested from the woods that grows specifically in this climate, and that makes a nice condiment for a whitefish," he explains.

Young is busy saving the world one jar of jam at a time, because he is into environmental preservation too. He built his house entirely from recycled materials. He stuffs his staff with certified-organic produce. One percent of his gross earnings, not just profits, go to environmental organizations.

Food for Thought is not open to the public, but you can visit their neck of the woods at www.giftsthatmatter.com.

The Homestead, America's Freshwater Resort, Wood Ridge Road, Glen Arbor, (231) 334-5000, www.thehomesteadresort.com. Just to watch the moods of Lake Michigan and the surrounding Sleeping Bear Dunes is worth a stay. You get flawless accommodations that embrace a country-rustic style, and a range of lodging types from the B&B Inn to vacation homes. See if you can't keep The Homestead a secret, either.

Snowbird Inn Bed and Breakfast, 473 North Manitou Trail West, Leland, (231) 256-9773, www.snowbirdinn.com. Turn-of-the-century farmhouse on 18 acres with pond and cherry orchard.

41. OCEANA COUNTY'S SEA OF GREEN

With sea-green leaves that flutter like the feathers of some exotic parrot, asparagus plants are among the prettiest of Midwestern crops. Theirs is a soft kind of beauty, with a delicacy that hints at the subtle taste of the slender spears. According to the National Asparagus Festival organizers, Michigan ranks third in the country among asparagus-growing states, and in Oceana County, the farmers grow more asparagus than any other county in Michigan. Here the pointy spears are bravely poking up from the sandy soil when spring days can still be miserable. Thus the locals get their first sign of spring just a little ahead of the rest of us. Surely they deserve it for growing such an abundant crop. Oceana County is located about halfway up the state on its sunset side, which is also the eastern shore of Lake Michigan. Oceana County butts right up against the water, so you are never far away from all the wet and wild opportunities that the lake has to offer.

So this spring, don't just wait for asparagus to pop up in your neighborhood grocery store. Go to the place where it originates in the American Heartland, to the fields, the stores, and the restaurants of Oceana County. You will see the asparagus fields on your way to and from the dunes at Silver Lake, but don't expect to find u-pick opportunities. This is a commercial growing region. While in the area, be sure to spend some time poking around the intriguing streets and shops of Pentwater (**Gustafson's** for gourmet cooking accessories, **Goodstuffs** for Pentwater Preserves), admiring the former home of a pioneering cherry grower in Hart, kicking up trail dust in New Era and Rothbury, and generally making waves on Lake Michigan or on one of the county's 65 inland lakes.

Celebrating Asparagus

For peak-season fun, plan your visit to Oceana County around the annual **National Asparagus Festival.** Every year as they have since 1974, the Oceana County towns of Hart and Shelby trade off hosting this celebration during the second weekend of June. This is nearing the end of the harvest season, when many of the tasks of growing and snapping are largely done, so everyone in town is eager to celebrate. The National Asparagus Festival features a three-day line-up of creative events. There is the asparagus food show competition in which members of the public get to be the judges, the asparagus pancake breakfast at the Oceana County Airport's Fly-In, various lunches and dinners featuring asparagus dishes and soups, the asparagus-eating contest, asparagus farm tours, and the Asparagus Royal Parade. Need more? Asparagus-themed souvenirs and cookbooks are for sale all weekend long.

Festival organizers report that Michigan growers harvest the spears by hand-

A typical feathery asparagus field in Oceana County.

snapping them above the ground. This method ensures a more tender and tasty eating experience, and it is a point of pride among Michigan growers. Spears that do not get picked are left to, as the growers say, go to fern, which means they can grow and replenish the perennial rootstock. Later in autumn or early the next spring, these mature plants get mowed down so a fresh crop of spears can start the cycle over again. Amazingly prolific once they get going, spears can grow up to 10 inches in a single day, and a field can be picked about 22 times in a single season. Farmers may harvest the plants' berries in order to start new fields, which take four years to become productive, but then can last for 15 to 20 years. In this area, only about 30 percent of the yield is sold fresh, as the bulk gets frozen or canned, and much of the processing is done locally.

Don't think that the local restaurants haven't noticed the bounty in their back-yard. In season, they offer recipes such as deep-fried asparagus, asparagus soup, and asparagus omelets. At **Fresh Catch Seafood**, 815 S. State Street, Hart, (231) 873-1936, a local farmer drops his spears off at the kitchen, where they know exact-ly what to do with them from early May to the Fourth of July weekend. They have tried to extend the season by substituting frozen and California asparagus, but just could not achieve the taste they wanted. So in the two months or so that the asparagus window is open, Fresh Catch deep-fries it in peanut oil for an appetiz-er that goes well with the cream of asparagus soup they also make. They also incor-porate it into the 80-item salad bar, pickling it with jalapeños, for example, or maybe slicing and blending it with French dressing.

While in Hart, stop by the deli counter at **Hansen Foods**, 3750 West Polk Road (Business Highway 31), Hart, (231) 873-2826, to pick up gourmet asparagus delicacies. Try pickled asparagus spears (grown in Oceana County) with their crunchy perfection preserved and enhanced in vinegar, dill, chopped garlic, and secret spices. A newer hot version, called Firecrackers, will test your mettle. Now let's talk about the little jars of Espárrago, www.bettersalsa.com, which is gourmet asparagus guacamole. The asparagus in this guac replaces avocado with zero percent fat and cholesterol, but no sacrifice of taste or texture. Also try the zingy asparagus salsa, which would be great with tortillas on the beach. These great products are made by a family of farmers in New Jersey. They have been farming since the 1840s, and first got a taste for asparagus in the 1970s.

Branching Out

But Hart is not just about asparagus. It is also home to **Rennhack Orchards Market**, 3731 West Polk Road, Hart, (231) 873-7523, where they sell their farm's own hand-harvested sweet and tart cherries and other stone fruits, along with sweet corn, squashes, and other vegetables. Cast a wider net and visit the various small museums of the **Oceana County Historical and Genealogical Society**. The Society's headquarters is at the Chadwick-Munger House, 114 S. Dryden Street, which was the home of Dr. L. P. Munger from 1897-1958. A physician, Dr. Munger also kept an orchard and was a huge early promoter of tart cherries (not asparagus). Located at Lincoln and Dryden streets, the house is not open for tours, but you can view it from the sidewalk. As a repository for local history, the society maintains clippings that yield asparagus-related tidbits such as these: The first mention of asparagus in the county dates from the late 1800s, but the vegetable was first grown here commercially about 1929. In 1969, the county's asparagus acreage totaled about three thousand acres; by 1974, it tripled to about nine thousand acres. No wonder they decided to start up the festival that year. Then in June 1977, an anonymous wag reported that given the variability of Michigan weather, anyone who planned to pick the crop should be prepared. That is, they should bring both a snowmobile suit and a bikini. At any rate, Hart's **Historic District**, which is two blocks east of the society headquarters, includes Schaner's Mill, which once ground flour but now houses mechanical dolls and a farmers' market. For information, call the Hart City Hall at (231) 873-2488.

Make this next stop in neighboring Mears. It is the **Silver Hills Antique Mall**, 6780 West Fox Road, Mears, (231) 873-3905, www.discoveroceana.com (click on Shopping and Antiques), and it is a little over five miles west of downtown Hart. They have moved all the cows out of the farm's century-old dairy barn and replaced them with antiques ranging from kitchenware and primitives to farm equipment and tools. Whatever treasure you are in the market for, you will enjoy hunting for it at this spacious, tree-shaded farm on a quiet road. If you have not seen a tin ladle or wood-and-zinc washboard in a while, this is your opportunity to bring some of these items back into your home. Take time out to study the dairy displays that mix nicely with the goods for sale and give a nod to the old days on the farm.

Also in Mears, stop in at **Morat's Old Tiffany Bake Shop**, 1983 North 56th Avenue, Mears, (231) 873-0192. Now into its third generation of bakers and sandwich makers, the business began with Granddad, who emigrated from Vienna, Austria. And stock up on seasonal produce at **Brubaker's Farm Market**, 2357 North 56th Avenue, Mears, (231) 873-1433. This cute, rustic roadside stand is tucked into an orchard. Afterward, you will definitely want to continue west on Fox Road toward the blue bowl that is Silver Lake. A beachy culture surrounds Silver Lake. It was inevitable. Massive piles of sand rise like dough along Silver Lake's western shore and extend beyond it to the north and to the south. It's a two-thousand-acre sandbox—room enough for kids of all ages to play with their toys, from boats to dune buggies.

Between Hart and Shelby, the paved, 22.5-mile Hart-Montague Bicycle Trail echoes the curve of the Lake Michigan shoreline before continuing south to the county line. It is a pleasant eight miles from Hart to Shelby, which is the other National Asparagus Festival host town. Here you can visit the **Cherry Point Farm and Market**, 9600 West Buchanan Road, Shelby, (231) 861-2029, to fill up on fresh-baked cherry strudel, pies, homemade fudge, and fresh produce. Go northeast for less than 2 miles to **The Barn Antiques**, 141 South 24th Avenue, Shelby, (231) 861-5038, which fills the stanchions and loft of a 130-something-year-old barn with pie safes, cupboards, farm items and tools, dinnerware, kitchen tools, and many more antiques. Enjoy refreshments on the order of fruit pie and lemonade in the seasonal Potting Shed Tea Room. The Barn Antiques is off the beaten path, just as a barn should be.

Got time for more? New Era has the **Country Dairy**, 3476 S. 80th Avenue, New Era, (231) 861-4636, where you can visit the barns, tour the processing plant, and enjoy the homemade ice cream, milk, and flavored cheeses. Hit the trail at **Rainbow Ranch**, 4345 South 44th Avenue, New Era, (231) 861-4445; find it one-half mile north of Stony Lake Road. This since-1949 stable offers reasonably priced trail rides through scenic woodlands. Also check out the **Claybanks Pottery**, 7060 South Scenic Drive, three miles south of Stony Lake on Scenic Drive (County Road B-15), New Era, (231) 894-4177. At this studio, the artisans whip up decorative and functional pieces, including one designed especially for your fresh fruits and vegetables (reason enough to go).

It is said that Oceana County got its name from its lakeside location. But if they were to come up with the name in the present day, they might also draw inspiration from a landside source. That would be the sea-green oceans of asparagus that every year hold the promise of outstanding flavor—and of spring.

Special Events

National Asparagus Festival, even-numbered years in Hart, odd-numbered years in Shelby, (231) 861-8110. Second weekend in June.

Pie Contest and Auction, Pentwater, www.pentwater.org, www.pentwater michigan.com. Early July. Anyone can enter!

Oceana County Fair, Hart, (800) 870-9786. Middle/end of August. Take in the tradition of a real county fair with midway rides, farm animal shows, and judgings including lots of horsey events, summer food, grandstand entertainment, and all the rest.

Hart Heritage Days, Hart. Early September. A variety of historic buildings have been moved into one locale where a historic district is beginning to emerge. Enjoy the weekend's activities.

Silver Lake Sand Dunes Apple Festival, Mears, (800) 874-3982, www.silverlake sanddunes.com. Mid-September. Apple trees love growing here as much as asparagus does, so the folks have decided to celebrate the autumn harvest with an apple pie contest, bobbing for apples, a fresh produce and apple market, a barbeque cookout, live entertainment, games, and a homemade craft show.

PLACES TO EAT

Dave's Kountry Kitchen, 7682 South Michigan Avenue, Rothbury, (231) 894-2426. Closed on Sundays. From-scratch cooking is the cornerstone at Dave's, as are all-day breakfasts and real mashed potatoes.

Fresh Catch Seafood/China Wok, 815 South State Street, Hart, (231) 873-1936. Catch all the freshness at this local favorite, from blueberry hot cakes to half-pound burgers and half-pound fish, including whitefish, lake trout, walleye, and lake perch. All-you-can-eat whitefish, lake trout, and pollack available too.

La Fiesta, 12 South State Street, Hart, (231) 873-4345. This local-favorite Mexican restaurant uses seasonal asparagus in its burritos.

The Brown Bear, 147 Michigan Avenue, Shelby, (231) 861-5014. Also in Pentwater. Try deep-fried asparagus with your Notorious Bear Burger, also try broasted chicken, steaks, Super Mombo Combo Brats, gourmet subs, and homemade soups.

PLACES TO STAY

Cocoa Cottage Bed and Breakfast, 223 South Mears Avenue, Whitehall, (231) 893-0674, (800) 204-7596, www.cocoacottage.com. Chocolate for breakfast? Yes, indeed, when it is the house-made gourmet hot fudge sauce over fresh strawberries. The coffee cakes and breads all feature some form of chocolate as well. Wine, cheese, and chocolate reception for newly arriving guests. Optional dinners during the quieter off-season. Four guestrooms, each named for a chocolate company. Authentically restored 1912 arts-and-crafts-style bungalow brings the outdoors in one county down from Oceana.

Double JJ Ranch and Golf Resort, 5900 Water Road, Rothbury, (800) 368-2535, www.doublejj.com. Play, stay, neigh, fairway.

Gateway Motel, 3781 North Oceana Drive (Old Highway 31), Hart,

(231) 873-2125, www.gatewaymotel.net. Sleep like a baby in the embrace of cherry and apple orchards that cradle this basic country motel. Located a short drive outside of Hart and nine miles from those dunes. Continental breakfast.

Sierra Sands at the Dunes, 7990 West Hazel Road, Mears, (231) 873-1008, (866) 873-1008, www.sierrasands.com. Scrubbed as clean as a sand dune, this pretty motel offers welcoming standard rooms and a beautifully furnished two-bedroom family suite that invites you to kick off your shoes and relax in the evenings with all the comforts of home. The suite's home-sized kitchen with full-size appliances is the perfect place to steam Oceana County asparagus, bake Lake Michigan white-fish, and wrap your lips around chocolate-covered cherries (yep, they're made in Hart). Outdoor heated pool and bubbling hot tub, grills, picnic tables, sandpit vol-leyball court, basketball area, and playground equipment. Continental breakfast. Oh, and a neighboring asparagus farm.

42. SWEET SHOPS AND SUGAR FARMS IN SAGINAW COUNTY

Frankenmuth is magical. The magic springs from the Bavarian heritage of this Michigan village. Visitors respond to the storybook charm that dates back to 1845 and has intensified in recent years. Today even new chain hotels get the half-tim-ber treatment. But even as Frankenmuth's enduring purpose is to celebrate a time gone by and a place far away, it is not a village that stands still except, of course, when the glockenspiel clock tower performs. Then everyone, well, every visitor any-way, stops to watch. Speaking of visitors, they come in droves to eat and to shop in ways that are only possible here. But they also enjoy the country charm of an in-town farm attraction and a recreated flour mill. Frankenmuth is rich with sugar and spice, but wait, it is not the only place in Saginaw County that is prepared to satisfy your appetite. So venture out to other parts of Saginaw County, and see how farmers grow unusual crops like navy beans for domestic use and international export, and sugar beets, whose roots are processed not into a vegetable product, but into refined white sugar. Farm tours are not available, but it is still interesting to see the crops in the fields, especially as they represent the unique agricultural heritage of this region.

First, let's get oriented. When in Saginaw County, you are just about at the thumb of the mitten that is Michigan, at the southern edge of Saginaw Bay of Lake Huron. The city of Saginaw is about halfway up the state, 36 miles north of Flint and about 100 miles northwest of Detroit.

Frankenmuth

Frankenmuth is fun. Most of its attractions are on South Main Street, so that is a good place to start. The Frankenmuth tasting room of Michigan's famous **Saint Julian Winery** is located at 127 S. Main Street, and offers free tasting and a video tour. A little south, you come to **Willi's Sausage Co.,** 316 South Main Street,

Admiring a freshly pulled sugar beet; its root contains the sugar.

Frankenmuth, (989) 652-9041, www.willissausage.com, with an amazing one hundred kinds of homemade sausages, including those made from ostrich or Michigan-raised buffalo. Try smoked and cooked apple sausage, seasonal cherry sausage, the bestselling cooked bratwurst, German hot dogs (coarser grind, heavier on the garlic, more character), horseradish sticks, also Hungarian, Italian, Polish, Swedish, and Ukrainian-style sausages and sticks. All smoking is done over natural smoke hickory chips in the computer-controlled smokehouse. **Frankenmuth Cheese Haus,** 561 South Main Street, Frankenmuth, (989) 652-6727, www.frankenmuth cheesehaus.com, invites you to watch the making of chocolate cheese, and packs its cases with another 140 types, from aged Cheddars to jumbo Goudas. The scads of sweet shops at this juncture are hard to pass up, especially the one that stretches pastel taffy in its window.

Frankenmuth has way more than two restaurants under its considerable belt, but the two highest profile among these are the **Bavarian Inn Restaurant,** 713 South Main Street, and **Zehnder's of Frankenmuth,** 730 South Main Street. These family-owned empires serve not only as delightful village anchors, but also rank among the country's top 10 in restaurant sales. Their combined seating capacity is over 2,500, and more than two million dinners are served annually. Are you sitting down? Each year over at the Bavarian Inn, they go through two tons of navy beans, 30 tons of beet sugar, and five tons of pastry flour; altogether, 412 tons of Michigan products in a conscious decision to help support the state's farmers. You know it is autumn in Frankenmuth when the Hubbard squashes roll down Main Street, piled high in the truck beds and headed straight for the kitchens of the Bavarian Inn. Both the Bavarian Inn and Zehnder's tempt you further with shops that stock their own specialty foods like seasonings, preserves, noodles, fruit pies, and chocolates.

Just south of the fabled restaurants and perched on the Cass River, there is the **Frankenmuth Mill,** 701 Mill Street, Frankenmuth, (989) 652-6850. The mill is a gift shop with gourmet items, kitchenware, and a remarkable history that goes back to the mid-nineteenth century. In 1847 a gristmill was first built on this site. Following a fire, a replacement was built in 1911, but torn down in 1956. In 1980, pillars of the community financed reconstruction, incorporating many of the previous mill's floorboards that were still in storage in a local barn. Today the mill is more shop than mill, but the equipment, waterwheel, and grinding stones are still in place. Downstairs, you can pull up a comfy rocker and watch the 15-minute educational video.

Grandpa Tiny's Farm, 7775 Weiss Street, Frankenmuth, phone November–March (989) 871-2937, phone April–October (989) 652-KIDS, www.grandpatinys farm.com, is a guided-tour experience. From the mill, it is just a little over a mile. Walk through the critter-filled barn that provides petting opportunities, and hop aboard the horse-drawn hay wagon for a narrated tour past fields of locally important crops like navy beans and sugar beets. Enjoy seasonal demonstrations of horse-powered plowing, planting, and harvesting.

You are likely to notice **Star of the West Milling Company** trucks lumbering down Main Street on their way to and from the commercial flour mill at the north end of town (you can't miss the 160-foot silo). The mill is not open for tours and its on-site retail store is history, but you can find its Nightingale brand of flours in the local Kroger stores. The mill is known for the excellent pastry and baking flours that it grinds from soft wheat. No small operation this, it is actually part of the multi-million dollar Star of the West Milling Company that serves brand-name customers across the country. The family that owns Star of the West was in business in Europe long before coming to Frankenmuth in the early twentieth century, and today owns five flour mills throughout Michigan, Indiana, Ohio, and New York. In addition to the fine flours, other Star of the West facilities process dry beans that come in from the local fields.

Around Saginaw County

Let's leave Frankenmuth now and get a taste of more of Saginaw County. Among all counties in Michigan, Saginaw County ranked third for sugar beets (360,000 tons) and fifth for dry beans in 2001. The numbers are significant considering that Michigan produces more navy beans and turtle beans than any other state, and is in the top 10 for sugar beet production. The folks at www.michigan.gov will tell you that the beans taste great baked, and also how to bake them. They suggest that to save overnight-soaking time and planning, you can cook a quantity, then drain and freeze it in meal-sized portions. Dry beans, they report, are a significant source of fiber, protein, calcium, iron, and thiamin, but have no cholesterol and only a small amount of fat. As for the sugar beets, it is the root that the farmers are after, and which processors refine into white sugar that is similar to the more commonly marketed cane sugar. The name to know around here is Michigan Sugar Company of Fairgrove, Michigan, which is a grower-owned cooperative that makes the Pioneer Sugar and Big Chief brands.

From Frankenmuth, drive south on Highway 83 (Gera Road) about 5 miles to **Wilderness Trails Animal Park**, 11721 Gera Road, Birch Run, (989) 624-6177, a 56-acre park with over 60 species of animals and petting and play areas. Continue 25 miles to Chesaning. The local harvest is available at IGA, 148 South Chapman Street, downtown Chesaning, (989) 845-3449. Look for dry navy beans that are sold in bulk or in bags, as well as the great local sugar. So now that you've got the finished products in hand, backtrack on Highway 57 and go north on Bishop Road. Cross Fergus Road and continue north on Bishop Road, looking to the right at what is now a regular farm field but what used to be the Prairie Farm. It was created on almost 7,500 acres in 1903 by the Owosso Sugar Company, then sold in 1933 to Joseph Cohen, a Jewish socialist who formed the **Sunrise Cooperative Farm Community**. This experiment was supposed to give 125 indigent urban Jewish families a fresh start, but failed after a few years. The residents were not, after all, farmers. Make a right on Fry Road and a left onto Highway 13, keeping an eye out for fields of sugar beets and navy beans along the way.

With the team at Grandpa Tiny's Farm, Frankenmuth.

The urban environment begins to intensify closer to Saginaw, which is the biggest city and the county seat, located 28 miles north of Chesaning. From I-675, look to the south over the Saginaw River, where you will see the **Jack Rabbit Beans** sign at the top of a grain elevator. The neon sign is still lit up at night thanks to locals who rescued the rabbit and pay its electric bill. Jack Rabbit was a brand of navy beans known to everyone in the area and still, apparently, much loved because of the rabbit.

For the most part, this tour highlights Frankenmuth, Saginaw County's big tourist draw and the ambassador of its German heritage. But there are also surrounding towns to take in and the countryside to wander, for views of sugar beet and navy bean fields. Many visitors are unaware of Michigan's sugar farms, and it comes as a surprise to find out that they do not have to venture farther than the good, old Midwest to find a producer of refined white sugar.

SPECIAL EVENTS

Frankenmuth Historic Farm Fest, Grandpa Tiny's Farm, 7775 Weiss Street, Frankenmuth, phone November–March (989) 871-2937, phone April–October (989) 652-KIDS, www.grandpatinysfarm.com. Early August. Go hog-wild with

Bulk dried navy beans, redskin potatoes, miniature pumpkins—fresh from the fields—for sale at the IGA in Chesaning.

a corn maze, hay wagon and stagecoach rides, threshing demonstration, machinery parade, cow-drop raffle, pedal tractor pull, agricultural demonstrations and exhibits, vegetable stand, farm store, and hearty foods like bean soup, brats, and kettle corn.

Frankenmuth Oktoberfest, Heritage Park, Frankenmuth, (800) FUN-TOWN, www.frankenmuthfestivals.com. Local and flown-in German bands (including cowbell song performances), authentic German bier and food, soft pretzels everywhere, pork sausages, grilled pork, grilled chicken and beef.

The Great Jack-O-Lantern Carnivale, Saginaw County Fairgrounds, Chesaning, (800) 255-3055. Mid-October. Enjoy pumpkin contests (weight-guessing, decorating), a harvest dance, arts/crafts, carnival rides, a children's sing-along with a jack-o-lantern, polka music, and lots of food. Barely noticeable admission.

PLACES TO EAT

Bavarian Inn Restaurant, 713 South Main Street, Frankenmuth, (989) 652-9941, (800) 228-2742, www.bavarianinn.com. Hearty German cuisine made from scratch in cavernous kitchens. All-you-can-eat family-style chicken dinners served with bread, butter, and homemade preserves, chicken noodle soup, seasonal salads, dressing, mashed potatoes and gravy, buttered noodles, fresh vegetables, and ice cream. Angus steaks, fish, and seafood. Famous harvest-time squash sides featuring Blue Hubbards specially grown for the restaurant using a vintage potato-planting machine.

Black Forest Brau Keller, 281 Heinlein Strasse, Frankenmuth, (989) 652-6400. Warm up inside with sausage sampler served with spicy brown mustard, and white Cheddar cheese and brown ale soup made with dry cured ham. Salmon salad includes Michigan dried cherries. Smoked pork barbeque sandwich has slow-roasted pork piled high on a crusty sourdough roll.

Sullivan's Food and Spirits, 5235 Gratiot Road, Saginaw, (989) 799-1940. Famous fish and chips served for over 50 years. Gets the "where the locals eat" award every time anyone asks.

The Chesaning Heritage House, 605 West Broad Street, Chesaning, (989) 845-7700. Classic fine dining in the historic home of a lumber baron. Stuffed pork tenderloin with fried apples, pork and mincemeat en croute. Steaks, seafood, and chicken choices for lunch and dinner. White and milk chocolate marble cheesecake with fudge topping. Tour all four levels and visit the 1908 Carriage Shoppe that once housed horses.

Zehnder's of Frankenmuth, 730 South Main Street, Frankenmuth, (800) 863-7999, www.zehnders.com. Sprawling white structure that could pass for a summer resort served its first all-you-can-eat chicken dinner in 1895 and today keeps it coming with noodle soup, cabbage salad, cheese spread and chicken liver pate with garlic toast, stollen and white breads and butter, preserves, cottage cheese, relish, dressing, mashed potatoes and gravy, vegetables, and ice cream. Menu items, served with many of the sides, include Black Forest pork chops that are apple-marinated, seasoned, and grilled over an open flame, and broiled Great Lakes whitefish in lemon-herb butter.

PLACES TO STAY

Bavarian Inn Lodge, One Covered Bridge Lane, Frankenmuth, (989) 652-7200, (888) 77-LODGE, www.bavarianinn.com. A long and interesting walk through seven acres of 355 guestrooms; five indoor pools (one with a waterfall, another adults-only); all the bleeps, bells, and whistles the kids will love (indoor 18-hole mini-golf, arcade games, stuff only the young can understand); two lounges with nightly entertainment; Oma's Restaurant (German/Continental).

Bonnymill Inn, 710 E. Broad Street, Chesaning, (989) 845-7780. When a 1920s grain elevator gets a makeover, the results are Cinderella-pretty with white wicker, extensive porches, a garden, white holiday lights, and spacious rooms. Kept hot within silver serving pieces, the breakfast buffet features sausages, French toast, potato chunks, a hot berry dish, and pastries galore. Huge, comfortable eating area with loads of window views, lots of woodwork, and a carousel horse.

Cinnamon Stick Farm Bed and Breakfast, 12364 North Genesee Road, Clio, (810) 686-8391, www.cinnamonstickfarmbnb.com. For the getaway or the get-together, this country farm home on 50 acres has a catch-and-release pond, Belgian draft horses (summer wagon rides may be arranged, time permitting), chickens, organic vegetable garden. Five guestrooms, four with private bath.

Montague Inn, 1581 South Washington Avenue, Saginaw, (989) 752-3937, www.montagueinn.com. 1930 mansion sprawls elegantly over 12,000 square feet and is surrounded by eight acres just two miles south of downtown. Robert Montague was successful enough in the development of a skincare product derived from sugar beets that he was able to build it. The family called it home until the 1950s, whereupon they sold the family business to the Andrew Jergens Company. Choose from a variety of guestrooms at this professionally run inn that is big on great food.

43. A FRUITFUL JOURNEY AROUND GRAND RAPIDS

With elevations topping out at some 800 feet and Lake Michigan just 25 miles to the west, the Fruit Ridge of Michigan yields fully 40 percent of the state's famous apples. That's plenty, considering Michigan is one of the country's largest producers. Sixty-six percent of the Fruit Ridge's 158 square miles sits in Kent County, putting it within 20 miles of vibrant Grand Rapids—good news for visitors who want a little culture with their country. But there is time too, to drive out to a great new farm museum and a 19th century mill.

To put it all into geographical perspective, Grand Rapids is about 50 miles north of Kalamazoo and 65 miles northeast of Lansing, which is the state capital.

Start your fruitful journey with the current growers' map; visit www.fruitridge market.com, which lists about 35 growers and sites of related interest. Not all do apples, though, and you are as likely to find yourself munching on peaches or sweet cherries as gazing into the timeless eyes of a bison. Many of the growers' retail shops operate out of comfortable old barns. So for the farm-freshest tastes and the opportunity to ask questions of the folks who grew the goods, nothing beats a run to the Ridge.

Up on the Fruit Ridge

It's not the people but the buffalo that eat the fruit at **The Buffalo Barn Meat and Gift Shop** of Twiss Centennial Bison, at the corner of North Kenowa Avenue and 20 Mile Road, two miles north of Casnovia, (616) 675-4286. The farm is a cow/calf operation that sells the calves and maintains a separate herd for the USDA-inspected meat products available on-site. The animals are raised in as natural a state as possible, munching on grasses all summer long and chewing hay in the winter, but they are never treated with growth hormones, steroids, or the like. Enjoy the mile-long view with members of the herd peacefully grazing as in pre-settlement times. The gift shop carries stuffed toy buffalos and related items like Native American arrows and dream catchers, buffalo jerky, buffalo burgers, and other lean meats that require less cooking time than traditional beef.

It is a short drive southeast to **Fruit Ridge Hayrides**, 11966 Fruit Ridge Avenue NW, Kent City, (616) 887-5052, www.fruitridgehayrides.com. For about a month

Barn at Ed Dunneback and Girls Farm, on the Fruit Ridge, Grand Rapids.

beginning in late September, enjoy autumn-harvest fun with horse-drawn hayrides through woods and orchards, farm animals, the Corn Confusion maze, u-pick apples and pumpkins. Especially for kids, they have a pig train and pony rides. From August to November, **Steffens Orchards**, 4344 13 Mile Road NW, Sparta, (616) 887-2404, has Honeycrisp, Gala, and Spy varieties that have been pre-picked and are ready to pop into your trunk. Simply drive south on Fruit Ridge (the road) and then a little west on 13 Mile Road. Continue south toward the city and **Hill Bros. Orchards and Cider Mill**, 6159 Peach Ridge Avenue NW, Grand Rapids, (616) 784-2767. Hill Bros. is unique for its cider mill and its farm market that carries gourmet products like fruit blend ciders, mustard horseradish, baking mixes in souvenir bags, lots of jams, jellies, and preserves, handcrafted soaps, cookbooks, and apple gadgets.

Meet some of the friendliest folks on the Ridge at **Ed Dunneback & Girls Farm**, 3025 Six Mile Road, Grand Rapids, (616) 784-0058, www.dunneback farm.com. The experience is u-pick and pre-picked, and you can find some of the bounty in the white barn. There are seasonal fruits and veggies, homemade jams, an apple cookbook, and much more to keep you happily browsing. From May to November, come for, in this order, asparagus, strawberries, sweet cherries, apples, and pumpkins. Drive east to **Brechting's Farm Market**, 1307 Six Mile Road NW, Comstock Park, (616) 784-0771. Open from August to November (Sunday afternoons during October only), this farm has been in the family forever and offers

Happy pumpkins at Brechting's Farm Market, Comstock Park.

u-pick tomatoes and pumpkins and a variety of seasonal produce including white potatoes and colorful peppers that are a special favorite of the European customers. The onions and tomatoes are popular among home salsa makers. Look for maple syrup that is made by Amish hands.

The scene begins to suburbanize in the southeastern chunk of the Fruit Ridge. Pull off Highway 37 at **Homrich's Under the Pines**, 6103 Alpine Avenue, Comstock Park, (616) 784-1020. It is a produce-packed and pine-shaded roadside stand that offers welcome respite from the increasingly fast-paced locale. Enjoy the variety of apples ("Paula Red, good for everything!" reads one sign), some squashes, colorful peppers in little baskets, beans, pickles, cukes, and more. A short drive north on Highway 37 takes you to **Country Basket**, 1185 Nine Mile Road, Sparta, (616) 785-9896. This September to October venue features a big red barn on a hill, a welcoming walkway, and a friendly barn cat or two. Look for northern-Michigan-made Cherry Republic products on the shelves, pumpkins in the bins, and fresh donuts before they fly out the barn doors. Don't miss the small petting zoo/barn out back, where calves, pigs, hens, chicks, rabbits, and goats wait for friendly customers. Spend time among the trees as you pick your own apples. It is always a treat to find a haven such as this within shouting distance of a highway, because it has a way of slowing you and everyone else down.

Robinette's Apple Haus, 3142 Four Mile Road NE, Grand Rapids, (616) 361-5567, (800) 400-8100, www.robinettes.com, is minivan-busy. The market and café are the big draws. No wonder, since these are the places where Robinette's purveys bagged apples, including the hot-selling Honeycrisp that was developed at the University of Minnesota and is sought after for its sweet-tart flavor and snappy crunch. And surely if Robinette's ever stopped making their homemade donuts, cider, and specialty breads (iced apple, cheese), the regulars would revolt. Consider, too, that the Robinette family had been tossing apples into bushels way back in 1912, and you realize that for many reasons, this is a special place, indeed. The farm market feeling can get lost in the crowds, but what Robinette's is selling is pure country, including horse-drawn hayrides on weekends.

In Coopersville

Coopersville is a must-stop town with a great farm museum and an excursion railroad. In October, kids who ride the Coopersville & Marne Railway's **Pumpkin Train** get a free pumpkin; call (616) 997-7000, or visit www.coopersvilleandmarne.org. Coopersville is 18 miles northwest of Grand Rapids, on the way toward the lakeshore. From Robinette's, jump on I-96 and zoom westward to Exit 19 (48th Avenue), and turn left onto Ironwood Drive, take a slight left onto Randall Street, turn right onto Eastmanville Road, and left onto Main Street. Opened in 2001, **The Coopersville Farm Museum**, 375 Main Street, Coopersville, (616) 997-8555, www. coopersvillefarmmuseum.org, offers an educational, hands-on comparison between agriculture's past and its future. Step right into the cement silo that was specially made for the museum, and view the photo of four generations of a farm family to whom the museum is dedicated. Study the local farming statistics, compare the competition's answer to John Deere tractors introduced over the years, and view the feed sacks and quilts. There is a farmers' market where little ones can pretend to purchase (and keep) a lollipop, seed packet, or other small treat, and a sandbox where model farm equipment just waits for little hands to plant and harvest the year's crop (*you* try tearing them away from this exhibit). The gift shop carries unusual *papier-mâché* livestock, a museum-exclusive WPA quilt-block postcard packet tied with a raffia bow, mostly-Deere models of farm machinery, Ertl farm sets, and more. Inquire about the museum's agricultural science workshops and pioneer craft programs.

The community of Coopersville offers other farm experiences. Visit **Steve-N-Sons Sustenance**, 14238 60th Avenue, Coopersville, (616) 997-8251, Steve-N-Sons-Sustenance.us, for cheese made from raw milk. The farm is about four and one-half miles south of the historical society museum. The farm's pasture-based method of raising livestock is ages-old but oddly *au courant* in terms of the gourmet approach to food. The cows, chickens, turkeys, rabbits, and lambs are raised in as natural an environment as possible, where they graze outdoors and are free of antibiotics or production hormones. You can buy their Gouda, Edam, and Brabander cheeses, along with brown eggs and other products. Also visit **Winkel Chestnut Farms**, 10788 Garfield Street, Coopersville, (616) 895-1332, www.chestnutfarms.com, where they keep an orchard full of chestnut trees and offer classes in woodworking and soap making. This farm is eight miles northwest of Steve-N-Sons, and you will be driving on some gravel.

In Grand Rapids

Grand Rapids is a clean, vibrant city that is worth exploring. From Coopersville, you are looking at a quick 22 miles to the 125-acre **Frederik Meijer Gardens and Sculpture Park**, 1000 East Beltline NE, Grand Rapids, (616) 957-1580, (888) 957-1580, www.meijergardens.org. This beautiful oasis is a project of grocery-store magnate Fred Meijer. Newly opened in 2003, the park's **Michigan's Farm Garden** replicates the childhood farmhouse of Fred Meijer's wife, Lena Rader Meijer. On these three tidy acres, families explore gardens abloom with period flowers like the cleome, fruitful orchards, and farm animal sculpture in a 1930s farm setting that symbolizes the working family farm. The farm animal sculptures are part of Fred Meijer's collection and actually precede the larger park's renowned pieces. The windmill is the original from Mrs. Meijer's childhood farm. The 1910 barn hails from a different Michigan farm. Partake of special activities like Chore Champions where kids can churn butter, dig potatoes, and perform other novel tasks; play the barn-based tool identification game where you can try to identify tools like the pig scraper; and listen to storytelling by volunteers who grew up on farms.

The **Grand Rapids Art Museum**, 155 Division Avenue North, at Pearl Street, 616-831-1000, www.gramonline.org, presents works by Mathias Alten (1871–1938), a German immigrant who settled in the area and frequently painted Grand River

A well-crafted billboard inside the Coopersville Farm Museum.

and rural scenes. The collection also includes works by artists who specifically chose to paint West Michigan's agricultural heritage. The museum is five miles east of the park; take I-196.

Let's go shopping. The **Grand Rapids Fulton Street Farmers' Market**, 1147 East Fulton Street, Grand Rapids, (616) 454-4118, is known for having a sociable bunch of farmers on weekends, as well as the fine produce from the fields north of town, that is to say, the Ridge. And **G. B. Russo & Son**, 2770 29th Street SE, Grand Rapids, (616) 942-2980, www.gbrusso.com, has been an international grocery since 1905. Discover its distinctive Italian, Middle Eastern, and regional-specialty tastes, and shop for wines (over three thousand available) and cookware. Closed on Sundays. Speaking of cookware, **The Clever Cook**, 6469 28th Street SE, Grand Rapids, (616) 575-8520, www.theclevercook.com, is a huge source for cookware, bakeware, gadgets, butcher blocks, pot racks, wine and serving accessories, coffee, tea, and cooking classes.

In the Country

Drive east out of Grand Rapids some 34 miles along I-196/I-96 to **Homestead Acres**, 6720 Ainsworth Road, Ionia, (616) 527-5910, www.homesteadacres.com. This working farm has rare, exotic farm animals, and offers farm tours and a retail store with fiber, yarns, sweaters, and alpaca teddy bears. Homestead Acres' animal menagerie includes llamas, alpacas, Shetland and Icelandic sheep, Dexter cattle, miniature donkeys, and magnificent Norwegian Fjord horses. What the owners especially like is that they can harvest valuable materials from their animals without harming them. Call in advance to make an appointment to visit.

And finally, you will want to visit **Historic Bowens Mills**, Middleville, (269) 795-7530, www.bowensmills.com. This rural heritage site is 40 miles southwest of Ionia and two miles north of Yankee Springs (Gun Lake) State Park; watch for the huge grindstone marker on Briggs Road. This 19-acre park with its 1864 gristmill is a working museum where the miller still grinds and sells cornmeal. The waterwheel is circa-1999, but the grinding process remains water-powered, which is somewhat unusual, and the grinding stones are original. Visit the 1840s plank house, 1850s schoolhouse, 1860s Victorian house, and the post-and-beam barn that stables Belgian draft horses.

From the Fruit Ridge to the concentrated flavors of Grand Rapids to the area's farther-flung farming attractions, you have to agree that, as always, Michigan can come through with almost more fun than you can pack into a single weekend.

SPECIAL EVENTS

Sugar Bush Saturdays and Sundays, Blandford Nature Center, 1715 Hillburn Avenue NW, Grand Rapids, (616) 453-6192. March. The sap from over one hundred maple trees is tapped into buckets and processed in the sugarhouse's evaporator. Sample the pure product and buy some to pour over pancakes back home. Also inspect the log cabin and blacksmith shop on a guided tour, and enjoy demonstrations of Native American and pioneer life. Return for the Fall Harvest Fair in September.

Rockford Harvest Festival, Rockford, (616) 866-2000. September. Cooler weather brings out apple cider, painted pumpkins, kids' corral, scarecrow-building contest, crafts, and entertainment.

It's Cider Time Festivals, Historic Bowens Mills, two miles north of Yankee Springs (Gun Lake) State Park; watch for the huge grindstone marker on Briggs Road, Middleville, (269) 795-7530, www.bowensmills.com. Mid-September through mid-October. Gate fee. They really know how to entertain, with a new, lavishly presented theme each weekend: Colonial Days and Fiber Fest Weekend, Steam and Gasoline Engine Show, Mountain Men Encampment, Civil War Days, and Harvest Festival and Quilt Show Weekend. All weekends include live, old-time music by the millstream, farm animals, horse-drawn wagon rides, cider-pressing demonstrations on a century-old press, and cornmeal grinding.

Kent Harvest Trails, Fruit Ridge, Kent County. Five weekends from the end of September through the end of October. The growers on the Ridge get together and throw open their barn doors, pumpkin patches, and friendly-critter yards to celebrate the harvest and welcome the visitors.

Red Flannel Festival, Cedar Springs, (616) 696-2662. Early October. So this is where they make the long johns! Yep, the folks of Cedar Springs have been flying by the seat of their pants—make that drop-seat—for over half a century, so why not celebrate? Wear red if you go, because the Keystone Cops jail anyone not thusly attired. Eat up at the lumberjack supper, which features hearty recipes from the old logging days.

PLACES TO EAT

Bistro Bella Vita, 44 Grandville Avenue SW (west of the Arena), Grand Rapids, (616) 222-4600. Fresh, from-scratch Italian, French, and Mediterranean fare, Michigan apple-wood-burning oven, grill, and rotisserie.

Country Café, 259 Main Street, Coopersville, (616) 997-6572.

Gibson's, 1033 Lake Drive SE, Grand Rapids, (616) 774-8535, www.gibsons restaurant.com. Upscale dining in Victorian surroundings restored to 1874 elegance. The emphasis on fresh, seasonal ingredients is fed by unique, locally grown produce. Romantically named for the wife of the original lumber-baron owner, a lady who epitomized the era's Gibson Girl. Consider Michigan brook trout sautéed with herb butter and crushed hazelnuts, Amish double breast of chicken dijonaise served with grilled asparagus, whipped potatoes, and parsnips, and roasted squash ravioli in a light cream sauce.

Herman's Boy Inc., 63 Courtland Street, Rockford, (616) 866-2900. Since 1901. Munch on their house-made, hand-waxed cheese, bagels, roasted nuts, and Mackinac-style fudge and chocolates.

Rose's Restaurant, 530 Lakeside Drive SE, East Grand Rapids, (616) 458-1122. Homemade root chips (made from veggies) with sandwiches, along with salads, pastas, wood-fired pizza, and Mediterranean-style fare. Free caramel corn is a legacy of the restaurant's popcorn-shop roots.

PLACES TO STAY

Fountain Hill Bed and Breakfast, 222 Fountain Street NE, Grand Rapids, (616) 458-6621, www.fountainhillbandb.com. 1874 Italianate home next to downtown. Four guestrooms with private baths; Jacuzzis; in-room TVs, VCRs, and telephones; A/C. Feather beds. Full breakfast with entrée of the day, cereal, yogurt, individual fresh fruit plates, breads, and rolls.

McGee Homestead B&B, 2534 Alden Nash Avenue NE, Lowell, (616) 897-8142, www.iserv.net/~mcgeebb. It starts with an 1880 brick farmhouse in the country, and continues with farm animals and orchards. Four big guestrooms, common area features a fireplace, kitchen, porch with hot tub, and full cookie jar. Country breakfast with the property's own fresh eggs.

Springhill Suites by Marriott, 450 Center Drive, Grand Rapids, (616) 785-1600, (888) 287-9400. Ultra-convenient to the Fruit Ridge and the city lights. All suites, arty décor, newer property.

The Madison Street Inn, 433 Madison Avenue SE, Grand Rapids, (616) 459-5954, (888) 618-5615. Feel the elegance of much woodwork, three-story oak staircase, stained glass windows, and ceiling medallions. Oh, and king feather beds and A/C. Full, cooked-to-order breakfast with homemade bread.

44. COUNTRY IN THE CITY: THIS IS KALAMAZOO-BATTLE CREEK?

Each summer in Battle Creek, the Kellogg Company, the Post Division of Kraft Foods, and Ralston Foods join forces to push hundreds of picnic tables together for the longest breakfast spread in America, and everyone is invited to tuck in a bib and dig in a spoon. Kellogg's also welcomes visitors into the super-sized Cereal City USA to learn all about the production, marketing, and surprising origins of cold cereal. To the west of Battle Creek, the greater Kalamazoo area offers agriculture-oriented experiences of a different nature—from fish hatching to celery farming to cow milking. And to the east, hungry folks are gobbling up the turkey as fast as Cornwell's Turkeyville USA can send it out of the kitchen.

This is Michigan's country-in-the-city (make that cities) tour. You are about to experience a range of attractions in keeping with the farms/foods theme, and an agricultural diversity that is so Michigan. Let's get geographically oriented. From Detroit, Battle Creek is about 120 miles due west, and Kalamazoo is another 25 miles west of that. This will put you in the southwest part of the state, and inland from the Lake Michigan shore.

Around Kalamazoo

Starting eight miles west of Kalamazoo, the **Wolf Lake Fish Hatchery Visitor**

Center, 34270 County Road 652, I-94 at Exit 66, Mattawan, (269) 668-2876, is a fun destination. Enjoy the educational exhibits that interpret the facility and teach about fishing, life cycles, and habitats. Take a guided hatchery tour, have a picnic, and, best of all, feed the fish. The Small Fry Fishing Frenzy event happens each Saturday from June through August.

From the hatchery, drive east toward Kalamazoo and then south into **Celery Flats Interpretive Center and Historical Area,** 7335 Garden Lane, about two miles south of I-94 Exit 76A, Portage, (269) 329-4522, www.portagemi.com. Take South Westnedge Avenue to Garden Lane, then go east one-half mile and follow the signs. This pretty little center has seen to it that the heritage of a relatively unknown form of farming as practiced by Dutch immigrants—celery farming— does not get forgotten. Celery farming was once very, very big around here, so big, in fact, that it earned Kalamazoo the nickname of Celery City. Guided tours start inside the Interpretive Center, taking visitors past historic photos, an ice cutting sleigh, medicinal bottles, and various tools. These are all that remain of a way of life that is gone forever from this area. Tools that were once important and self-explanatory are now historic and puzzling, and require name tags, never mind instructions.

The tour continues outdoors. There the Interpretive Center grows a fresh celery crop each year, painstakingly tending it in the old way of the Dutch immigrants, and giving visitors a real chance to understand their methods and imagine

Showing off the harvest-ready crop at Celery Flats Interpretive Center, Portage.

the plantings as they would have been seen on a far grander scale. As you are about to see, celery is a beautiful crop, with leafy tops the color of springtime and stalks that beg to be made into the child-pleasing snack Ants on a Log, or sliced more thinly and used in turkey stuffing. Find out why the area was so good for celery farming (hint: the site keeps its plot mucky). Find out why the celery farmers wanted some of their crops to be exceptionally light in color, and what they did to achieve this. Find out too, who benefits from the site's estimated two-thousand-pound annual harvest. Surrounding the Interpretive Center are restored historic buildings, including a 1931 grain elevator, the Hayloft Theatre, the 1856 Portage schoolhouse with its pot-bellied stove, and the 1846 Stuart Manor. After touring, take some time to join the happy locals and rent a canoe or bicycle surrey for a ride through the adjoining parklands.

East of Portage, you could visit **Scotts Mill Park**, 8451 South 35th Street, Scotts, (269) 626-9738, www.kalcounty.com, in order to tour a mid-nineteenth-century water-powered gristmill. Tours are available by advance arrangement, so call ahead. Once at the mill, you have driven 11 miles east of Celery Flats.

Why not have a bite to eat in Kalamazoo, then drive 5 miles north of downtown to **Kalamazoo Nature Center**, 7000 North Westnedge Avenue, Kalamazoo, (269) 381-1574, www.naturecenter.org. This 1,100-acre preserve is an environmental respite, but also celebrates rural roots with a summertime barnyard of farm animals. Back in your vehicle, rev it up and zoom northeast about 15 miles to a most

Kellogg's mammoth Cereal City in Battle Creek.

unusual car museum. Car museum? Just wait. The **Gilmore Car Museum**, Highway 43 at Hickory Road, Hickory Corners, (269) 671-5089, www.gilmorecarmuseum.org, houses over 140 cars inside the cavernous confines of antique and contemporary Michigan barns. The cars range from luxury imports to muscle cars, and the entire museum covers 90 acres of landscaped grounds. Enjoy a self-guided tour beginning in the replica 1930s Shell filling station. The barns alone are worthy of a tour. The C Barn, which is also called the Campania Barn, was built on a 1,600-acre Michigan mint farm in 1897. In fact, it became the biggest mint farm in the world, with the oils that were distilled from mint leaves going, in part, to P. J. Wrigley of chewing gum fame. No doubt the cars housed in this barn are all in mint condition. Some of the other barns are of more recent vintage and have been built specifically to house the museum's amazing collection.

Drive 4.5 miles east and south to **Kellogg Farm Dairy Center**, Michigan State University, 10461 North 40th Street, Hickory Corners, (269) 671-2507, www.kbs .msu.edu. The Dairy Center invites visitors to learn about modern dairy farming at this research, teaching, and working facility. Begin a self-guided tour within the milking parlor viewing room, where the action takes place three times daily. Farther on, learn about the corn, alfalfa, and soybeans grown on the university's 1,100-acre farm, and about the cows' feeding systems and requirements. Learn about the stages of life for heifers, calves, and cows. Finally, find out how the farm uses settling ponds, grass waterways, and irrigation to manage waste products.

Around Battle Creek

Let's go east to Battle Creek and **Kellogg's Cereal City USA**, 171 West Michigan Avenue (west end of downtown), Battle Creek, (269) 962-6230, www.kelloggscerealcity .com. It is a little over 13 miles from the Kellogg Farm Dairy Center; take Highway 89 to Michigan Avenue. Now really, does any other food company tell its story this well? Kellogg's needed 15,000 square feet of exhibit space to do it, and the result is that people of all ages are entertained and educated in a big way. It is as if Kellogg's carefully blended all of its cereals into one giant cereal box, and cooked up an experience that is sometimes fun, sometimes serious, and at all times great. Kellogg's beloved cartoon characters are all here in the colorful graphics and replays of the old commercials, as well as a roaming Tony the Tiger, who is always good for a high five.

The experience starts in the outdoor courtyard, with Kellogg's character show marking the hour in glockenspiel style, and a corn plot waving symbolically in the wind. Inside, the first floor has the Red Onion Grill and the 1930s-style Sullivan's eatery, where you can order ice cream or yogurt topped with favorite cereals. The first of three theaters is also here, this one being the Battle Creek Bijou, which gets everyone into the spirit with a multi-media presentation. Upstairs, the Historical Museum tells of flaked cereal's 1894 origins at the Battle Creek Sanitarium, which was a Seventh-Day Adventist hospital and health spa popular among the rich and famous. The Battle Creek Visitor and Convention Bureau reports that in order to help satisfy the institution's prescribed health regimen, Dr. John Harvey Kellogg and his brother, W. K. Kellogg, invented grain-based foods. One day when they were cooking wheat berries and got called away, they returned to find that the wheat was overdone. But they decided to run it through a roller as usual anyway, and instead of emerging as dough, each individual wheat berry was flattened into a flake. They baked the flakes, which tasted light and crisp.

The story continues with W. K. Kellogg inventing the corn-flaking process in 1898 and founding the Battle Creek Toasted Corn Flake Company in 1906. The Cereal Production Line features a self-guided video tour (learn which brands get which treatments, and how they work) and a free sample at the end, in the tradition of Kellogg's famous factory tours that ended, after an 80-year run, in 1986. Through old photos and signage, Cereal City gives a nostalgic nod to the memory of the old factory tours, so even those who never took one find themselves feeling a twinge of nostalgia. Finally, the Cereal City exhibit area is a hands-on, interactive environment with a computer game, a kids' craft project, and fun, oversized, and color-mad graphics.

While in the neighborhood, do not miss the unforgettable **Road to Wellness Tour** that is hosted by Heritage Battle Creek and which begins at Cereal City USA. Call (800) 397-2240 for details. Guides take you to the Federal Center (the former Battle Creek Sanitarium; existing building was rebuilt in 1903 following a fire); the W. K. Kellogg House; the Historic Adventist Village and Discovery Center, which tells the story of the Adventist pioneers who arrived in the 1850s; the Kimball House Museum with its exhibits of Mother Ella Eaton Kellogg, Dr. Kellogg's wife, who ran the Experimental Kitchen in the Sanitarium; The C. W. Post Monument, a 1917 bronze sculpture honoring C. W. Post; and Oak Hill Cemetery, where the long-lived Kellogg brothers and C. W. Post were buried. Post began producing his cereal products in 1895. Look for Mill Race Park (East Michigan Avenue), which commemorates the mile-long channel that once powered the city's 18 flour, saw, grist and woolen mills, and the Ward Mill Marker (Capital Avenue NE), where the 1849 Ward woolen mill was converted to flour milling in 1860.

Points East

Head east now on Michigan Avenue to **Ott Biological Preserve**, Arlington Avenue (left turn), Emmett Township, (269) 781-9841, www.ottpreserve.org. This 300-acre swath of green still has apple trees growing at the site of abandoned orchards. Enjoy trail hiking before resuming your eastward drive on Michigan Avenue to 11 Mile Road, where you will turn left (north) to visit **Southern Exposure Herb Farm**, 11269 N Drive North (Gorsline Road), Battle Creek, (269) 962-1255, (866) 554-HERB, www.southernmoon.com. Feast your eyes on the beauty as you stroll through the creative flower and herb gardens and enjoy a distant view of grazing cattle and the polite company of rescued pets. Shop for seasonal fresh herbs such as bee balm, dried herbs for culinary, medicinal, or decorative purposes, peppers in decorative bottles, and unique gift pieces. Southern Exposure does not run a restaurant, but register in advance for herbal specialty dinners scheduled for selected Friday nights and Sunday afternoons, when individuals can savor the gourmet flavors of, say, beef tenderloin with wild mushroom and sherry, and mashed potatoes with celery root and mascarpone cheese, as prepared by Southern Exposure's chef in the beautiful farm setting.

Continue east for about three miles on N Drive North to **Cornwell's Turkeyville USA**, 18935 15^1/$_2$ Mile Road, Marshall, (269) 781-4293, (800) 228-4315, www .turkeyville.com. They do more than talk turkey at this rural emporium. The 450-seat restaurant specializes exclusively in turkey that is raised by a Michigan farmer and fed according to proprietary specifications. This, combined with slow, overnight cooking of the whole bird, results in tender, juicy cuts for each day's meals. Gobble up the complete turkey dinner with stuffing, mashed potatoes and gravy, cranberries, coleslaw, and a roll. Order it chargrilled with braised Italian green beans and mushrooms, a tossed salad, cranberries, and a roll. Or choose stir-fry with plenty of vegetables. Sloppy Tom is a popular sandwich choice featuring Grandma Cornwell's own barbeque sauce. For dessert, choose from 13 homemade pies, including apple, blueberry, and cherry made from Michigan fruits.

Make an occasion of your visit with a dinner (or matinee) theater experience featuring Broadway-style musicals and comedies. There are five productions a year, six days a week, almost year-round, so planning should not be a problem. Stroll over to the Ice Cream Parlour with over 20 flavors of homemade ice cream including Turkey Tracks. Grandpa's General Store makes homemade fudge and old-fashioned candies like licorice pipes and candy necklaces, and Country Junction bakes specialty breads and stocks turkey specialties. Kids love the petting farm, game room, and outdoor playground. Turkeyville is closed on Thanksgiving Day, when the Cornwell family takes a break for their own Thanksgiving dinner of pork or venison or anything but turkey. For everyone else who cannot imagine having anything but turkey on Thanksgiving, you can pre-order whole dressed birds. Watch for a planned educational component to Turkeyville and learn about a working turkey farm, feed the animals in the barn, and find out how a farm used to be and how farm families lived.

Marshall is a nearby historic town with quaint specialty shops, grand brick mansions, and an upscale-Americana feel that makes autumn scarecrow-building an art form. Pick up the walking tour brochure, which lists 139 structures and a couple of outlying centennial farms. One of these farms was abandoned and rescued three times, and the other has a farmhouse and outbuildings that look like they did during the Civil War (when W. K. Kellogg was a toddler and Kellogg's Corn Flakes had yet to appear on America's breakfast tables, if you can imagine such a time).

This tour is a food lover's delight, from celery farming to farm-raised turkey dinners to cereal, and a whole lot more. After a visit, it will be easy to see why Battle Creek is known as Cereal City USA.

SPECIAL EVENTS

Barn Theatre, West Highway 96, Augusta, (269) 731-4121. Michigan's oldest resident Equity summer stock theatre has been setting the stage for great performances for half a century. Enjoy traditional plays and musicals in the big red barn.

Hayloft Theatre, Celery Flats Historical Area, 7335 Garden Lane, east of South Westnedge Avenue, Portage, (269) 329-4522. This turn-of-the-century barn became a theater in the 1940s and today stages musicals, comedies, and other presentations from May through August.

Breakfast with Tony, Kellogg's Cereal City USA, (800) 970-7020 x123. Various dates spring through autumn. Reservations required. Other special events throughout the season.

Maple Sugar Festival, Kalamazoo Nature Center, 7000 North Westnedge Avenue, Kalamazoo, (269) 381-1574, www.naturecenter.org. Tap into the fun at this early-season event.

Cereal Festival and World's Longest Breakfast Table, Downtown Battle Creek, (269) 962-4076, www.battlecreekvisitors.org. Second Saturday of June. Parade the night before. Children's activities and clowns in Mill Race Park, live entertainment.

Kalamazoo Valley Antique Tractor, Engine, and Machinery Show, on the grounds of the Gilmore Car Museum, Hickory Corners, (269) 371-5089, www.gilmorecarmuseum.org. End of June. Saw mill, steam engines, tractor parade, etc. Also, Red Barns Spectacular. Mid-August.

Calhoun County Fair, Calhoun County Fairgrounds, I-94, Exits 110, 112, Marshall, (269) 781-8161, www.calhouncountyfair.org. Second full week of August. Michigan's oldest fair with shaded grounds. Return in early October for the Harvest Festival: fresh produce booths, agricultural exhibits, horse-drawn wagon rides, pony rides, petting zoo, old-time kids' games, sawmill demo, horse pulling competition, wool spinning, lumberjack show, chili cook off, apple and pumpkin pie-baking contest.

Marshall Scarecrow Festival, (800) 877-5163, www.scarecrowfestival.com. Last three weekends in October. The population of Marshall swells as a thousand scarecrows suddenly take up residence and begin camping out, clipping hedges, playing in piles of leaves, snuggling romantically on front porches, repairing telephone lines, and generally running amok all over town. Even the crows come to gape. Enjoy the display and the special events that change each of the three weekends and include the harvest festival, pig roast, live scarecrows, haunted river walk, cemetery tour, corn maze, straw tunnel, hayrides, and more.

PLACES TO EAT

Arcadia Brewing Co., 103 West Michigan Avenue, Battle Creek, (269) 963-9690, www.arcadiabrewingcompany.com. Wood-fired oven fare (the oven hails from Naples, Italy and really cooks at 675–775 degrees) and British-style ales (grains from premium English maltsters), along with their own red and white wines. Pizzas, sandwiches, entrées. Saturday afternoon tours or by appointment.

Field to table

Enjoy these recipes from the past, courtesy of the city of Portage, Celery Flats Interpretive Center.

Celery Vinegar
3 ounces celery seed
1 quart cider vinegar or white wine vinegar

Put 3 ounces of celery seed into a quart bottle and fill with good cider vinegar or white wine vinegar. After a few days it is nice to flavor soups or gravies, or to use in place of celery salt on meats, etc. The more seed used, up to 4 ounces, makes stronger flavor. Diluted alcohol or brandy will suit some persons better than the vinegar. Let them use either, as they like best.
— from *Dr. Chase's Recipe Book*, Ann Arbor, 1884

Pea and Celery Croquettes
1 cup peas, plump
²/3 cup chopped celery
2 eggs (1 beaten)
Bread crumbs
Salt
Thyme

Add peas, celery, egg, and dough bread crumbs to make stiff enough for croquettes; salt and thyme to taste. Form in croquettes, roll in beaten egg and crumbs, and bake until slightly browned.
—from *Science in the Kitchen*, Battle Creek, 1892

Clara's on the River, 44 McCamly Street North, Battle Creek, (269) 963-0966, www.claras.com. Housed in the 1888 Michigan Central Railroad Depot, the atmosphere of this eatery drips with history, including artwork and photographs from the cereal world. Beef, pork, chicken, seafood, burgers, sandwiches, pastas, brunch, and Club Car Classics that feature classic railway fare, updated.

Club Car Restaurant, 6225 West D Avenue, Kalamazoo, (269) 342-8087. Dine on Midwestern cuisine within the 1910 Denver Rio Grande coach.

Schuler's Restaurant and Pub, 115 South Eagle Street, Marshall, (269) 781-

0600, www.schulersrestaurant.com. A regional classic since 1909.

PLACES TO STAY

Hall House Bed and Breakfast, 106 Thompson Street, Kalamazoo, (269) 343-2500, (888) 761-2525, www.hallhouse.com. This 1923 Georgian Revival has six guest rooms; two with fireplaces, all with private baths. Breakfast continental-plus on weekdays, full on weekends.

The National House Inn, 102 South Parkview Street, Marshall, (269) 781-7374, www .nationalhouseinn.com. Michigan's oldest inn was built in 1835 as a stagecoach stop and later served as a windmill factory. Travelers discover early American charm amid rough-hewn beams, hardwood floors, and antiques, and the boutique-inn style of hospitality that combines the professionalism of a hotel with the warmth of a B&B. Air-conditioned rooms with private baths and telephones, private Victorian sitting garden, sitting room lounge, afternoon tea, home-baked continental breakfast.

The Old Farmhouse Bed and Breakfast, 18992 18 Mile Road, Marshall, (269) 789-2349. Enjoy the country setting with amenities such as a TV and VCR in each of the three guest rooms.

45. SOUTHWESTERN MICHIGAN: THE PRODUCE SECTION

Michigan's lower left-hand corner has so many orchards, roadside stands, and farm markets under its Fruit Belt that you could not possibly visit all of them in a single weekend. Signs tacked onto telephone poles and stuck into the ground at the country crossroads will always tell you what season it is: "Asparagus, One Block," "Nectarines, Three Miles," "Pumpkins for Sale." For this is the country's largest non-citrus fruit-growing region, and a fresh and colorful produce section all its own. So find out when your favorite fruits and vegetables are scheduled to ripen, and drive out to where the vines, shrubs, and trees groan with the weight of the state's apple-to-zucchini harvest.

Starting in the Three Oaks area and meandering along a leisurely path, this tour takes in the produce farms and the little museums that have thought to include agriculture among their exhibits. You will be traveling through the three counties of Berrien, Cass and Van Buren. The general direction of travel is south to north, but don't expect neat, straight lines, because you're in the country now.

From the South

Three Oaks, located about seven miles east of New Buffalo and I-94 on Highway 12, has an unusual agricultural product lurking in its past. It seems that turkey feather quills were once the mainstay of local manufacturers of corset stays. Today, however, it is presumed that the good people of Three Oaks have found more civilized uses for the turkey feather quill, and other means of support

Ghostly white pumpkins at Dinges' Farm, Three Oaks.

for the local economy.

As for Michigan fruit, the proprietor of **Froehlich's**, 26 North Elm Street, Three Oaks, (269) 756-6002, knows that if you preserve Michigan fruit in beautiful German jars and bake artisan breads in the same kitchen, you've got a recipe for happy customers. And **Drier's Meat Market**, 14 South Elm Street, Three Oaks, (269) 756-3101, www.driers.com, is known far and wide for sawdust on the floor, homemade liver sausage, double-smoked holiday ham, bacon, and sausage that comes out of its century-old smokehouse. Pooches are known to love Drier's smoked steer femur bones that are available on a seasonal basis.

Drive several miles northeast to **Dinges' Farm**, 15219 Mill Road, Three Oaks, (269) 426-4034. Autumn brings a brilliant display of pumpkins and winter squashes to the grounds of this farm-based country market. The warm colors spill out from row after row of wooden crates that sit on the grass beneath old shade trees. Here is a great opportunity to stock up on the tried-and-true acorns and butternuts while also considering the more unusual Jarradales, Kuris, and Lacotas. Gourds are a house specialty that you can buy fresh for seasonal decorating or dried to make into birdhouses. One Dinges family member transforms rough, dull gourds into high-gloss artisanal pieces. The farm also offers sunflower heads, broom corn, Indian corn, strawberry popcorn, fresh-cut flowers, and a little-old-lady witch who threatens to turn unsuspecting customers into hags. Available foods include taffy apples, cider, hot dogs and brats, popcorn, candy, and hot and cold beverages including free coffee. Add tractor hayrides, horse-drawn hayrides on weekends, a haunted semi-truck, an educational corn maze, and a children's play area that immerses them in the farm experience as only a Corn Tunnel and Playhouse Pumpkin can do.

Next up, **Pears Mill Museum**, 121 South Oak Street, Buchanan, (269) 695-5525, can be found in downtown Buchanan between Oak Street and Days Avenue, about 17 miles east of Dinges' Farm. This working 1850s gristmill has been restored to its original and simple Italianate/Greek Revival design and still has its real beams and foundation. It was one of about 13 of the area's known water-powered mills of the nineteenth century. Take home stone-ground flour and cornmeal, and on weekend afternoons, enjoy free guided tours, as well as special-event demonstrations of blacksmithing and basket weaving.

Let's visit **Dodd's Sugar Shack**, 1654 Dodd Road, Niles, (269) 683-4835, which is located about seven miles northeast of Niles. Niles is a little over five miles east of the mill. Early in the year, they tap trees and process the sap into maple syrup that you can buy. They recommend using the darker grades of syrup for cooking; try making a glaze to enhance the natural sweetness of baked carrots, squash, or sweet potatoes. They also suggest mixing the syrup into milk shakes and eggnogs. Or, if you are in the Niles area during October, the **Niles Haunted House Scream Park** on Mayflower Road just east of Highway 31, Exit 5, (269) 687-FEAR, www.haunted.org, is prepared to scare the pants off you, and it has 44 acres of land area to accomplish this task. Attractions include the Field of Screams and the 20-minute

Dark TERRORtory Haunted Hayride. Local charities benefit from your fear.

Want a 100 percent rural setting in which to pick fruits? Then go a few miles north and slightly west from Niles to **Calderwood Farms,** 2993 East Lemon Creek Road, Berrien Springs, (269) 471-2102, where apples, tart cherries, and peaches grow in abundance. Even in late summer, autumn is in the air as machines hum and workers sort and pack the famous Michigan apples for shipment to major markets. Wholesale is big on this 1,200-acre spread, but individuals are welcome to pick their own cherries (first half of July), peaches (early August through early September), and apples. Of the 17 apple varieties, eight are available for u-pick as they come into season.

From Calderwood Farms, drive east on Lemon Creek Road, north on Red Bud Trail, and northwest on Highway 31 for a total of a little over one mile. U can't miss **Stover's U-Pic and Farm Market,** 7608 U.S. Highway 31, Berrien Springs, (269) 471-1401, www.stoversupic.com, (closed on Sundays) because its name is inlaid right into the roof of the red bank barn. It was built of wooden pegs about 150 years ago. Out front, the crop art of friendly hay bale characters (they stack 'em up with a forklift) welcomes autumn visitors to the fun. The season begins with cherries (sweet and tart), raspberries (red and black), and strawberries from June through July; heats up with apricots, blackberries, blueberries, and peaches from July through August; and goes out with a bang when the apples, grapes, Indian corn, popcorn, pumpkins, late raspberries, and sunflowers ripen from September through October. Try gourmet products like the asparagus guacamole

A friendly hay man at Stover's U-Pick and Farm Market, Berrien Springs.

and cherry salsa. Enjoy hayrides, tours, the corn maze, and Potawatomi stories.

While in the area, also visit **Andrews University Dairy Barn**, Dairy Drive, Berrien Springs, (800) 287-8502, www.andrews.edu/COT/Ag. Located just west of town (from Stover's go back southeast on Highway 31 for a little over one mile), the school milks 550 of its 1,200-head herd each day. Milking is done indoors beginning at 11:00 a.m. and 7:00 p.m., and self-guided viewing is open to the public during daylight hours.

For additional serious picking and plenty of outdoor fun, drive northeast of Berrien Springs through Eau Claire (it is almost five miles from town to town). Off County Road 62, turn left on County Road 140 toward the 400-plus acres of **Tree-Mendus Fruit U-Pick**, 9351 East Eureka Road, Eau Claire, (269) 782-7101, www.treemendus-fruit.com. Eureka, but this is a vast orchard! The trees march up and down the rolling hills. To pick, sign up in the market barn, where you will also be tempted to browse among the merchandise. Take your time here, because you will find stuff that is fresh and good and, in some cases, not available elsewhere. The house-made apple butter is free of added sugar, but cinnamon makes its way into some of the jars. Try their dark or light ciders and Grandma's secret-recipe pickles, and pack it all in a crate made from the orchard's own wood. Don't overlook the very special cherry juice concentrate (made from their own Montmorency cherries and processed off-site) that you can mix with water for cherry juice, pour onto pancakes, drizzle over ice cream, and just wallow in for all those antioxidants. They also carry blueberry and apricot vinegars from Round Barn Winery, Distillery, and Brewery at Heart of the Vineyard, which is located in the region. Have a field day picking fresh fruit, including cherries (almost 30 varieties, sweet and tart), apricots, peaches, nectarines, plums, pears, apples, and berries. The peaches are juicy and sweet, and the apples number over two hundred varieties, including antique/heirloom/heritage. Besides picking, you can also rent a family tree, tie the knot, or spit a pit.

On to **Wicks' Apple House**, 52281 Indian Lake Road, Dowagiac, (269) 782-7306, www.wicksapplehouse.com, located four miles northeast of Tree-Mendus. You gotta love a farm market that is run by people who figure it is a good idea to trade up to a cider mill that is older than the one they started with. It all began in 1950 when the Wicks' family started selling apples and cider from their farmhouse lawn. Then, once they built their market up to the point of becoming regionally famous, they sold it to current owners Jerry and Kelli Casey, who kept the traditions and are adding some of their own. The season starts with asparagus in the Fruit and Vegetable Market and warms the bones in autumn with pre-picked apples and Concord grapes. All the preserves, maple syrup, popcorn, caramel apples, cheese, and fudge you would expect are also found here. Enjoy the Country Kitchen Bakery, the Orchard View Restaurant (Monster Reuben sandwiches, etc.) and the Apple Tree Gift Shop. Now about that cider mill. From mid-September through October, you can watch as it produces Wicks' signature Apple Squeezin's, which is pure, sweet, pasteurized juice that can be frozen until ready to thaw, shake, and savor.

FIELD NOTES
Herb Teichman, Tree-Mendus
FRUIT U-PICK

Drop a casual complaint about the day's freezing temperature to a life-long orchardist, and you are bound to find out quickly that two weather systems are fighting, but that the apples ripening in the orchard could not be happier. "They pick up color and crispness," says Herb Teichman, orchardist at Tree-Mendus Fruit U-Pick in Eau Claire, as he pushes aside a few fruits that someone left on the seat of the pickup. With fur the color of pumpkin pie, Max, the orchard dog, gets as comfortable as he can among the thingamajigs that clank around in the truck bed.

Teichman settles the tires into the dirt track that winds through the orchard and warms up to his favorite subject. "We can raise more crops here than most any place other than California. It is because of Lake Michigan, and it is also because of the elevation changes. If this were flat land, frost would affect every location equally, because cold air settles into the valleys and warm air rises through the hills. Because of this irregular terrain, we can actually bank on that hole storing our cold air on a frosty night. If it lasts too long, the cold air will rise, but we still will be warmer up here. That's the reason why we can build a farm as diverse as this is in production," he explains.

Suddenly, a cold but bright sun lights up a stand of old fruit trees. Teichman is a practical farmer, but knows all the subtle changes of the light as it moves through his land. "In the evening and in the morning when the sun shines on this valley, the colors that come into it, it's just beautiful," he says, remembering.

He stops the truck, talks with a staff member. He plucks an apple from a tree and cuts a chunk of it for Max, who has been expecting this. Then the pickup arrives at the stands of peach trees. Swollen fruits sway from the branches, threatening to join those gathered on the ground like fuzzy tennis balls. Teichman pulls right up to one of the peach trees, reaches out the window, and harvests a handful of the fruits. He finds a paper bag in the pickup and immediately gives away the bag of gold. 🐾

And, from August to November, take the corn maze challenge.

For hands-on exploration of agriculture, history, science, and technology, visit **The Museum at Southwestern Michigan College**, 58900 Cherry Grove Road, Dowagiac, (269) 782-1374, www.smc.cc.mi.us/museum. It is less than 12 miles southeast of Wick's, and if you've ever smelled apple pie baking in the oven, you know why we are college-bound this weekend. The museum's collection of Round Oak Stoves is gorgeous, and these venerable appliances have, quite possibly, been responsible for more than one apple pie in their time. The gift shop has Round Oak items, including the museum's own book titled *Identification and Dating of Round Oak Heating Stoves.*

To the North

Heading in the opposite direction, drive about 6 miles northeast of where you pick up I-94 in Saint Joe to Exit 39 and Coloma. The area surrounding this exit is a cornucopia for those who want Michigan fruits and vegetables. That is because everything is so easily accessible from the interstate. You can't miss the huge, orange **Fruit Acres** sign, and you won't want to. It is a classic produce-packed stand and u-pick orchard with, well, everything. A few highlights: black cherries (July), super-sweet corn (mid-July into October), and sweet freestone peaches (August through September).

From the same exit, go 2 miles to **Jollay Orchards**, 1850 Friday Road, Coloma, (269) 468-3075, www.jollayorchards.com. This is a happy place where the family is well into its sixth generation of growers and working on its seventh. It is hard to believe you are so close to the interstate, but here it is, complete with satisfyingly bumpy hayrides, pumpkins, jellies and jams, a catch-and-release fishing pond with bamboo poles, and a friendly petting zoo. Fresh-baked apple-pie-in-a-bag scents the market, while goodies like Michigan-made Carp River Trading Company sauces and toppings enrich the shelves. Enjoy interactive caramel apples wherein you choose the apple you want, they dunk it in warm caramel, and you choose the toppings. If you have kids in tow, they are not likely to let you shop for long, because they will have already spotted the colorful climb-ons outside. One admission fee buys daylong fun at the various attractions. The additional-fee haunted house is chain-saw-free, black as pitch, and loaded with spooks. In the play area, children will love crawling through the blown-up caterpillar and petting the friendly critters in their spacious pen. Everyone will enjoy hopping aboard a hay bale and bumping along on a hayride through the orchard. Depending on the season, you might be picking cherries, apricots, peaches, apples, or pumpkins.

Another museum stop can be made at **North Berrien Historical Society Museum**, 300 Coloma Avenue (less than three miles from Jollay Orchards and across from Coloma High School on West Saint Joseph Street), Coloma, (269) 468-3330, which includes an exhibit of agricultural equipment and a display-filled barn.

Your tour in this area will indeed be a fruitful one. And oh, don't forget that the great lakeshore is around here somewhere, too.

SPECIAL EVENTS

Log Cabin Day, (held in part at) Pioneer Log Cabin Museum, South Broadway, Cassopolis, (269) 925-3836. Last Sunday in June. Enjoy family entertainment in this charming log cabin that was built in 1923 of logs donated by area farmers. The day celebrates 90 log structures and pioneer villages throughout Michigan, many on farms, some historic, others new. Tours and open houses are available at some sites; inquire at www.qtm.net/logcabincrafts.

Eau Claire Cherry Festival, Eau Claire, (269) 461-3976, www.eauclairecherry fest.org. Fourth of July. Cherry products, baking and pit spit contests, parade with original takes on the cherry theme, and antique farm implements.

International Cherry Pit Spitting Qualifying and Championship, Tree-Mendus Fruit U-Pick, 9351 East Eureka Road, Eau Claire, (269) 782-7101. Fourth-Fifth of July. U-spit.

Pickle Fest, Downtown and Grove Park, Berrien Springs, www.swmichigan.org. Late July. Pickle flinging, pickle tasting, pickle decorating, family pickle games, pickle parade, chocolate-covered pickles.

Coloma Glad-Peach Art Fair and Festival, Downtown Coloma, www.swmichi gan.org. Early August. It is all about good taste that can be found in works of art and regional agricultural products.

National Blueberry Festival, Downtown South Haven, (269) 637-5252. Mid-August. Blueberries pop up in the parade, the pie-eating contest, and all wrapped up in chocolate.

Four Flags Area Apple Festival, Niles, (269) 683-8870. Late September. Apple products tent, pie-eating contest, scarecrow contest, carnival.

Ciderfest, Wicks' Apple House, Dowagiac, (269) 782-7306. Columbus Day Weekend in October. Drink of the last harvest of the season with fresh cider, narrated wagon rides around the centennial farm, country music, and entertainment.

PLACES TO EAT

Day-Break Café, 126 East Ferry Street, Berrien Springs, (269) 471-5605. All-day breakfast, Friday night fish fry, and specials, all at prices that are not hard to swallow.

Kilwin's Chocolate, Fudge, and Ice Cream Shoppe, 316 State Street, center of downtown, Saint Joseph, (269) 982-1330. Locally owned shrine to the sweet tooth with old-fashioned malts and shakes, smoothies, 32 flavors of premium ice cream, homemade waffle cones, fudge, chocolates, gourmet caramel apples, caramel and peanut corn, chocolate-dipped cherries, strawberries, cookies, and pretzels.

Schuler's of Stevensville, 5000 Red Arrow Highway, Stevensville, (269) 429-3273, www.schulersrest.com. Regional menu items include signature salad of greens, red onion, pine nuts, dried Michigan cherries, and Maytag blue cheese from Iowa. The house specialty is slow-roasted prime rib with homemade Yorkshire pudding. The Grand Traverse Bay chicken is stuffed with rice, walnuts, and dried cherries, and topped with black currant sauce.

PLACES TO STAY

A Country Place Bed and Breakfast, 79 North Shore Drive North, South Haven, (269) 637-5523, www.csi-net.net/acountryplace.com. Located on part of one of the area's oldest fruit farms, with two woodland acres one-half block from Lake Michigan beach access. Full breakfast served fireside or on the deck. Complimentary refreshments are a B&B bonus.

Elmhurst Farm Inn, 634 64th Street, South Haven, (269) 637-4633. This 1870 Italianate centennial farmhouse is furnished with antiques and country charm. House was built by owner's great-grandfather and has been in the family for over 120 years. Rural environment. Three guestrooms.

White Rabbit Inn, 14634 Red Arrow Highway, Lakeside, (269) 469-4620, (800) 867-2224, www.whiterabbitinn.com. Very close to a beach and a few miles south of Warren Dunes State Park, where Fuller Pier once served the local logging industry. Casual, interesting breakfast with an array of preserves.

Torch Lake, Michigan.

ALPHABETICAL

Index

TYPE OF ESTABLISHMENT

*index">
Colony Store (Bishop Hill, IL), 201
Cook's Collection (Arcola, IL), 213
Cookery, The (LaPorte, IN), 249
Country Cheese and More (Arthur, IL), 215
Country Spice Shoppe (Arthur, IL), 215
Dutchman's Store (Cantril, IA), 172
E & S Sales (Shipshewana, IN), 254
Elegant Farmer, The (Mukwonago, WI), 57
Enchanted Cottage, The
  (Pequot Lakes, MN), 81
Esperance (Charlevoix, MI), 284
Frankenmuth Mill (Frankenmuth, MI), 303
Froehlich's (Three Oaks, MI), 326
G.B. Russo & Son (Grand Rapids, MI), 314
Galena Cellars Tasting Room & Gift Shop
  (Galena, IL), 181
Galena River Wine & Cheese Shop
  (Galena, IL), 181
Goodstuffs (Pentwater, MI), 296
Granary Emporium, The
  (South Amana, IA), 165
Greef General Store (Bentonsport, IA), 171
Gustafson's (Pentwater, MI), 296
Harvest Preserve, The (Nashville, IN), 266
Heart of Iowa Market Place
  (West Des Moines, IA), 152
High Amana General Store
  (High Amana, IA), 165
Kitchen Sink, The (Amana, IA), 163
Lakeside Fibers (Madison, WI), 38
Miller's Dry Goods (Arthur, IL), 214
Mount Horeb Mustard Museum
  (Mount Horeb, WI), 39
Norman General Store (Kewaunee, WI), 16
Norsland Lefse (Rushford, MN), 105
Old Mission General Store
  (Traverse City, MI), 289
Old School, The (Sullivan, IL), 212
Poppy Barn (Bishop Hill, IL), 201
Robert's European Imports
  (New Glarus, WI), 46
Rockome Store (Arcola, IL), 213
Schanz Furniture Refinishing Shop
  (South Amana, IA), 165
Seed Savers Garden Store (Madison, WI), 38
Seventh Avenue Outlet (Monroe, WI), 43
Sweet Sailing (Bayfield, WI), 4
Sweetie Pies (Fish Creek), 19
Trading Post, The (Park Rapids, MN), 64
Tschetter's Red Barn/Antiques
  (Oskaloosa, IA), 159
Walnut Grove Mercantile (Marshall, MN), 99

Weekend Innovations
  (Walnut Grove, MN), 97
White Water Valley Orchard Pie Shop
  (Saint Charles, MN), 113
Windy Corner Farm (Bishop Hill, IL), 201
Yoder Popcorn (Shipshewana, IN), 255

GROCERY, PHARMACY, OTHER
Dick's Pharmacy (Arthur, IL), 215
Hansen Foods (Hart, MI), 298
IGA (Chesaning, MI), 304,
  (Rushford, MN), 105
Ivey's Pharmacy (Mineral Point, WI), 47
Joynes Department Store and Ben Franklin
  (Grand Marais, MN), 73
K&S Foods (Decorah, IA), 120
Mall of America (Bloomington, MN), 89
Oneota Community Food Co-op
  (Decorah, IA), 121
Schaefer's Foods (Nisswa, MN), 80
Snyder's Park Pharmacy
  (Park Rapids, MN), 64

HORSES – TRAIL RIDES
BK Ranch (Nevis, MN), 61
Eagle Point Horseback Riding Farm
  (Milledgeville, IL), 188
Field Wood Farm
  (Washington Island, WI), 20
Kickapoo Valley Ranch (LaFarge, WI), 26
Rainbow Ranch (New Era, MI), 299
Red Ridge Ranch (Mauston, WI), 26
Rising Star Ranch (Park Rapids, MN), 65
Swinging W Ranch (Eagle, WI), 56

ICE CREAM, OTHER DAIRY PRODUCTS & ATTRACTIONS
Babcock Hall Dairy Store
  (Madison, WI), 37
Corner George Inn Sweet Shoppe
  (Maeystown, IL), 225
Country Dairy (New Era, MI), 299
Dairy View Country Store
  (Sturgeon Bay, WI), 19
J. Lauber's Old Fashioned Ice Cream Parlor
  (East Troy, WI), 57
Miller's Ice Cream House (Nashville, IN), 266
Pine River Dairy (Manitowoc, WI), 32
Snyder's Park Pharmacy
  (Park Rapids, MN), 64
Temple News Agency (LaPorte, IN), 249

PARKS, DRIVES, TOURS

WILD RICE SOURCES

More Great Titles
FROM TRAILS BOOKS & PRAIRIE OAK PRESS

ACTIVITY GUIDES
Biking Wisconsin: 50 Great Road and Trail Rides, *Steve Johnson*
Great Cross-Country Ski Trails: Wisconsin, Minnesota, Michigan & Ontario,
Wm. Chad McGrath
Great Iowa Walks: 50 Strolls, Rambles, Hikes, and Treks, *Lynn L. Walters*
Great Minnesota Walks: 49 Strolls, Rambles, Hikes, and Treks, *Wm. Chad McGrath*
Great Wisconsin Walks: 45 Strolls, Rambles, Hikes, and Treks, *Wm. Chad McGrath*
Horsing Around in Wisconsin, *Anne M. Connor*
Iowa Underground, *Greg A. Brick*
Minnesota Underground & the Best of the Black Hills, *Doris Green*
Paddling Illinois: 64 Great Trips by Canoe and Kayak, *Mike Svob*
Paddling Iowa: 96 Great Trips by Canoe and Kayak, *Nate Hoogeveen*
Paddling Northern Minnesota: 86 Great Trips by Canoe and Kayak,
Lynne Smith Diebel
Paddling Northern Wisconsin: 82 Great Trips by Canoe and Kayak, *Mike Svob*
Paddling Southern Wisconsin: 82 Great Trips by Canoe and Kayak, *Mike Svob*
Walking Tours of Wisconsin's Historic Towns,
Lucy Rhodes, Elizabeth McBride, Anita Matcha
Wisconsin's Outdoor Treasures: A Guide to 150 Natural Destinations, *Tim Bewer*
Wisconsin Underground, *Doris Green*

TRAVEL GUIDES
Classic Wisconsin Weekends, *Michael Bie*
Great Little Museums of the Midwest, *Christine des Garennes*
Great Minnesota Taverns, *David K. Wright & Monica G. Wright*
Great Minnesota Weekend Adventures, *Beth Gauper*
Great Weekend Adventures, *the Editors of Wisconsin Trails*
Great Wisconsin Romantic Weekends, *Christine des Garennes*
Great Wisconsin Taverns: 101 Distinctive Badger Bars, *Dennis Boyer*
Iowa's Hometown Flavors, *Donna Tabbert Long*
Sacred Sites of Minnesota, *John-Brian Paprock & Teresa Peneguy Paprock*
Sacred Sites of Wisconsin, *John-Brian Paprock & Teresa Peneguy Paprock*
Tastes of Minnesota: A Food Lover's Tour, *Donna Tabbert Long*
The Great Iowa Touring Book: 27 Spectacular Auto Trips, *Mike Whye*
The Great Minnesota Touring Book: 30 Spectacular Auto Trips, *Thomas Huhti*
The Great Wisconsin Touring Book: 30 Spectacular Auto Tours, *Gary Knowles*
Wisconsin Family Weekends: 20 Fun Trips for You and the Kids,
Susan Lampert Smith

Wisconsin Golf Getaways, *Jeff Mayers and Jerry Poling*
Wisconsin Lighthouses: A Photographic and Historical Guide,
Ken and Barb Wardius
Wisconsin's Hometown Flavors, *Terese Allen*
Wisconsin Waterfalls, *Patrick Lisi*
Up North Wisconsin: A Region for All Seasons, *Sharyn Alden*

HOME & GARDEN
Bountiful Wisconsin: 110 Favorite Recipes, *Terese Allen*
Codfather 2, *Jeff Hagen*
Creating a Perennial Garden in the Midwest, *Joan Severa*
Eating Well in Wisconsin, *Jerry Minnich*
Foods That Made Wisconsin Famous: 150 Great Recipes, *Richard J. Baumann*
Midwest Cottage Gardening, *Frances Manos*
North Woods Cottage Cookbook, *Jerry Minnich*
Wisconsin Country Gourmet, *Marge Snyder & Suzanne Breckenridge*
Wisconsin Garden Guide, *Jerry Minnich*

HISTORICAL BOOKS
Barns of Wisconsin, *Jerry Apps*
Duck Hunting on the Fox: Hunting and Decoy-Carving Traditions,
Stephen M. Miller
Grand Army of the Republic: Department of Wisconsin, *Thomas J. McCrory*
Portrait of the Past: A Photographic Journey Through Wisconsin 1865-1920,
Howard Mead, Jill Dean, and Susan Smith
Prairie Whistles: Tales of Midwest Railroading, *Dennis Boyer*
Shipwrecks of Lake Michigan, *Benjamin J. Shelak*
Wisconsin At War: 20th Century Conflicts Through the Eyes of Veterans,
Dr. James F. McIntosh, M.D.
Wisconsin's Historic Houses & Living History Museums, *Krista Finstad Hanson*
Wisconsin: The Story of the Badger State, *Norman K. Risjord*

GIFT BOOKS
Celebrating Door County's Wild Places, *The Ridges Sanctuary*
Fairlawn: Restoring the Splendor, *Tom Davis*
Madison, *Photography by Brent Nicastro*
Milwaukee, *Photography by Todd Dacquisto*
Milwaukee Architecture: A Guide to Notable Buildings, *Joseph Korom*
Spirit of the North: A Photographic Journey Through Northern Wisconsin,
Richard Hamilton Smith
The Spirit of Door County: A Photographic Essay, *Darryl R. Beers*
Uncommon Sense: The Life Of Marshall Erdman, *Doug Moe & Alice D'Alessio*

LEGENDS & LORE

Driftless Spirits: Ghosts of Southwest Wisconsin, *Dennis Boyer*
Haunted Wisconsin, *Michael Norman and Beth Scott*
The Beast of Bray Road: Tailing Wisconsin's Werewolf, *Linda S. Godfrey*
The Eagle's Voice: Tales Told by Indian Effigy Mounds, *Gary J. Maier, M.D.*
The Poison Widow: A True Story of Sin, Strychnine, & Murder, *Linda S. Godfrey*
The W-Files: True Reports of Wisconsin's Unexplained Phenomena, *Jay Rath*

YOUNG READERS

ABCs Naturally, *Lynne Smith Diebel & Jann Faust Kalscheur*
ABCs of Wisconsin, *Dori Hillestad Butler, Illustrated by Alison Relyea*
H is for Hawkeye, *Jay Wagner, Illustrated by Eileen Potts Dawson*
H is for Hoosier, *Dori Hillestad Butler, Illustrated by Eileen Potts Dawson*
Wisconsin Portraits, *Martin Hintz*
Wisconsin Sports Heroes, *Martin Hintz*
W is for Wisconsin, *Dori Hillestad Butler, Illustrated by Eileen Potts Dawson*

SPORTS

Baseball in Beertown: America's Pastime in Milwaukee, *Todd Mishler*
Before They Were the Packers: Green Bay's Town Team Days,
Denis J. Gullickson & Carl Hanson
Cold Wars: 40+ Years of Packer-Viking Rivalry, *Todd Mishler*
Downfield: Untold Stories of the Green Bay Packers, *Jerry Poling*
Great Moments in Wisconsin Sports, *Todd Mishler*
Green Bay Packers Titletown Trivia Teasers, *Don Davenport*
Mean on Sunday: The Autobiography of Ray Nitschke, *Robert W. Wells*
Mudbaths and Bloodbaths: The Inside Story of the Bears-Packers Rivalry,
Gary D'Amato & Cliff Christl
Packers By the Numbers: Jersey Numbers and the Players Who Wore Them,
John Maxymuk

For a free catalog, phone, write, or e-mail us.

Trails Books

P.O. Box 317, Black Earth, WI 53515
(800) 236-8088 • e-mail: books@wistrails.com